Dante's
Journey of
Sanctification

Antonio C. Mastrobuono

Regnery Gateway
Washington, D.C.

Library of Congress Cataloging-in-Publication Data

(TK)

Mastrobuono, A. C.
    Dante's Journey of Sanctification / Antonio Critodemo Mastrobuono
    p. cm.
    ISBN 0-89526-741-1
    1. Singleton, Charles Southward, 1909-   *Journey to Beatrice.*
    2. Dante Alighieri, 1265-1321. *Divina Commedia.*
    3. Dante Alighieri, 1265-1321--Symbolism.
    4. Grace (Theology) in Literature.
    I. Title.
    PQ4406.S53M36   1990
    851' .1--dc20   90-35108
                                                    CIP

Published in the United States by
Regnery Gateway
1130 17th Street, NW
Washington, DC 20036

Distributed to the trade by
National Book Network
4720-A Boston Way
Lanham, MD 20706

1990 printing
Printed on acid free paper
Manifactured in the United States of America
10 9 8 7 6 5 4 3 2 1

ACKNOWLEDGMENTS

I would like to express my sincere thanks to Tom Ruggiero for having written for me a long and complicated software program that made communication possible between my computer and printer (they were not designed to communicate with each other), thereby greatly facilitating the completion of the manuscript.

To Ernest Fortin (Professor of Theology: Boston College) goes my gratitude for an acutely expert reading of the manuscript, and for his intellectual support on difficult matters of Theology.

I am also grateful to Professor Nicolae Iliescu (Harvard University) for a thorough, critically sagacious reading of the entire manuscript, and for his generous availability as both a scholar and a friend.

My heartfelt appreciation for their warm encouragement, valuable scholarly advice, and generous friendship goes to: Michelangelo Picone, Louis LaFavia, Ruth El Saffar, Tibor Wlassics, and Paolo Cherchi.

To Paolo Cherchi I am also especially grateful for having been a catalyst for this project. It was he, in fact, who in 1981 commissioned me to write a review article on Giuseppe Mazzotta's book *Dante, Poet of the Desert* which, in turn, became the starting point for my complete reevaluation of Singleton's school of thought.

To my wife, Dinah, go my deep feelings of gratitude for a singularly beautiful illustration of Dante and Virgil at the Gates of Purgatory.

And finally, I am also very grateful to Susanna Carey for a meticulous and professional editing of the final draft of the manuscript.

PREFACE

Some thirty years ago, Charles Singleton (then a Harvard professor) published a book entitled: *Journey to Beatrice*. The main thesis of this book is that Dante's journey through Inferno and Purgatory under the guidance of Virgil is a preparation for sanctifying grace, which Dante supposedly receives at the advent of Beatrice on the mountaintop of Purgatory. In order to prove this thesis, Singleton quotes extensively from the *Summa* of St. Thomas Aquinas as interpreted by Henri Bouillard in the book *Conversion et grâce chez S.Thomas d'Aquin* (Paris: 1941), "to which," Singleton says, "I am greatly indebted" (p. 55). Bouillard's book, as we read in the Avant-Propos, was a doctoral dissertation ("Cette étude a été présentée comme thèse de doctorat à la Faculté de Theologie S. J. de Lyon-Fourvière"), which was severely criticized by one of the most eminent Thomists of the century, R. Garrigou-Lagrange, recognized by Jacques Maritain (*Degrees of Knowledge*: p. 474) as one of his masters. Singleton's book has remained the highest, undisputed interpretation of the *Comedy* in the United States for the past three decades. Indeed, Singleton was considered by some the "world's leading critic of the *Divine Comedy*."*

In the first chapter of the present work, "Sanctifying Grace: Justification and Merit," I have endeavored to demonstrate that Singleton's thesis of the *Comedy* is based on an erroneous interpretation of St. Thomas, and that Dante's journey under Virgil's guidance through Inferno and Purgatory is an effect of (not a preparation for) sanctifying grace, which Dante has already received before entering the world beyond.

In the second chapter of the present study "This is the Day the Lord has made," I introduce new evidence in support of my thesis (already expounded in my book, *Essays on Dante's Philosophy of History*) that the first day in Purgatory is not Easter Sunday as most critics believe. It is, instead, simply a day in Purgatory corresponding to the Vigil Night of Holy Saturday in Jerusalem. Professor Rocco Montano, in presenting my book to the Italian public ("Saggi sulla filosofia della storia in Dante," *Segni*: 1980), has accurately grasped the essential meaning of my thesis when he says: "Oltre a queste essenziali conferme il libro di Mastrobuono dà nuove, molto importanti indicazioni sulla natura dell'Antipurgatorio. Prima di tutto, ed è un merito grandissimo, ci viene mostrato, o rivelato, che il giorno del passaggio attraverso l'Antipurgatorio non è il giorno di Pasqua, come tutti ritengono, ma corrisponde alla notte della Vigilia a Gerusalemme" ("Over and beyond

---

Dante: A Collection of Critical Essays, Edited, and with an introduction by John Freccero. (Englewood Cliffs, N.J.: Prentice-Hall, 1965, p. 179).

these essential confirmations Mastrobuono's book gives new, very important information on the nature of the Ante-Purgatory. First of all, and this is a very great merit, Mastrobuono shows, or reveals, that the day of passage across the Ante-Purgatory is not Easter day, as everyone believes, but corresponds instead to the night of the Vigil in Jerusalem"). Evidently, however, some readers misunderstood my position and wrote Montano asking for further elucidation. This came in a subsequent issue of the journal ("L'alba dell'antipurgatorio," *Segni*: 1981) in which Montano in explaining, once again, my position also says: "La risposta che diamo non sappiamo se è condivisa dall'autore del libro (*Essays on Dante's Philosophy of History*), dal quale abbiamo tratto quelle pagine. . . . Il funzionamento disastroso delle nostre poste ci ha dissuasi dal tentare di ottenere il parere dell'autore del libro, che forse potrà anche venire in un secondo numero. Cerchiamo quindi di dare una nostra spiegazione. Forse altri, o lo stesso Mastrobuono, dirà cose più giuste" ("We do not know if the answer we give is shared by the author of the book—*Essays on Dante's Philosophy of History*—from which we have taken those pages. . . . The disastrous performance of our mail system has dissuaded us from trying to obtain the opinion of the author of the book, which could perhaps come in a second issue. Let us therefore try to give our explanation. Perhaps others, or Mastrobuono himself, will say something more accurate"). The present chapter, "This is the Day the Lord has made" is meant to be both: an elucidation and a further confirmation of my thesis. On the second day, as he stands in front of the Gates of Purgatory, Dante symbolically receives the Sacrament of Penance which, as Durandus confirms, is administered by the Church (symbolized by the keys of the Angel) at Easter time. Montano has also recently reiterated: "The fact that the day which starts with the landing of the two poets on the shore of Purgatory is not Sunday as it is commonly believed . . . has been demonstrated by Antonio Mastrobuono in his volume . . . The book offers the basis for a better understanding of the whole first part of *The Purgatorio* . . . the Ante-Purgatory is still a place and a time outside the world of the Church, it is a world of expectation" (R. Montano, *Dante's Thought and Poetry*, Regnery Gateway: Chicago, 1988, p. 510).

In the third chapter, "The Powerful Enigma: A Mortification of the Intellect," I propose a new approach to the age old problem of Beatrice's prophecy. In order to fully convey the extent and importance of this problem, it should suffice to say that Dante's philosophy of history remains incomplete as long as this prophecy remains unresolved. The *Enciclopedia Dantesca* gives the whole history of the enormous amount of scholarship that this problem has generated through the centuries. My approach to this problem consists, first of all, in rejecting the solution first proposed by Jacopo della Lana between 1324-1329, which has been followed to this day without a single exception. As is well known, della Lana's proposal was to translate Beatrice's prophecy into Roman numerals DXV, and subsequently hunt for possible meanings of these numerals or letters. This approach, I maintain, should be abandoned because it leads only to sterile external proofs.

Instead, I have proposed an internal proof—one that comes from the text of the *Comedy* itself. In this I have been fortunate since I have discovered an image in Dante's text the full meaning of which has gone hitherto unnoticed. This has to do with the image of the wax and the seal, which I have been able to trace all the way back to Aristotle's *De Anima*. In this book Aristotle presents his philosophy of knowledge, and the image of the wax and the seal plays a crucial role in distinguishing his position from those of Plato and Democritus. Dante was very well acquainted with the problem, and in the *Convivio* he explicitly sides with Aristotle quoting from Book II of *De Anima* where the image occurs. In my study, through a parallel analysis of the *Comedy* and *De Anima*, I have proposed a philosophical approach that makes the meaning of the prophecy proceed from the text of the poem.

*   *   *

As the final draft of the present study was about to go to press, I received in the mail (October 10, 1989) the latest issue of *Dante Studies* dedicated to the memory of Charles S. Singleton. In one of the essays, "The American Criticism of Charles Singleton" by Giuseppe Mazzotta, we read as follows:

Singleton's Dantean lesson, on which I shall linger, might seem to lack present currency under certain aspects, but under other aspects it continues viable still, and, for the most part, it gives rise to perplexities. Indeed, I find that perplexity is the fairest way in which to confront the power of an authentic work. The opposite of perplexity would be veneration. But there is nothing more violent than the veneration accorded the master by his epigones. Veneration does violence because it freezes the thinking of both the scholar and his epigones, it rigidifies it in fixed formulae and, in effect, destroys it.

Perplexity, on the other hand, belongs to a different order of ideas and intentions. The term, from the Latin *per-plectere*, means to interlace, mix together. To feel perplexities before Singleton's work, then, is not to point out errors in a polemical fashion or to offer corrections (a possible but fatuous exercise that places the corrector in the spiral of error). It means, if anything, exactly the opposite: to permit his range of questionings and certitudes to interpret ours while we approach his; to accompany him along the path of critical reflection. To have some perplexities, in short, means that we recognize that we do not understand him completely, that we do not know yet what is still viable in his work and what is its provenance (p. 28).

Mazzotta is aware of my critique of Singleton's thesis as he was present at a lecture ("Is 'Journey to Beatrice' a Preparation for Sanctifying Grace?") delivered by me at Yale University on May 2, 1988, where I distributed to Mazzotta and the rest of the audience a generous amount of key material from my manuscript. Now Mazzotta tells us that Singleton's work "for the most part . . . gives rise to perplexities," which, I am pleased to say, is certainly a good sign. But I would hasten to add that more than "perplexities" or a "mixing together" are required on Mazzotta's part. What is required, in fact, is nothing less than an honest, serious, reevaluation of one's own borrowings, especially if we consider that the validity of Mazzotta's interpretation of the structure of the *Comedy*, as expounded in his book *Dante, Poet of the Desert*, is totally dependent on Singleton's false claim that the Pilgrim Dante receives sanctifying grace with the advent of Beatrice in the Earthly Paradise. To say of Singleton and his work that "we do not understand him completely" or that "we do not know yet what is still viable in his work" is quite simply an untenable, highly questionable, evasion of the problem. This is so because the borrowings from him were fundamental philosophical and theological notions concerning the very structure of the *Comedy*, and, more importantly, these notions were accepted by Mazzotta with crystal clear understanding of how they were supposedly exemplified in Dante's poem. The following quotation from Mazzotta's book unmistakably testifies to his then steadfast assurance concerning the viability of Singleton's teachings:

> In order for man to be restored to his prelapsarian condition, he has to be healed by recovering the four cardinal virtues, prudence, justice, fortitude, and temperance. In the redemptive order, such a recovery is for Aquinas only the first stage toward complete justification. Such a stage, *gratia sanans*, justifies the soul insofar as it can make it acceptable to God. The second stage, *gratia sanctificans*, occurs when the soul in the Earthly Paradise is in possession of all the seven virtues (p. 36).

In the above quotation the word "virtues" is followed by foot note number 37 in which Mazzotta says "see C. S. Singleton . . . *Journey to Beatrice* pp. 159-83. Mazzotta erroneously believes that Dante's soul (or fallen man) is healed by the recovery of the four cardinal virtues rather than by sanctifying grace, as he says: "I have already, though in a general way, discussed the function of the four cardinal virtues to heal fallen man of the *vulnera naturae*" (p. 50). More specifically, concerning the structure of the *Comedy* Mazzotta believes that Dante's journey to the Earthly Paradise is a preparation for sanctifying grace which, supposedly, he receives with the advent of Beatrice. Here is what Mazzotta, echoing Singleton and without "perplexities," steadfastly affirms on the subject: "In the moral structure of the *Divine Comedy*, this ambiguity is dramatized by the pilgrim's movement through Purgatory as an ascetic preparation for grace until, later in the Garden, Beatrice finally comes as sanctifying grace" (p. 122). For a full explanation of Mazzotta's misunderstanding of St. Thomas (and therefore of Dante), see Chapter I, (section XIII) of the present book. A more complete evaluation of Mazzotta's book may be found in my review article "Criticism on Ambiguity," (*Italian Culture*, vol. V, 1984).

Also, I fail to see how anyone's difficult endeavor of trying to demonstrate, after years of patient meditation, that Singleton misunderstood St. Thomas (and as a consequence also Dante) could, in all honesty, be termed a "fatuous exercise." The charge could not be more inane or more patently ludicrous. As for the possibility that this endeavor "places the corrector in the spiral of error," it could be easily argued that only by a distorted kind of logic could Mazzotta claim as much.

In the same issue of *Dante Studies*, we find the essay "Charles S. Singleton: An Appraisal" by Dante Della Terza who says the following:

Six entire chapters of the book, *Journey to Beatrice*, are devoted to illustrating the "return" of Dante—and through him, of humanity—to Eden. Where the episodic *épaisseur* needs clarification, Singleton, in his highly controlled style, spares no effort in striving to amplify descriptions and solve dilemmas. In order to help us to see, face to face and not through a glass darkly, both background and foreground of Dante's "return" to Eden, he asks himself questions about the four stars inhabiting the celestial horizon of Purgatory; about the four rivers whose presence in Eden is acknowledged by Genesis; about the four inborn cardinal virtues known to the pagan world and the four infused cardinal virtues closely linked to the three theological ones—faith, hope, and charity.

In order to come to the rescue of the reader who by sticking to the letter of the text might not be able to understand the poem in all its implications, Singleton advises him to take into account both Augustinian trends, the one stressing the importance of allegorical reading (*De Genesi contra Manichaeos*) and the other emphasizing the irreversible value of the letter (*De Genesi ad Litteram*). For a significant reading of the poem we need, according to Singleton, not only an allegorical intelligence of the event, but also an awareness of the iconic substantiality of the letter (pp. 14-15).

In the chapter "Sanctifying Grace: Justification and Merit," I have shown that Singleton's interpretation of the "return" of Dante—and through him, of humanity—to Eden is based on a terrible confusion, on Singleton's part, between the order of nature and the order of grace. For a full explanation of the problem, I refer the reader to sections VIII, IX, and X of the chapter, but it might well be worth it to quote here some pages of concluding remarks on the subject:

Therefore, it should be clear that the idea of two kinds of justice within the process of justification itself—the "human justice" attained under Virgil's guidance, and the "transhuman justice" attained with Beatrice—is a pure invention of Singleton's. Justification is an effect of sanctifying (operating) grace, not a preparation for it as Singleton believes: "And so too in the matter of justification in the soul: first justice, then advent of grace, as to a place prepared."[43]

But Singleton has pushed this absurdity to the very extreme by saying that Dante, before the supposed advent of sanctifying grace with Beatrice, finds himself in a condition of "pure nature" similar to the one possessed by Adam at the time of creation, before Adam received the original justice, and therefore two steps before the Fall:

> What we are finally privileged to see is clear: Dante has continued to work with the metaphor "return to Eden" even in this respect. At the summit and end of the climb up the mountain, when Eden is reached, we may see history somehow repeating itself; as it was with Adam in his formation, so now with this man, so now with "man," in his reformation. Only now do we glimpse an aspect of the metaphor we might otherwise have missed. There had been a moment in Adam's formation when Adam was not yet in Eden, when Adam was formed outside of Eden in a first condition "secundum naturam." What corresponds to this, in a "return" to Eden is the moment when Virgil proclaims that Dante the Wayfarer is now reformed in justice, a justice discernible by the natural light. This then is the moment "secundum naturam" in the reformation.
>
> The pattern of the original formation of man is thus seen to repeat itself in the reformation of a man named Dante, who attains first to a condition of justice with Virgil, within the proportion of his nature and under the natural light, and then, in a second moment attains to Eden proper, crossing the river to a kind of justice with Beatrice that is truly beyond all human measure.[44]

These are Singleton's last words on the last page of his book *Journey to Beatrice*. Now, according to St. Thomas, and as duly acknowledged by Singleton, the state of "pure nature" never existed, since Adam "was created in grace, according to Eccles. vii. 30, *God made man right*" (I, q. 95, a. 1). Yet even if we suppose that the state of "pure nature" did exist before Adam was elevated by sanctifying grace, by what impossible, triple-backward somersault could Dante (or humanity symbolized by him) have returned to a similar state of pure nature? Dante was born in the state of fallen nature and is now redeemed—the new Adam is Christ, not Dante. But Singleton gives this quotation from St. Thomas: "original justice could not be without grace. . . .

Yet even supposing this opinion, such a reason is not conclusive: for even if original justice did not include grace, still *it was a certain disposition prerequisite to grace"* (Singleton's italics).[45] And this, of course, is enough for Singleton to say that the pattern of Adam's original formation repeats itself in the reformation of Dante, who attains first to a condition of justice with Virgil (within the proportion of human nature) and then to a justice (beyond human proportion) with Beatrice and sanctifying grace.

Now over and beyond the fact that Virgil's "human justice" as a preparation for Beatrice's "transhuman justice" is simply a case, as we have already noted, of putting the cart in front of the horse, what should be pointed out is that Singleton has actually confused the order of nature with the order of grace. Immediately following the above quotation from St. Thomas, Singleton, in order to strengthen his idea of a natural justice as a preparation to a supernatural one, works out an analogy whereby Adam's original formation, first in nature and then in grace, is analogous for him (for Singleton—and supposedly for Dante) to "the formation of every human creature since Adam":

Such a notion of a first moment or phase in the formation of man, followed by another completing moment, had good support, by analogy at least, in the view which we know Dante to have held respecting the formation of every human creature since Adam. The fact that Adam must be set apart from all others in this is what makes it a matter of analogy. For Adam was fashioned directly by God, body and spirit, was created "mature," fully formed as an adult; whereas Adam's children and all his posterity come into existence in a mother's womb, developing first as a foetus through a natural formation. Such in fact is the account of the genesis of the human creature which Statius (who can "see further" than Virgil) gives when he has joined the two wayfarers in their climb toward the summit of the mountain.[46]

What follows is a brief exposition of *Purgatory* XXV, where Statius expounds the Aristotelian doctrine of generation and embryology according to which the human fetus goes through two major stages of formation: the vegetative and the animal. This is a phase of preparation in nature for the infusion of the soul directly by God into the fetus when the latter has reached a perfect animal form. At this point the "animal creature" becomes the "human creature" by virtue of the immortal soul created directly by God. Statius gives here the Christian answer to Averroes' denial of the immortality of the individual soul. Then Singleton continues:

The relevance of such a view to the question of Adam's formation is evident. In the formation of every human creature, two moments or phases are made distinct by an emphatic line: first, there is the phase of nature, a moment of formation *in naturalibus* (and just so far Virgil could have carried the argument), followed by the moment "above nature" when God, happy (and almost proud!) of nature's handiwork within her own order, completes the genesis and full formation of the creature to be fashioned, by breathing in, infusing, the rational soul. It is a moment of grace. Might Adam's formation not have followed such a pattern, even though, in Adam's case, God and not nature is the *faber* at the first stage? (Singleton's italic).[47]

What should be remembered here is Singleton's major analogy in virtue of which Dante finds himself in a state of "human justice" (the preparation in nature) before the infusion of grace ("the transhuman justice" with Beatrice), just as Adam was created first in nature and then elevated to grace. Obviously, Singleton believes he has found confirmation of his analogy in the "formation of every human creature," since the latter is for him analogous to Adam's formation: "the relevance of such a view to the question of Adam's formation is evident." This must be so, according to Singleton, because: "in the formation of every human creature, two moments or phases are made distinct by an emphatic line: first there is the phase of nature, a moment of formation *in naturalibus* . . . followed by the moment 'above nature' when God . . . completes the genesis and full formation of the creature to be fashioned, by breathing in, infusing, the rational soul." This moment, according to Singleton, is "the moment above nature . . . It is a moment of grace." And here, exactly, is the confusion between the "order of nature" and the "order of grace." God's infusion of the soul into the fetus is an act of creation and not a "moment of grace," as Singleton believes. The soul is the natural *form* of the body, and as such it accounts for man's very being. God creates the soul by an act of common love—"whereby He loves all things that are." Sanctifying grace is the supernatural *form* of the soul created by God by an act of special love—"whereby He draws the rational creature above the condition of its nature to a participation of the divine good":

> And according to this difference of good the love of God towards the creature is looked at differently. For one is common, whereby He loves all things that are (Wis. xi. 25), and thereby gives things their natural being. But the second is a special love, whereby He draws the rational creature above the condition of its nature to a participation of the divine good; and according to this love, He is said to love anyone absolutely, since it is by this love that God wills absolutely the eternal good, which is Himself . . . accordingly, when a man is said to have the grace of God, there is signified something supernatural bestowed on man by God (I-II, q. 110, a. 1).

Also, as we have already noted, the good of creation terminates at the good of nature, whereas the good of justification terminates at the eternal good of a participation in God. That is why St. Thomas will say that the justification of the ungodly is God's greatest work, even greater than creation. And, indeed, by the time Dante meets Beatrice, not only has he received justification in the Prologue scene, but he will also have gone through a process of personal sanctification under cooperating grace on the mountain which, is itself a preparation for the transhuman process of deification that takes place with Beatrice in Paradise.

An analogy is always a question of "likeness in difference," so that we may say that the infusion of the soul into the fetus is analogous to the infusion of sanctifying grace into the soul, provided it is understood that the former is a process in the "order of nature" and the latter is a process in the "order of grace." But this is not what Singleton has done. For him, the infusion of the soul into the fetus is a "moment of grace" in no way different from the infusion of grace into the soul. The same error occurs when Singleton treats the problem of Dante's preparation for sanctifying grace. The model once again is Aristotle's scheme of generation:

Della Terza has apparently accepted Singleton's interpretation of Dante's "return" to Eden. He is convinced, as he says, that Singleton helps the reader "to see face to face and not through a glass darkly, both background and foreground of Dante's 'return' to Eden." This has happened, I believe, because Della Terza, in good faith, has taken Singleton at his word.

I agree completely with this penetrating critique of Singleton, Freccero, Mazzotta, and company, which shows conclusively that they either misunderstood Thomas or did not use him properly in their attempt to understand Dante. I have long had serious misgivings about Singleton and his overall approach. Mastrobuono puts his finger on a number of specific points that confirm my suspicions. **Ernest Fortin (Professor of Theology): Boston College.**

Mastrobuono brings to his study on Sanctifying Grace an overwhelming, clear, and complete amount of impeccable *textual* documentation that shows Singleton's shortcomings and outright errors in his selected use and interpretations of St. Thomas's writings on the subject of sanctifying grace. Singleton's studies on Dante have left many essential Thomistic concepts (will, intellect, power, essence) in a state of fragmentary and superficial analysis, and the reader, in good faith and insufficiently prepared in topics of this kind, has taken him at his word. Mastrobuono did not. He went to Singleton's aknowledged source of information, the *Summa Theologiae*, and found that what St. Thomas had said and how he had argued the question of the soul in relation to grace and salvation were erroneously understood and interpreted by Singleton. . . . Mastrobuono shows this beyond controversy. **Nicolae Iliescu: Harvard University.**

Professor Mastrobuono is a follower of the critical approach that reads the *Divine Comedy* as a work written according to the allegory of theologians rather than according to the allegory of poets. In this he finds himself in the mainstream of the most updated line of American Dante studies. His personal contribution to this hermeneutical trend is the demonstration that the analogical model, the cultural intertext according to which Dante's poem is constructed, is the Book of Salvation, the Bible, but as it is codified by the Christian Liturgy; in this particular case the liturgy of Holy Week. Some of the most persistent *cruces* of Dante's text are accordingly solved by Professor Mastrobuono. He does so by introducing the pertinent reference to the great code of Roman Rite, having Durandus as Baedeker. **Michelangelo Picone: McGill University.**

It is a work of high quality in which the author shows in detail that he has a deep and precise knowledge of the original sources on which he bases his work. . . . Among Dante scholars in the United States, it is very difficult to find someone who has a scholarly familiarity of Thomistic Theology, a familiarity that Professor Mastrobuono exploits to the fullest. For this reason I can almost predict that certain parts of his work will engender controversy. But as Thomism is also my field of expertise, I have been able to verify that Professor Mastrobuono's arguments are analytically valid and essentially correspond to the original meaning of his sources. **Louis LaFavia: The Catholic University of America.**

He is taking a position that puts him at variance with the most outstanding American Dantista, Charles Singleton, and he is doing it with such acumen and attention to detail—theological as well as literary—that he generates great interest and respect among those who have heard his presentations. . . . His, I am sure, is a name in Dante studies that will have to be reckoned with more and more, especially as his thesis on the structure of the *Commedia* comes to be better known. **Ruth El Saffar: The University of Illinois at Chicago.**

Mastrobuono's absolute command of the totality of background critical material; his rigor and vigor of argumentation; the depth and thoroughness of his scriptural studies; the enthusiasm and stylistic persuasion he manages to bring to his topic—all combine to produce a volume of great coherence (the essays complement and complete each other to produce a critical discourse of perfect unity), intimate persuasion, and pleasant accessibility. **Tibor Wlassics: The University of Virginia.**

Mastrobuono shows that Singleton's thesis is vitiated by a wrong assumption, namely that grace is conferred upon intellect and will, which he takes to be the essence of the soul rather than its faculties. Mastrobuono demonstrates that such an assumption is untenable in Thomistic terms as well as in those of Scholastic philosophy in general. With punctilious philological work, he shows how Singleton quotes St. Thomas incorrectly: quotations that stop at a point when the argument goes in a different direction; quotations taken from the wrong articles of the *Summa*; quotations that are taken from the *difficultates* of an article rather than from the *solutiones* . . . in sum, quotations that indicate an irresponsible use of St. Thomas's text. In a sagacious and genuinely learned manner Màstrobuono demolishes Singleton's theories and restores what I learned in my first days as a student, namely that grace is given to the pilgrim before the moment he sets foot in the other world. Does this seem too little? Anyone who has any familiarity with Dante studies in the United States (and these studies really form a tradition of their own) will appreciate the meaning of this reversal proposed by Mastrobuono: decades of scholarship will have to be rethought! **Paolo Cherchi: The University of Chicago.**

CONTENTS

Sanctifying Grace: Justification and Merit

The *Divine Comedy* opens with a confession: Dante confesses to having found himself in the dark wood of his personal sins because he had lost the straight path:

> Nel mezzo del cammin di nostra vita
> mi ritrovai per una selva oscura,
> ché la diritta via era smarrita.*
>
> *(Inf.* I, 1-3)
>
> In the middle of the journey of our life I came
> to myself in a dark wood where the straight
> way was lost.**

Within the fiction of the poem, Dante regains this straight path by undertaking the journey in the world beyond. On the shore of Purgatory we are told that he feels like one who is returning to his lost road, and until he reaches it he seems to go in vain:

> Noi andavam per lo solingo piano
> com' om che torna a la perduta strada,
> che 'nfino ad essa li pare ire in vano.
>
> *(Purg.* I, 118-120)
>
> We paced along the lonely plain, as one who
> returns to his lost road, and, till he reach it,
> seems to go in vain.

When Dante in the Prologue scene confesses to being a sinner, he is still on the stage of this world. He is then granted the special miracle of a journey through the world beyond in order to gain his salvation. But to have a specific understanding of what Dante gains because of the journey, we must probe into what he has lost because of his sins. More specifically, we must make the distinction that to cease from the act of sin is not the same as to rise from sin. To accomplish the latter, Dante has to regain what he has lost by sinning, that is, grace:

---

* Petrocchi's Edition.
** The Temple Classics.

Man by himself can in no way rise from sin without the help of Grace. For since sin is transient as to the act and abiding in its guilt, as was stated above, to rise from sin is not the same as to cease from the act of sin, but to rise from sin means that man has restored to him what he has lost by sinning (I-II, q. 109, a. 7).[1]

There are two thematic patterns involved here: one of sin, the other of grace. The two will be seen to coalesce in a single symmetrical perspective that will function as the unifying principle of this entire study. This approach to the *Comedy* may prove to be most advantageous since St. Thomas himself utilizes it in one of the questions in the *Summa* on "The Necessity of Grace." Having lost grace, Dante may be said to have incurred a further, triple loss by sinning: "Now man incurs a triple loss by sinning, as was shown above, viz., stain, corruption of natural good, and debt of punishment" (I-II, q. 109, a. 7). Dante has incurred a stain on his soul because, by sinning, he has forfeited the adornment of grace, which is later defined by St. Thomas as the splendor of the soul, as beauty is the splendor of the body: "He incurs a stain inasmuch as he forfeits the adornment of grace through the deformity of sin" (I-II, q. 109, a. 7). That Dante once possessed the "adornment of grace," which he has now lost through the deformity of his personal sins, is evident from the fact that he had received baptism, "ch'è porta de la fede che tu credi" (*Inf.* IV, 36), in his native Florence where he hoped to return and be crowned poet at the same font where he had entered into the faith that makes souls known to God:

> ritornerò poeta, e in sul fonte
> del mio battesmo prenderò 'l cappello;
>   però che ne la fede, che fa conte
> l'anime a Dio, quivi intra' io . . .
>
> (Par. XXV, 8-11)
>
> shall I return, a poet, and at the font of my
> baptism shall I assume the chaplet;
>   because into the Faith which maketh souls known
> of God, 'twas there I entered . . .

Dante's "natural good" has been corrupted by sinning. To understand how this may be so we should briefly recall that, according to St. Thomas, the good of human nature is threefold:

First, there are the principles of which nature is constituted, and the properties that flow from them, such as the powers of the soul, and so forth. Secondly, since man has from nature an inclination to virtue, as was stated above, this inclination to virtue is a good of nature. Thirdly, the gift of original justice, conferred on the whole human nature in the

Adam

person of the first (man,) may be called a good of nature. Accordingly, the first-mentioned good of nature is neither destroyed nor diminished by sin. The third good of nature was entirely destroyed through the sin of our first parent. But the second good of nature, viz., the natural inclination to virtue, is diminished by sin . . . Therefore, as sin is opposed to virtue, from the very fact that a man sins there results a diminution of that good of nature which is the inclination to virtue (I-II, q. 85, a. 1).

not destroyed
we have been
weakened

From the above quotation we may say that human nature as such remained intact after the fall of Adam: "Therefore, nature itself is not changed in itself through a change in the voluntary action; it is the inclination that is changed insofar as it is directed to its terminus" (I-II, q. 85, a. 1, R.Obj. 2). More specifically, the good of nature is corrupted in Dante because his will is not subject to God, since by sinning he has turned away from Him. As a consequence of this, his lower powers have rebelled against his will, thus diminishing his inclination to virtue: "Natural good is corrupted, inasmuch as man's nature is disordered because man's will is not subject to God's; and when this order is overthrown, the consequence is that the whole nature of sinful man remains disordered" (I-II, q. 109, a. 7). Lastly, by sinning, Dante has actually incurred a debt of punishment, which renders him deserving of eternal damnation: "there is the debt of punishment, inasmuch as by sinning man deserves eternal damnation" (I-II, q. 109, a. 7).

These then are the effects of sin in Dante's soul:

    I. Loss of Grace
    A. Stain on the soul
    B. Corruption of the good of nature
    C. Debt of eternal punishment

I therefore propose that, within the context of the poem, these effects of sin will be cancelled out by the infusion of sanctifying grace and its effects, according to the following pattern:

    I. Infusion of sanctifying grace

    A. Removal of stain:

"For since the adornment of grace comes from the illumination of divine light, this adornment cannot be brought back, except God give His light anew. Hence a habitual gift is necessary; and this is the light of grace" (I-II, q. 109, a. 7).

    B. Order of the good of nature restored:

"Likewise, the order of nature can be restored, i.e., man's will can be

passions
emotions

subject to God, only when God draws man's will to Himself, as was stated above" (I-II, q. 109, a. 7).

C. Guilt of eternal punishment remitted:

"So too, the guilt of eternal punishment can be remitted by God alone, against whom the offense was committed and Who is Man's Judge. And thus, in order that man rise from sin there is required the help of grace, both as regards a habitual gift, and as regards the internal motion of God" (I-II, q. 109, a. 7).

II

In more exact terms, St. Thomas speaks of a twofold splendor of the soul—the refulgence of the natural light of reason and the refulgence of the divine light of grace. By sinning, a man goes against the light of reason and the divine law. The resulting loss of splendor is what is metaphorically referred to as a stain on the soul:

Now man's soul has a twofold splendor: one from the refulgence of the natural reason, whereby man is directed in his actions; the other from the refulgence of the divine light, viz., of wisdom and grace, whereby man is also perfected for the purpose of doing good and fitting actions. Now, when the soul cleaves to things by love, there is a kind of contact in the soul; and when man sins, he cleaves to certain things against the light of reason and of the divine law, as was shown above. Therefore the loss of splendor, occasioned by this contact, is metaphorically called a stain on the soul (I-II, q. 86, a. 1).

The stain remains in the soul of the sinner, and is removed as soon as he returns to the light of reason and to the divine light:

The stain of sin remains in the soul even when the act of sin is past. The reason for this is that the stain, as was stated above, denotes a blemish in the splendor of the soul, because of its withdrawing from the light of reason or of the divine law. Hence, so long as man remains out of this light, the stain of sin remains in him; but as soon as, moved by grace, he returns to the divine light and to the light of reason, the stain is removed. For although the act of sin, by which man withdrew from the light of reason and the divine law, ceases, man does not at once return to the state in which he was before, but it is necessary that his will should have a movement contrary to the previous movement. Thus, if a man is separated from someone because of some sort of motion, he is not therefore brought any nearer when the motion ceases, it is still necessary for him to retrace his way by a contrary motion (I-II, q. 86, a. 2).

There are a number of important points in this quotation. First, we are told, the stain remains even when the act of sin is past. This should be a clear indication to us that Dante, as a confessed sinner, carries a blemish in his soul for at least two-thirds of his journey through the world beyond since, as St. Thomas says, a "man does not at once return to the state in which he was before, but it is necessary that his will should have a movement contrary to the previous movement." Now, the clearest evidence of an actual cleansing of this stain can be none other than the ascent of the mountain of Purgatory itself, where, at each terrace, a "P" is erased from Dante's forehead as a stain is erased from his soul. This is so because there are as many stains as there are kinds of sin:

> The stain is neither something positive in the soul, nor does it denote a pure privation; it denotes a privation of the soul's splendor in relation to its cause, which is sin. Hence, diverse sins cause diverse stains. We may say that stain is like a shadow, which is the privation of light through the interposition of a body, and which varies according to the diversity of the interposed bodies (I-II, q. 86, a. 1 R.Obj. 3).

Dante is then immersed by Matelda in the waters of the river Lethe, which possess the miraculous function of erasing or washing away any memory of the sins ("che toglie altrui memoria del peccato" (*Purg.* XXVIII, 128) that Dante has ever committed. For Singleton the river Lethe represents the line of demarcation between Virgil and Beatrice, which is to say a dividing line between nature and grace: "we come into the clear realization that one most prominent feature of the whole scene or stage-set at the summit is the river Lethe, that stream which seems to draw a dividing line between Virgil and Beatrice. It is readily felt to be some kind of boundary line, even before we understand how this must be so."[2] This must be so because, according to Singleton, Dante receives sanctifying grace only with the advent of Beatrice: "The light of grace flashes through the forest, from beyond the stream. And when, after contrition and confession, Dante may cross through the water to the far shore, to attain to Beatrice and the infused virtues, we know that he crosses to a condition of grace and justice beyond Virgil, and beyond nature."[3] I have tried to show elsewhere[4] that the line of demarcation between nature and grace on the stage of history falls between the first and second canto of the prologue scene. In the first canto Dante may be said to be symbolical of mankind leading up to the time of Christ, whereas in the second, he may be symbolical of mankind redeemed by Christ and looking forward to His second coming. In the course of this study I shall attempt to demonstrate that when Dante attains to Beatrice, he crosses to a condition of merit, which is an effect of grace. But before that occurs, the stains of sin must be washed from his soul, and this too is an effect of grace.

According to St. Thomas, the stain of sin is removed from the sinner when, "moved by grace, he returns to the divine light and to the light of reason." It should be kept in mind that a sinner must first of all be "moved by grace." Secondly, the light of reason and the divine light are said to be intimately related in this process. When the process is completed, Dante will attain to a condition of merit, for "no one existing in a state of mortal sin can merit eternal life unless first he be reconciled to God, through the forgiveness of his sin, which is brought about by grace. For the sinner deserves, not life, but death, according to Rom. VI, 23: *'The wages of sin is death'* " (I-II, q. 114, a. 2). More on the condition of merit later. For now, we shall focus our attention on Dante's descent into Hell, which he has to undertake as part of the price to be paid to satisfy the debt of punishment that weighs upon him. This is clear from the very beginning when Dante tells us that he alone among the living was preparing to bear the war of the journey and the torment:

> . . . e io sol uno
> m'apparecchiava a sostener la guerra
> sì del cammino e sì de la pietate

(Inf. II, 3-5)

> . . . and I, one alone,
> was preparing myself to bear the war both of the
> journey and the pity

If the journey is a kind of war, it is so because Dante is a sinner and, as such, he is under pain of death, as St. Paul has said: "the wages of sin is death." The debt of eternal punishment is equivalent to eternal spiritual death in Hell; and this too is confirmed by the text when St. Lucia tells Beatrice that Dante stands condemned to death in front of the she-wolf:

> "non vedi tu la *morte* che 'l combatte
> su la fiumana ove 'l mar non ha vanto?"

(Inf. II, 107-8)

> "Seest
> thou not the *death* which combats him upon
> the river over which the sea has no boast?"

The she-wolf, I have argued elsewhere,[5] should be interpreted as being symbolic of spiritual as well as physical death—the effects of original sin. These are the two faces of the same coin: moral as well as physical evil. Dante does not cross the path of the she-wolf, and therefore will enter the world beyond without suffering a physical death. This is so because of a special miracle that has been granted to him. But before he ascends the mountain of Purgatory in order to be regenerated, he will have to undergo an actual experience of the tribulation and anguish of Hell as punishment for the sins that he has committed. The descent into Hell is such a punishment that will renew Dante in humility as evidenced by the fact that Virgil, on the shore of Purgatory soon after they emerge from Hell, girds Dante with a branch from "l'umile pianta." The ascent of Purgatory is also punitive but more obviously regenerative. In Romans 2:9 we read: "Tribulation and anguish upon every soul of man that worketh evil." This is the very quotation used by St. Thomas in answer to the first article of question 87: "whether the debt of punishment is an effect of sin?" To work evil is to sin, he says. Therefore: "sin incurs a punishment, which is signified by the terms tribulation and anguish" (I-II, q. 87, a. 1).

To sin is an inordinate act and as such it is an offense against some order: "Hence he is put down, in consequence, by that same order; and this repression is punishment" (I-II, q. 87, a. 1). Accordingly, a man incurs a threefold punishment because the human will is subject to three orders. A man's nature is first of all subject to the order of his own reason; secondly, it is subject to another man who governs him temporally, or spiritually (state-household-Church); and thirdly, it is subject to the universal order of divine government:

> Each of these orders is disturbed by sin, for the sinner acts against his reason, and against human and divine law. Therefore, he incurs a threefold punishment: one, inflicted by himself, viz., remorse of conscience; another, inflicted by man; and a third, inflicted by God (I-II, q. 87, a. 1).

While sin incurs a debt of punishment through disturbing an order, the disturbance itself may be either reparable or irreparable. It becomes irreparable when the principle of the order itself is destroyed. The principle of the order between man and God is the "last end" to which man adheres by virtue of charity. Mortal sin turns a man away from God by destroying charity. He therefore incurs a debt of eternal punishment:

> Now in every order there is a principle by which one becomes a member of that order. Consequently, if a sin destroys the principle of the order by which man's will is subject to God, the disorder will be such as to be considered in itself irreparable although it is possible to repair it by the power of God. Now the principle of this order is the last end, to which man adheres by charity. Therefore whatever sins turn man away from God, so as to destroy charity, considered in themselves, incur a debt of eternal punishment (I-II, q. 87, a. 3).

The souls in Dante's *Inferno* are there not only because they sinned throughout their lives but also because, having fixed their "end in sin," they have the will to sin everlastingly, as in fact they do—Francesca, Farinata, and Ugolino are eternally sinning:

A man is said to have sinned in his own eternity, not only because he sinned throughout his whole life, but also because, from the very fact that he fixes his end in sin, he has the will to sin everlastingly. Therefore Gregory says that the wicked would wish to live without end, that they might abide in their sins forever (I-II, q. 87, a. 3, R.Obj. 1).

Punishment is proportioned to sin, therefore: "mortal sin deserves eternal punishment, whereas venial sin deserves temporal punishment" (I-II, q. 88, a. 6). The former may be called a pain of loss because the loss is the infinite good of God Himself, while the latter may be called a pain of sense:

Accordingly, insofar as sin consists in turning away from something, its corresponding punishment is the pain of loss, which is also infinite, because it is the loss of the infinite good, i.e., God. But insofar as sin turns inordinately to something, its corresponding punishment is the pain of sense, which also is finite (I-II, q. 87, a. 4).

The souls in Purgatory are suffering a temporal pain of sense and a temporal pain of loss and are therefore content to be in the fire because they hope to be among the blessed: "e vederai color che son contenti / nel foco, perché speran di venire / quando che sia a le beate genti" (*Inf.* I, 118-20), while the souls in Hell are suffering an eternal pain of sense and of loss and are therefore eternally dead: "vedrai li antichi spiriti dolenti, / ch'a la seconda morte ciascun grida" (*Inf.* I, 116-17). As for Dante's sins, he is still alive and thus, if he should receive an infusion of grace, by the exercise of the freedom of his choice, he can still determine his ultimate destiny. This in fact is the allegorical meaning of the poem as a whole. Dante is symbolic of humanity, and in the "Letter to Cangrande" we are told that the subject of the poem is "man as by good or ill deserts, in the exercise of the freedom of his choice, he becomes liable to rewarding or punishing justice."[6] But we learn from St. Thomas that the debt of punishment remains even after the sin has been forgiven: "Therefore a man is punished by God even after his sin is forgiven; and so the debt of punishment remains when the sin has been removed" (I-II, q. 87, a. 6). Dante's sins may have been forgiven by God because a Lady in Heaven (the Virgin Mary) interceded on his behalf:

> Donna è gentil nel ciel che si compiange
> di questo 'mpedimento ov' io ti mando,
> sì che duro giudicio là sù frange.
>
> (*Inf.* II, 94-96)
>
> There is a noble Lady in Heaven who has such
> pity of this hindrance, for which I send thee,
> that she breaks the sharp judgment there on high.

But a personal debt of punishment remains outstanding. Dante's descent into Hell and his ascent of Purgatory are the punishment or the satisfaction he has to pay. Two things may be considered in sin, says St. Thomas:

> The guilty act, and the consequent stain. Now it is evident that in all actual sins, when the act of sin has ceased, the guilt remains; for the act of sin makes man deserving of punishment, insofar as he transgresses the order of divine justice, to which he cannot return except he pay some sort of penal compensation which restores him to the equality of justice. Hence, according to the order of divine justice, he who has been too indulgent to his will, by transgressing God's commandment, suffers, either willingly or unwillingly, something contrary to what he would wish. This restoration of the equality of justice by penal compensation is also to be observed in injuries done to one's fellow men. Consequently, it is evident that when the sinful or injurious act has ceased, there still remains the debt of punishment (I-II, q. 87, a. 6).

The penal compensation paid by Dante is his experience of the tribulation and anguish of Hell as well as the pain and solace of Purgatory. Purgatory is punitive as well as regenerative: the same moment is at once a moment of pain and one of solace, as Forese says: "io dico pena, e dovria dir sollazzo" (*Purg.* XXIII, 72). The stain of sin is removed from Dante's soul by his descent into Hell and by his ascent of Purgatory. This is symbolically confirmed on many occasions, most notably as we have suggested, at each terrace of Purgatory, when an angel removes a "P" from Dante's forehead. As for the removal of the stain of sin pertaining to Hell, the culmination must surely be the removal of the infernal filth from Dante's face as he emerges from it:

> "Va dunque, e fa che tu costui ricinghe
> d'un giunco schietto e che li lavi 'l viso,
> sì ch'ogne sucidume quindi stinghe"
>
> (*Purg.*, I, 94-96)
>
> "Go then, and look that thou gird this man with
> a smooth rush, and that thou bathe his face
> so that all filth may thence be wiped away"

Moreover, the removal of the stain demands that the soul be actually united to God:

> But if we speak of the removal of sin as to the stain, it is evident that the stain of sin cannot be removed from the soul without the soul being united to God; since it was through being separated from Him that it suffered the loss of its splendor, in which the stain consists, as was stated above(I-II, q. 87, a. 6).

But to have the stain of sin removed, says St. Thomas, a man must of his own accord take upon himself the punishment of his past sins, or he must bear with patience the punishment that God inflicts upon him, because a man is united to God by his will:

> Now man is united to God by his will. Therefore the stain of sin cannot be removed from man unless his will accepts the order of divine justice, that is to say, unless either of his own accord he take upon himself the punishment of his past sin, or bear patiently the punishment which God inflicts on him; and in both ways punishment has the character of satisfaction (I-II, q. 87, a. 6).

Dante, of his own accord, undertakes the journey through Hell and Purgatory as a just punishment ("la guerra / sì del cammino e sì de la pietate") inflicted on him so that he may at last have the stain removed from his soul and be united to God.

A punishment whether undertaken voluntarily or inflicted by God has in both ways the character of satisfaction. Dante has to render satisfaction for his sins. His ascent of the mountain of Purgatory conveys more clearly such a character of satisfaction, since he finds himself on the same spiritual level as the spirits that he encounters who are, in fact, paying their debt of punishment to God:

> Non vo' però, lettor, che tu ti smaghi
> di buon proponimento per udire
> come Dio vuol che 'l debito si paghi.
>
> *(Purg.* X, 106-8)
>
> I would not, reader, that thou be scared from a
> good purpose through hearing how God wills
> that the debt be paid.

This debt of punishment is later called, more appropriately, a satisfaction:

> E qui convien ch'io questo peso porti
> per lei, tanto che a Dio si sodisfaccia,
> poi ch'io nol fe' tra' vivi, qui tra' morti.
>
> *(Purg.* Xl, 70-72)
>
> And here must I therefore bear this load among
> the dead, until God be satisfied, since I did it
> not among the living.

This is the reason why the pain of sense experienced by Dante on the mountain is a very real one. We should recall that on the Terrace of Lust the burning sensation from the flames is such that Dante would have gladly thrown himself in molten glass to cool off. But Dante's Purgatory is not simply punitive; it is also regenerative:

> It is the proclamation, the triumphant vindication, in agony but also in joy, of this reversed scale of values and their self-identification with the better past. Thus it is essential to Dante's conception of Purgatory that the pain itself shall be a relief, and therefore shall not be endured, but eagerly embraced, by the souls. That this is so they themselves repeatedly declare. They fling themselves upon their sufferings with the same eagerness now with which before they had flung themselves upon their evil gratifications. Their torment is itself their solace.[7]

III

This brings us to the all-important problem of Virgil's function in the *Comedy*. That Dante goes through a process of regeneration on the Mountain is unmistakably confirmed by the text when Virgil crowns him king and bishop over himself:

> "libero, dritto e sano è tuo arbitrio,
> e fallo fora non fare a suo senno:
>   per ch'io te sovra te corono e mitrio."
>
> > > > (*Purg.* XXVII, 140-42)
> > > > "Free,
> upright, and whole, is thy will, and 'twere a fault
> not to act according to its prompting; where-
> fore I do crown and mitre thee over thyself."

The key concepts in this quotation are "senno" and "arbitrio," which refer respectively to the two powers or functions of the soul, intellect and will. The object of the will is the good, whereas the object of the intellect is the truth; Dante's journey to God therefore will obviously involve both faculties. In fact, we learn from Beatrice that being blessed is founded first of all on the act that sees (intellect), and secondly on the act of love (will), which follows after:

> Quinci si può veder come si fonda
> l'esser beato ne l'atto che vede,
> non in quel ch'ama, che poscia seconda
>
> > > > (*Par.* XXVIII, 109-11)
> Hence may be seen how the being blessed is
> founded on the act that seeth, not that which
> loveth, which after followeth

Beatrice's words are most precise; they convey the Aristotelian Thom-istic idea of the primacy of the intellect:

Now the last end of man and of any intelligent substance is called *happi-ness* or *beatitude,* for it is this that every intellectual substance desires as its last end, and for its own sake alone. Therefore the last beatitude or happiness of any intellectual substance is to know God. Hence it is said (Math. v. 8): *Blessed are the clean of heart, for they shall see God;* and (Jo. XVII, v. 3): *This is eternal life, that they may know thee, the only true God.* Aristotle himself agrees with this judgement when he says that man's ultimate happiness is speculative, and this with regard to the high-est object of speculation (*Contra Gentiles*, III, 25).

Virgil's words are equally precise; they clearly confirm to us that at this stage of the journey one of the powers of Dante's soul—the will—is now free, upright, and whole: "libero, diritto e sano è tuo arbitrio," which indicates that a spiritual process has taken place on the mountain.

These are the facts. However, the problem arises when we interpret these facts. According to the widely accepted interpretation of Charles Sin-gleton, Dante's journey under Virgil's guidance on the mountain is a prepa-ration for sanctifying grace, which, supposedly, Dante receives only with the advent of Beatrice. This element is so pervasive that Singleton's book *Journey to Beatrice* could easily have been entitled "Journey to Sanctifying Grace":

What we have to see is what Dante has so well realized as poet: that jus-tification as it took place in history, and justification as it takes place now in the soul, are strikingly alike in essential outline. In the one, in justifi-cation of the soul, there are two basic features, as we know. First there is preparation, then there is that for which preparation has been made. Or, in the Aristotelian scheme of generation, we may say that a "matter" is prepared to receive a "form." Thus Virgil guides to the top of the mountain and his guidance is preparation. Virgil leads to justice, where-upon the "form" is given: Beatrice as sanctifying grace.[8]

In the pages that follow I shall propose that there are four basic features in justification, not two as Singleton maintains. I shall further propose that the Aristotelian "scheme of generation" has little to do with justification as such. Justification is a complex process of regeneration and not one of simple generation. Most importantly, I shall propose that justification is an effect of sanctifying grace, not a preparation for it as Singleton believes. I will also propose that, with Beatrice, Dante attains to a condition of merit, not to a condition of grace, which he has already received in the Prologue scene. Merit is an effect of sanctifying grace. Finally, I will show that Singleton un-derstands justification as a process in the "order of time." I shall propose, on the contrary, that justification is a process in the "order of nature." The difference of interpretation on these major thematic patterns could not be more divergent. And since Singleton has quoted extensively from St. Thomas, it will be necessary to examine his application of that philosopher's ideas to the structure of the *Comedy*.

I shall begin therefore with Singleton's first chapter, "The Allegorical Journey," which functions as a methodological preface for the entire book. It is here that Singleton proposes that Dante's journey to God should be seen in terms of intellect and will. Following a quotation from St. Thomas stressing the role of charity in uniting a man's mind to God, Singleton says:

> Yet Thomas insists that the soul achieves union with God not through love alone, which is an operation of the will, but through intellect as well. The two faculties function inseparably and simultaneously with respect to their proper end, which is God: "anima conjungatur Deo per intellectum et affectum," . . . the soul is united to God through intellect and love. Nor was Thomas alone in holding to this view. It is necessarily shared by all who think on such matters and in such terms, since the simple acknowledged truth is that the rational or intellective soul, the immortal part of the human creature, is made up entirely of these two faculties, intellect and will.[9]

For St. Thomas, then, the soul is united to God through intellect and will. This, although true, is not the whole truth, as we shall see later. But Singleton says much more than this. He goes on to assert that St. Thomas was not alone in holding this view for it was necessarily shared by all who thought on such matters in such terms. Note especially that Singleton does not give any quotations to substantiate his claim that, for St. Thomas, the rational soul is made up entirely of intellect and will. Nor, evidently, does he feel obliged to do so since he claims the matter to be a "simple acknowledged truth." The truth is not so simple nor was it ever acknowledged as such. In fact, St. Thomas insists that the faculties of the soul cannot constitute the essence of the soul because there stands between them the very same distinction that exists between "potency" and "act." The soul is act. The intellect and will are potencies. The intellect is like an empty blackboard: "But the human intellect, which is the lowest in the order of intellects and most remote from the perfection of the divine intellect, is in potentiality with regard to things intelligible, and is at first like a clean tablet on which nothing is written, as the Philosopher says" (I, q. 79, a. 2). Only in God—St. Thomas says—the intellect and will constitute essence because in Him alone operation and substance coincide. To the question "whether the essence of the soul is its power," St. Thomas answers:

> Now the operation of the soul is not in the genus of substance, for this belongs to God alone, whose operation is His own substance. Therefore

the divine potency or power which is the principle of His operation is the divine essence itself. This cannot be true either of the soul or of any creature, as we have said above when speaking of the angels. Secondly, this may also be shown to be impossible in the soul. For the soul by its very essence is an act (I, q. 77, a. 1).

Note that "the soul by its very essence is an act." The soul is the first act or substantial form of the body: "Now it is clear that the first thing by which the body lives is the soul," which "is the form of the body. This is the demonstration used by Aristotle" (I, q. 76, a. 1). All this means that the soul accounts for man's very being, whereas the intellect and will, as powers of the soul, account for man's acts as a rational being. In God alone is His act of understanding the same as His very Being:

> In accordance with what has been already shown, it is necessary to say that the intellect is a power of the soul, and not the very essence of the soul. For the essence of that which operates is then alone the immediate principle of operation, when operation itself is its being; for as power is related to operation as to its act, so is essence related to being. But in God alone is His act of understanding the same as His very Being. Hence, in God alone is His intellect His essence, while in other intellectual creatures the intellect is a power (I, q. 79, a. 1).

To have failed to draw the necessary distinction between the entitative and the operational aspects of the soul is indeed a significant omission on Singleton's part. The distinction is of paramount importance since it involves the fundamental problem of grace in the *Comedy*, and, as we shall see, many of Singleton's misinterpretations of Dante's poem may actually be traced back to this problem. We should now recall that in the *Paradiso* we meet none other than St. Thomas himself who teaches Dante (and by extension us) that in matters of philosophy and theology one must always proceed by way of proper distinction. This has to do with the famed story of Solomon, who had asked and had been granted a wisdom so profound that it was unequalled by any man:

> entro v'è l'alta mente u' sì profondo
> saver fu messo, che, se 'l vero è vero,
> a veder tanto non surse il secondo.
>
> (*Par.* X, 112-14)
>
> within there is the lofty mind, to which a wisdom
> so profound was granted, that, if the truth be
> true, no second ever rose to such full vision.

Three cantos later St. Thomas reads Dante's mind, which is naturally perplexed, for if Solomon's wisdom were unequalled by any man's, it would follow that his wisdom was even greater than Adam's and Christ's; this cannot possibly be since the latter possessed all human knowledge in perfection. The contradiction will prove to be apparent only once the proper distinction is introduced. We learn in fact that if one makes affirmations and negations without distinction, his opinion will surely lean towards falsehood:

> E questo ti sia sempre piombo a' piedi,
> per farti mover lento com' uom lasso
> e al sì e al no che tu non vedi:
>   ché quelli è tra li stolti bene a basso,
> che sanza distinzione afferma e nega
> ne l'un così come ne l'altro passo;
>   perch' elli 'ncontra che più volte piega
> l'oppinïon corrente in falsa parte,
> e poi l'affetto l'intelletto lega.

(Par. XIII, 112-20)

> And let this ever be lead to thy feet, to make
> thee move slow, like a weary man; both to
> the yea and nay thou seest not;
>   for he is right low down amongst the fools who
> maketh affirmation or negation without distinction between case and case;
>   wherefore it chanceth many times swift-formed
> opinion leaneth the wrong way, and then conceit bindeth the intellect.

But if we consider that Solomon did not ask for geometrical, or astronomical, or logical, or metaphysical wisdom, but only for regal wisdom proper to a king,

> Non ho parlato sì, che tu non posse
> ben veder ch'el fu re, che chiese senno
> acciò che re sufficïente fosse

(Par. XIII, 94-96)

> I have spoken so that thou mayst perceive
> he was a king, who chose such wit that as a
> king he might be adequate

the contradiction will obviously disappear, for Adam and Christ were not temporal kings, while of all those who ever became kings, none possessed a wisdom equal to Solomon's:

> Onde, se ciò ch'io dissi e questo note,
> regal prudenza è quel vedere impari
> in che lo stral di mia intenzion percuote.

(Par. XIII, 103-5)

> Wherefore (if this and all that I have said thou
> note) that insight without peer whereon the
> arrow of my intention smiteth, is regal
> prudence.

Thus, concerning the problem of grace in the *Comedy*, we should first of all ask, what is grace? Second, we should further ask, is grace a gift to the powers of the soul (intellect and will) or is it a gift to the essence of the soul? The two problems are obviously interrelated since the correct answer to the second question will depend by necessity on the correct answer to the first. Now, having said that the rational soul is united to God through intellect and will, and that it is made up entirely of these faculties, Singleton, quite naturally, cannot even begin to pose the question of whether grace is a gift to the soul itself or to the powers of the soul. His identification of the rational soul with intellect and will is quite clearly total and complete:

> If the goal to which Virgil leads, in this journey in soul, is essentially a condition of rectitude in the will, then that higher goal to which Beatrice leads in her turn is one in which intellect is primary, even as we have heard her say of the angels who are ever present at such a goal: "si fonda l'esser beato ne l'atto che vede." Hence, in even a fleeting glimpse of these matters, we take note of the necessity of realizing which faculties are involved, what moves in movement toward God. The very goals of the journey, whether intermediate or final, must be given and are given in terms of will and intellect. They are the coordinated and cooperating functions of the rational soul in all of its movements.[10]

As we have already noted, the intellect and will do not constitute the essence of the soul. The soul is first act and substantial form of the body; the powers are potencies. Thinking and willing demand a power that thinks and a power that wills, but also an immaterial substance in which these powers are rooted. What should be further considered is the fact that the soul has the power of understanding through its immateriality, and immateriality in a created, intelligent substance is not its intellect:

> The immateriality of a created intelligent substance is not its intellect; but rather through its immateriality it has the power of understanding. Therefore it follows, not that the intellect is the substance of the soul, but that it is its virtue and power (I, q. 79, a. 1, R.Obj. 4).

St. Thomas goes so far as to say that even if we grant, by hypothesis, that the soul were without its powers (which cannot be), the soul would still be called rational because it is so in its species:

> Since the powers of the soul are natural properties following upon the species, the soul cannot be without them. Yet, granted that it were with-

out them, the soul would still be called intellectual or rational in its species; not that it would actually have these powers, but because of the species of such an essence, from which these powers naturally flow (I-II, q. 110, a. 4, R.Obj. 4).

I have said that the distinction between the entitative and the operational aspects of the soul is of paramount importance because it involves the problem of grace in the *Comedy*. So, to the question of whether sanctifying grace is a gift to the soul itself, or to the powers of the soul, Singleton—as one would expect—will affirm that sanctifying grace is a gift to the intellect and will:

> But the advent of Beatrice is not merely advent of light. By such grace as she (in allegory) is, man's whole nature is transformed, elevated above the limits of what is natural to man. A *trasumanar* takes place, not in the intellect alone but also in the will. A new orientation of the inner man prevails, *itinerarium mentis* "turns" and moves in a new way. Through sanctifying grace the soul is uplifted and turned toward God as to its special object of beatitude. By such grace alone do we become the "adopted sons of God."[11]

Note especially: "man's whole nature is transformed"; "through sanctifying grace the soul is uplifted." And, most important: "a *trasumanar* takes place, not only in the intellect alone, but also in the will." The identification between the soul and its powers is once again complete. There can be no "trasumanar" that takes place either in the intellect or in the will unless sanctifying grace changes first of all the soul itself since it is a gift to the essence of the soul, and, as we have seen, the essence of the soul is constituted neither by the intellect nor by the will. The powers of the soul are the proper subject of virtues, such as faith and charity. Grace is not a virtue. Grace is a quality, and as such it may exist only in a substance, and the essence of the soul is in fact to be the substantial form of the body. St. Thomas is most precise on this subject. He says that, through his intellect, a man participates in the divine knowledge through the virtue of faith; whereas, through his will, he participates in the divine love through the virtue of charity. But it is through the very nature of the soul that a man participates in the divine nature—after the manner of a likeness—because it is the soul itself that has been regenerated, or recreated, by grace:

> This question depends on the preceding. For if grace is the same as virtue, it must necessarily be in the powers of the soul as in a subject; for the soul's powers are proper subject of virtue, as was stated above. But if grace differs from virtue, it cannot be said that a power of the soul is the subject of grace, since every perfection of the soul's powers has the na-

ture of virtue, as was stated above. Hence it remains that grace, being prior to virtue, has therefore a subject prior to the powers of the soul, so that it is in the essence of the soul. For just as man through his intellectual power participates in the divine knowledge through the virtue of faith, and through his power of will participates in the divine love through the virtue of charity, so also through the nature of the soul does he participate in the divine nature, after the manner of a likeness, through a certain regeneration or re-creation (I-II, q. 110, a. 4).

Grace is the splendor of the soul as beauty is the splendor of the body: "Grace is a certain splendor of the soul, which wins the divine love. But splendor of soul is a quality, even as beauty of body. Therefore grace is a quality" (I-II, q. 110, a. 2). Grace acts upon the soul itself by perfecting it after the manner of a formal cause: "Grace, as a quality, is said to act upon the soul, not after the manner of an efficient cause, but after the manner of a formal cause, as whiteness makes a thing white, and justice, just" (I-II, q. 110, R.Obj. 1). More stringently, grace is an accidental form of the soul: "And because grace is above human nature, it cannot be a substance or a substantial form; it is rather an accidental form of the soul. Now what is in God substantially comes to be accidentally in the soul participating in the divine goodness, as is clear in the case of knowledge" (I-II, q. 110, R.Obj. 2).

Singleton is aware, of course, that theologians have spoken of grace in terms of form. But once again he fails to make the necessary distinction between "substantial form" and "accidental form." He refers to grace simply as "form," which may be given either to the soul or to "some faculty of the soul":

Thus, if sanctifying grace is "form," as Philippe decided and as many another theologian conceded it to be, then must there not be some process that would culminate in the reception of such a form? Would there not be some "matter" which at a beginning point is deprived of that form, but which, on the established pattern of Aristotle, would "move" toward that form, being made ready to receive it? "Matter" in this case would surely be the soul, or some faculty of the soul. Thus sanctifying grace would be the form of the soul and there would be a movement of soul toward form, a process by which the soul is "disposed" to receive the form.[12]

Note especially that the matter being made ready to receive the form is "the soul or some faculty of the soul." How can this be? If grace is an "accidental form," and the essence of the soul is to be a "substantial form," the former can only be given to the latter since an "accident" can only exist in a "substance." Singleton, however, proceeds as if grace were a gift to the intellect:

But grace itself is a kind of light and as such must pertain directly to vision, to that operation of the intellect which precedes movement of the will in any *itinerarium mentis*.[13]

Or as if it were a gift to the will:

The matter which receives the form (when the form is habitual grace) is, broadly speaking, the soul. Or again, matter may be conceived as man's nature simply, in that sanctifying grace is said to "inform" the very nature of a man, uplifting it to a condition above nature. But in a more limited sense (in no way contradicting the broader view) the matter which receives the form in this case is thought to be the will. For this reason the whole question falls properly under the notion of conversion, which is movement of the will. It is thus the will which is made ready to receive the form.[14]

From the above quotation it begins to appear that Singleton is proceeding by way of vague approximations. Note especially, when he says the soul receives habitual grace, the expression "broadly speaking." Note also that in a more limited way "in no way contradicting the broader view" it is the will which is made ready to receive the form. Now, we have learned from St. Thomas that, "strictly speaking," sanctifying grace (habitual grace is another name for it) is received by the essence of the soul. This being the case, it becomes "in every way" contradictory to say that the will is made ready to receive the form. The truth of the matter is that intellect and will are indeed involved in the problem of sanctifying grace, but in a way diametrically opposed to how Singleton understands the matter to be. The simple truth is that grace is in the essence of the soul prior to being in the powers of the soul:

By grace we are born again sons of God. But generation terminates at the essence prior to the powers. Therefore grace is in the soul's essence prior to being in the powers (I-II, q. 110, a. 4).

There is a most important analogical correspondence between the essence of the soul and its powers on the one hand, and sanctifying grace and the infused virtues on the other:

For grace is the principle of meritorious works through the medium of the virtues, just as the essence of the soul is the principle of vital operations through the medium of the powers (I-II, q. 110, a. 4, R.Obj. 1).

What this means is that grace, like the soul, is not immediately operative. The essence of the soul is to the powers as grace is to the virtues. Just as the soul becomes operative through the vital operations of its powers, so grace becomes operative through the medium of the infused virtues. Therefore, it is not the will that is made ready to receive the form of sanctifying grace, as Singleton seems to believe; it is sanctifying grace, already existing in the essence of the soul that becomes operative through the medium of charity, and charity is a virtue of the will. Similarly, it is not the intellect that receives "directly" sanctifying grace as a kind of light, as Singleton seems also to believe. It is sanctifying grace, already existing in the essence of the soul, that becomes operative through the medium of faith; and faith is a virtue of the intellect.

IV

Having failed to make the distinction between the essence of the soul and the powers of the soul, it was inevitable that Singleton should also misunderstand the proper relationship between sanctifying grace and the infused virtues. The following note from his book reveals as much:

> Neither charity nor any of the other infused virtues may be without sanctifying grace, which is as their root. See Aquinas, *Summa Theol.*, I-II, q. 110, a. 3 resp. : "Manifestum est autem quod virtutes acquisitae per actus humanos . . . sunt dispositiones quibus homo convenienter disponitur in ordine ad naturam qua homo est. Virtutes autem infusae disponunt hominem altiori modo et ad altiorem finem; unde etiam oportet quod in ordine ad aliquam altiorem naturam. . . . Sicut igitur lumen naturalis rationis est aliquid praeter virtutes acquisitas, quae dicuntur in ordine ad ipsum lumen naturale: ita etiam ipsum lumen gratiae, quod est participatio divinae naturae, est aliquid praeter virtutes infusas, *quae a lumine illo derivantur*, et ad illud lumen ordinantur."
>
> The point is too clearly established everywhere in theology to require documentation.[15] (Singleton's italics.)

Now it is very true that sanctifying grace is the root and principle of the infused virtues, as St. Thomas clearly states: "Grace is reduced to the first species of quality; and yet it is not the same as virtue, but rather a certain disposition, which is presupposed to the infused virtues, as their principle and root" (I-II, q. 110, a. 3, R.Obj. 3). However, this does not mean that "Neither charity nor any of the other infused virtues may be without sanctifying grace," as Singleton believes. The very opposite is true. It is sanctifying grace that may not be without the infused virtues because, once sanctifying grace is possessed, the infused virtues are also possessed. The infused virtues flow from grace as the powers of the soul flow from the essence of the soul. Once the soul is possessed, the powers are also possessed.

> Just as from the essence of the soul flow its powers, which are the principles of operations, so likewise the virtues, whereby the powers are moved

to act, flow into the powers of the soul from grace. And thus grace is compared to the will as the mover to the moved, which is the same comparison as that of a horseman to the horse—but not as an accident to a subject (I-II, q. 110, a. 4, R.Obj. 1).

Infused virtues such as faith and hope—but with the exception of charity—may in fact be without sanctifying grace:

> If grace is a virtue, it would seem before all to be one of the three theological virtues. But grace is neither faith nor hope, for these can be without sanctifying grace. Nor is it charity, since grace fore-runs charity, as Augustine says in his book *On the Predestination of the Saints*. Therefore grace is not a virtue (I-II, q. 110, a. 3).

My last quotation comes from *S Th.* I-II, q. 110, a. 3, exactly two paragraphs above the Latin quotation from the same article given by Singleton. Yet Singleton says that the infused virtues may not be without sanctifying grace and that "the point is too clearly established everywhere in theology to require documentation." The very Latin words that Singleton has italicized, "*quae a lumine illo derivantur,*" contradict what he says. Infused virtues are derived from grace; it is not grace that is derived from the infused virtues.

This whole discussion is of considerable importance, since it shows that Singleton has actually effected a reversal in the order of nature, so much so that his book *Journey to Beatrice* may be viewed as a continuous exercise of a reversal in the order of nature imposed on the *Comedy*.

To say that the infused virtues may not be without sanctifying grace is one such reversal. The infused virtues are habits properly belonging to the powers of the soul. Sanctifying grace is a supernatural form or quality properly existing in the essence of the soul. Now, being precedes operation, since a thing must first of all be before it can be said to operate. Sanctifying grace is an accidental form of the soul, and as such it has two principal effects upon the soul, the first of which is being, the second operation:

> But if grace is taken for the habitual gift, then again there is a double effect of grace, even as of every other form, the first of which is being, and the second, operation. Thus, the work of heat is to make its subject hot, and to give heat outwardly (I-II, q. 110, a. 3).

When viewed from the perspective of being, sanctifying grace acts upon the soul after the manner of a formal cause by conferring a supernatural being, that is a supernatural form or quality, on the soul, whereby man, through the nature of the soul, participates in the divine nature, after the manner of a likeness, through a certain regeneration: "Grace, as a quality, is said to act upon the soul, not after the manner of an efficient cause, but after the man-

ner of a formal cause, as whiteness makes a thing white, and justice, just."
"And because grace is above human nature, it cannot be a substance or a
substantial form; it is rather an accidental form of the soul. Now, what is in
God substantially comes to be accidentally in the soul participating in the divine goodness, as is clear in the case of knowledge." Sanctifying grace heals
and perfects the soul, which thus becomes the supernatural form of the soul
as the soul itself is the natural form of the body. Man needs sanctifying grace
as "a habitual gift whereby corrupted human nature is healed, and after being
healed is lifted up so as to work deeds meritorious of eternal life, which exceed the capability of nature" (I-II, q. 109, a. 9). Therefore, when sanctifying
grace is viewed from the perspective of operation, it acts upon the soul after
the manner of an efficient cause—as "the principle of meritorious works
through the medium of the virtues," so much so that "the virtues, whereby
the powers are moved to act, flow into the powers of the soul from grace." In
this sense, sanctifying grace is compared to the will as the "mover" to the
"moved," which is the same comparison as that of a horseman to the horse.
Thus sanctifying grace makes the works performed by man meritorious of
eternal life, which is an end exceeding the proportion of human nature:

> Now eternal life is an end exceeding the proportion of human nature, as
> is clear from what we have said above. Hence man, by his natural pow-
> ers, cannot produce meritorious works proportioned to eternal life; but
> for this a higher power is needed, viz., the power of grace. And thus,
> without grace, man cannot merit eternal life (I-II, q. 109, a. 5).

Sanctifying grace brings about a new orientation of the natural powers of
the soul through the medium of the infused virtues that flow from it:

> For as the acquired virtues enable a man to walk in accordance with the
> natural light of reason, so the infused virtues enable a man to walk as
> befits the light of grace (I-II, q. 110, a. 3).

The analogy is this: acquired virtues are to the light of reason as infused
virtues are to the light of grace. But, since being always precedes operation,
the proper order will therefore be: light of reason (acquired virtues) walking
in accordance with reason; similarly: light of grace (infused virtues) walking
as befits grace. The light of reason and the light of grace must first of all be
(possessed) before a man may be said to walk (operate) in accordance with
them. And so it is always from sanctifying grace itself that the infused virtues
flow to the powers of the soul by which the powers are moved to their acts.
The proper order is therefore the following: sanctifying grace—infused
virtues—powers, all flowing from the essence of the soul. If infused virtues
may not be without sanctifying grace, as Singleton believes, the order would
be: powers—infused virtues—sanctifying grace, all floating in the air without

being grounded in the essence of the soul, since Singleton believes that sanctifying grace may be given to the powers of the soul. The order of efficient causality cannot be reversed. It is not the horse that makes the horseman move, but the other way about. Similarly, it is not the infused virtues (with the exception of charity, which is called the proximate principle of merit, whereas sanctifying grace is the radical principle of merit) that make the works of man meritorious of eternal life. The personages of the Old Testament lived in faith and hope of a Messiah to come, but it was the grace of Christ that drew them out of Limbo and "feceli beati" (*Inf.* IV, v. 61), made them blessed in Heaven where they now possess eternal life.

It should be emphasized that Singleton's starting point itself is one of operation rather than being. The soul is united to God through intellect and love, he says. And, on the supposition that the soul is made up entirely of these two faculties, he writes chapters such as "Three Lights," where he traces Dante's journey to God exclusively in terms of the intellect; or "Three Conversions," where he will view the journey in terms of the will exclusively.

> It will be our first concern, therefore, to distinguish two master patterns or paradigms in this matter of a journey to God in the soul, and they are two for the reason noted, namely, that the faculties involved are two, intellect and will. Only by seeing such broad patterns may we then recognize those which are subordinate to them as parts of the whole, and see how these shapes of doctrine are made manifest in the concrete substance of a poem.[16]

Everything is subordinate to intellect and will, as parts to a whole, because Singleton has it on the authority of St. Thomas that "anima conjungatur Deo per intellectum et affectum." Where does this quotation come from and, more important, what is the exact meaning that St. Thomas has ascribed to it? It does not seem likely that St. Thomas would have made an unqualified affirmation without the necessary distinctions.

V

The quotation comes from an obscure article of the *Summa* dealing with "Whether the Ceremonial Precepts are Figurative." Let us quote the paragraph in its entirety so as to preserve the integrity of its meaning:

> As was stated above, the ceremonial precepts are those which refer to the worship of God. Now the divine worship is twofold: interior and exterior. For since man is composed of soul and body, each of these should be applied to the worship of God, the soul by an interior worship, and the body by an outward worship. Hence it is written (Ps. lxxxii. 3): *My heart and my flesh have rejoiced in the living God.* And just as the body is

ordained to God through the soul, so the exterior worship is ordained to the interior worship. *Now interior worship consists in the soul being united to God by the intellect and by affection.* Therefore, according to the various ways in which the intellect and the affection of the man who worships God are rightly united to God, his exterior actions are applied in various ways to the divine worship (I-II, q. 101, a. 2). (Italics mine.)

Clearly, we can see from the above that Singleton's quotation from St. Thomas (anima conjungatur Deo per intellectum et affectum) is both fragmented and out of context. The complete statement by St. Thomas is the following: "Now interior worship consists in the soul being united to God by the intellect and affection." The interior act of worship involves prayer and devotion. But devotion is a promptness of the will in those things that concern the worship of God: "the will to give oneself readily to things concerning the worship of God" (II-II, q. 82, a. 1),[17] whereas prayer is an act of the intellect, as "the lifting up of the mind to God."[18] It is therefore right for St. Thomas to say that in worship the soul is united to God through intellect and love. This is a qualified affirmation concerning the function of intellect and will as they are involved in the particular act of worship. By eliminating the words, "Now interior worship consists in," Singleton has changed a "particular" affirmation of St. Thomas into a "universal" affirmation without qualification. Singleton seems to be unaware that, for St. Thomas, grace is in the soul's essence prior to being in the powers.

Consequent upon an infusion of sanctifying grace in the essence of the soul, there are then several effects that take place:

Now there are five effects of grace in us. Of these, the first is, to heal the soul; the second, to desire good; the third, to carry into effect the good proposed; the fourth, to persevere in good; the fifth, to reach glory. And hence grace, inasmuch as it causes the first effect in us, is called prevenient with respect to the second, and inasmuch as it causes the second it is called subsequent with respect to the first effect. And as one effect is posterior to this effect, and prior to that, so grace may be called prevenient and subsequent because of the same effect viewed in relation to other and different effects (I-II, q. 111, a. 3).

It should be understood, however, that grace is one as to its essence, and that it is divisible only in its effects:

The division into prevenient and subsequent grace does not divide grace in its essence, but only in its effects, as was already said of operating and cooperating grace. For subsequent grace, inasmuch as it pertains to glory, is not numerically distinct from prevenient grace whereby we are at present justified. For even as the charity of earth is not voided in heaven, so must the same be said of the light of grace, since the notion of neither implies imperfection (I-II, q. 111, a. 3, R.Obj. 2).

The above passage from the *Summa* is of considerable importance for I will attempt to prove shortly that Singleton has failed to make a fundamental distinction concerning sanctifying grace itself. As a consequence, he has also failed to distinguish two different effects of sanctifying grace and has actually confused one with the other. This is of paramount importance since it changes the whole perspective of the *Comedy* as regards the most significant element of the poem: the element of structure. Singleton maintains that Dante will receive an infusion of sanctifying grace at the mountaintop of Purgatory with the advent of Beatrice. On the contrary, I propose that Dante has already received an infusion of sanctifying grace at the beginning of the journey, in the second half of the Prologue scene, on the stage of this life, before he enters the world beyond. Let us see what Singleton says:

> To pass from Virgil to Beatrice must mean to pass from the first natural light to the second, which is supernatural. It means to pass out of a first conversion into a second, wherein the soul attains to that meritorious justice which is given with sanctifying grace and the infused virtues. On such a test, we see the truth of what was noted at the outset: that we may understand a part of this journey to God only if we see that part within the pattern of the whole. Thus justification finds its proper and enlightening measure within the whole pattern of the three lights and three conversions, as a part thereof.[19]

We are, at this point, on page 67 of Singleton's book. He is directing our attention to "the truth of what was noted at the outset," the outset, that is, of his book. This truth is that the whole pattern of Dante's journey to God is constituted by the three lights (a journey of the intellect) and three conversions (a journey of the will). This must be so, according to Singleton, because the rational soul "is made up entirely of these two faculties" and the soul is united to God through intellect and will: "anima conjungatur Deo per intellectum et affectum." Those are Singleton's major premises, the fallacy of which I have already noted in detail. The first is true only of God, in whom alone the will and intellect are His very essence. As for Dante, his intellect and will do not constitute the essence of his soul. The second premise is true only as it concerns the function of the intellect and will in the particular act of worship. But in relation to sanctifying grace, Dante's journey to God involves, first of all, the essence of his soul, which receives the infusion of grace. Justification, Singleton says, is only part of the whole—"a part thereof." More on this later, since the powers of the soul are also involved in justification, but not in the same way as I have already noted concerning the virtues of faith and charity. By his intellect, man participates in the divine knowledge through the virtue of faith; whereas, by the power of his will, he participates in the divine love through the virtue of charity. This is a special ordering of the human mind to God. In justification, the intellect and will are involved in a justice that "expresses a general rectitude of order":

> Faith and charity express a special ordering of the human mind to God by the intellect and will; whereas justice expresses a general rectitude of order. Hence this transmutation is named from justice rather than from charity or faith (I-II, q. 113, a. 1, R.Obj. 2).

According to Singleton, in passing from Virgil to Beatrice, Dante's soul "attains to that meritorious justice which is given with sanctifying grace and the infused virtues." The point of special interest here is the expression, "meritorious justice," which is an indication that Singleton might have confused the process of "merit" with the process of "justification." Justification and Merit are two distinct, principal effects of sanctifying grace. And here is the crux of the matter: in virtue of these two effects, sanctifying grace may be divided into Operating Grace and Cooperating Grace. Justification is the effect of operating grace; Merit is the effect of cooperating grace:

> But if grace is taken, for the habitual gift, then again there is a double effect of grace, even as of every other form, the first of which is being, and the second, operation. Thus, the work of heat is to make its subject hot, and to give heat outwardly. In this way, habitual grace, inasmuch as it heals and justifies the soul, or makes it pleasing to God, is called operating grace; but inasmuch as it is the principle of meritorious works, which proceed from free choice, it is called cooperating grace (I-II, q. 111, a. 2).

It should be clearly understood, however, that operating grace and cooperating grace are one and the same. It is sanctifying grace viewed from two different perspectives: "Operating and cooperating grace are the same grace, but they are distinguished by their different objects, as is plain from what has been said" (I-II, q. 111, a. 2, R.Obj.4).

Against St. Thomas's best advice, as given in the *Paradiso*, which is in fact the best advice of Dante himself, Singleton, once again has failed to make a necessary distinction. He has fused together two different effects of sanctifying grace, which is the same as confusing the order of being with the order of operation. In the order of being it is God who operates. It is He who heals the soul, justifies the soul, and makes it pleasing to Himself; and he does all this by an infusion of the form of sanctifying grace which, from this perspective, may now be called operating grace. Justification is an effect of operating grace because a cause is prior to its effect:

The cause is naturally prior to its effect. Now the infusion of grace is the cause of whatever is required for the justification of the ungodly, as was stated above. Therefore it is naturally prior to it (I-II, q. 113, a. 8).

Dante is justified by operating grace. One important aspect of justification is constituted by a reestablished harmony whereby Dante's reason is made obedient to God (order of part to whole), and his lower powers are made obedient to his reason (order of part to part):

> Justice is so called inasmuch as it signifies a certain rectitude of order in the interior disposition of man, insofar as what is highest in man is subject to God, and the inferior powers of the soul are subject to the superior, i.e., to the reason; and this disposition the Philosopher calls justice metaphorically speaking (I-II, q. 113, a. 1).

This certain rectitude of order in the interior disposition of man is the "good of nature," or the "natural inclination to virtue" that was corrupted by original sin in the sense that it was diminished, although not destroyed. This rectitude of order in the soul (this justice) is reestablished by the grace of Baptism with the sole infusion of grace, since as infants we are not capable of the movement of free choice:

> Infants are not capable of the movement of free choice, and so it is by the sole information of their souls that God moves them to justice (I-II, q. 113, a. 3, R.Obj. 1).

Dante has lost this baptismal grace because of actual personal sins. The poem opens with a confession of sin. Therefore, "as sin is opposed to virtue, from the very fact that a man sins there results a diminution of that good of nature which is the inclination to virtue." After being healed Dante is lifted up so as to work deeds meritorious of eternal life:

> And thus human nature, undone by reason of the act of sin, remains no longer integral, but corrupted, as was stated above; nor can it be restored, by itself, even to its connatural good, and much less to the good of supernatural justice. . . . Hence man cannot be restored by himself, but requires the light of grace to be poured upon him anew, as if the soul were infused into a dead body for its resurrection (I-II, q. 109, a. 7, R.Obj. 3 & 2).

Dante, as the poem opens, stands in need of a new infusion of sanctifying grace that would justify him, i.e., would heal his soul by reestablishing a certain rectitude of order, which consists in his reason (intellect and will) being subject to God, and the inferior powers subject to his reason. It should be pointed out, however, that even in this state Dante's carnal appetite would not be entirely healed. He would be able to abstain from all mortal sin but not from all venial sin, because while he would be resisting one, another would arise just as St. Paul, speaking as a person already healed by grace, says: "I myself, with the mind, serve the law of God, but with the flesh, the law of sin."

> We may speak of man in two ways: first, in the state of integral nature; secondly, in the state of corrupted nature. Now in the state of integral nature, man, even without habitual grace, could avoid sinning either mortally or venially, since to sin is nothing else than to stray from what is according to our nature—and in the state of integral nature man could avoid this. Nevertheless, he could not have done it without God's help upholding him in good, since if this had been withdrawn, even his nature would have fallen back into nothingness.
>
> But in the state of corrupted nature man needs grace to heal his nature in order that he may entirely abstain from sin. And in the present life this healing is wrought first in the mind, since the carnal appetite is not yet entirely healed. Hence the Apostle (Rom. vii. 25) says in the person of one who is healed: *I myself, with the mind, serve the law of God, but with the flesh, the law of sin.* And in this state man can abstain from all mortal sin, whose source is in the reason, as was stated above; but man cannot abstain from all venial sin because of the corruption of his lower appetite of sensuality. For man can, indeed, repress each of its movements (and hence they are sinful and voluntary), but not all, because, while he is resisting one, another may arise, and also because the reason is not always alert to avoid the movements, as it was said above (S T. I, II, q. 109 a. 8).

But we should inquire as to when Dante does receive this justice in the *Comedy*. Singleton maintains that Dante receives it when he meets Beatrice: "the soul attains to that meritorious justice which is given with sanctifying grace and the infused virtues." I maintain instead that Dante receives this justice in the second half of the Prologue scene, for the simple reason that merit and justification are two distinct effects of sanctifying grace that involve the distinction between being and operation. Justification is an effect of operating grace—God conferring supernatural being. Merit is an effect of cooperating grace, whereby God cooperates with Dante, who is already justified, in the free performance of good works meritorious of eternal life. Merit is the right to the reward of eternal life that Dante earns by performing works proceeding from free choice. Sanctifying grace is called cooperating grace, "inasmuch as it is the principle of meritorious works, which proceed from free choice." God may have justified Dante in the Prologue scene, but Dante must now participate in the process of his own sanctification by freely undertaking the journey through the world beyond in order to earn the right to the reward of eternal life. Beatrice comes on the mountain of Purgatory in order to lift Dante up to Heaven so that he may have a foretaste of the reward of Heaven. There is no such thing as "meritorious justice," as Singleton maintains. The justice of justification cannot be merited, whereas the justice of merit, which is the right to the reward of eternal life, is earned after one has been justified. But this involves operation, and in this sense "grace is the principle of meritorious works through the medium of the virtues, just as the essence of the soul is the principle of vital operations through the medium of the powers." Sanctifying grace is the radical principle of merit. The virtues—principally charity—are the proximate principles:

> For we must first bear in mind that eternal life consists in the fruition of God. Now the human mind's movement to the fruition of the divine good is the proper act of charity, by which all the acts of the other virtues are ordained to this end, since all the other virtues are commanded by charity. Hence the merit of eternal life pertains first to charity, and secondly to the other virtues, inasmuch as their acts are commanded by charity. It is likewise manifest that what we do out of love we do most willingly. Hence, even inasmuch as merit depends on voluntariness, merit is chiefly attributed to charity (I-II, q. 114, a. 4).

But the justice that is given as an effect of operating grace cannot be merited. That justice is a free gift from God. No one, in fact, can merit for himself the first actual or habitual grace:

> The gift of grace can be considered in two ways. First, in the nature of a gratuitous gift, and thus it is manifest that all merit is repugnant to grace, since, as the Apostle says (Rom. XI, 6), if by grace, it is not now by works. Secondly, it may be considered according to the nature of the thing given, and thus, also, it cannot come under the merit of him who has not grace, both because it exceeds the proportion of nature, and because prior to grace a man in the state of sin has an obstacle to his meriting grace, viz., sin. But when anyone has grace, the grace already possessed cannot come under merit, *since reward is the term of work, whereas grace is the principle of all our good works,* as was stated above. But if anyone merits a further gratuitous gift by virtue of the preceding grace, it would not be the first grace. Hence it is manifest that no one can merit for himself the first grace (I-II, q. 114, a. 5). (Italics mine.)

By failing to distinguish between operating grace and cooperating grace, Singleton gives rise to at least three other major reversals in the order of nature that he imposes on Dante and on the very structure of the *Comedy* (more on this later). Once again, the problem is Singleton's point of departure, his major premises. He has taken an isolated quotation from the

Summa of St. Thomas, and then has proceeded to apply the content to the entire structure of the *Comedy*. Compounding the problem is the fact that the quotation comes from a part of the *Summa* that has nothing to do with the specific problem of sanctifying grace as it pertains to man—the most fundamental problem in the *Divine Comedy*. We have noted this already in the case of his major premise, that "the soul is united to God through intellect and love." The quotation comes from an obscure article of the *Summa* having to do with "whether the Ceremonial Precepts are Figurative." The very same is true with Singleton's failure to distinguish between operating grace and co-operating grace. Let us see how. Singleton opens the chapter "The Three Conversions" with the following quotation from St. Thomas:

> Every movement of the will toward God can be termed a conversion to God. And so there is a threefold turning to God. The first is by the perfect love of God; this belongs to the creature enjoying the possession of God; and for such a conversion, consummate grace is required. The next turning to God is that which merits beatitude; and for this there is required habitual grace, which is the principle of merit. The third conversion is that whereby a man disposes himself so that he may have grace; for this no habitual grace is required, but an operation of God, Who draws the soul toward Himself, according to *Lam.* 5.21: "Convert us, O Lord, to thee, and we shall be converted." Hence it is clear that there is no need to go on to infinity.[20]

Since Dante's journey to God takes place with the assistance of three guides—Virgil, Beatrice, and St. Bernard—Singleton immediately proceeds to apply the above quotation from the *Summa* to the entire structure of the *Comedy* by matching St. Thomas's threefold turning to God with the phases of the journey under the three guides. The phase under Virgil thus becomes a conversion "whereby a man disposes himself so that he may have grace; for this no habitual grace is required, but an operation of God, Who draws the soul toward Himself." The whole journey under Virgil's guidance is analyzed by Singleton in terms of the Aristotelian concept of "generatio," which is a movement toward form, the form being sanctifying grace, which Dante supposedly will receive with Beatrice: "the whole area of Virgil's guidance in the *Comedy* is that of *praeparatio ad gratiam*.[21] We shall see shortly that the whole area of Virgil's guidance in the *Comedy* is not a "preparation for grace," as Singleton believes, but an effect of sanctifying grace.

The second phase of the journey, under Beatrice's guidance, corresponds for Singleton with St. Thomas's: "The next turning to God is that which merits beatitude; and for this there is required habitual grace, which is the principle of merit." But Beatrice comes as the bringer of the reward that Dante has merited because of the good works he has performed. In fact, Dante's journey (the work) under Virgil's guidance is meritorious of the reward of beatitude because he has already received an infusion of sanctifying grace, which makes it (the journey) meritorious in the first place:

> And hence it is that no created nature is a sufficient principle of an act meritorious of eternal life, unless there is added a supernatural gift, which we call grace (I-II, q. 114, a. 2).

The third phase of Dante's journey, under the guidance of St. Bernard, is made by Singleton to correspond with the conversion "by the perfect love of God; this belongs to the creature enjoying the possession of God; and for such a conversion, consummate grace is required."

But we should now inquire about the origin of the quotation. It comes from *S.T.* I, q. 62, a. 2, reply obj. 3, and the title of the article is "Whether an Angel needed grace in order to turn to God?" What should first of all be noted is that the quotation is a reply to the third objection of the article. The main concern of the article is the need of grace as it pertains to an angel, so that if St. Thomas, in the restricted scope of a reply to an objection will say anything about grace as it may pertain to man, he will obviously do so in the most condensed and concise manner. He cannot stop to elaborate. And this is indeed what he does. These are the lines he devotes here to sanctifying grace and merit: "The next turning to God is that which merits beatitude; and for this there is required habitual grace, which is the principle of merit." Habitual grace is another name for sanctifying grace. St. Thomas cannot be expected to stop here in order to write a digression on how sanctifying grace may further be distinguished into operating grace and cooperating grace, because the distinction is too fundamental to be simply touched upon in passing. He will explain later in his "Treatise on Grace" that the principle of meritorious works is, specifically cooperating grace: "In this way, habitual grace, inasmuch as it heals and justifies the soul, or makes it pleasing to God, is called operating grace; but inasmuch as it is the principle of meritorious works, which proceed from free choice, it is called cooperating grace" (I-II, q. 111, a. 2). It is surprising that Singleton would extract two lines from an article dealing with the need of grace as it pertains to an angel, and think that he thus had it on St. Thomas's authority that sanctifying grace is a principle of merit, and that he should have therefore felt justified in applying these two lines to the entire *Comedy*. Having done this, it was inevitable, therefore, that Singleton should fuse together the process of justification with the process of merit and say that when Dante meets Beatrice, he will attain "to that meritorious justice which is given with sanctifying grace and the infused virtues." Justification is an effect of operating grace and is, therefore, given. Merit is an effect of cooperating grace and is, therefore, earned. Dante receives justification in the second half of the Prologue scene. Dante earns merit (the right to the reward of beatitude) by freely undertaking the journey. Beatrice is the bringer of beatitude, of that happiness of Heaven that is beyond the propor-

tion of human nature, and it is through her (mostly through her eyes) that
Dante is made to partake of that beatitude. But Singleton proceeds without
ever suspecting that there is a distinction to be made within sanctifying grace
itself:

> While we take note of this difference as we turn from the highest conver-
> sion with St. Bernard to the next lower conversion with Beatrice, we re-
> mark also the similarity between the two moments: for even as the light
> of glory is that same consummate grace by which the final conversion of
> the will is realized, so now is the light of sanctifying grace that same
> lesser grace by which the second conversion of the will takes place, a
> turning to God which merits beatitude. Only through habitual grace, as
> St. Thomas tells us above, can such merit be obtained; and habitual grace
> is but another name for sanctifying grace. Beatrice is such grace, and her
> advent is predominantly in terms of light for that reason. She is *lumen
> gratiae*, the light of grace descending to the wayfarer who attains to the
> summit of the mountain and is made ready to receive her. Beatrice is
> thus that grace by which a man is made "pleasing" to God, as the name
> in Latin most commonly used to denote it explicitly affirms: gratia gra-
> tum faciens.[22]

Note especially: "Only through habitual grace, as St. Thomas tells us
above, can such merit be obtained." There is no mention of "meritorious
works." Note also: "Beatrice is thus that grace by which a man is made
'pleasing' to God." The fusion of being and operation is complete. The making of Dante "pleasing" to God is an effect of operating grace—God operating, conferring supernatural being on Dante's soul. Merit is an effect of cooperating grace—God cooperating with Dante in the free performance of his
meritorious works. "Merit is related to sanctifying grace in the same way as
operation follows being,"[23] or to put it once again in St. Thomas's words: "but
inasmuch as it is the principle of meritorious works which proceed from free
choice, it is called cooperating grace." Singleton obviously thinks that Dante
is sanctified by an infusion of sanctifying grace alone. Of the works of charity
required, there is not even a shadow. But Paul said: "God will render to every
man according to his works" (Rom. 2:6). Dante's journey is the work of a
penitent, whereby the pilgrim expiates the debt of punishment he has incurred because of his sins, as St. Thomas says: "for there is a reward for thy
work. Now the reward for the work of the penitent is complete pardon for sin
both as to guilt and punishment" (III, q. 84, a. 9). This is so because a man in
the state of grace (as Dante is) may sin simply by failing to make use of the
grace that he possesses: "consequently the movement of grace does not impose necessity; but he who has grace can fail to make use of it, and can sin"
(I, q. 62, a. 3). What Singleton seems to be unaware of is the distinction that,
under operating grace, the human mind is moved by God "to become con-

verted to its final supernatural end," whereas under cooperating grace the human mind is moved by God "to determining to exercise the infused virtues."[24]

VI

Let us consider more closely this specific function of cooperating grace in the following quotation:

> We now come to the question of cooperative grace. This is conferred for good works in which our will is not only moved, but moves itself, that is, when already actually willing the final supernatural end, it converts itself to willing the means conducive to that end. This act is said to be external, although it may be only internal, since it is commanded by the will in virtue of a previous efficacious act of the same order. Thus it is in the use of the infused virtues, by deliberation properly so called, that the act is performed in the human mode, for example, when the will commands an act of justice or religion or fortitude or temperance, by virtue of a previous act of love of God. Not only are these acts vital, free, and meritorious, but the will properly moves toward them or "determines itself to will this or that," as is said in the well-known reply to the third objection, Ia, IIae, q. 9, a. 6.[25]

This, I believe, describes Dante's condition in the second half of the Prologue scene when his will, having already consented to be converted to its final supernatural end, converts itself to willing the means conducive to that end. Sanctifying grace is present in both of its aspects of operating grace and cooperating grace. By one of the most beautiful images in the entire *Comedy*, Dante conveys to the reader that a profound spiritual regeneration has taken place in the depth of his soul: the light of grace, as St. Thomas would say, is "poured upon him anew, as if the soul were infused into a dead body for its resurrection." This is the only meaning that I could ascribe to the image of the flowers that remain bent down and closed because of the chill of the night; but when the morning sun whitens them, they lift themselves up, all open on their stems—suddenly revivified. So too Dante, with his tired "soul," suddenly feels so much good daring running into his heart, that he begins, as a person set free:

> Quali fioretti dal notturno gelo
> chinati e chiusi, poi che 'l sol li 'mbianca,
> si drizzan tutti aperti in loro stelo,
>   tal mi fec' io di mia virtude stanca,
> e tanto buono ardire al cor mi corse,
> ch'i' cominciai come persona franca:

(*Inf.* II, 127-32)

> As flowerets, by the nightly chillness bended
> down and closed, erect themselves all open
> on their stems when the sun whitens them:
>   thus I did, with my fainting courage; and so
> much good daring ran into my heart, that I
> began as one set free:

Dante's will has consented, "come persona franca," to be converted to its final supernatural end. This freedom is a direct effect of sanctifying grace: "The entire justification of the ungodly consists, as to its origin, in the infusion of grace. For, it is by grace that free choice is moved and guilt is remitted" (I-II, q. 113, a. 3). A conversion has taken place as an effect of operating grace. Dante's soul (the essence of his soul) has now received an infusion of sanctifying grace. Therefore, Dante's will, already actually willing the final supernatural end, converts itself to willing the means conducive to that end, and the means conducive to that end is the journey itself that he now wills to undertake. "You have disposed my heart," he says to Virgil, "with so much desire to go, / that I have returned to my first purpose." / "Now go," he tells Virgil, "for we both have one will." By this "now go" Dante's will converts itself to willing the means conducive to his final supernatural end:

> "Or va, ch'un sol volere è d'ambedue"
>
> *(Inf.* II, 139)
>
> "Now go, for both have one will"

This is an effect of cooperating grace whereby Dante cooperates with God and God cooperates with Dante in the process of the latter's personal sanctification. From this instant onwards, Dante's journey takes place not as a preparation for sanctifying grace as Singleton maintains, but as an effect of it: "The same instant the form is acquired, the thing begins to operate with the form" (I-II, 113 a.7, R.Obj. 4). This is confirmed in the *Letter to Cangrande*, where we are told by Dante himself that he undertook the journey for two specific, personal reasons, the first of which was "conversion," the second "punishment":

> But if they should rail at the ordering of so great an exaltation through the fault of the speaker, let them read Daniel, wherein they will find that even Nebuchadnezzar, by divine inspiration saw something terrible to sinners, and then forgot it. For He "who maketh his sun to rise on the evil and on the good, and sendeth rain on the just and the unjust,"—sometimes compassionately, for their *conversion*, sometimes severely, for their *punishment*,—more or less, according as it pleaseth Him, doth manifest His glory even to those who live evilly.[26] (Italics mine.)

Note especially: "sometimes compassionately for their conversion, sometimes severely for their punishment—more or less, according as it pleaseth Him." Conversion or justification is an effect of operating grace, which involves a movement of faith, and therefore must occur right here and now, on the stage of this life, in the Prologue scene. Faith, according to Dante himself, is the substance of things hoped for, and the argument of things which are not seen: "fede è sustanza di cose sperate / e argomento de le non parventi" (*Par.* XXIV, 64-5). By faith, Dante must hold that he may be converted through Christ before he is even allowed to enter the world beyond:

> The effect of operative grace is justification of the wicked, as stated in Ia IIae, q. 113, a. 1-3, which [justification] consists not only in the infusion of grace and the remission of sins, but also a movement of the free will toward God, which is the act of formed faith, and a movement of the free will in relation to sin, which is the act of penance. But these human acts are present as effects of operative grace, produced in the same way as the remission of sins. Hence, the remission of sin is not accomplished without an act of the virtue of penance, even if it is the effect of operative grace.[27]

What should be clearly understood here is the fact that conversion, or justification, is the work of God alone. An act of formed faith is required so that we may believe that God justifies us through the mystery of Christ: "As the Apostle says (Rom. 4: 5), to him that . . . believeth in Him that justifieth the ungodly his faith is reputed to justice, according to the purpose of the grace of God. Hence it is clear that in the justification of the ungodly, an act of faith is required in order that a man may believe that God justifies man through the mystery of Christ" (I-II, q. 113, a. 4, R.Obj. 3). Similarly, since justification is a movement from the state of sin to the state of justice, the human mind, while it is justified, must withdraw from sin and draw near to justice. Therefore, there must be two movements of free choice, one towards God, the other against sin:

> As we have stated above, the justification of the ungodly is a certain movement whereby the human mind is moved by God from the state of sin to the state of justice . . . Hence the human mind, while it is being justified, must, by a movement of free choice, withdraw from sin and draw near to justice. Now, to withdraw from sin and to draw near to justice, in a movement of free choice, means detestation and desire. . . . Hence in the justification of the ungodly there must be two movements of the free choice, one whereby it tends to God's justice, the other whereby it hates sin (I-II, q. 113, a. 5).

More specifically, since a movement of faith is made perfect by a movement of charity, a movement of charity is also infused. This is what is called an act of "formed faith," which is faith directed by charity: "The movement of faith is not perfect unless it is quickened by charity, and so in the justification of the ungodly, a movement of charity is infused together with the movement of faith." And since the same act of free choice may spring from different virtues, "an act of filial fear and an act of humility also concur" (I-II, q. 113, a. 4, R.Obj. 1).

Now, as we turn once again to the Prologue scene, we should not have any difficulty in realizing that Dante does in fact express a deep feeling of humility when he says that neither he nor others consider him worthy of the journey:

> "Ma io, perché venirvi? o chi 'l concede?
> Io non Enëa, io non Paulo sono;
> me degno a ciò né io né altri 'l crede.
>
> <div align="right">(<i>Inf.</i> II, 31-33)</div>
>
> "But I, why go? or who permits it? I am not
> Æneas, am not Paul; neither myself nor others
> deem me worthy of it.

He fears, in fact—and this is indeed an act of filial fear—that if he should let himself go, his going might prove to be an act of folly:

> "Per che, se del venire io m'abbandono,
> temo che la venuta non sia folle.
> Se' savio; intendi me' ch'i' non ragiono."
>
> <div align="right">(<i>Inf.</i> II, 34-6)</div>
>
> "Wherefore, if I resign myself to go, I fear my
> going may prove foolish; thou art wise, and
> understandest better than I speak."

But now Virgil speaks, saying that he was called by a lady, "beata e bella," with eyes brighter than the stars, who, speaking to him softly and gently with "angelica voce," had asked that he go and rescue her friend, "l'amico mio e non de la ventura," who was so impeded in his way upon the desert shore that he had turned back because of fear, she fears that he might have already gone too far astray: "e temo che non sia già sì smarrito." This lady turns out to be none other than Beatrice, who makes Virgil go: "I' son Beatrice che ti faccio andare." This is clearly an indication of operating grace, God operating alone, as distinguished from cooperating grace whereby God cooperates with Dante. Grace is a special act of God's love, to be distinguished from the common act of God's love whereby He gives being: "And according to this difference of good the love of God towards the creature is looked at differently. For one is common, whereby He loves all things that are (Wis. 11:25), and thereby gives things their natural being. But the second is a special love, whereby He draws the rational creature above the condition of its nature to a participation of the divine good. . . . accordingly when a man is said to have the grace of God, there is signified something supernatural bestowed on man by God." This special act is the eternal act of love called the grace of predestination: "nevertheless, the grace of God sometimes signifies God's eternal love in which sense it is also called the grace of predestination, inasmuch as God gratuitously, and not from merits, predestines or elects some" (I-II, q. 110, a. 1). Beatrice now confirms that it was in fact love that moved her and makes her speak: "amor mi mosse che mi fa parlare." More specifically, she is a lady of virtue through whom alone mankind may go beyond all that is contained within the sphere of the moon:

> "O donna di virtù sola per cui
> l'umana spezie eccede ogne contento
> di quel ciel c'ha minor li cerchi sui!"
>
> *(Inf.* II, 76-8)
>
> "O Lady of virtue, through whom alone man-
> kind excels all that is contained within the
> heaven which has the smallest circles!"

Sanctifying grace is known as the grace of the virtues and gifts: "Hence sanctifying grace is identical here with the 'grace of the virtues and gifts with their proportionate helps,' which St. Thomas speaks of (III a, q. 62, a.1),"[28] as it is also clear that through sanctifying grace alone may mankind go beyond the proportion of nature:

> Now eternal life is an end exceeding the proportion of human nature, as it is clear from what we have said above. Hence man, by his natural powers, cannot produce meritorious works proportioned to eternal life; but for this a higher power is needed, viz., the power of grace. And thus, without grace, man cannot merit eternal life (I-II, q. 109, a. 5).

Beatrice insists that she is made by God—"I' son fatta da Dio"—who alone is the cause of grace: "Now the gift of grace surpasses every capability of created nature, since it is nothing short of a partaking of divine nature, which exceeds every other nature. And thus it is impossible that any creature should cause grace. For it is as necessary that God alone should deify, by bestowing a partaking of the divine nature through a participated likeness, as it is impossible that anything save fire should enkindle" (I-II, q. 112, a. 1). And finally, we learn that St. Lucia calls Beatrice "true praise of God": "Beatrice, loda di Dio vera," inasmuch as the good of grace in one man—St. Thomas says—"is greater than the good of nature in the whole universe" (I-II, q. 113, a. 9, R.Obj. 2). The justification of the ungodly through grace is God's greatest work, even greater than creation, for creation terminates in a good of the natural order, whereas justification "terminates at the eternal good of a participation in God. . . . Hence, Augustine, after saying that *for a just man to be made from a sinner is greater than to create heaven and earth,* adds, *for heaven and earth shall pass away, but salvation and the justification of the predestined shall endure* (I-II, q. 113, a. 9). And better still: "He hath predestinated us into the addition of children . . . *unto the praise of the glory of his grace*" (I-II, q. 110, a. 1). (Italics mine.)

Then Virgil asks: Why do you lodge so much coward fear in your heart, "perché tanta viltà nel core allette," when three such blessed ladies care for you in the court of Heaven, and my words promise you so much good?

> "poscia che tai tre donne benedette
> curan di te ne la corte del cielo,
> e 'l mio parlar tanto ben ti promette?"
>
> (Inf. II, 124-26)
>
> "when three such blessed Ladies care for thee in
> the court of Heaven, and my words promise
> thee so much good?"

Immediately following this terzina, we find the famous simile of the little flowers revivified by the sun, a simile that, without a doubt, conveys a spiritual regeneration of Dante's soul. As we have noted, an act of humility and an act of filial fear also occur with an infusion of sanctifying grace, and are clearly identifiable in the scene. Now what of a "movement of free will toward God, which is an act of formed faith, and a movement of free will in relation to sin, which is the act of penance?" May these two movements, which are intrinsically concurrent with justification, also be found in the scene? I think so. We should recall that an act of formed faith is an act of faith directed by Charity:

> Faith of itself, cannot transcend its properly intellectual nature; it opens the door on supernatural truth, but nothing more. For this knowledge to be raised up outside the strictly intellectual sphere and directed to the good—and therefore to the ultimate goal—of the whole man, something other than faith must do the directing. And it is in exactly this manner that faith is directed by charity. It is charity which orders the acts of all the virtues to the true ultimate goal of man. Faith, then, loses its imperfection, becoming transformed from a dead to a living faith, from faith unformed to faith formed only when the will orders it to the goal of the whole man under the influence of charity.[29]

We have noted in St. Thomas that "the human mind's movement to the fruition of the divine good is the proper act of charity, by which all the acts of the other virtues are ordained to this end." Now we find a clear indication of this formed faith when Dante, immediately following the image of the flowers, breaks into a moving expression of faith.

> "Oh pietosa colei che mi soccorse!
> e te cortese ch'ubidisti tosto
> a le vere parole che ti porse!"
>
> (Inf. II, 133-35)
>
> "O compassionate she, who succoured me! and
> courteous thou, who quickly didst obey the
> true words that she gave thee!"

Dante indicates that Virgil had quickly obeyed the true words that Beatrice gave him: "alle vere parole che ti porse." This is unmistakably an expression of an act of faith in Beatrice's words, but not yet an act of formed faith, which requires charity. And, indeed, charity follows, when Dante immediately adds that his heart has been so disposed by Virgil with a desire to go on that he has returned to his first purpose:

> "Tu m'hai con desiderio il cor disposto
> sì al venir con le parole tue,
> ch'i' son tornato nel primo proposto."
>
> (Inf. II, 136-38)
>
> "Thou hast disposed my heart with such desire
> to go, by what thou sayest, that I have returned
> to my first purpose."

It should be clearly noted here that Dante's heart is not being disposed with desire for a simple good of the natural order. His heart is disposed with desire to undertake the journey that brings him to the fruition of the divine good. This is an act of charity, since the object of charity is the last end—God Himself: "Now the human mind's movement to the fruition of the divine good is the proper act of charity" (I-II, q. 114, a. 4). And the act of faith becomes meritorious only through charity: "The act of faith is not meritorious unless faith . . . worketh by charity" (I-II, q. 114, a. 4, R.Obj. 3). Most importantly for us, as we are trying to establish that Dante receives sanctifying grace before he enters the world beyond and not on the mountaintop of Purgatory as Singleton maintains, is the fundamental consideration that an act of faith guided by charity actually constitutes the first act by which sanctifying grace is manifested:

Augustine calls faith that worketh by charity grace, since the act of faith of him that worketh by charity is the first act by which sanctifying grace is manifested (I-II, q. 110, a. 3, R.Obj. 1).

Clearly, then, the journey to Beatrice is not a journey to sanctifying grace as Singleton believes. If Dante has received here and now—before he enters the world beyond—an infusion of grace as confirmed by an act of formed faith, which is said to be "the first act by which sanctifying grace is manifested," then the journey to Beatrice must by necessity be taking place as an effect of sanctifying grace. This, as I have said, is of fundamental importance since it changes the whole perspective of the *Comedy*.

Now let us consider whether the other concurrent movement in the process of justification is also present on the scene. This, as we recall, is the "movement of the free will in relation to sin, which is the act of penance." And, in this connection, we should further recall that to withdraw from sin and to draw near to justice, "in a movement of free choice, means detestation and desire. . . . Hence, in the justification of the ungodly there must be two movements of the free choice, one, whereby it tends to God's justice, the other whereby it hates sin." This "detestation and desire" on the part of the protagonist is conveyed when he tells Virgil that he has returned to his first purpose:

> "ch'i' son tornato nel primo proposto."
>
> *(Inf.* II, 138)
>
> "that I have returned to my first purpose."

This verse follows immediately the expression of "formed faith" in lines 133-37. Dante's "primo proposto" is in fact an act of detestation and an act of desire. To see how this may be so, we should go back to the end of the first canto, where the "first purpose" was expressed.

Dante is being told by Virgil that he will be shown the doleful spirits of Hell, "Ch'a la seconda morte ciascun grida," and the spirits of Purgatory, "che son contenti / nel foco perché speran di venire quando che sia a le beate genti." Then, Virgil adds, if he still desires to ascend, there will be a worthier spirit than he (Beatrice) who will be his guide. This must be so because the Emperor that reigns above does not allow Virgil to enter his city. Happy is the one whom God chooses for that place, "oh felice colui, cu' ivi elegge," Virgil concludes. Whereupon Dante breaks in a movement of detestation for sins:

> "a ciò ch'io fugga questo male e peggio"
>
> *(Inf.* I, 132)
>
> "in order that I may escape this ill and worse"

and in a movement of desire to see the door of St. Peter, i.e., a movement of free choice whereby it tends to God's justice:

> "che tu mi meni là dov'or dicesti,

sì ch'io veggia la porta di san Pietro
e color cui tu fai cotanto mesti."

(Inf. I, 133-35)

"lead me where thou now hast said, so that I may
see the Gate of St. Peter, and those whom
thou makest so sad."

This "evil and worse"—"questo male e peggio"—refers of course to the
evil symbolized by the she-wolf, which ought to be understood as moral evil
as well as physical evil, since that is man's condition after the Fall. It should
be understood, however, that we are here concerned with the act of detestation for sins, and the act of tending toward God's justice as expressed by the
verse "ch'io son tornato nel primo proposto," which occurs concurrently with
the process of justification in the second canto, and is identified by St.
Thomas as "the act of penance." What takes place at the end of the first
canto is another act of detestation for sins and another act tending toward
God's justice, but these two acts are not concurrent with the process of justification that takes place later. This is of considerable importance, as we shall
see shortly when we consider the problem of preparation for grace.

A clear indication that Dante has already received sanctifying grace may
also be found in *Purgatory* where Guido del Duca, unlike Cavalcante in Hell
who thinks that Dante is making the journey "per altezza d'ingegno," is
keenly aware that God's grace is shining forth in Dante's soul as a kind of
splendor:

Ma da che Dio in te vuol che traluca
tanto sua grazia, non ti sarò scarso;
però sappi ch'io fui Guido del Duca.

(Purg. XIV, 79-81)

But since God wills that so much of his grace shine
forth in thee, I will not be chary with thee;
therefore know that I am Guido del Duca.

As for *Inferno* X, a most lucid study by Paolo Cherchi argues convincingly, and in my opinion conclusively, that "il disdegno di Guido" is actually
"il disdegno per Guido," inasmuch as the cause of Dante's journey is tran-
scendental, not immanent, as Cavalcante had erroneously thought. According
to Cherchi, and I agree, Dante is allowed to visit the world beyond because
he has already received "una grazia attiva."[30]

By now, Dante's sins have been forgiven. His soul has been made
"pleasing to God" inasmuch as it has been healed and justified. This is the
effect of sanctifying grace in the order of being: "In this way, habitual grace,
inasmuch as it heals and justifies the soul, or makes it pleasing to God, is
called operating grace" (I-II, q. 111, a. 2). So far I have been concerned with

establishing that Dante did in fact receive an infusion of sanctifying grace in the Prologue scene. I have therefore dealt with some of the articles listed by St. Thomas in question 113, "On the Effects of Grace." It should be noted, however, that St.Thomas, as is typical of him, proceeds by reiterating first of all the distinction within sanctifying grace itself:

> We have now to consider the effects of grace: (1) concerning the justification of the ungodly, which is the effect of operating grace; and (2) concerning merit, which is the effect of cooperating grace" (I-II, q. 113).

The problem of merit is treated by St. Thomas in question 114 in ten articles. Merit is the effect of sanctifying grace in the order of operation: "but inasmuch as it is the principle of meritorious works, which proceed from free choice, it is called cooperating grace" (I-II, q. 111, a. 2). There will be more on this later, since it actually involves the whole ascent of Purgatory. For now I shall list the articles of question 113 in order to point out that we have already covered some of them as they pertain to Dante's condition in the Prologue scene:

> Under the first head there are ten points of inquiry: (1) What is the justification of the ungodly? (2) Whether grace is required for it? (3) Whether any movement of free choice is required for it? (4) Whether a movement of faith is required for the justification of the ungodly? (5) Whether a movement of free choice against sin is required for it? (6) Whether the remission of sins is to be reckoned with the foregoing? (7) Whether the justification of the ungodly is a work of time or is sudden? (8) Of the natural order of the things concurring to justification. (9) Whether the justification of the ungodly is God's greatest work? (10) Whether the justification of the ungodly is miraculous? (I-II, q. 113).

From the above list, the reader will recognize that we have already spoken of all the articles concerning things that are concurrent with the process of justification itself. Further elucidation is, however, necessary in order to show how Singleton has imposed on Dante and the structure of the *Comedy* some glaring reversals in the order of nature. A case in point is the problem of sin and its effects.

VII

According to Singleton, Dante receives an infusion of sanctifying grace with Beatrice's advent on the mountaintop of Purgatory, and Virgil's guidance is a preparation for sanctifying grace: "Thus, Virgil guides to the top of the mountain and his guidance is preparation. Virgil leads to justice, whereupon the "form" is given: Beatrice as sanctifying grace."[31] However, Singleton maintains that before Dante may receive the "form" of "sanctifying grace," his sin and the consequence of sin in the soul must first be put off:

> Regeneration is complex. It is a matter of a man rising out of his sinful nature and out of his own burden of actual sin, to attain to justice. Sin and the consequence of sin in the soul must first be put off, before justice (which is the form, in this instance) may be received in the soul.[32]

There is a confusion here between cause and effect. Singleton thinks of justice as the form: "justice (which is the form, in this instance)." Yet sanctifying grace is the form; justice is an effect of sanctifying grace. If Dante had to rise "out of his sinful nature" and "out of his burden of actual sin," and if his "sin and the consequence of sin in the soul must first be put off" before he can receive sanctifying grace (supposedly with Beatrice), what does he need sanctifying grace for? To think, as Singleton does, that Dante could do all this with his or Virgil's power of natural reason is sheer absurdity:

> The natural reason is not the sufficient principle of the health that is in man by justifying grace. The principle of this health is grace, which is taken away by sin. Hence man cannot be restored by himself, but requires the light of grace to be poured upon him anew, as if the soul were infused into a dead body for its resurrection (I-II, q. 109, a. 7, R. Obj. 2).

Singleton is evidently unaware that "to rise" from sin and "to cease" from the act of sin are not the same thing; he is also unaware that sin is "transient" as to the act but "abiding" as to the effect (guilt). To rise from sin, grace is needed:

> Man by himself can in no way rise from sin without the help of grace. For since sin is transient as to the act and abiding in its guilt, as was stated above, to rise from sin is not the same as to cease from the act of sin; but to rise from sin means that man has restored to him what he lost by sinning (I-II, q. 109, a. 7).

In the next page, Singleton becomes even more adamant. He goes so far as to invoke the authority of St. Thomas for the statement that all impediments must be removed before the reception of the form:

> The wayfarer is led through one terrace of Purgatory after another, and as he moves, a burden of sin and the consequence of sin is put off. *Impedimenta* to the reception of the form, *as St. Thomas would say*, [Italics mine] are removed, and all the while there are varying statements in metaphor of what those obstacles are: they are "stains," "knots," "blemishes," left in the soul or the will through sinful acts. And the seven

letters "P" inscribed upon Dante's forehead are the visible sign of those impedimenta. These are marks which must be erased in the long hard climb.[33]

Again, according to Singleton, the "burden of sin," and the "consequence of sin," the "stains," the "knots," and the "blemishes" all must be removed before the infusion of sanctifying grace that, as he says, comes with Beatrice. Singleton seems to be unaware that Dante finds himself in the same spiritual condition as the souls of Purgatory, whose sins have already been forgiven by an infusion of grace on earth (as Dante's sins are forgiven with an infusion of grace in the Prologue scene), and who are now washing away the stains of sin from their souls, "Ben si de' loro atar lavar le note / che portar quinci, sì che, mondi e lievi, / possano uscire a le stellate ruote" (*Purg.* XI, 34-36), as Dante is in the process of having the stains of sin erased from his own soul: "Fa che lavi, / quando se' dentro, queste piaghe" (*Purg.* IX, 113-4). The verbs "lavar" and "lavi" convey, without a doubt, that a cleansing process is taking place for the souls as well as for Dante. The souls of Purgatory (as also Dante) are actually expiating the punishment demanded by God's justice: "Moreover, punishment is requisite in order to restore the equality of justice" (I-II, q. 87, a. 6, R.Obj. 3). And this is so because "a man is punished by God even after his sin is forgiven; and so the debt of punishment remains, when the sin has been removed" (I-II, q. 87, a. 6). Singleton erroneously thinks of the seven "P"s on Dante's forehead as impediments to be removed before the infusion of sanctifying grace with Beatrice: "And the seven letters 'P' inscribed upon Dante's forehead are the visible sign of those impedimenta. These are marks which must be erased in the long hard climb." The letters on Dante's forehead are instead symbolic of the stains of sin that remain in the soul even after the guilt of sin has been forgiven by an infusion of sanctifying grace. In fact, St. Thomas says that the duration of punishment corresponds to the duration of the stain:

> The duration of punishment corresponds to the duration of fault, not indeed on the part of the act, but on the part of the stain, for as long as this remains, the debt of punishment remains (I-II, q. 87, a. 4, R.Obj. 3).

and Dante, of course, is in perfect agreement with St. Thomas when he makes Statius say that the mountain of Purgatory quakes when some soul feels herself cleansed and is therefore released from punishment:

> Tremaci quando alcuna anima monda
> sentesi, sì che surga o che si mova
> per salir sù; e tal grido seconda.
> De la mondizia sol voler fa prova,
> che, tutto libero a mutar convento,

l'alma sorprende, e di voler le giova.
Prima vuol ben, ma non lascia il talento
che divina giustizia, contra voglia,
come fu al peccar, pone al tormento.

(Purg. XXI. 58-66)

It quakes here when some soul feeleth herself
cleansed, so that she may rise up, or set forth, to
mount on high, and such a shout follows her.
Of the cleansing the will alone gives proof, which
fills the soul, all free to change her cloister,
and avails her to will.
She wills indeed before, but that desire permits it
not which divine justice sets, counter to will,
toward the penalty, even as it was toward the sin.

Therefore, the fact that on each terrace of Purgatory a stain is erased from Dante's soul as a "P" is removed from his forehead is in itself proof that Dante's soul had already received an infusion of sanctifying grace before he entered the world beyond. For St. Thomas, there is first an infusion of sanctifying grace, which brings about the forgiveness of sins, and, subsequently, the expiation of the debt of punishment as a just satisfaction, which brings about the removal of the effects of sin (the stains) from the soul: "He first forgives sin through operating grace; and afterwards, through cooperating grace, he takes away sin's after-effects little by little" (III, q. 86, a. 5). For Singleton, on the other hand, Dante has to remove the stains of sin from his soul before he supposedly receives an infusion of sanctifying grace with Beatrice, which is simply another case of putting the cart in front of the horse and of falsifying the whole structure of the *Comedy*.

Note also that St.Thomas's authority is invoked by Singleton to support his own argument that the "impedimenta to the reception of form, as St. Thomas would say, are removed." There is a note for the word "removed," and when we turn to that note (p. 70 n. 8) we expect, since Singleton is treating of Dante's sins in relation to grace, to find a quotation from one of the questions in St. Thomas's Treatise on Grace. Yet there is no quotation from any of those questions in Singleton's note. Singleton merely says: "'Remotio impedimentorum' is, in fact, the standard phrase with St. Thomas. See *In IV Sent.* d. xvii q. 1 a. 4, sol. 1." An incomplete and out of context quotation follows where it is apparent that Singleton has seriously misrepresented St. Thomas's text. The following is the incomplete quotation from St. Thomas as it appears in note 8 of Singleton's text:

". . . quia secundum genus causae materialis materia est causa formae quasi sustentans ipsam, et forma est causa materiae quasi faciens eam esse actu secundum genus causae formalis. Ex parte autem causae materialis se tenet secundum quemdam reductionem omne illud per quod materia efficitur propria huius formae, sicut dispositiones et remotiones impedimentorum. . . ."

What follows, instead, is the complete quotation where it becomes self-evident that Singleton is quoting selectively from St. Thomas:

> Dicendum ad primam quaestionem quod omnis prioritas secundum ordinem naturae aliquo modo reducitur ad ordinem causae et causati; quia principium et causa sunt idem. In causis autem contigit quod idem est causa et causatum, secundum diversum genus causae, ut patet in II *Phys.*, (β 3. 195ª, 5; l. 5, n. 7); et in V *Metaph.*, (δ 2. 1013ª, 23; l. 2): sicut ambulatio est causa efficiens sanationis, et sanatio est causa finalis ambulationis. Et similiter de habitudine quae est inter materiam et formam; *quia secundum genus causae materialis materia est causa formae quasi sustentans ipsam, et forma est causa materiae quasi faciens eam esse actu, secundum genus causae formalis.*
>
> *Ex parte autem causae materialis se tenet secundum quemdam reductionem omne illud per quod materia efficitur propria hujus formae, sicut dispositiones et remotiones impedimentorum.* Et ideo in generatione naturali quando corruptio unius est generatio alterius per hoc quod forma una inducitur et alia expellitur, remotio formae praeexistentis se tenet ex parte causae materialis. Et ideo secundum ordinem causae materialis praecedit naturaliter introductionem alterius formae, sed secundum ordinem causae formalis est e converso.[34] (Italics mine.)

Note that Singleton ends his quotation with the word "impedimentorum," whereas St. Thomas ends the paragraph with the word "converso." In fact, St. Thomas says: "but according to the order of formal cause it is the converse"("sed secundum ordinem causae formalis est e converso"). Singleton does not seem to understand that the formal cause of justification is, precisely, sanctifying grace. This means that the removal of both—the guilt of sin and the stain of sin—from Dante's soul is an effect of sanctifying grace, not a preparation for it. More specifically, the removal of the guilt of sin is an effect of operating grace, whereas the removal of the stain of sin is an effect of cooperating grace:

> As was said in the *Secunda Pars*, grace in man is operating with regard to his justification, and cooperating with regard to his living rightly. Therefore, pardon for sin and guilt of eternal punishment is the work of operating grace; but the release of the burden of temporal punishment, that of cooperating grace, in the sense namely that with the help of divine grace, a person is absolved from the debt of temporal punishment also because of bearing suffering patiently. Therefore, just as the effect of op-

erating grace comes before the effect of cooperating grace, so also the remission of sin and of eternal punishment comes before the full release from temporal punishment. Each is from grace, but the first is from grace alone; the other from grace and free will (III, q. 86, a. 4, R.Obj. 2).

But Singleton, who has never distinguished between operating and cooperating grace, has gone his own way: "*Impedimenta* to the reception of the form, as St. Thomas would say, are removed; and all the while there are varying statements in metaphor of what those obstacles are: they are 'stains,' 'knots,' 'blemishes,' left in the soul or the will through sinful acts." The word "acts" is followed by yet another note (p. 70 n. 9), and as we turn to that note, Singleton says:

See "nota" in *Purgatorio* XI, 34 ff.; "velo" and "nebbia," *Purgatorio* XXX, 3. The terms are out of established theology and refer to what is most commonly called a "macula" or a "detrimentum nitoris."

And this time Singleton does not even feel obliged to give a quotation from St. Thomas since he maintains that these terms are out of "established theology," just as he did not feel obliged to give a quotation in support of his false claim that the rational soul was "made up entirely" of intellect and will. He merely said that it was a "simple acknowledged truth."

VIII

Another reversal of the order of nature has to do with Virgil's function in the *Comedy*. According to Singleton:

In the journey with Virgil through Purgatory, right order is restored in the passions and lower powers.[35]

This is a kind of justice (justification) in the soul that, says Singleton, must precede the attainment of grace:

And so too in the matter of justification in the soul: first justice, then advent of grace, as to a place prepared.[36]

In fact, Singleton goes so far as to postulate two kinds of justice: natural (human) attained with Virgil:

To attain to justice with Virgil must mean to come to a justice which is discernible by the natural light of reason and without benefit of the light of sanctifying grace; or shall we not say, discernible *before* the light of grace is had, for when Virgil dismisses Dante, Beatrice has not yet come, though she is expected. . . . To move with Virgil means to move "within the proportion of man's nature," as Thomas Aquinas liked to express it. To journey with Virgil is to journey by that natural light which may not extend beyond such confines.[37] (Singleton's italics.)

The second is supernatural (transhuman) and is attained with Beatrice, i.e., sanctifying grace:

Since this is represented as an attainment, first with Virgil, then with Beatrice, the two "justices" become two successive moments in a forward movement. Virgil leads to Beatrice. The question then comes to be: Is the human justice of Virgil "ordered to" the transhuman justice attained with Beatrice?[38]

It is so ordered, says Singleton, because between Virgil and Beatrice there is the dividing line of a river—the Lethe—which, as we have already noted, Singleton has interpreted as the line of demarcation between nature and grace:

As for the first, the justice of Virgil, we are now in a position to understand it for what it is. Virgil's justice is justice according to the philosophers, justice as Plato and Aristotle had conceived it by the natural light of reason. This is the only conception of justice that may be had by such a light as theirs. "Più oltre non discerno." But when the wayfarer can cross the stream which Virgil may not cross, and can enter into the company of Beatrice and her handmaids, this is then nothing less than that highest subjection of personal justice given through Christ's grace and through charity alone, and known only by the light of grace. Between the two justices is the line of a river. Whereupon we have only to turn back to that definition of justice by Thomas Aquinas which we were examining to see what the line of this river in Eden means; for we may view it as a line drawn within and through that very formulation.[39]

Immediately following the above, Singleton gives the following quotation from St. Thomas:

Justice is so called inasmuch as it implies a certain rectitude of order in the interior disposition of man, in so far as what is highest in man is subject to God || and the inferior powers of the soul are subject to the superior, i.e., to the reason; and this disposition the Philosopher calls justice *metaphorically speaking*.[40] (Singleton's italics.)

This is of the utmost importance. Singleton is performing a very delicate surgical operation here—one that is impossible to perform. Note the two vertical bars after the word "God." These two bars have been placed there by Singleton himself, and represent for him the line of demarcation between the "human justice" that Dante supposedly attains under Virgil's guidance ("in the journey with Virgil through Purgatory, right order is restored in the passions and lower powers") and the "transhuman justice attained with Beatrice," which for Singleton is "nothing less than the highest subjection of personal justice given through Christ's grace and through charity alone, and known only as the light of grace." The river Lethe, which separates Virgil and Dante from Beatrice, should be understood as having the same function as the vertical bars that Singleton has drawn within St. Thomas's definition of justice:

> The line of the river, in Dante's scene at the summit, falls exactly where we may see a line drawn through the definition. And with this we understand better what Dante has done. Thomas Aquinas chose to take no notice at this point of the fact that the Philosopher had not and could not have conceived of the highest subjection of justice, named first in his definition. Such a subjection, in which what is highest in man is ordered to God, lies quite beyond the philosopher's range of vision. Thomas draws no line here, though at many another time he did. Dante did draw the line in his poem. In staging the event of justice attained, Dante drew that line in the shape of a stream, a limit for Virgil. Virgil may go only so far as Aristotle's conception actually went, to that justice which is the second and lower subjection only, or, in the ascending order of the journey, to the first justice to be reached.[41]

Now, we should preface by saying that there are indeed two kinds of justice with sanctifying grace. The first is the justice of justification, which is an effect of operating grace; the second is the justice of merit (the right to a supernatural reward), which involves God's distributive-commutative justice and is an effect of cooperating grace. But this is not what Singleton is saying because he has never made the distinction, in sanctifying grace, between operating and cooperating grace. What Singleton has actually postulated is two kinds of justice within the process of justification itself, which is a pure invention of Singleton's imagination for the very simple reason that the process of justification does not take place in succession, as he believes, but in an instant:

> The entire justification of the ungodly consists, as to its origin, in the infusion of grace. For it is by grace that free choice is moved and guilt is remitted. Now, the infusion of grace takes place in an instant and without succession. . . . Therefore, since the divine power is infinite, it can instantaneously dispose any created matter to its form; and much more man's free choice, whose movement is by nature instantaneous. Therefore the justification of the ungodly by God takes place in an instant (I-II, q. 113, a. 7).

Singleton does not seem to be aware that justification is a process in the order of nature, and not a process in the order of time as he believes. A process in the order of nature is a process of cause and effect. A process in the order of time is a process of a before and an after: "in every change there is a before and an after. Now the before and after of movement is reckoned by time. Consequently every movement is in time" (I, q. 53, a. 3). But in the process of justification, the human mind is above time:

> Now the human mind, which is justified, is, in itself, above time, but is subject to time accidently, inasmuch as it understands with continuity and time, in keeping with the phantasm in which it considers the intelligible species, as was stated above. We must, therefore, decide from this about its change as regards the condition of temporal movements, i.e., we must say that there is no last instant that sin inheres, but a last time; whereas there is a first instant that grace inheres, but in all the time previous sin inhered (I-II, q. 113, a. 7, R.Obj. 5).

This is exactly Dante's condition in the Prologue scene. At the moment of justification, the same instant is the first nonexistence of sin and the first existence of sanctifying grace. But since Dante's mind is accidentally in time by virtue of the intellect and will, "we must, therefore, decide from this about its change as regards the condition of temporal movements," and indeed we do, since as we have seen, there has been a movement of the intellect and a movement of the will inasmuch as there was an act of faith directed by an act of charity. This constitutes the very proof that Dante has received an infusion of sanctifying grace in the Prologue scene, since, once again, "Augustine calls faith that worketh by charity grace, since the act of faith of him that worketh by charity is the first act by which sanctifying grace is manifested."

God is the cause of grace. Therefore, what is required of us is to be attentive to the inner logic of the concatenation of the effects of grace in Dante's soul:

> The cause is naturally prior to its effect. Now the infusion of grace is the cause of whatever is required for the justification of the ungodly, as was stated above. Therefore it is naturally prior to it.
>
> The aforesaid four things required for the justification of the ungodly are simultaneous in time, since the justification of the ungodly is not successive, as was stated above; but in the order of nature, one is prior to another. According to the order that is natural among them, the first is the infusion of grace; the second, the movement of free choice towards God; the third, the movement of free choice against sin; the fourth, the remission of guilt.
>
> The reason for this is that, in every movement the motion of the mover is naturally first; the disposition of the matter, or the movement of the

moved, is second; the end or term of the movement in which the motion of the mover rests, is last. Now the motion of God the mover is the infusion of grace, as was stated above; the movement or disposition of the moved is the double movement of free choice; and the term or end of the movement is the remission of sin, as was stated above. Hence, in their natural order, the first in the justification of the ungodly is the infusion of grace; the second is the movement of free choice towards God; the third is the movement of free choice against sin, for he who is being justified detests sin because it is against God, and thus the movement of free choice towards God naturally precedes the movement of free choice against sin, since it is its cause and reason; the fourth and last is the remission of guilt, to which this transmutation is ordained as to an end, as was stated above (I-II, q. 113, a. 8).

It should be stressed again that while in the order of nature one effect of grace may be naturally prior to another, in the order of time they are simultaneous:

As was stated above, there is nothing to prevent two things from being understood at once, in so far as they are somehow one. Thus, we understand the subject and predicate together, inasmuch as they are united in relation to one affirmation. And in the same manner, free choice can be moved to two things at once in so far as one is ordained to the other. Now the movement of free choice against sin is ordained to the movement of free choice towards God, since a man detests sin as contrary to God, to Whom he wishes to cling. Hence, in the justification of the ungodly, free choice simultaneously detests sin and turns to God, even as a body approaches one point and withdraws from another simultaneously (I-II, q. 113, a. 7, R.Obj. 2).

In a most beautiful analogy, St. Thomas says that in justification the infusion of grace and the remission of guilt should be understood as the propagation of light and the receding of darkness occurring simultaneously in time:

The withdrawal from one term and approach to another may be looked at in two ways. First, on the part of the thing moved, and thus the withdrawal from a term naturally precedes the approach to a term, since in the subject of movement the opposite which is put away is prior to the opposite which the subject moved attains to by its movement. But on the part of the agent, it is the other way about, since the agent, by the form preexisting in it, acts for the removal of the opposite form. And thus, the sun by its light acts for the removal of darkness, and hence, on the part of the sun, illumination is prior to the removal of darkness; but on the part of the atmosphere to be illuminated, to be freed from darkness is, in the

order of nature, prior to being illuminated, although both are simultaneous in time. And since the infusion of grace and the remission of guilt are
referred to God Who justifies, hence in the order of nature the infusion
of grace is prior to the remission of guilt. But if we look at what takes
place on the part of the man justified, it is the other way about, since in
the order of nature liberation from guilt is prior to the obtaining of justifying grace—or it may be said that the term 'whence' of justification is
guilt, and the term 'whereto' is justice, and that grace is the cause of the
forgiveness of sin and of the obtaining of justice (I-II, q. 113, a. 8, R.Obj.
1).

It should be noted that in the order of nature, on the part of the man
being justified, liberation from guilt is prior to the obtaining of justifying
grace, whereas, on the part of God Who justifies, the infusion of grace is
prior to the remission of guilt. However, in the order of time, the infusion of
grace is simultaneous with the expulsion of guilt, just as the same instant is, at
one and the same time, an instant of propagation of light and an instant of
recession of darkness. Similarly, in the order of nature, the subjection of
Dante's mind to God precedes the acquisition of grace, but it follows the infusion of grace. This means that, in the instant of justification, the subjection
of Dante's mind to God is an effect of grace which, in turn, simultaneously
causes the subjection of Dante's lower powers to his mind since our love of
God is the cause of our contrition. Grace is the cause of both the forgiveness
of sin and the obtaining of justice, that is, the justice of the double subjection:
"Hence, in the justification of the ungodly, free choice simultaneously detests
sin and turns to God, even as a body approaches one point and withdraws
from another simultaneously." The following is a most lucid explanation of
the above passage by Garrigou-LaGrange where it becomes apparent that
Singleton has confused a "process in the order of nature" for a "process in
the order of time":

> Why does the movement of free will toward God precede contrition?
> Because we detest sin inasmuch as it is against God; our love of God is
> the cause of our contrition, which is the cause of the remission of guilt.
> Hence our Lord says of Mary Magdalen: "Many sins are forgiven her,
> because she hath loved much" (Luke 7:47); but He adds: "To whom less
> is forgiven, he loveth less." This is explained by St. Thomas' second con-
> clusion which concerns the movable element or material cause.
>
> The second conclusion refutes the first objection as follows: With re-
> gard to the movable element or the justified man, freedom from guilt is
> prior in the order of nature to the acquisition of grace. Observe well that
> St. Thomas uses the terms liberation from guilt rather than remission of
> guilt, and acquisition of grace rather than infusion of grace, since he is
> here considering the matter from the standpoint of the man justified and

not of God who justifies. (Consult the answer to the first objection.)

Proof. On the part of the object moved, withdrawal from the *terminus a quo* precedes the approach to the *terminus ad quem*. For instance, with regard to the lighting up of the atmosphere, the dispelling of darkness precedes the arrival of the light, not by a priority of time but of nature, whereas on the other hand, in relation to the sun, illumination is prior by nature to the removal of darkness. Therefore, from the standpoint of man, liberation from guilt precedes the acquisition of grace, whereas, from the standpoint of God, the infusion of grace precedes the remission of guilt.

Again, St. Thomas says in answer to the second objection: "The movement of free will precedes in the order of nature the acquisition of grace for which it disposes one, but it follows the infusion of grace."[42]

It should be abundantly clear by now that Singleton's surgical cutting through of St. Thomas's definition of justification is a sheer absurdity. The subjection of Dante's reason to God and the subjection of his lower powers to his reason take place in an instant, and has already taken place in the Prologue scene. The two subjections are inseparable (one causes the other—"thus the movement of free choice towards God naturally precedes the movement of free choice against sin, since it is its cause and reason") and constitute the single justice of justification whereby the harmony, the good of nature, the inclination to virtue that was diminished but not destroyed by original sin, is once again reestablished (though not entirely) by an infusion of sanctifying grace into the essence of the soul. This must be so because it was the essence of the soul that was involved with original sin:

> Original sin is called a sin of nature, as was stated above. Now the soul is the form and nature of the body according to its essence and not according to its powers, as was stated in the First Part. Therefore the soul is the subject of original sin chiefly according to its essence (I-II, q. 83, a. 2).

Furthermore:

> Even original justice pertained primarily to the essence of the soul, because it was God's gift to human nature, to which the essence of the soul is related before the powers. For the powers seem rather to regard the person, inasmuch as they are the principles of personal acts. Hence they are the proper subjects of actual sin, which are the sins of the person (I-II, q. 83, a. 2, R.Obj. 2).

But original justice was not a natural gift, it was an endowment of grace, the effect of which was the double subjection of the mind to God and the lower powers to the reason, a subjection that can be reestablished only by an infusion of sanctifying grace into the essence of the soul:

> For this rectitude consisted in his reason being subject to God, the lower powers to reason, and the body to the soul. Now the first subjection was the cause of both the second and the third, since while reason was subject to God, the lower powers remained subject to reason, as Augustine says. Now it is clear that such a subjection of the body to the soul and of the lower powers to reason was not from nature, or otherwise it would have remained after sin; for even in the demons the natural gifts remained after sin, as Dionysius declares. Hence it is clear that also the first subjection, by virtue of which reason was subject to God, was not a merely natural gift, but a supernatural endowment of grace; for it is not possible that the effect should be of greater efficacy than the cause (I, q. 95, a. 1).

Therefore, it should be clear that the idea of two kinds of justice within the process of justification itself—the "human justice" attained under Virgil's guidance, and the "transhuman justice" attained with Beatrice—is a pure invention of Singleton's. Justification is an effect of sanctifying (operating) grace, not a preparation for it as Singleton believes: "And so too in the matter of justification in the soul: first justice, then advent of grace, as to a place prepared."[43]

IX

But Singleton has pushed this absurdity to the very extreme by saying that Dante, before the supposed advent of sanctifying grace with Beatrice, finds himself in a condition of "pure nature" similar to the one possessed by Adam at the time of creation, before Adam received the original justice, and therefore two steps before the Fall:

> What we are finally privileged to see is clear: Dante has continued to work with the metaphor "return to Eden" even in this respect. At the summit and end of the climb up the mountain, when Eden is reached, we may see history somehow repeating itself; as it was with Adam in his formation, so now with this man, so now with "man," in his reformation. Only now do we glimpse an aspect of the metaphor we might otherwise have missed. There had been a moment in Adam's formation when Adam was not yet in Eden, when Adam was formed outside of Eden in a first condition "secundum naturam." What corresponds to this, in a "return" to Eden is the moment when Virgil proclaims that Dante the Wayfarer is now reformed in justice, a justice discernible by the natural light. This then is the moment "secundum naturam" in the reformation.

The pattern of the original formation of man is thus seen to repeat itself in the reformation of a man named Dante, who attains first to a condition of justice with Virgil, within the proportion of his nature and under the natural light, and then, in a second moment attains to Eden proper, crossing the river to a kind of justice with Beatrice that is truly beyond all human measure.[44]

These are Singleton's last words on the last page of his book *Journey to Beatrice*. Now, according to St. Thomas, and as duly acknowledged by Singleton, the state of "pure nature" never existed, since Adam "was created in grace, according to Eccles. vii. 30, *God made man right*" (I, q. 95, a. 1). Yet even if we suppose that the state of "pure nature" did exist before Adam was elevated by sanctifying grace, by what impossible, triple-backward somersault could Dante (or humanity symbolized by him) have returned to a similar state of pure nature? Dante was born in the state of fallen nature and is now redeemed—the new Adam is Christ, not Dante. But Singleton gives this quotation from St. Thomas: "original justice could not be without grace. . . . Yet even supposing this opinion, such a reason is not conclusive: for even if original justice did not include grace, still *it was a certain disposition prerequisite to grace*."[45] (Singleton's italics.) And this, of course, is enough for Singleton to say that the pattern of Adam's original formation repeats itself in the reformation of Dante, who attains first to a condition of justice with Virgil (within the proportion of human nature) and then to a justice (beyond human proportion) with Beatrice and sanctifying grace.

Now over and beyond the fact that Virgil's "human justice" as a preparation for Beatrice's "transhuman justice" is simply a case, as we have already noted, of putting the cart in front of the horse, what should be pointed out is that Singleton has actually confused the order of nature with the order of grace. Immediately following the above quotation from St. Thomas, Singleton, in order to strengthen his idea of a natural justice as a preparation to a supernatural one, works out an analogy whereby Adam's original formation, first in nature and then in grace, is analogous for him (for Singleton—and supposedly for Dante) to "the formation of every human creature since Adam":

Such a notion of a first moment or phase in the formation of man, followed by another completing moment, had good support, by analogy at least, in the view which we know Dante to have held respecting the formation of every human creature since Adam. The fact that Adam must be set apart from all others in this is what makes it a matter of analogy. For Adam was fashioned directly by God, body and spirit, was created "mature," fully formed as an adult; whereas Adam's children and all his posterity come into existence in a mother's womb, developing first as a foetus through a natural formation. Such in fact is the account of the genesis of the human creature which Statius (who can "see further" than Virgil) gives when he has joined the two wayfarers in their climb toward the summit of the mountain.[46]

What follows is a brief exposition of *Purgatory* XXV, where Statius expounds the Aristotelian doctrine of generation and embryology according to which the human fetus goes through two major stages of formation: the vegetative and the animal. This is a phase of preparation in nature for the infusion of the soul directly by God into the fetus when the latter has reached a perfect animal form. At this point the "animal creature" becomes the "human creature" by virtue of the immortal soul created directly by God. Statius gives here the Christian answer to Averroes's denial of the immortality of the individual soul. Then Singleton continues:

> The relevance of such a view to the question of Adam's formation is evident. In the formation of every human creature, two moments or phases are made distinct by an emphatic line: first, there is the phase of nature, a moment of formation *in naturalibus* (and just so far Virgil could have carried the argument), followed by the moment "above nature" when God, happy (and almost proud!) of nature's handiwork within her own order, completes the genesis and full formation of the creature to be fashioned, by breathing in, infusing, the rational soul. It is a moment of grace. Might Adam's formation not have followed such a pattern, even though, in Adam's case, God and not nature is the *faber* at the first stage? (Singleton's italic.)[47]

What should be remembered here is Singleton's major analogy in virtue of which Dante finds himself in a state of "human justice" (the preparation in nature) before the infusion of grace ("the transhuman justice" with Beatrice), just as Adam was created first in nature and then elevated to grace. Obviously, Singleton believes he has found confirmation of his analogy in the "formation of every human creature," since the latter is for him analogous to Adam's formation: "the relevance of such a view to the question of Adam's formation is evident." This must be so, according to Singleton, because: "in the formation of every human creature, two moments or phases are made distinct by an emphatic line: first there is the phase of nature, a moment of formation *in naturalibus* . . . followed by the moment 'above nature' when God . . . completes the genesis and full formation of the creature to be fashioned, by breathing in, infusing, the rational soul." This moment, according to Singleton, is "the moment above nature . . . It is a moment of grace." And here, exactly, is the confusion between the "order of nature" and the "order of grace." God's infusion of the soul into the fetus is an act of creation and not a "moment of grace," as Singleton believes. The soul is the natural *form* of the body, and as such it accounts for man's very being. God creates the

soul by an act of common love—"whereby He loves all things that are."
Sanctifying grace is the supernatural form of the soul created by God by an
act of special love—"whereby He draws the rational creature above the condition of its nature to a participation of the divine good":

> And according to this difference of good the love of God towards the
> creature is looked at differently. For one is common, whereby He loves
> all things that are (Wis. xi. 25), and thereby gives things their natural
> being. But the second is a special love, whereby He draws the rational
> creature above the condition of its nature to a participation of the divine
> good; and according to this love, He is said to love anyone absolutely,
> since it is by this love that God wills absolutely the eternal good, which is
> Himself . . . accordingly, when a man is said to have the grace of God,
> there is signified something supernatural bestowed on man by God (I-II,
> q. 110, a. 1).

Also, as we have already noted, the good of creation terminates at the
good of nature, whereas the good of justification terminates at the eternal
good of a participation in God. That is why St. Thomas will say that the justification of the ungodly is God's greatest work, even greater than creation.
And, indeed, by the time Dante meets Beatrice, not only has he received justification in the Prologue scene, but he will also have gone through a process
of personal sanctification under cooperating grace on the mountain, which is
itself a preparation for the transhuman process of deification that takes place
with Beatrice in Paradise.

An analogy is always a question of "likeness in difference" so that we
may say that the infusion of the soul into the fetus is analogous to the infusion of sanctifying grace into the soul, provided it is understood that the former is a process in the "order of nature" and the latter is a process in the
"order of grace." But this is not what Singleton has done. For him, the infusion of the soul into the fetus is a "moment of grace" in no way different
from the infusion of grace into the soul. The same error occurs when Singleton treats the problem of Dante's preparation for sanctifying grace. The
model once again is Aristotle's scheme of generation:

X

> *Generatio* is essentially a movement toward form. Such literally, is the
> most general definition of the term; "generatio est motus ad formam."
> What moves toward "form" is of course, some "matter." The movement
> itself is essentially an alteration, a process of change in a given matter by
> which that matter is prepared to receive the form.
> . . . "Matter" in this case would surely be the soul, or some faculty of the
> soul. Thus sanctifying grace would be the form of the soul, and there
> would be a movement of soul toward form, a process by which the soul is
> "disposed" to receive the form.[48]

Since, according to Singleton, Dante will receive the form of sanctifying grace only with the advent of Beatrice on the mountain, the whole area of Virgil's guidance within the structure of the poem must be a preparation for grace:

> This clearly becomes a point of very particular interest to our consideration of the substance and basic structural progression of Dante's poem, when we realize that the whole area of Virgil's guidance in the *Comedy* is that of *praeparatio ad gratiam*, and that had the Aristotelian notion of *generatio* not prevailed so generally in the thought of the poet's time, the event of the journey would not have been at all as it is.
>
> If, then, sanctifying grace is "form" and if the process of conversion is construed on such a pattern of *generatio*, what exactly are we to understand the "matter" to be which is made ready to receive that form? The matter is, in the broadest sense, some human creature.[49]

The human creature is, of course, Dante. Note, first of all, that "generatio" is a movement toward form. The movement itself is an alternation—a process of change in Dante's soul (the matter) by which that soul is made ready to receive the form of sanctifying grace. Justification, or conversion, is construed on such a pattern of generation. This Aristotelian pattern of generatio is a process that takes place in the order of time: "One thus conceives a process which has extension in time and manifests two successive moments or phases. The first is the moment of preparation, the second the moment of completion, at the end, when form is attained."[50] The whole area of Virgil's guidance constitutes for Singleton the phase of "praeparatio ad gratiam," whereby Dante "attains first to a condition of justice with Virgil, within the proportion of his nature and under the natural light, and then, in a second moment, attains to . . . a kind of justice with Beatrice that is truly beyond all human measure." Now, since the fetus's phase of preparation for the infusion of the soul is within the proportion of nature, and since Singleton believes that Dante's phase of preparation for the infusion of grace under Virgil is also within the proportion of nature, the two preparations are thought by Singleton to be essentially the same in every respect. The mistake should be obvious by now. As Singleton mistakenly believed that the two infusions (the soul into the fetus and grace into the soul) were both a "moment of grace," so will he believe, equally mistakenly, that the two preparations are both within the proportion of nature. And so, just as the fetus was naturally brought to a perfect preparedness "in naturalibus," as Singleton says, before it could receive the infusion of the soul, so also Dante's soul, before it may receive an infusion of grace, must be brought to a perfect preparedness of natural justice which, for Singleton, means that Dante must rise: "out of his sinful nature and out of his own burden of actual sin . . . sin and the consequences of sin in the soul must first be put off." All the obstacles such as "stains, knots, blemishes left in the soul or the will through sinful acts" must be erased.

All of this, according to Singleton, is within the proportion of Dante's nature to accomplish, aided, of course, by Virgil's natural light of reason. Once again there is a confusion between the order of nature and the order of grace. The preparation of the soul for grace, and the infusion of grace are within the supernatural order just as the preparation of the fetus for the soul and the infusion of the soul are within the natural order. Singleton does not seem to understand that the natural reason symbolized by Virgil is an immanent power, and as such is absolutely impotent to erase the effects of sin from Dante's soul. For this, Dante needs the transcendent power of grace. Since it does in fact happen that on the mountain of Purgatory the effects of sin (the stains) are erased from Dante's soul, as the "P"s are erased from his forehead, that in itself is proof, as we have noted, that Dante has already received an infusion of sanctifying grace before he entered the world beyond. The erasing of the effects of sin from Dante's soul is an effect of sanctifying grace, not a preparation for it, which also means that the whole area of Virgil's guidance through the world beyond is an effect of sanctifying grace, not a preparation for it as Singleton also believes. We should also note that Singleton thinks of justification as a process in the order of time: "one thus conceives of a process which has extension in time, and manifests two successive moments or phases," whereas we have seen with St. Thomas that Dante's soul, which is justified, is, in itself, above time.

As for the initial (note I say initial) preparation for grace, we are not to think, says St. Thomas, that a "complete rising from sin precedes the illumination of grace" as Singleton believes:

> To man is bidden that which pertains to the act of free choice, as this act is required in order that man should rise from sin. Hence when it is said, *Arise, and Christ shall enlighten thee,* we are not to think that the complete rising from sin precedes the illumination of grace; but that when man by his free choice, moved by God, strives to rise from sin, he receives the light of justifying grace (I-II, q. 109, a. 7, R.Obj. 1).

This is exactly Dante's condition in the first half of the Prologue scene. Here in the first canto, Dante may be said to be in search of God's beatitude, since he is striving to reach the light (lumen Christi) on the hill: "Arise, and Christ shall enlighten thee." He is, however, stopped by the she-wolf, which, as I have proposed in my first book, should be interpreted as moral evil (sin) as well as physical evil (death). A man must first of all die before he may receive the final justice of reward in Heaven. But Dante does not die—he does not cross the path of the she-wolf. Instead, Virgil (the first Heaven-sent guide) comes to his rescue and proposes that Dante, for his own best interest ("per lo tuo me"), should follow him along another road. This clearly constitutes the very first help on the part of God to draw Dante to Himself in order to convert him. This is the beginning of the initial preparation for conver-

ay speak in fact of two kinds of preparation: a preparation to
.ightly and to enjoy God," for which an actual infusion of habitual
.ing) grace is needed; and a preparation for receiving sanctifying
.tself:

> The preparation of the human will for good is twofold: the first whereby
> it is prepared to operate rightly and to enjoy God; and this preparation
> of the will cannot take place without the habitual gift of grace, which is
> the principle of meritorious works, as was stated above. There is a sec-
> ond way in which the human will may be taken to be prepared for the gift
> of habitual grace itself. Now in order that man prepare himself to receive
> this gift, it is not necessary to presuppose any further habitual gift in the
> soul, otherwise we should go on to infinity. But we must presuppose a
> gratuitous gift of God, Who moves the soul inwardly, or inspires the
> good wish. For it is in these two ways that we need the divine assistance,
> as was stated above (I-II, q. 109, a. 6).

According to Singleton, the whole area of Virgil's guidance in the *Comedy* takes place as a preparation for sanctifying grace. This at least is his
starting point. But then he will end up by surgically cutting in two the effect
of sanctifying (operating) grace itself: the subjection of Dante's mind to God
and the subjection of Dante's lower powers to his mind; and he will say that
the latter is the preparation for sanctifying grace, since he believes that, "in
the journey with Virgil through Purgatory, right order is restored in the passions and lower powers." Evidently Singleton mistakenly thinks that sanctifying grace brings about only the highest subjection of Dante's mind to God
which, according to him, is had only with Beatrice:

> At this point in the journey, when Virgil dismisses Dante, the completion
> of justification in its highest subjection is not yet. That completion lies
> beyond Virgil, is had with Beatrice and the infused virtues; it lies on the
> farther side of a stream in Eden, over which Virgil may not cross. Virgil
> thus leads Dante to justice as ancient wisdom had conceived it—so far
> and no farther. And that justice, if we measure it against the pattern of
> three subjections of original justice, is precisely the subjection which cor-
> responds to the second, or middle one; the rule of reason over the lower
> powers.[51]

I propose, on the contrary, that Dante's initial preparation takes place in
the first half of the Prologue scene, and that Dante, as evidenced by an act of
formed faith, receives an actual infusion of sanctifying grace in the second
half of the Prologue scene, since sanctifying grace itself is a preparation "to
operate rightly and to enjoy God." Only after Dante has received an infusion
of grace, which is the "principle of meritorious works," does the journey itself

assume the character of a work meritorious of God's beatitude of which Dante is allowed to partake when he ascends with Beatrice into the Celestial Paradise. The process of sanctification under sanctifying (cooperating) grace on the mountain of Purgatory is a preparation for the process of deification that takes place in Paradise. Dante earns merit—that is, the right to the supernatural reward of beatitude in Purgatory—whereas he is given justification in the second half of the Prologue scene. Dante has been "moved by God." A divine help (Virgil) has been offered (sent) to him. An act of free choice must now take place on the part of Dante. This is an act of striving to rise from sin—"when man by his free choice, moved by God, strives to rise from sin"—which in fact takes place when Dante expresses his free choice to see the door of St. Peter (a movement of free choice toward God), and go away from the she-wolf (a movement of detestation toward sin):

> E io a lui: "Poeta, io ti richeggio
> per quello Dio che tu non conoscesti,
> a ciò ch'io fugga questo male e peggio,
> che tu mi meni là dov' or dicesti,
> sì ch'io veggia la porta di san Pietro
> e color cui tu fai cotanto mesti."

(Inf. I, 130-35)

> And I to him: "Poet, I beseech thee by that
> God whom thou knowest not, in order that
> I may escape this ill and worse,
> lead me where thou now hast said, so that I may
> see the Gate of St. Peter, and those whom
> thou makest so sad.

What should be clearly noted here is the fact that Dante, in the first canto, is "striving to rise from sin," and this constitutes the initial preparation for justification. Only with an actual infusion of sanctifying grace in the essence of Dante's soul, in the second canto, will he begin to "rise from sin." But this is the process of justification itself that, as we have seen, involves a final disposition through an act of living faith (an act of faith directed by charity), a movement of free choice tending towards God's justice, and a movement of detestation toward sin. And all this takes place in the very instant of justification. It is simply not possible, as Singleton believes, that Dante could "rise from sin" during the phase of preparation for the sanctifying grace that, according to him, Dante will receive only with Beatrice. What Singleton has not understood is that the phase of initial preparation is a way to justification but not the substance of justification:

> The movement of free choice, which concurs in the justification of the ungodly, is a consent to detest sin, and to draw near to God; and this

consent takes place suddenly. Sometimes, indeed, it happens that deliberation precedes, *yet this is not of the substance of justification, but a way
to justification; just as local movement is a way to illumination, and alteration to generation* (I-II, q. 113, a. 7, R.Obj. 1).

Note that deliberation precedes justification but is not of the substance
of justification. And this is precisely what takes place in the scene. Dante is
deliberating whether or not to undertake the journey, as is evident from the
following verses, where we learn that he feels like the one who "unwills what
he willed":

> E qual è quei che disvuol ciò che volle
> e per novi pensier cangia proposta,
> sì che dal cominciar tutto si tolle,
>   tal mi fec' ïo 'n quella oscura costa,
> perché, pensando, consumai la 'mpresa
> che fu nel cominciar cotanto tosta.
>
> *(Inf.* II, 37-42)
>
> And as one who unwills what he willed, and
> with new thoughts changes his purpose, so that
> he wholly quits the thing commenced,
>   such I made myself on that dim coast: for with
> thinking I wasted the enterprise, that had
> been so quick in its commencement.

If we are to believe Singleton, who maintains that the whole area of Virgil's
guidance in the *Comedy* is a preparation for grace, we should naturally think
of this phase as a process of deliberation. And on the terraces of Purgatory,
are we to think that the "P"s erased from Dante's forehead (as the stains are
erased from his soul) are acts of deliberation? Obviously not! These erasures
are the effects of sanctifying grace.

What should be especially noted is that "alteration" is a way to
"generation." This is of considerable importance, since St. Thomas is here
formulating a most precise analogy: preparation is to justification as alteration is to generation. But preparation is not of the substance of justification
just as alteration is not of the substance of generation. Conversely, it is of the
substance of justification that the form of sanctifying grace is produced in an
instant, just as it is of the substance of generation that the form is also produced in an instant. This is the proper analogy that St. Thomas proposed, as
Garrigou-Lagrange points out:

A form is impressed upon a previously disposed subject in an instant
when the agent does not require time to overcome the resistance of the
subject. But justification is the impressing of habitual grace upon a pre-

viously disposed subject by God, who requires no time. Therefore justification, inasmuch as it is the infusion of grace, is effected in an instant.

We are here supposing the disposition to be primary in time, not final, since justification is understood as signifying only the infusion of grace, and God almighty requires no other disposition than that which He produces and which He can also effect at the very instant when He produces grace itself, as He did in St. Paul, or gradually and successively; but this does not pertain to justification taken in the sense of the infusion of grace. What does pertain to it, as we shall see in the following article, is the final disposition through an act of living faith and contrition at the very instant of justification. Therefore justification, taken in this sense, is effected in an instant.

The major is verifiable even in the natural order, inasmuch as, once the disposition for the substantial form is present in the matter, this form, of which the specific difference is indivisible, is produced in an instant; for example, an animal either is a lion or is not a lion; and again, transparency which is predisposed can be suddenly illuminated. The minor is clear with reference to the infusion of grace in its precise acceptation. Indeed, God sometimes produces in an instant, under extraordinary circumstances, the preliminary dispositions for grace, since acts of free will can be made instantaneously.

Confirmation. (*De veritate*, q. 8, a. 9.) When there is no mean between the extremes of a change, just as there is no mean in the substantial change between being and nonbeing (for example, between the being of the form of a lion and not being), then the transition is made instantaneously. But between the extremes involved in justification, habitual grace on the one hand and deprivation of habitual grace on the other, there can be no mean; for a man either possesses habitual grace or he does not; if he does, even in the least degree, he is already justified. Therefore:

Reply to first objection. The deliberation which precedes by a priority of time is the way to justification but not the substance of justification, for which there is required the final, instantaneous consent of the deliberation to detest sin and be united to God.[52]

This long quotation is necessary to show that Singleton mistakenly thinks of the initial preparation under Virgil as a phase belonging to "the substance of" justification, something that St. Thomas would expressly exclude, as confirmed by Garrigou-Lagrange. The initial preparation is a way to justification just as alteration is a way to generation. There is, however, a final preparation, which is indeed of the substance of justification and takes place in the very instant of justification. This, as we have already noted and as Garrigou-Lagrange confirms, is "the final disposition through an act of living faith and contrition at the very instant of justification. Therefore justification, taken in this sense, is effected in an instant." The difference between the "initial preparation" and the "final preparation" is that the first precedes in time the infusion of grace, whereas the second is simultaneous with the infusion of grace. Also, most importantly, the "initial preparation" does not carry merit whereas the "final preparation" does in fact carry it; and this merit is the right to the supernatural reward of the glory of beatitude:

> A certain preparation of man for grace is simultaneous with the infusion of grace; and this operation is meritorious not indeed of grace, which is not yet possessed. But there is another imperfect preparation, which sometimes precedes the gift of sanctifying grace, which yet is from God's motion. But it does not suffice for merit, since man is not yet justified by grace, and merit can only arise from grace, as will be seen farther on (I-II, q. 112, a. 2, R.Obj. 1).

The reason why this is so may be explained by yet another distinction. The initial preparation is caused by a gratuitous grace called "a divine help," whereas the final preparation is caused by sanctifying grace itself: "grace may be taken in two ways. First, as a divine help, whereby God moves us to will and to act; secondly, as a habitual gift divinely bestowed on us" (I-II, 111, a. 2). The effect of the "divine help" is a "passing motion" in Dante's mind: "the will which hitherto willed evil, begins to will good," (I-II, q. 111, a. 2) whereas the effect of sanctifying grace is a supernatural quality permanently abiding in the essence of Dante's soul. The soul, which is the natural form of the body, is raised to a supernatural level and is moved by God to acquire eternal good, as Dante is moved to undertake the journey:

> As we have stated above, there is understood to be an effect of God's grace in whoever is said to have God's grace. Now it was stated that man is aided by God's gratuitous will in two ways. First, inasmuch as man's soul is moved by God to know or will or do something, and in this way the gratuitous effect in man is not a quality, but a movement of the soul; for motion is the act of the mover in the moved, as it is said in *Physics* iii. Secondly, man is helped by God's gratuitous will inasmuch as a habitual gift is infused by God into the soul; and this for the reason that it is not fitting that God should provide less for those He loves, that they may acquire supernatural good, than for creatures whom He loves that they may acquire natural good. . . . Much more, therefore, does He infuse into those whom He moves towards the acquisition of supernatural good certain supernatural forms or qualities, whereby they may be moved by Him sweetly and promptly to acquire eternal good. Hence the gift of grace is a quality (I-II, q. 110, a. 2).

Singleton has never distinguished between the essence of the soul and the powers of the soul; he has therefore never spoken of sanctifying grace as a permanent quality existing in the essence of Dante's soul. Likewise, he has never considered that sanctifying grace as a form has a double effect in the soul—the first of which is being, and the second operation. His whole approach to the problem of grace in the *Comedy* is one of operation, whereby he maintains that Dante's journey to God is through intellect and will, and justification itself, he says, is part of this whole. This is his major premise and his major fault.

XI

I should also point out that Singleton has actually confused what distinguishes "common conversion" from "miraculous conversion." To the question, "whether the justification of the ungodly is a miraculous work," St. Thomas answers that "the justification of the ungodly is not miraculous, because the soul is naturally capable of grace; since by the fact of having been made to the likeness of God, it is fit to receive God by grace, as Augustine says" (I-II, q. 113, a. 10). This is called the "common and wanted course of justification." But justification may at times be miraculous, as it was for St. Paul:

> And in this sense the justification of the ungodly is sometimes miraculous and sometimes not. For the common and wanted course of justification is that God moves the soul interiorly and that man is converted to God, first by an imperfect conversion, and afterwards reaches a perfect conversion; because charity begun merits increase, so that when increased it may merit perfection, as Augustine says. Yet God sometimes moves the soul so vehemently that it reaches the perfection of justice at once, as took place in the conversion of Paul, which was accompanied at the same time by a miraculous external prostration. Hence the conversion of Paul is commemorated in the Church as miraculous (I-II, q. 113, a. 10).

But how is common conversion to be distinguished from miraculous conversion? Common conversion is characterized by two preparations—one initial, the other final—which take place at different times. The initial preparation is a call from God, a passing divine help: "grace may be taken in two ways. First, as divine help, whereby God moves us to will and to act; secondly, as a habitual gift divinely bestowed on us" (I-II, q. 111, a. 2). The final preparation whereby Dante's soul was brought by God to a perfect preparedness involves grace "as a habitual gift divinely bestowed on us" and is simultaneous with the infusion of sanctifying grace itself: "a certain preparation of man for grace is simultaneous with the infusion of grace." These two preparations constitute, in the words of St. Thomas, first an imperfect conversion, and afterwards a perfect one. In miraculous conversion, on the other hand, these two preparations take place in an instant, as Garrigou-Lagrange says:

"Indeed God sometimes produced in an instant, under extraordinary circumstances, the preliminary dispositions for grace, since acts of free will can be made instantaneously." This was the miraculous conversion of St. Paul: "God almighty requires no other disposition than that which He produces and which He can *also* effect at the very instant when He produces grace itself, as He did in St. Paul." (Italics mine.) Note the italicized word "also," which serves to indicate that in common ordinary conversions the initial preparation precedes in time the infusion of grace. This is the difference. Conversely, however, we should also consider the likeness that exists between common conversion and miraculous conversion, so that we may have a balanced view of the matter.

The likeness between these conversions is constituted by the fact that they both require a "final preparation" whereby the soul is brought to a state of perfect preparedness for the infusion of the form of sanctifying grace. This final preparation takes place through an act of living faith (an act of faith directed by charity) and an act of penance (a movement of detestation toward sin). Moreover, in both kinds of conversion, this final preparation takes place in the same instant of justification and is simultaneous with the infusion of sanctifying grace. And this is precisely what Singleton has not understood. He is under the mistaken impression that the final preparation (the perfect conversion), whereby the soul is brought to a perfect preparedness, is something that belongs exclusively to miraculous conversion. Having made the mistake, Singleton will naturally propose that before Dante may receive the form of sanctifying grace with Beatrice, his soul must be brought to a state of perfect preparedness under Virgil's guidance: "In this conception, Virgil's justice is the preparation for grace. And once more we may refer this to the Aristotelian scheme of generation, now so familiar, which provides precisely for two such moments: 1) a preparation for the form, and 2) reception of the form."[53] The reader will recall that Virgil's justice is, for Singleton, a perfect preparation, since, "in the journey with Virgil through Purgatory, right order is restored in the passions and the lower powers." There has been an obvious transference of powers from the supernatural to the natural. But to see how Singleton has actually ascribed to Virgil divine powers that properly belong to God, we should now follow the concatenation of his thought as it unfolds in the text. Let us consider the following passage:

> This is the more evident, indeed, when we realize that Thomas was ready to grant that the attainment of sanctifying grace could be instantaneous, if God so willed. In terms of "preparation for grace," God may bring about a perfect preparation for grace which is instantaneous and simultaneous with the infusion of the grace; or God may grant that there be a first imperfect *praeparatio* or process, extended in time, through which the soul, or more specifically the will, is gradually made ready to receive and is brought to perfect preparedness. Thus, to the question "whether

any preparation or disposition for grace is required on man's part," Thomas replies as follows—making, it will be noted, an essential distinction between habitual grace and the grace which is operative during the phase when the soul is being made ready to receive it.[54]

There we have it! The soul is brought to perfect preparedness during the initial preparation: "God may grant that there be a first imperfect preparation or process, extended in time, through which the soul, or more specifically the will, is gradually made ready to receive and is brought to perfect preparedness." The reason for the confusion, however, is not yet apparent. What follows in Singleton's text is a quotation from the *Summa* I-II, q. 112, a. 2, distinguishing grace as a "habitual gift" from grace as a "help from God." His text then continues in this fashion:

> Then, in two replies to objections in the same article, Thomas uses the terms, "imperfect preparation," and comes to the notion that there can be a perfect preparation from God which is instantaneous, simultaneous with the infusion of habitual grace, as happened to Paul on the road to Damascus.[55]

The confusion is here apparent. Singleton is ascribing the perfect preparation, which is instantaneous with the infusion of sanctifying grace, only to the miraculous conversion of St. Paul: "as happened to Paul on the road to Damascus." But even if the confusion is apparent, the reason for it is not yet so. What follows Singleton's text is two replies by St. Thomas to objections one and two—spliced together by Singleton himself—which in fact explains the confusion. Here they are as they appear in Singleton's text:

> A certain preparation of man for grace is simultaneous with the infusion of grace and this operation is meritorious, not indeed of grace, which is already possessed, but of glory which is not yet possessed. But there is another imperfect preparation, which sometimes precedes the gift of sanctifying grace, and yet it is from God's motion. But it does not suffice for merit, since man is not yet justified by grace, and merit can only arise from grace.
>
> Since a man cannot prepare himself for grace unless God . . . move him to good, it is of no account whether anyone arrive at perfect preparation instantaneously, or step by step. For it is written (Eccles. II. 23): *It is easy in the eyes of God of a sudden to make the poor man rich.* Now it sometimes happens that God moves a man to good, but not perfect good, and this preparation precedes grace. But He sometimes moves him suddenly and perfectly to good, and man receives grace suddenly. . . . And thus it happened to Paul, since, suddenly, when he was in the midst of sin, his heart was perfectly moved by God to hear, to learn, to come; and hence he received grace suddenly.[56]

We should preface by saying that Singleton never uses the expressions "common conversion" and "miraculous conversion," and this in itself is an indication that he is unaware of the fact that the above spliced replies deal with common and miraculous conversion respectively. An objection in the *Summa* is always a case of reasoning that is faulty either formally or materially, or a combination of both. This being so, the reply to the objection is always restricted simply to "disentangling" the confusion of the objection. St. Thomas therefore will not say more than what is actually required by the context. This is so because he will later expand on the subject by devoting, for example, an entire article to the question of "whether the justification of the ungodly is a miraculous work," which, as we have seen, is article 10 of question 113. If Singleton had read this later article, he would probably have realized his mistake. But it should be said that in article 2 of question 112 (quoted above by Singleton), St. Thomas himself has intentionally created the confusion between "common conversion" and "miraculous conversion" in the mind of the hypothetical objector who voices objections 1 and 2. And the replies to these objections are meant of course to disentangle the confusion. How has St. Thomas done this? By splicing together two objections in one confused train of thought. Let us therefore read the objections themselves:

> Objection 1. It would seem that no preparation or disposition for grace is required on man's part, since, as the Apostle says (Rom. IV.4), *To him that worketh, the reward is not reckoned according to grace, but according to debt.* Now a man's preparation by free choice can be only through some operation. Hence it would do away with the notion of grace.

> Objection 2. Further, whoever continues sinning is not preparing himself to have grace. But to some who continue sinning grace is given, as is clear in the case of Paul, who received grace while he was *breathing out threatenings and slaughter against the disciples of the Lord* (Acts ix. 1). Hence no preparation for grace is required on man's part (I-II, q. 112, a. 2, R.Obj. 1 & 2).

It is clear from the above that the hypothetical objector is confused. In the first objection he is denying (for whatever reasons that cannot interest us at this time) that a preparation for grace is required on man's part. This is "further" confirmed for him (and herein is the confusion between the two kinds of conversion) by the fact that St. Paul was converted without preparation. St. Thomas's reply to the first objection is designed to inform the objector that not one but two preparations are required for conversion. The first is an initial "imperfect preparation," which precedes the gift of sanctifying grace but is nonetheless caused by God's motion. This kind of grace, or divine help, does not suffice for merit, since the individual has not yet received an infusion of sanctifying grace, which not only justifies but, once received, is the principle of meritorious works; this "will be seen farther on," St. Thomas says, with an obvious reference to q. 114, a. 2, a reference omitted by Singleton, who ends the paragraph with the word "grace . . . " The second preparation, which by obvious implication is the "perfect preparation," is simultaneous with an infusion of grace and is meritorious, not of grace that has just been received, but of glory, since, as we have seen elsewhere, sanctifying grace itself is a preparation "to operate rightly and to enjoy God" (I-II, q. 109, a. 6). This final "perfect preparation," as we have also noted, takes place through an act of formed faith and an act of penance. And all this pertains to common conversion.

In the reply to the second objection, St. Thomas is careful to reiterate that "a man cannot prepare himself for grace unless God prevent and move him to good," which is to say that a "preparation precedes grace." But in the case of a miraculous conversion, it all takes place suddenly, without a preceding disposition in priority of time: "But He sometimes moves him suddenly and perfectly to good, and man receives grace suddenly. . . . and thus it happened to Paul, since, suddenly, when he was in the midst of sin, his heart was perfectly moved by God to hear, to learn, to come; and hence he received grace suddenly." The following summary of article 10, question 113, by Garrigou-Lagrange, will further confirm that a "perfect preparation" is common to both kinds of conversion:

> But justification, inasmuch as it commonly comes to pass, is within the ordinary course of supernatural providence; that is, imperfect conversion takes place first, which is the disposition for perfect conversion. The soul is naturally, by reason of its obedient power, "capable of grace," and is made "capable of God by Grace." Certain immanentists misunderstood these words of St. Thomas: "the soul is naturally capable of grace"; it does not possess within itself the germ of grace but only an obediential power, as St. Thomas declares in several places; cf. ad. 3.
>
> Sometimes, however, justification or conversion is miraculous, according as God, operating outside the usual order of His providence, suddenly moves a sinner to perfect conversion, without any preceding disposition in priority of time. This occurred in the conversion of St. Paul which is commemorated by the Church as a miracle for two reasons: 1. because, as St. Thomas says, St. Paul "suddenly attained to a certain perfection of justice"; and because a miraculous external prostration was also added to it.[57]

It is clear from all this that Singleton has kept intact the built-in confusion of the objections by simply splicing together the two replies that were meant to disentangle the confusion in the first place. He is under the mistaken impression that both replies refer to St. Paul, since he believes that a miraculous conversion is constituted by the fact that "there can be a perfect preparation from God which is instantaneous, simultaneous with the infusion of habitual grace, as happened to Paul on the road to Damascus." Note especially, "there can be a perfect preparation." The truth of the matter is that there is always a perfect preparation in common as well as miraculous conversion. What distinguishes miraculous conversion is the fact that there is no "preceding disposition in priority of time."

It should be understood here that I am not talking about a misinterpretation of a single canto of the *Comedy*. This fundamental error on the part of Singleton is responsible for his false interpretation of the entire structure of the *Comedy*. He has transferred divine powers from God to Virgil. Dante's soul, according to Singleton, must be brought to "perfect preparedness" during the first preparation under Virgil's guidance: "God may grant that there be a first imperfect 'praeparatio,' or process, extended in time, through which the soul, or, more specifically, the will, is gradually made ready to receive and is brought to perfect preparedness." Furthermore, Singleton is convinced that if this were not so, Virgil would have no function in the poem whatsoever: "Take away the preparation which is step by step, and all of Inferno and almost all of Purgatorio, insofar as they are conceived as a journey, must vanish. And Virgil would have no function whatsoever in the poem."[58]

But it should be said at this time that Singleton's interpretation of grace in the *Comedy* is heavily dependent on a doctoral dissertation (as we read in the Avant-Propos: "Cette étude a été présentée comme thèse de doctorat à la Faculté de Theologie S. J. de Lyon-Fourvière") on St. Thomas written by Henri Bouillard, as Singleton himself says: "For 'conversion' as understood by the theologians of the 13th century and by St. Thomas in particular, see Henri Bouillard, *Conversion et grace chez S. Thomas d'Aquin,* to which I am greatly indebted."[59] And in this connection I should point out that Henri Bouillard has been criticized by Garrigou-Lagrange precisely on the question of the "perfect preparedness" for grace. There is an analogy, says Garrigou-Lagrange, between the final disposition of the soul brought about by the infusion of grace and the final disposition of the body brought about by the infusion of the soul into the fetus.

> Proof from the authority of St. Thomas . . . "The final disposition of the subject precedes the reception of a form, in the order of nature, but it follows the action of the agent whereby the subject itself is disposed. Therefore the movement of free will precedes in the order of nature (on the part of the subject) the acquisition of grace, but it follows the infusion of grace." Cf. also Ia IIae, q. 113, a. 6, 7 ad 1. . . . In the same way, the body is organized finally only by the soul, and this organization is the disposition for receiving the soul. Ia, q. 76, a. 4 ad 1.[60]

In a less technical vein, he further explains:

In the same way, air will not enter a room unless a window is opened, nor can the window be opened without the air entering. So does God knock at the door of the heart and it opens, and at the same time, we open it by consenting. Actual grace suffices for a disposition which is not final, but the final disposition is effected at the very instant when the form is produced and, although as a disposition it precedes it in the genus or order of material cause, it nevertheless follows it in the genus or order of formal, efficient, and final cause.[61]

Then, in a note, Garrigou-Lagrange says the following:

Father Henri Bouillard, S. J., in his recent book, *Conversion et grâce chez S. Thomas d'Aquin,* Paris 1944, coming to the heart of the problem, writes (pp. 169-79): "It will be observed that St. Thomas, Ia, IIae, q.113, a. 8 ad 1, no longer has recourse to reciprocal causality. In the works of his youth he did so." On the contrary, as we have remarked (a. 8), St. Thomas clearly resorts to reciprocal causality, as all Thomists agree. In fact, this mutual causality always comes into play when the four causes are involved. Cf. above, pp. 204 ff. Nor can we admit to the opinions expressed in Father Bouillard's volume on pages 212, 219, 221, 224.[62]

In a later note[63] Garrigou-Lagrange gives detailed arguments for disagreeing with the opinions expressed by Bouillard in those pages. For now, I would like to go back to a previous remark by Garrigou-Lagrange concerning certain immanentists: "The soul is naturally, by reason of its obediential power, 'capable of grace' and is made 'capable of God by grace.' Certain immanentists misunderstood these words of St. Thomas: 'the soul is naturally capable of grace'; it does not possess within itself the germ of grace but only an obediential power, as St. Thomas declares in several places; cf. ad 3."[64] This is similar to what Singleton has said. He thinks that Dante is brought to perfect preparedness for grace by the immanent natural power of reason symbolized by Virgil:

Thus the first conversion, though natural, is directed to what is above nature: sanctifying grace. It is even more essentially directed to such grace in that it is a preparation to receive it. St. Thomas is given to using another term for this aspect of the matter: *habilitas ad gratiam.* For the "matter," in this case is a nature able to receive the "form" when made ready to receive it. Such a "making ready to receive" is the first of the three conversions.[65]

Note especially: "a nature able to receive the 'form' *when* made ready to receive it." (Italics mine.) But St. Thomas says that: "the justification of the ungodly is not miraculous, because the soul is naturally capable of grace;

since by the fact of having been made to the likeness of God, it is fit to receive God by grace, as Augustine says" (I-II q. 113 a. 10). This means that the justification of the ungodly is within the order of supernatural providence. There is no question here of "when," as Singleton believes. The soul is naturally capable of grace independently of whether or not it will actually be made fit to receive it. All souls are naturally capable of grace because they are all made in the likeness of God. This is the reason why the justification of the ungodly is not miraculous. However, only those souls which are made fit to receive God by grace will actually be justified. For Singleton, on the other hand, "being capable of receiving" grace is made dependent upon "making ready to receive it," which supposedly takes place, for Dante, during the first conversion under Virgil's guidance: "Such a 'making ready to receive' is the first of the three conversions." "Habilitas ad gratiam" is only an obediential power. Singleton has misunderstood it to mean the ability to prepare for sanctifying grace under the actual exercise of the immanent power of reason symbolized by Virgil, whereby, as he says, Dante's "soul, or more specifically the will, is gradually made ready to receive and is brought to perfect preparedness." "The order is natural," Singleton also says, "in that it is within confines which do not exceed human nature."[66]

What Singleton has not considered is the fact that a man may naturally acquire wisdom and science by his own talent and study. But it is, however, miraculous when this same man comes to possess that same wisdom and science outside the natural order. The same cannot be said of common conversion and miraculous conversion because in both cases the state of perfect preparedness is brought about by God Himself. There is therefore no parity:

> A man naturally acquires wisdom and science from God by his own talent and study. Hence it is miraculous when a man comes to possess wisdom or science outside this order. But a man does not naturally acquire justifying grace by his own action, but by God's. Hence there is no parity (I-II, q. 113, a. 10, R.Obj. 3).

But since Singleton mistakenly believes that instantaneous perfect preparedness for grace belongs exclusively to miraculous conversion, he has equally mistakenly assumed that in common conversion Dante must come to this same perfect preparedness, step by step, under Virgil's guidance, "within the proportion of his nature and under the natural light, and then, in a second moment attain(s) to Eden proper, crossing the river to a kind of justice with Beatrice that is truly beyond all human measure."

Apparently Singleton's misinterpretation of the relationship between nature and grace in the *Comedy* may be traced back to the book by Bouillard, who, according to Garrigou-Lagrange, seems to have had similar difficulties:

> If these various degrees of divine motion are carefully studied according to St. Thomas, it will be easy to reply to several difficulties recently pro-

posed by Father H. Bouillard, S. J., *Conversion et grâce chez S. Thomas d'Aquin,* 1944.[67]

However, what has been even more revealing to me was to learn that Bouillard rejected the possibility that grace may be a permanent gift in the essence of the soul. According to Garrigou-Lagrange, Bouillard thought of grace as a motion:

> Is sanctifying grace a permanent gift in the just, like the infused virtues? Of recent years an opinion has been expressed according to which sanctifying grace is not a form or a permanent, radical principle of supernatural operations, but rather a motion.[68]

In the above quotation, the word "motion" is followed by a note number (13), and at the bottom of page (411) we find that Garrigou-Lagrange is referring to Bouillard's work. And this might explain why Singleton's whole interpretation of the *Comedy* is one of operation, as he says: "the soul is united to God through intellect and love." Singleton has completely neglected the fact that, for St. Thomas, sanctifying grace as a form has two effects on the soul, the first of which is being, the second operation, and, most importantly, that operation follows being. This means that the soul is perfected first ontologically, then morally.

XII

Another parallel problem that has equally contributed to Singleton's fundamentally false interpretation of the entire structure of the *Comedy* is constituted by his peculiar understanding of the analogy between the Aristotelian scheme of generation and the Thomistic concept of justification. We have seen that for St. Thomas, justification is analogous to generation, inasmuch as in both cases the form is produced instantaneously. The initial preparation, St. Thomas says, "is not of the substance of justification, but a way to justification; just as local movement is a way to illumination, and alteration to generation." Singleton, on the other hand, has made the phase of preparation under Virgil of the very essence of justification by surgically cutting the process of justification into two phases. He has postulated, as we have seen, two kinds of justice within justification itself: the human justice that Dante supposedly acquires under Virgil, consisting in the subjection of the lower powers of Dante's soul to his reason, and the transhuman justice that Dante supposedly acquires with sanctifying grace at the advent of Beatrice, consisting in the subjection of Dante's reason to God. Here Singleton has simply constructed his own theology, since the two subjections are inseparable and take place in an instant: "The movement of free choice, which occurs in the justification of the ungodly, is a consent to detest sin, and to draw near to God; and this consent takes place suddenly." All this, I believe, stems in part from Singleton's misunderstanding of the relationship between generation and justification. In fact, according to Singleton, St. Thomas himself has supposedly cast the whole notion of justification into the mold of "generatio":

> Thomas is following Aristotle, not only in taking generation to be the mold in which the whole notion of justification is cast, but in the very conception of justice which is thought to lie at the end, as the form.[69]

The truth of the matter is otherwise. For St. Thomas, generation is not "the mold in which the whole notion of justification is cast." The notion of justification, St. Thomas explicitly says, is cast into the mold of a movement between two contraries. We find the following quotation from St. Thomas in Singleton's book:

> Justification taken passively implies a movement towards justice, as heating implies a movement towards heat. But since justice, by its nature, implies a certain rectitude of order, it may be taken in two ways:—First, inasmuch as it implies a right order in man's act, and thus justice is placed among the virtues. . . . Secondly, justice is so called inasmuch as it implies a certain rectitude of order in the interior disposition of a man, in so far as what is highest in man is subject to God, and the inferior powers of the soul are subject to the superior, i.e., to the reason; and this disposition the Philosopher calls *justice metaphorically speaking* (*Ethics*, v. 11). Now this justice may be in man in two ways:—First, by simple generation, which is from privation to form; and thus justification may belong to such as are not in sin, when they receive this justice from God, as Adam is said to have received original justice. Secondly, this justice may be brought about in man by a movement from one contrary to the other, and thus justification implies a transmutation from the state of injustice to the aforesaid state of justice. And it is thus we are now speaking of the justification of the ungodly, according to the Apostle (Rom. iv. 5): "But to him that worketh not, yet believeth in Him that justifieth the ungodly," etc. And because movement is named after its term *whereto* rather than from its term *whence*, the transmutation whereby anyone is changed by the remission of sins from the state of ungodliness to the state of justice, takes its name from its term whereto, and is called *justification of the ungodly*.[70]

This quotation comes from the *Summa* I-II, q. 113 a. 1. The truth is under his eyes but Singleton does not see it. Note especially that justice may be in man in two ways. The first is by simple generation, as it took place when Adam, who was not in sin, received original justice. After Adam, according to St. Thomas, only Christ has received justice by way of simple generation

(Thomas did not admit the Immaculate Conception of the Virgin Mary).[71] The second way, says St. Thomas, is "by a movement from one contrary to the other," which implies a transmutation from the state of injustice (sin) to the state of justice (grace). And, most importantly, *"it is thus we are now speaking of the justification of the ungodly, according to the Apostle."* (Italics mine.)

But Singleton has gone his own way, deciding that since justification "can be defined as 'movement towards justice,'" the movement must mean "alteration" and justification must follow the pattern of "generatio":

> The answer to the latter question is readily found in theological doctrine following the triumph of Aristotle with the schoolmen of the thirteenth century. "Movement," in this instance, must mean "alteration" (*alteratio*) taking place in a given subject or "matter"; movement will mean change in the "matter" with respect to an end. That is to say, obviously, that justification is to be conceived on the pattern of the Aristotelian conception of *generatio*, which we now know, is "motus ad formam." This being so, one must think of such a process in terms of the two elements involved, matter and form. Movement to form is thus change on the part of the matter to the end that it may receive the form. By such a change a given matter is "made ready," is "disposed," to receive. The whole movement ends when form is received by the matter which has been prepared for it. One thus conceives a process which has extension in time, and manifests two successive moments or phases. The first is the moment of *preparation*, the second the moment of *completion*, at the end, when form is attained.[72]

What has happened? Once again, Singleton has performed a delicate surgical operation. St. Thomas says: "Justification taken passively implies a movement towards justice." Singleton says, on the other hand: "justification can be defined as 'movement towards justice.'"[73] What is missing from Singleton's definition is the all-important expression "taken passively." This constitutes a difference, since justification "taken actively" signifies the infusion of sanctifying grace on the part of God: "The entire justification of the ungodly consists, as to its origin, in the infusion of grace. For it is by grace that free choice is moved and guilt is remitted" (I-II, q. 113 a. 7). This explains why, having taken the scheme of generation as the mold for the whole notion of justification, Singleton will transfer divine powers from God to Virgil, and thus say that the subjection of the lower powers of Dante's soul will take place under Virgil's guidance, whereas the subjection of Dante's mind to God will take place with sanctifying grace at the advent of Beatrice. God's active role in justification has been divided between Virgil and Beatrice. And here, of course, we have the major surgical operation, cutting through the process of justification itself. Virgil's justice, says Singleton, is justice according to the philosophers, whereas Beatrice's justice is justice according to the Apostle:

Virgil's justice is justice as the "philosophers" had understood it, it is justice according to Aristotle and Plato; whereas justice with Beatrice is quite beyond their conceptions and is the justice of which the Apostle speaks, the justice Christ brought to sinful man for his redemption.[74]

This, as we have seen, is a singularly absurd notion, since the two subjections constitute the single justice of justification and take place simultaneously in the very instant of justification: "Hence, in the justification of the ungodly, free choice simultaneously detests sin and turns to God, even as a body approaches one point and withdraws from another simultaneously" (I-II, q. 113, a. 7, R.Obj. 2).

Therefore, for St. Thomas, the whole mold for justification is not "generatio," as Singleton claims, but a movement between two contraries in which we have God (the mover) and Dante (the moved); the point of departure (the state of injustice—sin) and the point of arrival (the state of justice—grace). For Singleton, who has patterned justification on the notion of "generatio," there are only two elements involved in the process: "This being so, one must think of such a process in terms of two elements involved, matter and form." For St. Thomas, who has patterned justification on the notion of motion between two contraries, there are four elements involved in the process:

There are four things which are accounted to be necessary for the justification of the ungodly, viz., the infusion of grace, the movement of free choice towards God by faith, the movement of free choice against sin, and the remission of guilt. The reason for this is that, as was stated above, the justification of the ungodly is a movement whereby the soul is moved by God from a state of sin to a state of justice. Now in the movement whereby one thing is moved by another, three things are required:—first, the motion of the mover; secondly, the movement of the moved; thirdly, the consummation of the movement, or the attainment of the end. On the part of the divine motion, there is the infusion of grace; on the part of free choice which is moved, there are two movements—of departure from the term "whence," and of approach to the term "whereto"; while the consummation of the movement or the attainment of the end of the movement is signified in the remission of guilt; for in this is the justification of the ungodly completed (I-II, q. 113, a. 6).

We should say at this time that even Bouillard, whom Singleton claims to have followed, admits that for St. Thomas the notion of matter and form of "generatio" plays a subordinate role in the process of justification:

Désormais la notion de forme créée est subordonnée à celle d'action divine. La disposition de la matière est identifiée au mouvement du mobile et la première notion est subordonnée à la seconde. Le schème matière-forme se subordonne au schème mobile-moteur.[75]

It should be clear by now that Singleton has not only violated the Thomistic concept of justification but also the entire structure of Dante's poem. To have cut the two instantaneous and simultaneous subjections (the mind to God and the lower powers to the mind) in two phases, extended in time, and to have said that the whole area of Virgil's guidance corresponds to the first phase, whereby Dante acquires a human justice before receiving sanctifying grace with Beatrice, amounts to a total and complete distortion of both Dante's *Comedy* as well as St. Thomas's *Treatise on Grace*.

XIII

The full extent of Singleton's erroneous interpretation of the *Comedy* assumes an even broader dimension when we consider that he has created a school of thought. A case in point is John Freccero (a student of Singleton) who says:

Justice is achieved in the pilgrim's soul when he reaches the earthly paradise and his will is at last enabled to follow his reason's discernment. Virgil dismisses his charge with a circular blessing.[76]

And in a note, he adds: "For the theological concept of Justice and its relevance to Dante's poem, see C. S. Singleton, Dante Studies 2: *Journey to Beatrice* . . . pp. 55-71."[77] Freccero has accepted Singleton's interpretation of the structure of the *Comedy* as being modeled on the Aristotelian scheme of "generatio":

In their search to give the theology of grace a basis in natural philosophy, they turned to the teachings of Aristotle for a rationalization of the process of justification. Sanctifying grace was interpreted as an accidental form of the soul; justification was therefore a real change, a generation of a new form—"generatio ad formam." Charles Singleton has shown the relevance of the Aristotelian philosophy of becoming, "generatio et corruptio," to Dante's drama of justification, the *Purgatorio*. We need only review some of the principles established by Singleton's essay in order to show. . . . [78]

But, while Singleton has applied the notions of " 'generatio et corruptio' to Dante's drama of justification, the *Purgatorio*," Freccero, determined to improve on his master, will propose that the exact point in the poem where corruption meets generation (that is to say, Dante's regeneration) should be identified with the center of the earth, where Satan is found, and which he calls the "zero point":

To phrase the matter differently, in terms of the opposites that Aristotle used abstractly and Dante used in concrete detail, the change from one form to another requires first a mutation from black to non-black, *corruptio* of the old, and then a mutation from non-white to white, *generatio* of the new. The zero point is neither black nor white: "Io non mori' e non rimasi vivo" (*Inf.* XXXIV, 25).

The pilgrim is approaching the central point where descent meets ascent and death meets Resurrection. Singleton has demonstrated that the continuous movement of the pilgrim from sin to justification is a *motus ad formam*. We need only add that such a movement implies two mutations: the leaving behind of sin, *terminus a quo*, and the movement to grace, *terminus ad quem*. Satan is the zero point where corruption meets generation, which is to say the pilgrim's regeneration.[79]

This quotation is a clear indication that Freccero's understanding of the structure of the *Comedy* and of how it is related to the analogy between the process of generation and justification is quite simply the outcome of pure improvisation on his part. Singleton's interpretation has at least the great advantage of being rigorously coherent throughout his book. For him, the form of sanctifying grace comes with the advent of Beatrice. Everything before that (the whole area of Virgil's guidance) is a preparation for it in the order of nature. Singleton might have made a terrible mistake, but he is consistent. Freccero's attempt at a philosophical explanation of how the change (from one form to another) of generation is analogous to the change (from sin to grace) of justification displays a high degree of sophistication, which might easily give the impression of a profound proof. At a closer look, however, this sophistication reveals itself for what it actually is—an exercise in sophistry.

Let us, first of all, recall that Freccero starts off from second-hand information: "we need only review some of the principles established by Singleton's essay." These principles, as we have seen, constitute Singleton's false claim that supposedly, for St. Thomas, generation is "the mold in which the whole notion of justification is cast." But in order to prove his point, in two consecutive notes to these pages, Freccero invokes the authority of Aristotle's *Physics* (I, vii) and of Maurizio Flick: "For a discussion of these points and appropriate references to the *Physics*, see M. Flick, '*L'attimo della giustificazione*,' . . . esp. pp. 23-26: 'Il passaggio dallo stato di peccato allo stato di grazia.'"[80]

Had Freccero gone beyond page 26 of Flick's book, he would have discovered that, for St. Thomas, justification involves "real opposites," such as "black and white," and not "logical opposites," such as "black to non-black" and "non-white to white," as he believes.

The argument is based on the criterion used to distinguish actually, one from the other—two mutations. Mutations, it is explained, are distinguished according to their terms. Those mutations, then, are really distinguished whose terms are actually opposed in virtue of a positive reality like white and black. On the contrary, those mutations in which one of the terms is simply the negation of the other, like white and non white, are distinguished only by reason. "Now, the Angelic Doctor continues, the term of the infusion of grace is the presence of grace in the soul (gratia inesse); the term of the remission of guilt is the absence of guilt (culpam non esse) . . . It is clear, then, that if guilt is not in any way something positive, the infusion of grace is actually identified with the remission of guilt, from which it is distinguished only by a distinction of reason. If, on the contrary, guilt posits something positive, not only according to reason but in a real sense, the remission of guilt is distinguished from the infusion of grace, if considered as a mutation, for as movement they are the same thing, as has been said already. But guilt posits something positive and not only the absence of grace."[81]

Note especially that the state of sin is not simply the privation of grace. It is further explained that sin is not related to grace as an affirmation to a negation or a privation to a habit. This is so because sin as to its act is transient, whereas sin as to its effect is abiding. The effect of sin is guilt, which remains in the soul after the act has passed. And this precisely is the reason why we may speak of two mutations that take place at the instant of justification: the corruption of sin (the cancellation of guilt) and the generation of justice. Sin and grace are therefore "real opposites," like "black and white," and not "logical opposites," like "black to non-black" and "non-white to white," as Freccero believes:

We must now determine what that positive reality might be to which the remission of sin is directed, in virtue of which one may speak of a corruption of the state of sin, distinct from the generation of justice, and the justification of the sinner results to be a real movement including two mutations. One certainly cannot think of the act itself of sin which is essentially transient and therefore cannot belong to the constitutive elements of the state of sin. But it must be noted that, the act of sin having passed, man remains guilty of the sin itself, in God's eyes, until he has repaired. To this "guiltiness," which is a reality of the moral order, St. Thomas makes appeal in the Commentary in order to explain the opposition that exists between the state of justice and the state of sin. To a difficulty in fact that wishes to prove the uselessness of enumerating the remission of guilt after the infusion of grace, inasmuch as the removal of a privation is nothing but the positing of the opposite habit, he answers thus: "Sin and grace are not in relation one to the other as an affirmation and a negation, or as a privation and a habit. In fact, one may be without grace and nevertheless be without sin, as can be seen in Adam according to the opinion of those who say that he might not have been created in grace, because sin supposes something to be or to have been in the sinner (peccatum aliquid ponit vel esse vel fuisse in peccante). In fact, the act of sin having passed, somehow the offense of the previous sin still remains in the sinner, inasmuch as because of it he is made guilty before God, as meritorious acts also remain, as was said above in distinction XIV."[82]

It should be obvious that the formula of "logical opposites" is not applicable to the problem of justification as Freccero has done. What is not yet obvious is the fact that, by utilizing the above formula, Freccero has actually postulated an absurdity. This has to do with his notion of "zero-point"—as he says: "The zero-point is neither black nor white: Io non mori,' e non rimasi vivo." There is no such notion as a "zero-point" in generation, and much less in justification. According to St. Thomas, substantial form is responsible for the very being of a thing: "But the substantial form gives being absolutely, and hence by its coming a thing is said to be generated absolutely, and by its removal to be corrupted absolutely" (I, q. 76, a. 4). This means that a thing cannot exist without the form. So that, if there were a "zero-point" in generation, as Freccero maintains, the thing undergoing substantial change would actually collapse into nothingness. For example, the food we eat becomes our organism. What existed before under the form of, say bread, now exists under the new form of organism. The principle of sameness is therefore prime matter, whereas the principle of change is the form. If then, there were a "zero-point of neither black nor white," as Freccero says, or in our case, a "zero-point of neither bread nor organism," the thing would simply dissolve into nothingness.

The movement of corruption, St. Thomas says, tends towards non-being, whereas the movement of generation tends towards being. So that, since the new form is said to exist in the instant it is introduced, while the old form ceases to exist in the instant it is expelled, and since a matter cannot be without this or that form, it must be concluded that the expulsion of the old form and the introduction of the new one take place in the same instant. The same is true of justification. Guilt is expelled in the same instant in which grace is infused:

"The expulsion of a form, he explains, tells of the term of that movement which is ordered to corruption, and the introduction of a form tells similarly of the term of that movement which precedes generation, because generation and corruption are both terms of movement. Now, all that which moves, when it is at the term of movement, is disposed according to that to which the movement is ordered. Therefore since the movement of corruption tends to non-being, and that of generation to being, in the instant in which the form is introduced it exists; in the instant in which it

is expelled it does not exist. Since, then, it is said that the form is introduced when it exists for the first time, and that it is expelled when for the
first time it does not exist, matter cannot be without this or that form,
and thus we have, here and now, the expulsion of a form and the introduction of another. Since, then, similarly, the soul cannot be without guilt
and without grace, the expulsion of guilt and the infusion of grace take
place together."[83]

It should be clear by now that Dante cannot remain without guilt and
without grace, not even for an instant, since neither generation nor justification admit the possibility of a "zero-point," of "neither black nor white," as
postulated by Freccero. But Freccero is convinced that the center of Hell
constitutes an "Infernal Inversion and Christian Conversion," where the
"crux diaboli"—he says—"marks the transition from sin to penance, through
a first 'conversion,'"[84] as he is also equally convinced that Dante receives
grace only with the advent of Beatrice: "the second part of the journey also
ends in a conversion, with the theological motifs of sanctifying grace whose
presence has been convincingly demonstrated by Singleton."[85]

Freccero's understanding of the whole structure of the *Comedy* is obviously based on a metaphysical impossibility. St. Thomas is very precise on the
subject: "Poichè dunque similmente l'anima non può essere senza colpa e
senza grazia, insieme avviene l'espulsione della colpa e l'infusione della
grazia." Since the infusion of grace and the expulsion of guilt take place in
the same instant—at the instant of justification—Dante's soul cannot be
without guilt and without grace not even for an instant. Freccero, on the
other hand, maintains that Dante remains without guilt and without grace
from the center of Inferno to the mountaintop of Purgatorio. The zero-point,
Freccero says, constitutes the beginning of the preparation for grace:
"Justification *simpliciter*, however, is simply the infusion of grace, the preparation for which begins at the 'zero-point.'"[86] In an essay of 1983, "Infernal
Irony" ("Infernal Inversion and Christian Conversion" is of 1965), Freccero
is still convinced that the goal of the first part of the journey (the descent into
Hell) implies the destruction of an anterior form: "Conversion is a metamorphosis, which implies the destruction of an anterior form, the goal of the first
part of the journey."[87] An "anterior form" destroyed by what?—we might
ask. And since Freccero thinks that Dante receives grace only with Beatrice,
it then becomes apparent that he is not aware that the effects of sin can be
destroyed only by sanctifying grace. In an essay of 1961 ("Pilgrim in a Gyre"),
Freccero reveals himself to be equally unaware that the soul can be healed
only by sanctifying grace when he says that Dante's soul is "partially healed"
by his journey through hell: "After the will has accepted Divine Justice by its
journey through hell, it clings unswervingly to God, for south of the point 'al
quale ogni gravezza si rauna' (to which all heaviness is gathered), sin ceases
to exist and the soul is partially healed. There remains the painful work of

purgation, with the soul's powers in their proper order."[88] Note the expression: "sin ceases to exist and the soul is partially healed." What ceases to exist when a soul is healed is not sin, as Freccero believes, but guilt. This is so because sin, by its very nature, is transient, whereas guilt abides in the soul when the sin has passed. Freccero does not seem to be aware of the distinction between sin and the effects of sin. He is, therefore, also unaware that to cease from the act of sin is not the same as to rise from sin, as St. Thomas says: "Man by himself can in no way rise from sin without the help of Grace. For since sin is transient as to the act and abiding in its guilt, as was stated above, to rise from sin is not the same as to cease from the act of sin, but to rise from sin means that man has restored to him what he has lost by sinning" (S.T. I-II, q. 100, a. 7). Dante's purgation on the mountain is a process of rising from sin. Freccero, however, mistakenly believes that purgation can be accomplished without sanctifying grace, for, as we read elsewhere in the book, he thinks of the journey to Beatrice as a process within the natural order: "The implication seems to be that the preparation for grace lies within the competence of man, in the purely natural order. However, only Beatrice can bring the pilgrim the grace that is needed to accomplish a death and resurrection."[89] The last sentence is an obvious contradiction. If only Beatrice can, supposedly, bring the pilgrim the grace that is needed to accomplish a death and resurrection, and Beatrice comes at the mountaintop of Purgatory, how can Freccero say that the pilgrim's soul is "partially healed" at the center of Hell? Freccero seems to lack an organically coherent, comprehensive, vision of the Comedy. His major fault, I believe, is to have blindly accepted Singleton and to have desperately tried to improve on him.

In an essay of 1983 ("The Significance of Terza Rima"), it becomes even more apparent that the incoherence of Freccero's position concerning the process of justification within the structure of the Comedy is partly due to his inability to set himself free from Singleton's false interpretation of the Aristotelian-Thomistic concept of generation: "Here again, I must make reference to Singleton's work on the Purgatorio, where he explores the attempts in the Middle Ages to describe conversion, death, and resurrection, in Aristotelian terms, as movement toward form."[90] Freccero does not even suspect, of course, that Singleton, as we have shown, had completely misunderstood St. Thomas. This being the case, any attempt at improving on a mistake will inevitably compound the mistake. This is precisely Freccero's predicament. In the same essay (The Significance—1983), Freccero, in the obvious attempt to improve on Singleton, makes matters even worse this time by contradicting his own interpretation of the entire structure of the Comedy as he had proclaimed it for almost two decades. He does this by re-working an old formula of 1965 (The Sign of Satan), and by adding an isolated, appended sentence that has all the flavor of an awkward afterthought: "When the pilgrim says 'Io non mori' e non rimasi vivo' (Inf. XXXIV, 25) (I did not die and did not remain alive), he indicates a purely logical point that marks the destruction of an anterior form and the beginning of the generation of a new form, sancti-fying grace. *From the standpoint of theology, the two processes take place to-gether.*"[91] (Italics mine.)

There is a factual error involved here. The line "Io non mori' e non ri-masi vivo" is spoken by the poet, not the pilgrim as Freccero mistakenly be-lieves. This makes for a considerable difference since only the poet possesses an objective perspective of the entire journey:

> Com' io divenni allor gelato e fioco,
> nol dimandar, lettor, ch'i' non lo scrivo,
> però ch'ogne parlar sarebbe poco.
>
> Io non mori' e non rimasi vivo;
> pensa oggimai per te, s'hai fior d'ingegno,
> qual io divenni, d'uno e d'altro privo.
>
> (*Inf.* XXXIV, 22-27)

> How icy chill and hoarse I then became, ask
> not, O Reader! for I write it not, because all
> speech would fail to tell.
>
> I did not die, and did not remain alive: now
> think for thyself, if thou hast any grain of
> ingenuity, what I became, deprived of both
> death and life.

It is self-evidently clear from the above that the poet is here addressing the reader. However, Rachel Jacoff tells us that: "Freccero's way of deducing and implying the whole from a detail recalls Spitzer's conviction that every crux is potentially the totality to which it belongs ("Das Ganze im Frag-ment")."[92] But if the detail as interpreted by Freccero is a factual mistake, it follows that "deducing and implying the whole" of Dante's *Commedia* be-comes an exercise in futility. Had Freccero read Leo Spitzer's *Addresses to the reader in the Commedia*[93] he would have realized his mistake. Also, the line does not indicate "a purely logical point" as Freccero contends. It con-veys, instead, the metaphysical (spiritual) condition of the pilgrim who is about to escape the eternal death of Hell, but has not yet gained the eternal life of Heaven. The expression "d'uno e d'altro privo" means "della morte e della vita" ("deprived of both death and life"—Sapegno). This is confirmed elsewhere in the poem when Dante tells Nino Visconti that he is still in his first life, though by his journeying he gains the other, i.e. the eternal life:

> "Oh!" diss' io lui, "per entro i luoghi tristi
> venni stamane, e sono in prima vita,
> ancor che l'altra, sì andando, acquisti."
>
> (*Purg.* VIII, 58-60)

> "Oh," said I to him, "from within the places of
> woe came I this morn, and am in my first life,
> albeit by this my journeying I gain the other."

As for the statement that, "from the standpoint of theology, the two processes take place together," we are not to think that Freccero has finally realized (after having pushed for almost two decades his theory of the "zero-point" of "neither black nor white") that the destruction of the anterior form (guilt) and the generation of the new one (grace) take place, literally, in one instant—at the instant of justification—as we have learned from St. Thomas. What Freccero really means is that each step of Dante's journey is at one and the same time a moment of destruction of the old form and a moment of generation of the new one (and this of course is another absurdity), since the first step toward salvation is the first step away from sin. Freccero, in fact, thinks of conversion as a dialectics of death and resurrection supposedly analogous to "the dialectics of the poem, wherein pilgrim and narrator are created at the same time," as he says:

> Logically, conversion implies a destruction of a previous form and the creation of a new form. Like the process of autobiography, conversion begins with two subjects: the sinner who is and the saint who will be, like the pilgrim who is and the author who will be. The evolution of the sinner is toward destruction, the evolution of the saint is toward regeneration. Logically, the movement is twofold, chronologically it is one, for the first step toward salvation is the first away from sin. Like the dialectics of the poem, wherein pilgrim and narrator are created at the same time, conversion is a dialectic of death and resurrection. We may observe in passing that this theological paradox is illustrated in the poem by the symmetry and asymmetry of hell and purgatory. The center of the universe is no space-occupying place in the coordinates of moral theology, but simply the logical zero-point of a moral dialectic that leads from mountaintop to mountaintop, from the prologue scene to the ending of *Purgatorio*.[94]

What should be noted here is the fact that Freccero speaks of conversion as a moral process in the order of time. He does not seem to be aware that conversion is a process in the order of nature whereby the mind being converted is above time, as St. Thomas says: "the human mind, which is justified, is, in itself, above time" (I-II, q. 113, a. 7). Conversion is a movement between two contraries (guilt-grace), which takes place in one instant just as the propagation of light and the recession of darkness take place in the same instant. Also, it should be considered that in "the same instant the form is acquired, the thing begins to operate with the form" (I-II, q. 113, a. 7 R.Obj. 4), just as Dante begins the journey in the world beyond as a man set free:

"cominciai come persona franca" (*Inf.* II, 132). This freedom, as we have already noted, is a direct effect of sanctifying grace: "the entire justification of the ungodly consists, as to its origin, in the infusion of grace. For it is by grace that free choice is moved and guilt is remitted" (I-II, q. 113, a. 3).

Freccero, as also Singleton, is under the mistaken impression that Dante may ascend into Heaven (and partake of the glory of Heaven) solely with the infusion of sanctifying grace, which Dante supposedly receives with the advent of Beatrice. This is diametrically opposed to what Dante himself has explicitly affirmed in the *Paradiso*. In answer to a question on the nature of hope put to him by St. James, Dante, in strict theological terms that exclude even the possibility of a doubt, affirms that for a man to gain the glory of Heaven, grace and merit, not grace alone as Freccero and Singleton believe, are necessary:

> "Spene," diss' io, "è uno attender certo
> de la gloria futura, il qual produce
> grazia divina e precedente merto."
>
> *(Par.* XXV, 67-69)
>
> "Hope," said I, "is a certain expectation of
> future glory, the product of divine grace and
> precedent merit."

Dante's definition of hope is closely related to Peter Lombard's: "Est . . . spes certa exspectatio futurae beatitudinis, veniens ex Dei gratia et ex meritis praecedentibus" (*Sent.* III, dist. 26, I—Sapegno). As for the merits that Dante is here referring to, there is, of course, no doubt: they are the merits earned by a Christian through his works, as Sapegno rightly says: "precedente merto: i meriti acquisiti dal cristiano con le sue opere."

It should be pointed out, however, that in both Dante's and Peter Lombard's definitions, hope as a virtue cannot be received because of preceding merits; hope, like grace itself, is an absolute gift from God, as St. Thomas explains:

When hope is said to derive from merits what is meant is not the virtue itself but its object, i. e. the thing expected, as in this present example beatitude is hoped for from grace and merits. Or it is possible that Peter Lombard means the act of hope issuing from the virtue in so far as it is informed by charity. As for the very habit of hope itself, the act of which is the expectation of beatitude, this is in no way caused from merits but is a pure gift of grace (II-II, q. 17, a. 1, R.Obj. 2).

Freccero seems to be completely unaware that Dante's process of sanctification and his long journey to Beatrice are one and the same process—a supernatural process that can take place only as an effect of sanctifying grace whereby the effects of sin (the stains) are erased from Dante's soul as he pays his debt of punishment. Freccero seems to have confused justification (a process in the order of nature taking place in one instant) with sanctification (a process in the order of time taking place throughout the journey to Beatrice). This confusion arises from the fact that Freccero, like Singleton before him, speaks of sanctifying grace unqualifiedly, and is therefore unaware of the distinction between operating and cooperating grace, whereby conversion is first of all a metaphysical problem before being a moral one, as St. Thomas says: "But if grace is taken for the habitual gift, then again there is a double effect of grace, even as of every other form, the first of which is being, and the second, operation" (I-II, q. 111, a.2). The key concept here has to do with sanctifying grace as an accidental form (the level of being) that "inasmuch as it heals and justifies the soul, or makes it pleasing to God, is called operating grace." This is the time of justification whereby guilt is expelled from the soul at the same instant that grace is infused. As we have seen, Dante is justified in the second half (*Inf.* II) of the prologue scene. After Dante is formally justified (as St. Thomas says: "inasmuch as grace is a certain accidental quality, it does not act upon the soul efficiently, but formally, even as whiteness makes a surface white"), he can subsequently express the freedom of his choice (the moral level—as Dante had said in the Letter to Cangrande) to undertake the journey whereby he will merit the justice of reward to enter Heaven, just as St. Thomas says: "but inasmuch as it is the principle of meritorious works, which proceed from free choice, it is called cooperating grace" (I-II, q. 111 a. 2). These are some of the reasons why Dante's journey to Beatrice is an effect of sanctifying grace, not a preparation for it as both Singleton and Freccero believe. But Singleton's scholarship, as we have already noted, has at least the merit of being consistent. If he is wrong, he is consistently wrong. Freccero's scholarship, on the other hand, is characterized by a maze of vague formulas of approximation and generalities that become devoid of any meaning once they are applied to the structure of the *Comedy*. The following is a typical example of one among many such formulas: "The center of the universe is no space-occupying place in the coordinates of moral theology, but simply the logical zero-point of a moral dialectic that leads from mountaintop to mountaintop, from the prologue scene to the ending of the *Purgatorio*." There is no such thing as a "logical zero-point" either in justification or generation. In both cases, as we have seen, it is simply a metaphysical impossibility.

Furthermore, it is equally important to stress that there is no "logical zero-point of a moral dialectic" in the process of sanctification either. Sanctification is a process involving cooperating grace, whereby Dante willingly submits to divine justice in paying a penal compensation in order to have his soul cleansed of the stains of sins even after they have been forgiven: "a man is punished by God even after his sin is forgiven; and so the debt of punishment remains when the sin has been removed. . . . Two things may be considered in sin: the guilty act, and the consequent stain. Now it is evident that in all actual sins, when the act of sin has ceased, the guilt remains; for the act of sin makes man deserving of punishment, insofar as he transgresses the order of divine justice, to which he cannot return except he pay some sort of penal compensation which restores him to the equality of justice" (I-II, q. 87, a. 6). Dante undertakes his journey for personal conversion as well as for punishment: "sometimes compassionately, for their conversion, sometimes severely, for their punishment—more or less according as it pleaseth Him" (*Letter*). At this stage of the journey, and for the entire first day on the shore of Purgatory, Dante, as part of his expiation, is made to experience a deep spiritual longing to ascend the Mountain where the stains of sin will be cleansed from his soul. As we have already noted, the first day corresponds to the spiritual suspension of the Vigil night in Jerusalem, and is ultimately historically justified by the spiritual suspension on the stage of history between the Crucifixion and the Resurrection, when mankind hung—in a literal sense—spiritually suspended, longing for the Resurrection.

This does not mean, however, that Dante is without grace. He has already received sanctifying grace in the second half of the Prologue scene when he is justified and his sins are forgiven. What it does mean is that the pilgrim has not yet earned the merit (an effect of cooperating grace), which is the right to the glory of eternal life. Dante will have earned this right only at the completion of the ascent of Purgatory, which is the remaining penal compensation that will restore him to the equality of justice.

This is so because the grace of glory is not numerically distinct from sanctifying grace: "For subsequent grace, inasmuch as it pertains to glory, is not numerically distinct from prevenient grace whereby we are at present justified" (I-II, q. 111, a. 3). Sanctifying grace is the seed of beatitude: "Now it is evident that sanctifying grace bears the same relation to beatitude as the seedlike form in nature does to the natural effect; and hence grace is called the seed of God" (I, q. 62, a. 3). Most importantly, St. Thomas says that glory is the end of the operation of nature helped by grace. Therefore, Dante could not receive sanctifying grace at the end of the operation, which is to say at the end of Virgil's guidance "the preparation for grace in the natural order,"[95] as Freccero believes. Dante has already received sanctifying grace before entering the world beyond because, as the principle of right operation, sanctifying grace itself is the principle that makes Dante's freely undertaken journey a work meritorious of eternal life:

> Although in the order of nature grace comes midway between nature and glory, nevertheless, in the order of time, glory is not simultaneous with nature within the created nature; because glory is the end of the operation of nature helped by grace. *But grace stands, not as the end of operation, because it is not from works, but as the principle of right operation* (I, q. 62, a. 3, R.Obj. 3). (Italics mine.)

And elsewhere we read that for a work to be meritorious of eternal life, it must proceed from grace, first of all because God has so ordained, and second because the more perfect the principle, the more perfect the action:

> God ordained human nature to attain the end of eternal life, not by its own power, but by the help of grace; and in this way its act can be meritorious of eternal life.
> Without grace, a man cannot have a work equal to a work proceeding from grace, since the more perfect the principle, the more perfect the action (I-II, q. 114, a. 2, R.Obj. 1 & 2).

Sanctifying grace, it is once again stressed, may not be equal to glory in act, but, like the seed of a tree, it is equal to it virtually:

> The grace of the Holy Ghost which we have at present, although unequal to glory in act, is equal to it virtually, like the seed of a tree, wherein the whole tree is virtually. So likewise by grace the Holy Ghost dwells in man; and He is a sufficient cause of life everlasting. Hence he is called the pledge of our inheritance (I-II, q. 114, a. 3, R.Obj. 3).

It should be clear by now that Virgil's guidance in the *Comedy* takes place as an effect of sanctifying grace and not as preparation for it, as Singleton and Freccero maintain. What should be again stressed here is that we are confronted by an interpretation of the structure of the *Comedy* that is given not by a single author, but by a whole school of thought. Another case in point is provided by Giuseppe Mazzotta (a student of Freccero's), who has gone so far as to say that, during the first stage of Dante's journey, human nature is healed by the recovery of the four cardinal virtues rather than by sanctifying grace: "I have already, though in a general way, discussed the function of the four cardinal virtues to heal fallen man of the *vulnera naturae*."[96] And this, he says, is in conformity with—incredibly—none other than St. Thomas himself:

> In order for man to be restored to his prelapsarian condition, he has to be healed by recovering the four cardinal virtues, prudence, justice, fortitude, and temperance. In the redemptive order, such a recovery is for Aquinas only the first stage toward complete justification.[97]

Mazzotta is unaware, of course, that St. Thomas does not speak of the four *acquired* cardinal virtues as possessed by the pagans, but of the four *infused* cardinal virtues as possessed by the Christians together with sanctifying grace, as Gilson says: "As to what moral virtues St. Thomas is actually speaking about in the *Summa*, the answer in principle is simple. He is speaking of the infused supernatural moral virtues and not of the acquired natural moral virtues."[98] Most importantly, Gilson also explains, in a very cogent manner, that the natural morality described by St. Thomas pertains to a nature already healed by grace: "To attempt to disentangle the virtues in this theological organism so as to arrive at purely natural virtues is dangerous indeed . . . to dissociate the virtues from grace is not to take them back to the state of nature, but the state of fallen nature . . . because in its fallen state nature is wounded in its power to move toward the good and to fortify itself with genuine virtues . . . hence the natural morality which St. Thomas describes pertains to a nature healed by grace . . . those who would attempt such a study should be on their guard against the fundamental error of considering each moral virtue to be crowned with a theological double whose function is to do the same thing in a better way. The natural virtues remain what they were; it is the one who possess them who has changed."[99]

Mazzotta also thinks, as a final point of arrival of his methodology, that the *Comedy*: "tells the story of the persistent ambiguity of metaphoric language in which everything is perpetually fragmented and irreducible to any unification."[100] If in Dante's poem, as he maintains, everything is perpetually fragmented and irreducible to any unification, it cannot even be said that the *Comedy* is a "Christian poem" because once we pronounce the word "Christian" we have already introduced a principle of unification. Mazzotta's position on the *Comedy* is clearly an untenable form of irrationalism or nihilism.

XIV

We should now investigate the relationship postulated by St. Thomas between the three degrees of divine motion in the natural order, as compared with the three degrees of divine motion in the supernatural order, and how the latter may actually be exemplified in the very structure of the *Comedy*. However, it should be clearly noted from the start that we are not dealing here with three distinct kinds of grace as Mazzotta does when he speaks of healing grace and sanctifying grace as two distinct kinds of grace: "The two stages, insofar as they are emblems of the pilgrim's growth, will be fulfilled at the top of Purgatory where their theological coordination comes into clearer perspective because it is there that healing grace is transformed into sanctifying grace."[101] Mazzotta, like Singleton and Freccero before him, is here inventing his own personal theology. This, once again, is like putting the cart in front of the horse for the very simple reason that healing grace is not a distinct kind of grace that is supposedly "transformed into sanctifying grace," as Mazzotta erroneously believes, but an effect of sanctifying grace that is indivisible in its essence. We are dealing, instead, with one selfsame sanctifying grace, viewed from the operating or cooperating aspect, as the case may be, since sanctifying grace is divisible only in its effects. Garrigou-Lagrange says that,

According to the terminology of St. Thomas there are three degrees of divine motion in the natural order and three corresponding degrees in the supernatural; for in both the natural and the supernatural order divine motion is either before our deliberation or after it or above it.

Before our deliberation, as long as we naturally desire to be happy, we are moved to desire happiness in general. For, since this desire is the first act of our will, we are not moved to it by virtue of a previous act of deliberation. There is something similar in the supernatural order when we are moved to our final supernatural end, for we cannot be moved to it by virtue of a previous higher act by way of deliberation.

After deliberation, or at its end, we are moved toward some good (on which we have deliberated) by virtue of a previous act; for by intending the end we are moved to choose the means to the end under divine co-operating concursus; this indeed, whether in the natural order or in the supernatural by the exercise of the infused virtues.

Above deliberation we are moved toward some object which surpasses our powers. Thus, in the natural order, under special inspiration of God, the author of nature, great geniuses in the philosophic, poetic, or strategic sphere as well as great heroes are moved. There is something similar and even more frequent in the supernatural order, when a just man is moved by special inspiration of the gifts of the Holy Spirit; this is properly above discursive deliberation and the human mode of operation.[102]

In the first mode of divine motion in the natural order, "God moves man's will as the Universal Mover, to the universal object of the will, which is good. And without this universal motion, man cannot will anything" (I-II, q. 9, a. 6, R.Obj. 3).[103] We find an echo of these words of St. Thomas in the context of the *Comedy* when Virgil recognizes that there is indeed an inclination to the prime objects of appetite, but he does not know whence it may come: "Però, là onde vegna lo 'ntelletto / de le prime notizie, omo non sape, / e de' primi appetibili l'affetto" (*Purg.* XVIII, 55-57). This is so because, as Virgil has already explained to Dante, he is able to explain only so far as reason can see, but beyond that point, since it is a matter of faith, Dante must await Beatrice: "Ed elli a me: 'Quanto ragion qui vede, / dir ti poss'io; da indi in là t'aspetta / pur a Beatrice, ch'è opra di fede.'" (*Purg.* XVIII, 46-48). He knows, however, that in this first act of the will (in which the will does not move itself in its desire for happiness) there can be no praise or blame since we are not free not to desire our happiness: "e questa prima voglia / merto di lode o di biasmo non cape" (*Purg.* XVIII, 59-60).

Similarly, in the first mode of divine motion in the order of grace: "at the moment when a sinner is justified, God as the Author of grace moves the sinner's free will to be converted to his supernatural last end. Under this divine motion and by it the sinner is made just or is justified, and begins to act no longer merely in view of happiness naturally desired, but for God supernaturally loved above all things."[104] This, as we have seen, takes place in the second half of the Prologue scene when Dante receives an actual infusion of sanctifying grace, whereby he is justified—he is made pleasing to God. Dante's expressed act of formed faith (faith directed by charity) should be taken, of course, as conclusive evidence for this: "since the act of faith of him that worketh by charity is the first act by which sanctifying grace is manifested." It should be noted, however, that Dante's justification (like that of any sinner) takes place specifically as an effect of operating grace: "This supernatural motion first of all prepares the sinner to receive sanctifying grace, and justifies him through the infusion of this grace and of charity by moving him to a free act of faith, charity and repentance. In this case, the free will does not, strictly speaking, move itself to this act of living faith and charity; it is moved thereto by operating grace."[105] That Beatrice comes, in the Prologue scene, as sanctifying (operating) grace, is also confirmed by Dante's farewell address to her in the *Paradiso* where it is clearly recognized that it was by the power of her grace that she endured to leave her footprints in Hell for Dante's salvation:

> "O donna in cui la mia speranza vige,
> e che soffristi per la mia salute
> in inferno lasciar le tue vestige,
>   di tante cose quant' i' ho vedute,
> dal tuo podere e da la tua bontate
> riconosco la grazia e la virtute."

(Par. XXXI, 79-84)

> "O Lady, in whom my hope hath vigour, and
> who for my salvation didst endure to leave
> in Hell thy footprints;
>   of all the things which I have seen I recognise
> the grace and might, by thy power and by thine
> excellence."

We should recall that "habitual grace, inasmuch as it heals and justifies the soul, or makes it pleasing to God, is called operating grace," just as we are also informed that Beatrice has healed Dante's soul, and has drawn him from slavery to liberty:

> "Tu m'hai di servo tratto a libertate
> per tutte quelle vie, per tutt' i modi
> che di ciò fare avei la potestate.
>   La tua magnificenza in me custodi,
> sì che l'anima mia, che fatt' hai sana,
> piacente a te dal corpo si disnodi."

(Par. XXXI, 85-90)

>"Thou hast drawn me from a slave to liberty
>by all those paths, by all those methods by
>which thou hadst the power so to do.
>   Preserve thy munificence in me, so that my soul,
>which thou hast made sound, may unloose
>it from the body, pleasing unto thee."

This first movement in the order of grace resembles the first movement in the natural order, by which we desire happiness. Since this is the first efficacious act of love of the supernatural end, it is not preceded by personal merit but opens the way to merit, which is an effect of cooperating grace pertaining to the second mode of divine motion in the order of grace:

> In this act there cannot be sin; on the contrary, there is hatred of sin. This act is freely produced under the impulse of efficacious grace. Although entirely free, this supernatural movement of the will resembles the first natural movement by which we wish happiness. Strictly speaking, man cannot move himself; that would suppose an efficacious anterior act of the same order. This anterior act does not exist, since the question here concerns the first efficacious act of love of the supernatural end. This act is not preceded by personal merit; rather it opens the way of merit. It is, as it were, the threshold of the order of grace, or the first step in the execution of divine predestination.[106]

In the second mode of divine motion in the order of nature "our free will, still in the natural order, determines upon a true good or an apparent good. This movement of our will is not only vital but free, and to produce it the will moves itself in virtue of an anterior act; hence it can sin in this case,"[107] or, in the words of St. Thomas, "man determines himself by his reason, to will this or that, which is true or apparent good."[108] God is the first cause of our good act, whereas we are the second cause of our good act: "what hast thou that thou hast not received," says St. Paul.[109] However, while God is the cause of the physical act of sin, we alone are the cause of its malice, just as the defect of limping may be caused by a crooked leg whereas the motion itself springs from the vital energy of the man:

> Again, every action is caused by something existing in act, since nothing produces an action save in so far as it is in act; and every being in act is reduced to the First Act, viz., God, as to its cause, Who is act by His Essence. Therefore God is the cause of every action, in so far as it is an action. But sin denotes a being and an action with a defect. But this defect is from a created cause, viz., free choice, as falling away from the order of the First Cause, viz., God. Consequently, this defect is not reduced to God as its cause, but to free choice; just as the defect of limping is re-

duced to a crooked leg as its cause, but not to the power of locomotion, which causes whatever there is of movement in the limping. Accordingly, God is the cause of the act of sin; and yet, He is not the cause of sin, because He does not cause the act to have a defect (I-II, q. 79, a. 2).

Virgil, likewise, recognizes that those whose reasoning went to the foundation of reality, perceived that there is an innate freedom in us whereby we are able to choose this real or that apparent good, and this indeed constitutes the very principle of our merit or demerit:

> "Quest' è 'l principio là onde si piglia
> ragion di meritare in voi, secondo
> che buoni e rei amori accoglie e viglia.
>   Color che ragionando andaro al fondo,
> s'accorser d'esta innata libertate;
> però moralità lasciaro al mondo."
>
> (Purg. XVIII, 64-69)
>
> "This is the principle whence is derived the reason
> of desert in you, according as it garners and
> winnows good and evil loves.
>   Those who in their reasoning went to the
> foundation, perceived this innate freedom,
> therefore they left ethics to the world."

Virgil, however, hastily adds that Dante should ask Beatrice for further elucidation on this matter:

> "La nobile virtù Beatrice intende
> per lo libero arbitrio, e però guarda
> che l'abbi a mente, s'a parlar ten prende."
>
> (Purg. XVIII, 73-75)
>
> "By the noble virtue Beatrice understands Freewill,
> and therefore, look that thou have this in mind,
> if she betake her to speak with thee thereof."

Similarly, in the second mode of divine motion in the order of grace: "God moves a just man to act well supernaturally by using the infused virtues as he ought. In this movement of the free will, the will is moved and moves itself by virtue of an anterior supernatural act. Here there is deliberation, properly so called, regarding the means in view of the end, and a human manner of acting under the direction of reason enlightened by faith. Moreover, this grace is called cooperating grace,"[110] or in the words of St. Thomas, "in that effect in which our mind both moves and is moved, the operation is not only attributed to God, but also to the soul; and it is with reference to this that we speak of cooperating grace."[111] Human freedom, however, is not destroyed: "When this grace is efficacious, free will can still resist if it wishes, but it never wills to do so. In fact, it cannot happen that sin is produced in the very use of grace, when man is moved by efficacious actual grace. Thus, he who is seated can indeed rise, but he cannot at one and the same time be seated and standing. Liberty is not destroyed because God, who is infinitely powerful and closer to us than we are to ourselves, moves our will according to its natural inclinations freely to will one thing or another,"[112] or, once again, in the words of St. Thomas, "The divine will extends not only to the doing of something by the thing which He moves, but also to its being done in a way which is fitting to the nature of that thing. And therefore it would be more repugnant to the divine motion for the will to be moved of necessity, which is not fitting to its nature, than for it to be moved freely, which is becoming to its nature."[113]

We find the expression of this cooperating grace in the *Comedy* when Dante, having been justified and already intending the end, is now moved to choose the means conducive to that end—which is to say that he now wills the journey that will bring him face to face with God:

> "Or va, ch'un sol volere è d'ambedue"
>
> (*Inf.* II, 139)
>
> "Now go, for both have one will"

In fact, from this point onward, and covering all of Virgil's guidance in the *Comedy*, the journey to Beatrice takes place as an effect of cooperating grace. It is Beatrice that makes him go: "Io son Beatrice, che ti faccio andare," but Dante is freely cooperating with her, just as St. Thomas says: "in that effect in which our mind both moves and is moved, the operation is not only attributed to God, but also to the soul; and it is with reference to this that we speak of cooperating grace." And this indeed is also the reason why the journey itself acquires the character of a meritorious work: "but inasmuch as it is the principle of meritorious works which proceed from free choice, it is called cooperating grace."

Now, since the journey to Beatrice involves a descent into Hell, and an ascent of the mountain of Purgatory, we find further confirmation of this divine cooperation, not once, but twice. In two symmetrically placed cantos—*Inferno* IX and *Purgatorio* IX—that put Dante, respectively, at the gate of the city of Dis and at the gate of Purgatory, it is confirmed to us that both the descent and the ascent do indeed take place with divine cooperation, i.e., cooperating grace. In the first instance, Dante is being denied access to the city of Dis by more than a thousand fallen angels who close the gates on Virgil's breast. This is of course revealing, since Virgil, as the first guide and as the symbol of the natural light of reason, seems to be utterly powerless against the evil of the devils. The case is not resolved until a messenger of

Heaven comes with a wand and the gate opens with no resistance: "non v'ebbe alcun ritegno" (v. 90). And here precisely, just before the messenger appears, Dante invites the readers with sane intellects to consider the doctrine, which conceals itself under the veil of the strange verses:

> "O voi ch'avete li 'ntelletti sani,
> mirate la dottrina che s'asconde
> sotto 'l velame de li versi strani!"
>
> (*Inf.* IX, 61-63)
>
> "O ye, who have sane intellects, mark the
> doctrine, which conceals itself beneath the
> veil of the strange verses!"

The doctrine—"la dottrina"—is of course an obvious reference to the doctrine of sanctifying grace, whereby it is postulated that we may be justified by operating grace, but we must earn merit (the right to the reward of eternal life) by cooperating grace, just as Dante is doing, since "God, by cooperating with us, perfects what He began by operating in us, since He who perfects by cooperation with such as are willing, begins by operating that they may will," or "He operates that we may will; and when we will, He cooperates that we may accomplish" (I-II, q. 111, a. 2).

In the second instance, we even know the name of the messenger from Heaven. Her name is St. Lucia who, while Dante is asleep and dreaming of being taken up to the sphere of fire by an eagle (symbol of both justice and baptismal regeneration), takes Dante in her arms and deposits him by the gate of Purgatory so that she might, as she says, help him on his way:

> venne una donna, e disse; "I' son Lucia;
> lasciatemi pigliar costui che dorme;
> sì l'agevolerò per la sua via."
>
> (*Purg.* IX, 55-57)
>
> came a lady and said: "I am Lucy, let me take
> this man who sleepeth, so will I prosper him
> on his way."

The divine cooperation is here confirmed both by the physical action itself and by the verb "agevolare," which means "to facilitate," "to make easy," "to help forward." In fact, if we also consider her role in Heaven, St. Lucia may well be the symbol of cooperating grace, while Beatrice is the symbol of operating grace.

In the second mode of divine motion in the order of grace, we are dealing with a man who has already been justified and is now moved by God "to act well supernaturally by using the infused virtues as he ought." Moreover, this is a "human manner of acting under the direction of reason enlightened by faith." This last information is of paramount importance since it distinguishes the second from the third mode of divine motion in the order of grace. The third mode, as we shall see, involves the gifts of the Holy Spirit.

At the moment of justification in the Prologue scene, Dante has received not only an infusion of sanctifying grace, but also the infused virtues, theological as well as cardinal. Acquired cardinal virtues are caused by repetitive acts of virtue. On the other hand, the cause of infused cardinal virtues is God Himself: "Whether any moral virtues are in us by infusion? . . . It is written (Wis. viii. 7)":

> She teacheth temperance and prudence and justice and fortitude. . . . Effects must needs be proportioned to their causes and principles. Now all virtues, intellectual and moral, that are acquired by our actions, arise from certain natural principles preexisting in us, as was stated above. In the place of these natural principles, God bestows on us the theological virtues, by which we are directed to a supernatural end, as was stated above. Therefore, we need to receive from God other habits annexed proportionately to the theological virtues, which are to the theological virtues what the moral and intellectual virtues are to the natural principles of the virtues (I-II, q. 63, a. 3).

The mean in the acquired cardinal virtues is fixed by reason, whereas in infused cardinal virtues the mean is fixed by divine rule: "Now it is evident that the mean that is appointed, in such concupiscences, according to the rule of human reason, is of a different nature than the mean which is fixed according to the divine rule. For instance, in the consumption of food, the mean fixed by human reason is that food should not harm the health of the body, nor hinder the use of reason; whereas, according to the divine rule, it behooves man to chastise his body, and bring it into subjection (I Cor. ix, 27), by abstinence in food, drink and the like. It is therefore evident that infused and acquired temperance differ in species; and the same applies to the other virtues" (I-II, q. 63, a. 4). And finally, they also differ as to the things to which they are directed: "In the same way, too, those infused moral virtues, by which men behave well in relation to their being fellow-citizens with the saints, and of the house-hold of God (Ephes. ii. 19), differ from the acquired virtues by which man behaves well in relation to human affairs" (I-II, q. 63, a. 4).

The main difference that I wish to emphasize here is the fact that the infused cardinal virtues are caused by God, whereas the acquired cardinal virtues are caused by repetitive, virtuous acts. This all-important difference will explain why Virgil is able to understand Dante's perspective. By this I mean that only at the end of the process, having witnessed that Dante has indeed performed numerous acts of virtue, is Virgil able to know that Dante does indeed possess the cardinal virtues. In reality, however, Dante was given all seven infused virtues (theological and cardinal), together with sanctifying grace, even before he entered the world beyond. This is so because, in his ascent of the mountain of Purgatory, Dante is undergoing a process of personal sanctification by way of purgation. In this process the effects of his sins (the stains) are erased from his soul as the "P"s are erased from his forehead, since "sanctification is effected by all the virtues, by which also sins are taken away" (I-II, q. 70, a. 3), but Virgil could not possibly conceive of this. As far as Virgil is able to understand, Dante's spiritual process is taking place entirely within the order of nature. However, the many crucial failings of Virgil as guide throughout the journey should be taken as ample proof that the truth is otherwise than he thinks. But Virgil is the guide and is able to lead the way because he is the symbol of the highest natural perfection of reason, which he now possesses in a fulfilled manner; in a more perfect manner than the three theological virtues are possessed by Dante:

> Now man's reason is perfected by God in two ways: first, with its natural perfection, namely, the natural light of reason; secondly, with a supernatural perfection, namely, the theological virtues, as we have stated above. And though this latter perfection is greater than the former, yet the former is possessed by man in a more perfect manner than the latter; because man has the former in his full possession, whereas he possesses the latter imperfectly, since we love and know God imperfectly (I-II, q. 68, a. 2).

Virgil is in full possession of the acquired cardinal virtues—he possesses them in a fulfilled manner. However, he is not the only guide in Purgatory. At a certain point in the journey, the Christian poet Statius, who can see far beyond Virgil, and in a certain sense takes over as guide, should be understood as the symbol of reason enlightened by faith, as Montano accurately points out:

> Statius will give the assistance provided by a philosophy which, although remaining on the level of rational demonstration, thanks to directives given by revelation, can go farther in the conquest of truth. The moment is precisely symbolical of the Christian Philosophy that St. Thomas, in the medieval world, had formulated with more rigor than anyone else, and had been the basis for the great philosophical refutation of the errors of the Gentiles, which is the *Summa contra Gentiles*.[114]

It should be added that Statius has undergone a long purgation and is therefore already purified. Dante, on the other hand, is still a wayfarer, and in that condition both his reason and the theological virtues possessed by him are not enough to safeguard him against folly, ignorance, dullness of mind, and hardness of heart, as is apparent throughout his descent into the Inferno and his ascent of Purgatory. As remedies to these defects, Dante stands in need of the gifts of the Holy Ghost, as St. Thomas points out:

> Whether we consider human reason as perfected in its natural perfection, or as perfected by the theological virtues, it does not know all things, nor are all things possible to it. Consequently, it is unable under all circumstances to avoid folly and other like things mentioned in the objection. God, however, to Whose knowledge and power all things are subject, by His motion safeguards us from all folly, ignorance, dullness of mind and hardness of heart, and the rest. Consequently, the gifts of the Holy Ghost, which make us amenable to His instigation, are said to be given as remedies to these defects (I-II, q. 68, a. 2, R.Obj. 3).

This is so because, in the second mode of divine motion in the order of grace, the infused virtues (theological and cardinal) still operate in the human mode of reason enlightened by faith:

> The infused moral and theological virtues, even when they have reached a high degree, without a special help of the Holy Ghost, still operate according to the human mode of the faculties in which they are received. Faith makes us know God in a way which is still too abstract, too exterior, in *speculo et in aenigmate*, by excessively narrow formulas that must be multiplied. . . . Hope and Charity, which are directed by faith, share in this imperfection of faith. These two virtues of the will lack vitality and keep too much of the human manner as long as they are directed only by reason illumined by faith. . . . because our supernatural virtues must be adapted to the human mode of our faculties, they leave us in a state of inferiority with respect to the supernatural end toward which we should advance with greater eagerness.[115]

According to St. Thomas, the gifts of the Holy Ghost are actually necessary for salvation: "For none can receive the inheritance of that land of the blessed, except he be moved and led thither by the Holy Ghost. Therefore, in order to reach this end, it is necessary for man to have the gift of the Holy Ghost" (I-II, q. 68, a. 2). The gifts of the Holy Ghost surpass the virtues in the mode of operation, but not in the kind of works: "The gifts surpass the ordinary perfection of the virtues, not as regards the kind of works, but as regards the manner of working, according as man is moved by a higher principle" (I-II, q. 68, a. 2, R.Obj. 1). And finally, the gifts are necessary because the infused virtues do not completely perfect man in relation to this last end: "By the theological and moral virtues man is not so perfected in relation to his last end as not to stand in continual need of being moved by the yet higher instigation of the Holy Ghost, for the reason already given" (I-II, q. 68, a. 2, R.Obj. 2).

Does Dante possess the gifts of the Holy Ghost? The answer is in the affirmative, although the "gifts" are not really gifts, but divine "inspirations":

> Accordingly, in order to differentiate the gifts from the virtues, we must be guided by the way in which Scripture expresses itself, for we find there that the term employed is "spirit" rather than "gift." For thus it is written (Isa. xi. 2,3.): "The spirit . . . of wisdom and of understanding . . . shall rest upon him, etc." From these words we are clearly given to understand that these seven are there set down as being in us by divine inspiration. Now inspiration denotes motion from the outside. For it must be noted that in man there is a twofold principle of movement, one within him, viz., the reason, the other extrinsic to him, viz., God, as we have stated above (I-II, q. 68, a. 1).

More specifically, the gifts are infused habits whereby man is disposed to obey readily the Holy Ghost, just as moral virtues dispose the appetitive powers to obey reason: "Accordingly, the gifts of the Holy Ghost are related to man in his relation to the Holy Ghost as the moral virtues are related to the appetitive power in its relation to reason. Now the moral virtues are certain habits by which the powers of the appetite are disposed to obey reason promptly. Therefore, the gifts of the Holy Ghost are habits by which man is perfected to obey readily the Holy Ghost" (I-II, q. 68, a. 3). Also, more importantly, "just as the moral virtues are united together in prudence, so the gifts of the Holy Ghost are connected together in charity; so that whoever has charity, has all the gifts of the Holy Ghost, none of which can be possessed without charity" (I-II, q. 68, a. 5). From this we may infer that Dante does indeed possess the gifts, since we have witnessed an expression of formed faith (faith directed by charity) on his part at the very beginning of the journey. This, as we have also noted, was the first act that manifested sanctifying grace in Dante.

There is, however, stronger evidence to suggest that Dante may be receiving the gifts of the Holy Ghost, one by one, as he ascends each terrace of Purgatory. Dante, after all, is still alive, and the function of the gifts is to give us protection against evil in this life and to perfect us in good in the state of glory: "Gregory is speaking there of the gifts according as they belong to the present state, for it is thus that they afford us protection against evil temptations. But in the state of Glory, where all evil will have ceased, we shall be perfected in good by the gifts of the Holy Ghost" (I-II, q. 68, a. 6). This is indeed the status of souls in Dante's *Paradiso* in which Dante will participate in his ascension there with Beatrice. But here in Purgatory Dante is still in the process of purgation, which means that he is still in the process of earning merit—the right to the reward of eternal life. Only at the mountaintop of Purgatory will Dante have achieved the status of "equality of justice," which will be a confirmation of his sanctification.

At each terrace of Purgatory, just as a "P" is erased from Dante's forehead by the angel, so too the effect of sin (a stain) is erased from his soul. Moreover, like an echo of a sweet sound, immediately following the wiping away of each letter from Dante's forehead, the angel also utters one of the beatitudes. This is of considerable importance, since a beatitude is related to a gift as an act to a habit:

> Now a man is moved towards the end which is happiness, and approaches to it by works of virtue, and above all by the works of the gifts, if we speak of eternal happiness, for which our reason is not sufficient, since we need to be moved by the Holy Ghost, and to be perfected with His gifts that we may obey and follow him. Consequently, the beatitudes differ from the virtues and gifts, not as habit from habit, but as an act from a habit (I-II, q. 69, a. 1).

Moreover, because of their perfection, the beatitudes are assigned to the gifts rather than to the virtues: "the beatitudes are none but perfect works, and which, by reason of their perfection, are assigned to the gifts rather than to the virtues, as we have already stated" (I-II, q. 70, a. 2). This is so because the gifts actually perfect the virtues: "The gifts perfect the virtues by raising them above the human mode; as the gift of understanding perfects the virtue of faith."[116] The theological virtues, however, are said to be superior to the gifts inasmuch as they regulate them: "The theological virtues (uniting us to the Holy Ghost) are superior to the gifts which they regulate, and nevertheless receive a new perfection from them."[117] "Hence Gregory says that the 'seven sons,' i.e., the seven gifts, 'never attain the perfection of the number ten, unless all that they do be done in faith, hope and charity'" (I-II, q. 68, a. 8). Therefore, a beatitude proceeds from a virtue perfected by a gift: "The operation which proceeds from the virtue perfected by the gift is called a beatitude."[118]

It should be clear from all this that the beatitudes are indeed directly connected to the gifts of the Holy Ghost, and since we hear a beatitude at each terrace of Purgatory, it should be reasonable for us to assume that Dante is receiving or, is now revealing an already received gift corresponding to each beatitude.

This may be further confirmed if we consider that each beatitude is made up of two parts, the first of which pertains to merit: "Blessed are the poor in spirit," and the second to reward: "for theirs is the Kingdom of Heaven." But the final goal of merit is eternal life, which is possessed in Heaven, assured in Purgatory, and earned in this life:

> In order to make the matter clear, we must note that hope of future happiness may be in us for two reasons. First, by reason of our having a preparation for, or disposition to, future happiness, and this is by way of

merit; secondly, by a kind of imperfect inchoation of future happiness in holy men, even in this life. For it is one thing to hope that the tree will bear fruit when the leaves begin to appear, and another, when we see the first signs of the fruit.

Accordingly, those things which are set down as merits in the beatitudes are a kind of preparation for, or a disposition to happiness, either perfect or inchoate; while those that are assigned as rewards may be either perfect happiness itself, and thus refer to the future life, or some beginning of happiness, such as is found in those who have attained perfection, in which case they refer to the present life. For when a man begins to make progress in the acts of the virtues and gifts, it is to be hoped that he will arrive at perfection both as a wayfarer and as a citizen of the heavenly kingdom (I-II, q. 69, a. 2).

Note especially: "those things which are set down as merits in the beatitudes are a kind of preparation for, or disposition to, happiness, either perfect or inchoate." This passage is a perfect description of Dante's condition on the Mountain. On each terrace, with one possible exception, the angel utters that part of the beatitude which pertains to merit, thereby confirming that Dante is indeed in the process of earning the right to the reward of eternal life: "*Beati pauperes spiritu!*" (*Purg.* XII, 110); "*Beati misericordes!*" (*Purg.* XV, 38); "*Beati pacifici*"(*Purg.* XVII, 68-69); "*Qui lugent*' affermando esser beati, / ch'avran di consolar l'anime donne" (*Purg.* XIX, 50-52); "e quei c'hanno a giustizia lor disiro, / detto n'avea beati, e le sue voci / con '*sitiunt*', sanz'altro, ciò forniro." (*Purg.* XXII, 4-6); "Beati cui alluma / tanto di grazia, che l'amor del gusto / nel petto lor troppo disir non fuma, / esurïendo sempre quanto è giusto!" (*Purg* XXIV, 151-54); "*Beati mundo corde!*" (*Purg.* XXVII, 8); Dante, as we have noted, will have a foretaste of the beatitude of Heaven when he ascends there with Beatrice. The symbolic meaning is therefore clear: Dante, as a wayfarer, is the symbol of all mankind, and the perfection reached by him on his journey should be understood as something open to all mankind here on earth, since "when a man begins to make progress in the acts of the virtues and the gifts, it is to be hoped that he will arrive at perfection, both as a wayfarer and as a citizen of the heavenly kingdom," even if this is a "kind of imperfect inchoation of future happiness."

However, for a man to partake of the "imperfect inchoation of future happiness," or for Dante to partake of the happiness of Heaven under the guidance of Beatrice, he must first of all be brought to a state of "equality of justice," which is an effect of cooperating grace. This is so because a man is judged according to the works that he performs: "God will render to every man according to his works" (Rom. 2:26), or "As to the rest, there is laid up for me a crown of justice, which the Lord, the just judge, will render to me in that day" (II Tim. 4:8).[119] This, of course, is in perfect agreement with the allegorical meaning of the *Comedy* as a whole, since Dante himself declares,

"But if the work is considered according to its allegorical meaning, the subject is man, liable to the reward or punishment of Justice, according as through the freedom of the will he is deserving or undeserving."[120]

Several conditions, however, must be satisfied before a work may be called meritorious. Accordingly, Dante's journey itself must satisfy the following conditions:

> From the preceding four articles of St. Thomas can now be drawn the conditions necessary for merit. There are six here enumerated proceeding in order from the more general to the more particular. Thus we may construct a very clear and complete definition of a meritorious work according to remote and proximate genus and specific difference. But it is attained only at the end of the hunt or inquisition which was pursued through the foregoing articles.
>
> A meritorious work must be: 1. free; 2. good; 3. in submission or obedience to the rewarder (this is true even for merit in the human order, such as a soldier's merit); 4. the work of a wayfarer; 5. proceeding from sanctifying grace and charity; 6. ordained by God to a promised reward. We shall explain each of these conditions briefly. They are all necessary for merit "de condigno"; in the course of the explanation it will be indicated which are not absolutely necessary for merit "de congruo."[121]

Merit "de condigno" (merit of equivalence) is merit according to justice; either "strict justice," which "implies in itself absolute equality to the reward; such was the merit of Christ, inasmuch as, by reason of the divine person, He is equal to the Father," or "proportionate justice," which "implies a value not equal to the reward, but proportionate to it, according to a divine ordination and promise, without which promise there would be no strict right."[122] Better still, in the words of St. Thomas:

> Now justice is a kind of equality, as is clear from the philosopher, and hence justice exists absolutely between those that are absolutely equal; but where there is no absolute equality between them, neither is there absolute justice, but there may be a certain manner of justice as when we speak of a father's or a master's right, as the Philosopher says. And hence when there is justice absolutely, there is the character of merit and reward absolutely. But when there is nothing absolutely just, but only relatively, there is no character of merit absolutely, but only relatively, in so far as the character of justice is preserved there; since the child merits something from his father and the slave from his lord.
>
> Now it is clear that between God and man there is the greatest inequality; for they are infinitely apart, and all man's good is from God. Hence there can be no justice of absolute equality between man and God, but only of a certain proportion, inasmuch as both operate after

their own manner. Now the manner and measure of human virtue is in man from God. Hence man's merit with God exists only on the presupposition of the divine ordination, so that, namely, man obtains from God, as a sort of reward of his operation, what God gave him the power of operation for, even as natural things by their proper movements and operations obtain that to which they were ordained by God. There is a difference, however, since the rational creature moves itself to act by its free choice; and so its action has the character of merit, which is not the case in other creatures.

In three consecutive replies, St. Thomas further elucidates:

Man merits, inasmuch as by his own will he does what he ought; or otherwise the act of justice whereby anyone discharges a debt would not be meritorious.

God seeks from our goods not profit, but glory, i.e., the manifestation of His goodness; even as He seeks it also in His own works. Now nothing accrues to Him, but only to ourselves, by our worship of Him. Hence we merit from God, not that by our works anything accrues to Him, but inasmuch as we work for His glory.

Since our action has the character of merit only on the presupposition of the divine ordination, it does not follow that God is made our debtor absolutely, but His own, inasmuch as it is owing that His will should be carried out (I-II, q. 114, a. 1, R.Obj. 1, 2, 3).

Merit "de congruo" (merit of fitness) is either merit "based on friendship, by friendly right to the reward, [which] presupposes the state of grace"; or merit "based on the bounty or mercy of God, [which] does not presuppose the state of grace, but a certain disposition for grace, or prayer, as it exists in the sinner."[123]

It should be clear that the justice of merit is not to be confused with the metaphorical justice of justification. It must, however, be noted that "metaphorical" does not mean "fictional." In fact, metaphorical justice expresses a general rectitude of order in the soul whereby the subjection of the mind to God, and of the lower powers to the mind, constitute a real harmony. It is called "metaphorical" because it speaks of the powers of the soul as if they were persons. However, what distinguishes one from the other is the fact that metaphorical justice pertains to the powers of the soul, whereas the justice of merit pertains to the works produced by the powers of the soul, or, better still, produced by the man. Dante, as we have seen, has already been justified in the Prologue scene. By undertaking the journey in the world beyond, he is now in the process of earning the justice of merit. But it should be stressed once again that both metaphorical justice and the justice of merit are effects of sanctifying grace. The former is an effect of sanctifying (operating) grace, whereas the latter is an effect of sanctifying (cooperating) grace. It is simply not true, as Singleton maintains, that Dante acquires justice in the soul before receiving sanctifying grace with Beatrice: "And so too in the matter of justification in the soul: first justice, then advent of grace, as to a place prepared."[124]

Now let us examine more closely the conditions necessary for merit in a work.

1. The work must be free. Otherwise, as St. Thomas says, it would not be meritorious: "Man merits, inasmuch as by his own will he does what he ought; or otherwise the act of justice whereby anyone discharges a debt would not be meritorious." Similarly, Dante undertakes the journey as a man set free: "ch'i' cominciai come persona franca" (*Inf.* II, 132).

2. It must be a good work: "In fact, a meritorious work must possess supernatural goodness proportioned to the supernatural reward."[125] Similarly, Dante undertakes the journey for both personal and universal reasons. Dante's mission, as explicitly stated by Beatrice, is to write a poem for the benefit of mankind that lives in sin: "Però, in pro del mondo che mal vive, / al carro tieni or li occhi, e quel che vedi, / ritornato di là, fa che tu scrive" (*Purg.* XXXII, 103-5).

3. The work must be done "under submission or obedience to the rewarder . . . otherwise there would be no reason for expecting a reward from God."[126] Similarly, Dante undertakes the journey under submission or in obedience to Beatrice: "Oh pietosa colei che mi soccorse! / e te cortese, ch'ubidisti tosto / a le vere parole che ti porse!" (*Inf.* II, 133-34). Note especially the verb "ubidisti." As Virgil obeyed Beatrice, so now Dante is obeying her by obeying Virgil: "Or va, ch'un sol volere è d'ambedue" (*Inf.* II, 139).

4. The work must be the act of a wayfarer: "Merit and progress belong to this present state of life. . . . to merit belongs to the imperfect charity of this life; whereas perfect charity does not merit but rather enjoys the reward" (I, q. 62, a. 9, & R.Obj. 1). Similarly, Dante is making the journey as he is in this life. More specifically, the journey is conceived by Dante as a pilgrimage: "ma noi siam peregrin come voi siete" (*Purg.* II, 63).

5. The work must proceed from sanctifying grace and charity: "If I . . . have not charity, I am nothing . . . it profiteth me nothing" (I Cor. 13:2 f).[127] Also, as St. Thomas says: "hence it is that no created nature is a sufficient principle of an act meritorious of eternal life, unless there is added a supernatural gift, which we call grace . . . without grace, a man cannot have a work equal to a work proceeding from grace, since the more perfect the principle, the more perfect the action" (I-II, q. 114, a. 2, R.Obj. 2). Grace is the root principle, whereas charity is the proximate principle, since "charity, inasmuch as it has the last end for its object, moves the other virtues to act" (I-II, q. 114, a. 4, R.Obj. 1). Similarly, as we have seen throughout this study, Dante's journey is undertaken as an effect of cooperating grace and an act of formed faith—an act of faith directed by charity—which constitutes the first act of

manifestation of sanctifying grace. We have Dante's act of faith concerning the veracity of Beatrice's words: "a le vere parole che ti porse" (*Inf.* II, 135). And Dante's act of charity in willing his last end: "Tu m'hai con disiderio il cor disposto / sì al venir con le parole tue, / ch'i' son tornato nel primo proposto" (*Inf.* II, 136-38).

6. The work must be "ordained by God toward a promised reward; cf. q. 114, a. 1, ad 3: 'Our action has no reason for merit except on the presupposition of a divine ordination; [wherefore] it does not follow that God becomes our debtor absolutely [who hath first given to Him?], but rather His own, so far as it is due to Him that His ordination should be fulfilled.' Again in article 2 c: 'The merit of a man depends on divine ordination,' since 'all good in man comes from God,' and man has no right before God unless he receives such a right from God. Hence without this divine ordination and promise, our good works would give us no right to a reward, since they are already due to God by several other titles, such as creation, supreme dominion, final end. Therefore, even if God had not promised us a reward, man ought to love God above all things. . . . Thus St. Thomas says at the beginning of article 4 of the present question: 'A human act has the nature of meriting . . . by divine ordination whereby an act is said to be meritorious of that good toward which man is divinely ordained.'"[128]

Similarly, Dante has been promised a reward by three blessed ladies from Heaven:

> "Dunque: che è? perché, perché restai,
> perché tanta viltà nel core allette,
> perché ardire e franchezza non hai,
>   poscia che tai tre donne benedette
> curan di te ne la corte del cielo,
> e 'l mio parlar tanto ben ti promette?"
>
> (Inf. II, 121-126)
>
> "What is it then? why, why haltest thou? why
> lodgest in thy heart such coward fear? why
> art thou not bold and free,
>   when three such blessed Ladies care for thee in
> the court of Heaven, and my words promise
> thee so much good?"

Note especially the last verse: "e 'l mio parlar tanto ben ti promette" (and my words promise you so much good) where the verb "promette" clearly conveys a promise of a reward: "tanto ben."

It should be clear by now that Dante's journey does indeed satisfy all the necessary conditions that would qualify it as a work meritorious of reward. The reward is the contemplative, eternal life of Heaven of which Dante will have a foretaste with Beatrice. But, since a meritorious work must be the act of a wayfarer, it follows that a preparation for contemplative life may be constituted only by an active life. This is in fact confirmed by the very last beatitude that is heard on the mountain: *"Beati mundo corde"* ("Blessed are the pure in heart," (*Purg.* XXVII, 8), and to see how this may be so, we should once again recall that a beatitude is made up of two parts: the first pertains to merit: "Blessed are the pure in heart," and the second pertains to the reward: "for they shall see God." Moreover, we have also seen that the gifts of the Holy Ghost (wisdom, science, understanding, counsel, fortitude, piety, and fear) are all directly connected with the beatitudes. Specifically, the gifts are connected with the beatitudes inasmuch as they pertain either to merit, which belongs to the active life, or to reward, which belongs to the contemplative life:

> The acts of the gifts which belong to the active life are indicated in the merits themselves, but the acts of the gifts pertaining to the contemplative life are indicated in rewards, for the reason given above. For to "see God" corresponds to the gift of understanding; and to be like God, by being adopted "children of God," corresponds to the gift of wisdom (I-II, q. 69, a. 3, R.Obj. 1).

However, the effect of the active life as pertaining to virtues and gifts of personal perfection can be none other than a cleansing of a man's heart, which, moreover, must be done as a preparation for contemplation. This cleansing has to take place for Dante in Purgatory before he may be allowed to ascend into Heaven.

> Those things which concern the contemplative life are either final beatitude itself, or some beginning thereof; and therefore they are included in the beatitudes, not as merits, but as rewards. Yet the effects of the active life, which dispose man for the contemplative life, are included as merits in the beatitudes. Now the effect of the active life, as regards those virtues and gifts by which man is perfected in himself, is the cleansing of man's heart, *so that it is not defiled by the passions*. Hence the sixth beatitude is: "Blessed are the clean of heart" (I-II, q. 69, a. 3). (Italics mine.)

But, it should also be mentioned in passing that: "as regards the virtues and gifts by which man is perfected in relation to his neighbor, the effect of the active life is peace, according to Isaiah xxxii. 17: *The work of justice shall be peace*. Hence the seventh beatitude is: *Blessed are the peacemakers*" (I-II, q. 69, a. 3).

At this stage of the journey, Dante dreams of Leah and Rachel, the two Old Testament types of active and contemplative life respectively. This is clear indication that a change is about to take place. In fact, Dante's active life is about to come to a completion under the guidance of Virgil, and his contemplative life will soon begin under the guidance of Beatrice. However, before Dante may actually ascend into Heaven with Beatrice, he will have to be symbolically crowned and mitred emperor and bishop over himself by Virgil, and later he will have to be submerged in the waters of Lethe and Eunoë by Matelda.

According to Singleton, by Virgil's symbolic act of crowning Dante, we are supposed to understand that:

> To attain.to justice with Virgil must mean to come to a justice which is discernible by the natural light of reason and without benefit of the light of sanctifying grace; or shall we not say, discernible *before* the light of grace is had, for when Virgil dismisses Dante, Beatrice has not yet come, though she is expected.[129] (Singleton's italics.)

It is not true, of course, that there can be justice with Virgil "without benefit of the light of sanctifying grace," or "before the light of grace is had," as Singleton believes. This, once again, is like putting the cart in front of the horse. The truth of the matter is that Singleton, as we have shown, has failed to draw a necessary distinction within sanctifying grace itself. Had he done so, he would have known that the metaphorical justice of justification involves the double subjection of Dante's mind to God, and of the lower powers to his mind, since the latter is caused by the former upon an infusion of operating grace taking place in one single instant. Dante was justified in the second half of the Prologue scene as an effect of operating grace. Then, under cooperating grace, he undertook a journey through the world beyond which, by the time he crosses the rivers of Lethe and Eunoë, has not only purified him of the stains of sin, but has also satisfied all necessary conditions for merit—and merit, once again, is an effect of cooperating grace. This means that Dante the pilgrim has by now reached a state of equality of justice, which is to say that he has earned the right to the reward of Heaven. Dante has undertaken the journey for personal and universal reasons as well. The journey, therefore, is at one and the same time the just price Dante has to pay to satisfy his personal debt of punishment and a work of charity for the benefit of mankind that lives in sin: "Però, in pro del mondo che mal vive . . . ritornato di là fa che tu scrive" (*Purg.* XXXll, 103-5). This is so because more is required for merit than for satisfaction. Merit depends on an equality of proportion between the good work and the excellence of the reward, whereas satisfaction depends on an equality between punishment and guilt: "more is required for merit than satisfaction, which depends upon an equality between the punishment and the guilt, not upon an equality of proportion between the good work and the excellence of the reward."[130] But Virgil could not possibly know that Dante's journey is a work of charity because, by the time the above words are spoken, he has already left the scene: "Ma Virgilio n'avea lasciati scemi / di sé, Virgilio dolcissimo patre, / Virgilio a cui per mia salute die'mi"

(*Purg* XXX, 49-51). Virgil can understand the journey only from the perspective of the debt of punishment, a fact confirmed by his opening words: "Il temporal foco e l'etterno / veduto hai, figlio; e se' venuto in parte / dov' io per me più oltre non discerno" (*Purg*. XXVII, 127-29). Virgil discerns no more than human justice. Nevertheless, he is able to understand that Dante has paid a price, because the equality of justice in the order of grace is analogous to the equality of justice in the judicial order. In both cases a penal compensation must be paid in order to satisfy the requirements of justice:

> The act of sin makes man deserving of punishment, in so far as he transgresses the order of divine justice, to which he cannot return except he pay some sort of penal compensation which restores him to the equality of justice. Hence, according to the order of divine justice, he who has been too indulgent to his will, by transgressing God's commandment, suffers, either willingly, or unwillingly, something contrary to what he would wish. *This restoration of the equality of justice by penal compensation is also to be observed in injuries done to one's fellow men.* Consequently, it is evident that when the sinful or injurious act has ceased, there still remains the debt of punishment (I-II, q. 87, a. 6). (Italics mine.)

XV

It should be noted, however, that there is a distinction to be made between Dante's justification in the second half of the Prologue scene and Dante's purification on the mountain of Purgatory. Justification and purification are both said to be sanctifying. However, in justification Dante is "imperfectly" sanctified, whereas in purification he is "perfectly" sanctified: "Hence, the passive purification of the spirit renews once more, and much more profoundly what takes place in the justification of sinners; both of them are sanctifying, the first imperfectly, the second perfectly."[131] This is so because in justification, as St. Thomas says, metaphorical justice expresses only a "general rectitude of order" (I-II, q. 113, a. 1 R.Obj. 2) inasmuch as "what is highest in man is subject to God, and the inferior powers of the soul are subject to the superior, i.e., to the reason" (I-II, q. 113, a. 1).

By the time Virgil crowns Dante with the words "Free, upright, and healed is your will":

> "Libero, dritto e sano è tuo arbitrio"
>
> (*Purg*. XXVll, 140)

a process of purification has already taken place on the mountain of Purgatory inasmuch as the pilgrim's soul was cleansed of the stains of sin as the "P"s were erased from his forehead. This means that, by now, Dante's will has been healed in a perfect manner for, as St. Thomas says,

When the stain is removed, the wound of sin is healed as regards the will. But punishment is still requisite in order that the other powers of the soul be healed, since they were disordered by the sin committed. In other words, punishment is still requisite so that the disorder may be remedied by the contrary of that which caused it. Moreover, punishment is requisite in order to restore the equality of justice, and to remove the scandal given to others, so that those who were scandalized at the sin may be edified by the punishment, as may be seen in the example of David quoted above (I-II, q. 87, a. 6, R.Obj. 3).

Now, as we have already shown, the function of Matelda (who might possibly symbolize the active life of the Church) is not only to cleanse Dante's soul of the memory of sin, but also to refresh Dante's soul with the memory of all the good works that he has ever done so that he may be pure and ready to ascend to the stars: "puro e disposto a salire a le stelle" (*Purg.* XXXlll, 145). But before this may take place, the other powers of Dante's soul stand in need of purification, since, as St. Thomas says, only the will is healed when the stain is removed. This is clearly confirmed in the text when Virgil tells Dante that his will is now free, upright, and healed. The other powers of Dante's soul are, of course, the intellect, the concupiscible, and the irascible. These powers were disordered by Dante's sins and need to be purified by the contrary of that which caused the disorder: "punishment is still requisite in order that the other powers of the soul be healed, since they were disordered by the sin committed. In other words, punishment is still requisite so that the disorder may be remedied by the contrary of that which caused it." This punishment is constituted by an intense act of mortification, which may also be called "active purification"—a requirement necessary for the development of spiritual progress: "This progress should, in fact, be brought about by the purification from sin, from its results, and from imperfections. It is twofold: an active purification or mortification which we impose on ourselves; and a passive purification which has its origin in the divine action within us."[132]

Dante's dream of Leah and Rachel suggests, as we have seen, that a change from the active to the contemplative state of life is about to take place under the guidance of Beatrice. But contemplation requires preparation, and mortification is actually an integral part of this process: "The soul cannot by its own efforts reach this infused contemplation, but it ought to prepare itself to receive it. This it should do by prayer and mortification."[133] And this precisely is what takes place when Dante meets Beatrice. The other powers of Dante's soul become purified through an intense act of mortification. That this is the case is clearly confirmed by the text when Beatrice tells Dante that when self-accusation of sin (mortification) bursts from one's own cheeks in our Court, the grindstone is turned back against the edge, which is to say that mortification has the effect of blunting the edge of God's sword of justice:

> Ma quando scoppia de la propria gota
> l'accusa del peccato, in nostra corte
> rivolge sé contra 'l taglio la rota.
>
> (Purg. X
>
> But when self-accusation of sin bursts from the
> cheeks in our Court, the grindstone is turned
> back against the edge.

Mortification is here clearly understood as a form of active which is further confirmed when Beatrice tells Dante that he shame for his transgressions: "Tuttavia, perché mo vergogna pc errore" (*Purg.* XXXl, 43-44). And indeed we are told that Dan child, dumb with shame, standing in front of Beatrice and lister fixed to the ground, self-confessing, and repentant:

> Quali fanciulli, vergognando, muti
> con li occhi a terra stannosi, ascoltando
> e sé riconoscendo e ripentuti,
>   tal mi stav' io . . .
>
> (Purg. XXXl, 64-67)
>
> As children, dumb with shame, stand listening
> with eyes to earth, self-confessing, and re-
> pentant,
>   such stood I . . .

The motif of shame is already present in the preceding canto when Dante, unable to look upon Beatrice, sees himself in the clear waters of the river but has to withdraw his gaze since he is overwhelmed by much shame:

> Li occhi mi cadder giù nel chiaro fonte;
> ma veggendomi in esso, i trassi a l'erba,
> tanta vergogna mi gravò la fronte.
>
> (Purg. XXX, 76-78)
>
> Mine eyes drooped down to the fount, but
> beholding me therein, I drew them back to the
> grass, so great a shame weighted down my brow.

Specifically, we should now treat of the particular acts of the intellect and of the concupiscible and irascible powers in order to see how they may possibly be purified through the punishment of mortification.

With the concupiscible and irascible powers we are dealing, of course, with the passions of man. And the passions, as we have learned from St. Thomas, need to be cleansed as a preparation for the contemplative life: "Yet the effects of the active life, which dispose man for the contemplative life, are included as merits in the beatitudes. Now the effect of the active life, as regards those virtues and gifts by which man is perfected in himself, is the cleansing of man's heart, *so that it is not defiled by the passions*" (I-II, q. 69, a. 3). (Italics mine.) These passions exist in pairs. For the concupiscible we have: love-hate, desire-aversion, joy-sorrow; whereas for the irascible: hope-despair, courage-fear, and anger. In the words of St. Thomas, in the movement of the concupiscible appetite:

> Good has, as it were, a force of attraction, while evil has a force of repulsion. In the first place, therefore, good causes, in the appetitive power, a certain inclination, aptitude or connaturalness in respect of good: and this belongs to the passion of *love*: the corresponding contrary of which is *hatred* in respect of evil. Secondly, if the good be not yet possessed, it causes in the appetite a movement towards the attainment of the good beloved: and this belongs to the passion of *desire* or *concupiscence*: and contrary to it, in respect of evil, is the passion of *aversion* or *dislike*. Thirdly, when the good is obtained, it causes the appetite to rest, as it were, in the good obtained: and this belongs to the passion of *delight* or *joy*: the contrary of which, in respect of evil, is *sorrow* or *sadness*.

[margin handwritten: its almost second nature for you to love it]

whereas, in the movement of the irascible appetite:

> The aptitude, or inclination to seek good, or to shun evil, is presupposed as arising from the concupiscible faculty, which regards good or evil absolutely. And in respect of good not yet obtained, we have *hope* and *despair*. In respect of evil not yet present we have *fear* and *daring*. But in respect of good obtained there is no irascible passion: because it is no longer considered in the light of something arduous, as stated above. But evil already present gives rise to the passion of *anger*.
>
> Accordingly it is clear that in the concupiscible faculty there are three couples of passions; viz., love and hatred, desire and aversion, joy and sadness. In like manner there are three groups in the irascible faculty; viz., hope and despair, fear and daring, and anger which has no contrary passion.
>
> Consequently there are altogether eleven passions differing specifically; six in the concupiscible faculty, and five in the irascible; and under these all the passions of the soul are contained (S.T. I-II, q. 23, a. 4).[134]

What should be noted in the above quotation, as Gilson says, is that "the concupiscible has for its object whatever it is pleasant for the senses to apprehend" whereas "the irascible has for its object not the agreeable but the difficult and arduous" and that "the irascible is ordered to the concupiscible, for it is its guardian and defender. The animal had to vanquish its foes, by means of its irascible, so that the concupiscible might enjoy its agreeable objects in peace."[135]

Now, of all the passions, love assumes, of course, a primary importance, since it is actually the root of them all: "Every agent acts with some end in view, as we have seen. Now a person's end is the good that he desires and loves. Every agent whatsoever, therefore, performs every action out of love of some kind" (I-II, q. 28, a. 6).[136] We are dealing here with love as a passion of our animal nature rather than with charity (a higher form of love), which is a theological virtue of the will. This is the same kind of love of which Virgil speaks purely from a philosophical standpoint: "Quanto ragion qui vede, / dir ti poss' io" (*Purg.* XVlI, 46-47) immediately adding that Dante should ask Beatrice for a higher (theological) explanation of it: "da indi in là t'aspetta / pur a Beatrice, ch'è opra di fede." Virgil knows, however, that this love is the law of the universe common to both, the creator and the creature:

> "Né creator né creatura mai,"
> cominciò el, "figliuol, fu sanza amore,
> o naturale o d'animo; e tu 'l sai."
>
> *(Purg.* XVlI, 91-93)*
>
> "Nor Creator, nor creature, my
> son, was ever without love, either natural or
> rational; and this thou knowest."

This love is, in itself, morally neutral: "e questa prima voglia / merto di lode o di biasmo non cape" (*Purg.* XVlll, 59-60). It may, however, become morally evil if it is not regulated by reason, which discerns good loves from evil ones: "all sense pleasure is good or evil according to whether or not it is in accord with the demands of reason,"[137] as Virgil also knows:

> Quest' è 'l principio là onde si piglia
> ragion di meritare in voi, secondo
> che buoni e rei amori accoglie e viglia.
>
> *(Purg.* XVlll, 64-66)*
>
> This is the principle whence is derived the reason
> of desert in you, according as it garners and
> winnows good and evil loves.

Dante is, of course, guilty of having experienced evil loves, of having pursued false visions of good, for which Beatrice now sternly reproaches him:

> e volse i passi suoi per via non vera,
> imagini di ben seguendo false,
> che nulla promission rendono intera.
>
> *(Purg.* XXX, 130-32)*
>
> and he did turn his steps by a way not true,
> pursuing false visions of good, that pay back
> no promise entire.

But the passion of joy that Dante must have felt in pursuing and enjoying so many false visions of good must now be purified by mortification. This means that Dante must be mortified by making the experience of the opposite passion of joy, which is to say sorrow. In fact, the sorrow now experienced must be proportionate to the joy he felt in committing the sin:

> onde la mia risposta è con più cura
> che m'intenda colui che di là piagne,
> perché sia colpa e duol d'una misura.

> wherefore my answer is with greater care, that
> he who yonder doth weep may understand
> me, so that sin and sorrow be of one measure.
>
> (*Purg,* XXX, 106-8)

The sorrow that Dante experiences, is now so intensely felt that he bursts into a torrent of tears and sighs:

> sì scoppia' io sottesso grave carco,
> fuori sgorgando lagrime e sospiri,
> e la voce allentò per lo suo varco.
>
> (*Purg.* XXXI, 19-21)
> so burst I under this heavy charge, pouring forth
> a torrent of tears and sighs, and my voice died
> away in its passage.

That Dante had sinned through his concupiscible appetite is something that he himself must now confess by admitting that it was in fact the false pleasure of present things that turned him away from Beatrice as soon as she had died:

> Piangendo dissi: "Le presenti cose
> col falso lor piacer volser miei passi,
> tosto che 'l vostro viso si nascose."
>
> (*Purg.* XXXI, 34-36)
> Weeping I said: "Present things with their
> false pleasure turned away my steps soon as
> your face was hidden."

After Beatrice had died, Dante fell prey to despair—the worst passion of the irascible appetite because it destroys all hope:

> quai fossi attraversati o quai catene
> trovasti, per che del passare innanzi
> dovessiti così spogliar la spene?
>
> (*Purg.* XXXI, 25-27)

what pits didst find athwart thy path, or what
chains, that thou needs must strip thee of the
hope of passing onward?

Dante, after the death of Beatrice, had stripped himself of all hope of passing onward to the thought of God, and was therefore in despair for which fault he now gives a bitter sigh: "Dopo la tratta d'un sospiro amaro" (v. 31). The function of mortification in purifying the irascible and concupiscible powers of Dante's soul has been fully realized when we are told that all the things that Dante loved most have now become most hateful to him—love purified by hate:

Di penter sì mi punse ivi l'ortica
che di tutte altre cose qual mi torse
più nel suo amor, più mi si fé nemica.

(*Purg.* XXXl, 85-87)

The nettle of repentance here so did sting me,
that of all other things, that which turned me
most to love of it became most hateful to me.

so much so that Dante, gnawed at his heart by so much remorse, falls vanquished: "Tanta riconoscenza il cor mi morse, / ch'io caddi vinto" (vv. 88-89). Then he is immersed by Matelda in the river Lethe, which takes away the memory of sin: "che toglie altrui memoria del peccato," and when he emerges on the other shore, he is led directly within the dance of the four handmaidens of Beatrice symbolizing the four "perfected" (more on this later) infused cardinal virtues:

Indi mi tolse, e bagnato m'offerse
dentro a la danza de le quattro belle;
e ciascuna del braccio mi coperse.

(*Purg.* XXXl, 103-5)

Then drew me forth, and led me bathed within
the dance of the four fair ones, and each did
cover me with her arm.

This last symbolic act confirms most clearly that the passions of the irascible and concupiscible powers of Dante's soul have been purified since it is a fact that the passions of man are regulated by the cardinal virtues: "Such are the basic passions which are, as it were, the matter on which the virtues are exercised."[138] Another, no less important indication of this process of purification is given in the context when Dante, who is about to be immersed in the river, hears voices chanting a verse of Psalm 51 so sweetly that he cannot remember it, much less describe it:

> Quando fui presso a la beata riva,
> "*Asperges me*" sì dolcemente udissi,
> che nol so rimembrar, non ch'io lo scriva.
>
> (*Purg.* XXXI, 97-99)
>
> When I was nigh unto the blessed bank
> "*Asperges me*" so sweetly I heard that I cannot
> remember it, much less describe it.

Note especially: "*Asperges me*," "Sprinkle [purify] me." Note also that the full text of the verse conveys unmistakably that a purification is indeed taking place:

> Purify me with hyssop, and I shall be cleansed:
> Wash me, and I shall be made whiter than snow.
>
> (Ps. 51:9)

Now, let us recall once again that the irascible and the concupiscible, the intellect and will are the four powers of man's soul. So far we have seen how Dante's will was healed when the stains of sin were erased from his soul even as the "P"s were erased from his forehead. We have also seen how Dante's irascible and concupiscible powers have been purified through an intense mortification. What of Dante's intellect? Does this power also need to be purified by mortification? The answer to this question is of course in the affirmative, but this will be fully grasped only if we consider how even reason (a function of the intellect) may be said to sin. According to St. Thomas:

> Reason has a twofold act: one is its proper act in relation to its proper object, and this is the act of knowing a truth; the other is the act of reason as directing the other powers. Now in both of these ways there may be sin in the reason. First, in so far as it errs in the knowledge of truth, which error is imputed to the reason as a sin when it is in ignorance or error about what it is able and ought to know;—secondly, when it either commands the inordinate movements of the lower powers, or deliberately fails to check them (I-II, q. 74, a. 5).

Dante's reason may have sinned in so far as it erred in the knowledge of truth, which error—says St. Thomas—"is imputed to the reason as a sin when it is in ignorance or error about what it is able and ought to know." Now, according to Dante himself, an error may be either material or formal. A material error derives from a false assumption, a formal one from faulty reasoning: "as the Philosopher says in his treatise on Fallacies, the way to win an argument is to expose an error. Now since error can lie either in the substance or the form of an argument, there are two kinds of fallacies: assuming what is false or inferring incorrectly."[139] In my book *Essays on Dante's Phi-*

losophy of History, I have argued that Dante's fallacy in the *Monarchy* is constituted precisely by a false assumption. His error was to assume that human reason (an immanent power) could deduce: "truths that no one else has considered,"[140] which is to say, God's specific plan of history ordained by Divine Providence. This is, of course, an absurdity since Divine Providence is, after all, God's transcendent plan of history. I also said that this is like wanting to prove by reason that which transcends reason, for if man could have known God's plan by philosophical deductions there would obviously have been no need for revelation.

Now, as Dante emerges from the river Lethe we are not to think that he is completely purified, since only after he crosses the second river, Eunoë, we are told that he feels like a tree renewed with new foliage—pure and ready to mount to the stars:

> Io ritornai da la santissima onda
> rifatto sì come piante novelle
> rinovellate di novella fronda,
>   puro e disposto a salire a le stelle.
>
> (*Purg.* XXXIll, 142-45)
>
> I came back from the most holy waves, born
> again, even as new trees renewed with new
> foliage, pure and ready to mount to the
> stars.

In between the two rivers, the fourth power of Dante's soul, i.e., the intellect, will have to undergo a process of purification through an intense mortification. Dante's reason sinned because his intellect—as a God given power—was able to know and ought to have known that man's reason cannot deduce God's specific plan of history since this plan is infinitely beyond man's reach. This is precisely what St. Thomas says—an error is "imputed to the reason as a sin when it is in ignorance or error about what it is able and ought to know." And this precisely is the essence of Beatrice's reproach to Dante who, mortified in his power of understanding, complains to her: "Ma perché tanto sovra mia veduta / vostra parola disïata vola?" (But why does your longed-for word soar so far beyond my sight? vv. 82-83) to which Beatrice answers: so that you may see that your human way (of knowing) is as distant from the divine way (of knowing) as Heaven is distant from earth, which is to say that Divine knowledge is infinitely different from human knowledge:

> "e veggi vostra via da la divina
> distar cotanto, quanto si discorda
> da terra il ciel che più alto festina."
>
> (*Purg.* XXXIll. 88-90)

"and mayst see thy way so far distant from the
divine way, as the heaven which highest
speeds is removed from earth."

Now Dante's complaint (Ma perché tanto sopra mia veduta—v. 82) follows immediately the image of the wax and the seal:

E io: "Sì come cera da suggello,
che la figura impressa non trasmuta,
segnato è or da voi lo mio cervello."

(Purg. XXXlll, 79-81)

And I: "Even as wax under the seal, that
the imprinted figure changeth not, my brain
is now stamped by you."

which, as it will be shown in the third chapter, constitutes the very key for
unlocking the meaning of Beatrice's prophecy. This is a strong indication that
the prophecy itself is the means by which the fourth power of Dante's soul
must be purified. Dante's intellect must be mortified by a prophecy whose
meaning cannot be resolved without recourse to the second degree of abstraction, which constitutes, in fact, a very important difference between the
human way of knowing and the divine way of knowing. Man knows the universe and God by degrees of abstraction. God knows the universe and man as
His own ideas.

By the time Dante emerges from the river Eunoë, he is completely purified in his sensitive as well as spiritual part of the soul, because this is in fact
an absolute requirement for entering into Heaven:

According to Christian tradition, absolute purity is necessary for entering
into Heaven; all the dust and rust which have encrusted the soul must be
removed before it can be raised to the beatific vision, in other words,
before it can see God as he sees Himself. This purification must therefore affect not only the sensual part, but also the spiritual part, of the
soul. . . . St. Thomas says (Contra Gentiles, Bk. lV, chp. 91): "Ad vi-
sionem Dei creatura rationalis elevari non potest, nisi totaliter fuerit
depurata . . . unde dicitur de Sapientia quod nihil inquinatum in ea incur-
rit."[141]

XVI

So far, I have analyzed the second mode of divine motion in the order of
grace, which is constituted by reason enlightened by faith. In this mode God
moves a man already justified: "a just man to act well supernaturally by using
the infused virtues as he ought." Most importantly, in this movement, "the

will is moved and moves itself by virtue of an anterior supernatural act," which is to say that this is the area of cooperating grace encompassing Dante's journey to Beatrice. There is however a third mode of divine motion in the order of grace that will encompass the whole of the *Paradiso*, but since it falls outside the scope of this essay it must be addressed at another time. I should, however, give at least a brief description of it, since it involves the gifts of the Holy Ghost, especially those pertaining to contemplative life.

First of all it should be mentioned that there is also a third mode of divine motion in the *natural* order: "The Philosopher likewise says in the chapter 'On Good Fortune' that for those who are moved by divine instigation there is no need to take counsel according to human reason, but only to follow their inner promptings, since they are moved by a principle higher than human reason" (I-II, q. 68, a. 1). Accordingly, "Aristotle speaks of heroes, such as Hector, who 'because of the excellence of their courage are called divine . . . for there is something superior to human nature in them,' or to human science."[142] This is not only the sphere of heroes but also of geniuses such as poets, scientists, philosophers and great leaders who are moved by special inspiration of God toward some object that surpasses their powers.

Similarly, "the third mode of the divine motion in the order of grace is that by which God especially moves the free will of a spiritual man, who is disposed to the divine inspiration by the gifts of the Holy Ghost. Here the just soul is immediately directed, not only by reason enlightened by faith, but by the Holy Ghost Himself in a superhuman manner. This motion is not only given for the exercise of the act, but for its direction and specification; consequently it is called illumination and inspiration. It is an eminent mode of operating grace which thus leads to the highest acts of the virtues and of the gifts";[143] or, according to St. Albert (as quoted by St. Thomas): "the gifts perfect man for acts which are higher than the acts of virtue" (I-II, q. 68, a. 1).

Note particularly that what is involved here is "an eminent mode of operating grace which thus leads to the highest acts of the virtues and of the gifts." This, as we shall see shortly, pertains to Beatrice as she comes escorted by her maidens who symbolize the seven infused virtues. Note also that, "here the just soul is immediately directed, not only by reason enlightened by faith, but by the Holy Ghost Himself in a superhuman manner."

This last indication should bring to mind Dante the pilgrim in the very first canto of the Paradiso, where, as he gazes upon Beatrice, a metamorphosis takes place in his soul analogous to the one that changed Glaucus from a man into a sea-god:

> Nel suo aspetto tal dentro mi fei,
> qual si fé Glauco nel gustar de l'erba
> che 'l fé consorto in mar de li altri dèi.

> (*Par.* I, 67-69)

Gazing on her such I became within, as was
Glaucus, tasting of the grass that made him
the sea-fellow of the other gods.

That Dante has undergone a radical change from the human to the divine mode is further confirmed by Dante himself when he says that to pass beyond humanity may not be told in words, wherefore let the example satisfy him for whom grace reserveth the experience:

Trasumanar significar *per verba*
non si poria; però l'essemplo basti
a cui esperïenza grazia serba.

(Par. I, 70-72)

To pass beyond humanity may not be told in
words, wherefore let the example satisfy him
for whom grace reserveth the experience.

Note especially the words "grazia" and "trasumanar," the latter a verb Dante himself invented in order to convey his passing from a human to a divine mode of spiritual contemplation under the direct inspiration of the Holy Ghost. There is strong evidence to suggest, as we have noted, that on the mountain of Purgatory Dante may have already received the gifts of the Holy Ghost, one by one, as he ascended from terrace to terrace. This evidence is constituted by the fact that the gifts of the Holy Ghost are directly connected with the beatitudes, and it was there, on the mountain, that we heard the first part of each beatitude, which pertains to merit belonging to the active life. The second part of each beatitude, which pertains to reward belonging to the contemplative life, was not heard on the mountain. This suggests that Dante, in his ascent into Paradise with Beatrice, is made to partake of the rewards of the Beatitudes, and of the acts of the gifts pertaining to reward, since, as we have seen, "the acts of the gifts which belong to the active life are indicated in the merits themselves, but the acts of the gifts pertaining to the contemplative life are indicated in the rewards, for the reason given above. For to 'see God' corresponds to the gift of understanding; and to be like God, by being adopted 'Children of God,' corresponds to the gift of wisdom." As for the theological virtues: "faith, illumined by the gift of understanding, becomes much more penetrating and contemplative; hope, enlightened by the gift of knowledge as to the vanity of all that is transitory, becomes perfect confidence and filial abandonment to Providence; and the illuminations of the gift of wisdom invite charity to the intimacy of the divine union."[144] Similarly, faith in the Trinity shines in Dante's soul like a fixed star in Heaven: "Quest' è 'l principio, quest' è la favilla / che si dilata in fiamma poi vivace, / e come stella in cielo in me scintilla" (*Par.* XXIV, 145-147). The Church Militant has no child with greater hope than Dante, for which reason it was granted that

corruption ← ← *purity*

he should come from Egypt to Jerusalem before his prescribed time: "La Chiesa militante alcun figliuolo / non ha con più speranza . . . però li è conceduto che d'Egitto / vegna in Ierusalemme per veder, / anzi che 'l militar li sia prescritto" (*Par.* XXV, 52-57). And finally, of all Dante's loves, the sovereign one is reserved for God: "d'i tuoi amori a Dio guarda il sovrano" (*Par.* XXVI, v. 48). *so all your loves the sovereign one must be for god*

The gifts are given, as we have seen, as remedies for the defects of folly, ignorance, dullness of mind and hardness of heart, since, "whether we consider human reason as perfected in its natural perfection, or as perfected by the theological virtues, it does not know all things, nor are all things possible to it." According to St. Thomas, the gifts bring about a new disposition in the powers of the soul: "The theological virtues are those whereby man's mind is united to God; the intellectual virtues are those whereby reason itself is perfected; and the moral virtues are those which perfect the powers of the appetite for obedience to the reason. On the other hand, the Gifts of the Holy Ghost dispose all the powers of the soul to be amenable to the divine motion" (I-II, q. 68, a. 6). The powers of the soul are in fact perfected by the Gifts of the Holy Ghost:

> Therefore whatever powers in man can be the principles of human actions, can also be the subjects of gifts, even as they are the reason and appetite.
> Now the reason is speculative and practical, and in both we find the apprehension of truth, which pertains to the discovery of truth and to the judgement concerning the truth. Accordingly, for the apprehension of truth, the speculative reason is perfected by *understanding*; the practical reason, by *counsel*. In order to judge rightly, furthermore, the speculative reason is perfected by *wisdom*; the practical reason by *science*. The appetitive power, in matters touching a man's relations to another, is perfected by *piety*; in matters touching himself, it is perfected by *fortitude* against the fear of dangers, and against inordinate lust for pleasures, by *fear*, according to Prov. XV. 27: *By the fear of the Lord every one declineth from evil,* and Ps. cxviii. 120: *Pierce Thou my flesh with Thy fear: for I am afraid of Thy judgements.* Hence it is clear that these gifts extend to all those things to which both the intellectual and moral virtues extend (I-II, q. 68, a. 4).

Perfect virtues may be possessed only at the level of the third mode of divine motion in the order of grace. This brings us to a consideration of the cardinal virtues. We should recall that Beatrice comes to Dante escorted by seven handmaidens, of whom three on one side symbolize the theological virtues and four on the other side the cardinal virtues.

However, a question arises as to whether the four handmaidens symbolize the acquired cardinal virtues or the infused ones. Singleton favors the second interpretation: "Coming as the handmaidens of Beatrice, they come as the infused cardinal virtues given in personal justice through Christ";[145] this is so for Singleton, of course, because he believes that Beatrice comes on the Mountain as sanctifying grace in order to justify Dante.

Once again, Singleton is proceeding without making the proper distinction. It is not enough to distinguish the cardinal virtues into acquired and infused virtues, since we may speak of four kinds of cardinal virtues and not simply two, as Singleton believes. This is so because the cardinal virtues exist first of all in God as exemplary virtues:

> Consequently the exemplar of human virtue must needs pre-exist in God, just as in Him pre-exist the exemplars of all things. Accordingly, virtue may be considered as existing originally in God, and thus we speak of *exemplar* virtues, so that in God the divine mind itself may be called prudence; while temperance is that which conforms concupiscence to reason. God's fortitude is His unchangeableness, and His justice is the observance of the Eternal Law in His works, as Plotinus states (I-II, q. 61, a. 5).

Second, the cardinal virtues exist in man as they regulate his conduct within the sphere of human affairs, and for this reason they may be called "political" virtues:

> Again, since man by his nature is a political animal, these virtues, insofar as they are in him according to the condition of his nature, are called *political* virtues; since it is by reason of them that man deports himself well in the conduct of human affairs (I-II, q. 61, a. 5).

In the third place, the cardinal virtues may be called the "perfecting virtues," inasmuch as they are possessed by a man who is still "in via," and tending toward the divine likeness. These are, of course, the infused cardinal virtues that Dante has received at the time of justification in the Prologue scene. The exercise of these infused cardinal "perfecting virtues" belongs to the second mode of divine motion in the order of grace. Here "God moves a just man to act well supernaturally by using the infused virtues as he ought." This is the area of cooperating grace encompassing the whole journey to Beatrice, since this is also the principle of meritorious works that proceed from free choice, even as Dante's journey was undertaken as a free choice:

> But since it belongs to man to do his utmost to strive onward to divine things, as the Philosopher also declares in *Ethics* X, and as Scripture often admonishes us (for instance: *Be ye . . . perfect, as your heavenly Father is perfect* (Matt. v. 48), we must needs place some virtues between the political virtues, which are human virtues, and the exemplar virtues,

which are divine. Now, these intermediate virtues are distinguished by reason of a difference of movement and term. Thus, some are virtues of men who are on their way and tending towards the divine similitude, and these are called perfecting virtues. Thus prudence, by contemplating the things of God, counts as nothing all things of the world, and directs all the thoughts of the soul to God alone; temperance, so far as nature allows, neglects the needs of the body; fortitude prevents the soul from being afraid of neglecting the body and rising to heavenly things; and justice consists in the soul's giving a whole-hearted consent to follow the way thus proposed (I-II, q. 61, a. 5).

In the fourth place, the cardinal virtues may be called "perfect virtues," inasmuch as they are possessed by the blessed in Heaven and, in this life, by those who have reached the summit of their perfection, which is to say that their souls have already been purified:

> Besides these there are the virtues of those who have already attained to the divine likeness. These are called *perfect virtues* (literally, "virtues of a now cleansed soul"). Thus, prudence now sees nought else but the things of God; temperance knows no earthly desires; fortitude has no knowledge of passion; and justice, by imitating the divine mind, is united thereto by an everlasting covenant. Such are the virtues attributed to the blessed, or, in this life, to some who are at the summit of perfection (I-II, q. 61, a. 5).

In a more synthetic form, we might say that political virtues check the passions; perfecting virtues uproot the passions, as obviously happens to Dante in Purgatory; and perfect virtues forget the passions altogether as, again, is the case with Dante in Paradise:

> Human virtues, that is to say, virtues of men living together in this world, are about the passions. But the virtues of those who have attained to perfect beatitude are without passions. Hence, Plotinus says that *the political virtues check the passions,* i.e., they bring them to the mean; *the second kind* viz., the perfecting virtues, *uproot them; the third kind,* viz., the perfect virtues, *forget them; while it is impious to mention them in connection with virtues of the fourth kind,* viz., the exemplar virtues (I-II, q. 61, a. 5, R.Obj. 2).

The question whether the handmaidens escorting Beatrice symbolize the acquired or infused cardinal virtues is ill-posed to begin with. What needs to be distinguished are the infused virtues themselves; once this is done, the answer must surely be that the handmaidens symbolize the perfected infused cardinal virtues.

As for Beatrice, she comes to Dante now on the mountaintop of Purgatory as she came to him then, in the Prologue scene: as operating grace. That is to say that Beatrice comes the first time as operating grace in the first mode of divine motion in the order of grace (justification) whereas she comes the second time as operating grace in the third mode of divine motion in the order grace. The latter is an eminent mode of operating grace whereby Beatrice can now lead Dante to the highest acts of the virtues and of the gifts pertaining to the rewards of the beatitudes as they are enjoyed by the Blessed in their contemplative life of Heaven. In between, there stands the second mode of divine motion in the order of grace (sanctification) whereby Dante, by freely undertaking the journey as an effect of cooperating grace, has by now earned merit, which is the right to the reward of Heaven. This, as we have already noted, is clearly confirmed by Dante himself on two separate occasions. The first time, in answer to a question by Nino Visconti, Dante tells him that he is still in this life and that by his journeying he gains the other, i. e., the eternal life:

> "Oh!", diss' io lui, "per entro i luoghi tristi
> venni stamane, e sono in prima vita,
> ancor che l'altra, sì andando, acquisti."
>
> *(Purg.* Vlll, 58-60)
>
> "Oh," said I to him, "from within the places of
> woe came I this morn, and am in my first life,
> albeit by this my journeying I gain the other."

It is clear, from the above, that Dante conceives of his journey as a means for earning merit, which is the right to the glory of Heaven. On the second occasion, Dante uses strict theological terms which convey unmistakably the fact that grace and merit, not grace alone, are necessary for a man to gain the glory of Heaven:

> "Spene," diss' io, "è uno attender certo
> de la gloria futura, il qual produce
> grazia divina e precedente merto."
>
> (Par. XXV, 67-69)
>
> "Hope," said I, "is a certain expectation of
> future glory, the product of divine grace and
> precedent merit."

The above terzina is conclusive evidence that Dante is in perfect harmony with St. Thomas on the problem of sanctifying grace in its metaphysical as well as moral dimensions. St. Thomas had said: "There is a double effect of grace, even as of every other form, the first of which is being, and the second, operation." At the level of being, God creates the new form of grace which, "inasmuch as it heals and justifies the soul, or makes it pleasing to God, is called operating grace." This is the time of justification. Once the soul is justified, the moral process begins whereby Dante, in the exercise of the freedom of his choice, will cooperate with God in the process of his self-sanctification by performing works of charity in order to earn the merit of his future glory: "But inasmuch as it is the principle of meritorious works, which proceed from free choice, it is called cooperating grace." Justification is an effect of operating grace, whereas merit is an effect of cooperating grace. Dante's journey, therefore, takes place as an effect of—not a preparation for—sanctifying grace.

NOTES

1. St. Thomas, *Summa Theologica,* The Basic Writings of St. Thomas Aquinas, vol. 1 & 2, Ed. Anton C. Pegis (Random House: New York, 1954). Also, *Summa Theologiae,* Blackfriars (McGraw-Hill: New York & London, 1967) and *Summa Theologica,* (Christian Classics: P.O. Box 30, Westminster, Maryland, 1981).

2. Charles Singleton, *Journey to Beatrice,* (Harvard University Press: Cambridge, Mass., 1967), p. 267.

3. Ibid., p. 283.

4. Antonio C. Mastrobuono, *Essays on Dante's Philosophy of History,* (L. Olschki: Firenze, 1979), Chp. 2.

5. Ibid., Chp. 2.

6. Dante, "Letter to Cangrande," from *Dante's Eleven Letters,* (Houghton Mifflin: Cambridge, 1891), p. 195.

7. Philip Wicksteed, *Dante and Aquinas,* (J. M. Dent, London, 1913), p. 234.

8. Singleton, *Journey,* p. 88.

9. Ibid., p. 9.

10. Ibid., p. 11-12.

11. Ibid., p. 42.

12. Ibid., p. 46.

13. Ibid., p. 30.

14. Ibid., p. 47.

15. Ibid., p. 220, n. 16.

16. Ibid., p. 12.

17. *S.T.* II-II, q. 82, a. 1 in Francis L. B. Cunningham, O.P., *The Christian Life* (Priory Press: Dubuque, 1959), p. 565.

18. St. John Damascene, *On True Faith,* Bk. III, Chp. 4 in *Christian Life,* p. 566.

19. Singleton, *Journey,* p. 67.

20. Ibid., p. 39.

21. Ibid., p. 46.

22. Ibid., pp. 41-42.

23. Reginald Garrigou-LaGrange, *Grace: Commentary on the Summa Theologica of St. Thomas,* Ia, IIae, q. 109-14, (B. Herder: St. Louis, 1952) p. 363.

24. Ibid., p. 170.

25. Ibid., p. 172.

26. Dante, Op. Cit. p. 213-14.

27. S.T. IIa, q. 86, a. 6, ad. 1 in G. LaGrange, *Grace,* p. 169.

28. G. LaGrange, *Grace,* p. 153.

29. Cunningham, Op. Cit. p. 335.

30. Paolo Cherchi, "Il Disdegno per Guido: Una Proposta," *L'Alighieri,* XI, (1970), p. 35: "Nella sua risposta Dante riprende il paragone fra sé e Guido, ma lo basa su una certezza diversa, sul fatto, cioè, che non la sua altezza d'ingegno gli permetta di visitare il mondo infernale, ma una grazia attiva . . . a questo preciso momento del suo itinerario Dante si riferisce con il "da me non vegno," e vi si riferisce con tutta la consapevolezza d'essere stato dotato d'una grazia. Per rintuzzare Cavalcante egli deve cominciare col negare recisamente le premesse del suo discorso, sostituendo all'immanentistica causa del viaggio addotta dall'epicureo, una causa trascendentale. Così Dante declina ogni merito e responsabilità personali per demandare ad una volontà superiore l'iniziativa del suo viaggio."

31. Singleton, *Journey,* p. 88.

32. Ibid., p. 63.

33. Ibid., p. 64.

34. Thomas Aquinas, *Scriptum super libros sententiarum magistri Petri Lombardi Episcopi Parisiensis,* Ed. nova / cura R. P. Mandonnet, (Parisiis, Sumptibus P. Lethielleux, 1929-1947), v. 4, pp. 845-46.

35. Singleton, *Journey*, p. 116.
36. Ibid., p. 107.
37. Ibid., pp. 257 and 269.
38. Ibid., p. 269.
39. Ibid., p. 268.
40. Ibid., p. 268.
41. Ibid., p. 268.
42. Garrigou-LaGrange, *Grace*, p. 354
43. Singleton, *Journey* p. 107.
44. Ibid., p. 283.
45. Ibid., p. 279.
46. Ibid., p. 279.
47. Ibid., p. 280.
48. Ibid., pp. 45-46
49. Ibid., p. 46.
50. Ibid., p. 58.
51. Ibid., pp. 263-64
52. R. Garrigou-LaGrange, *Grace*, pp. 350-51.
53. Singleton, *Journey*, p. 68.
54. Ibid., pp. 50-51.
55. Ibid., p. 51.
56. Ibid., pp. 51-52.
57. Garrigou-LaGrange, *Grace*, p. 360.
58. Singleton, *Journey*, p. 52.
59. Ibid., p. 55, n. 2.
60. Garrigou-LaGrange, *Grace*, p. 357.
61. Ibid., p. 358.
62. Ibid., p. 358, n. 10.
63. Ibid., p. 412, n. 14. The following are the contents of note 14: Father Bouillard (op. cit., p. 212) writes: "Grace is conceived by St. Thomas as a form, that is, not only as an inherent quality but as a principle of operation inclining the soul to produce certain determined actions. Evidently the notions used by St. Thomas are simply Aristotelian notions applied to theology." They are human notions such as those of nature, essence, constituent form. Moreover, it is the Council of Trent which itself declares that sanctifying grace is the formal cause of justification; by not maintaining this, one denies it and no longer preserves the meaning of the Council's affirmation. Father Bouillard says (p. 220): "Notions change but affirmations abide." What an illusion! An affirmation which unites two notions by the verb "to be" cannot abide if the two notions change and remain forever unstable. One might as well insist on using a grappling hook to fasten the waves of the ocean. If, for example, the notion of transubstantiation changes, and is no longer maintained in its ontological sense, which transcends phenomena, the affirmation: "The real presence depends on transubstantiation" cannot abide. And if one continues to speak of "the real presence," it will no longer be such as conceived by tradition and the councils. The examples we have used are well known; they are not of our selection.

Father Bouillard writes (p. 219): "A theology that is not abreast of the times would be a false theology," and he adds (p. 224): "By renouncing Aristotelian physics, modern thought has given up the notions . . . which had no meaning except in terms of the former." The reader is led to conclude that a theology which still makes use of the notion of form is no longer abreast of the times and is therefore false. We should thus be led to change even the notion and definition of truth and thus return to Modernism by asserting that truth is not the agreement of the judgement with extra-mental reality and its immutable laws, but the agreement of thought with the demands of a perpetually evolving human life. Thus the nature of theology and of dogma itself are changed; cf. Denz., nos. 2058, 2025, 2079, 2080. In line with the same tendency, some would change the notion of original sin so that it would no longer depend upon a single fault committed by Adam at the beginning of humanity's history, but upon the personal faults of men in the course of centuries which have rebounded on humanity as a whole. Thus we revert to Modernism; and it is a more serious matter to return to a condemned error than to fall into it for the first time.
64. Ibid., p. 360.
65. Singleton, *Journey*, p. 54.
66. Ibid., p. 54.

67. Garrigou-LaGrange, *Grace*, p. 35, n. 15.
68. Ibid., p. 411, n. 13.
69. Singleton, *Journey*, p. 58.
70. Ibid., p. 59-60.
71. Maurizio Flick, S.J. *L'attimo della giustificazione secondo S. Tommaso.* Analecta Gregoriana, vol. XL, Sectio B (n. 17). (Apud Aedes Universitatis Gregorianae; Rome, 1947), p. 25, n. 45.
72. Singleton, *Journey*, pp. 57-58.
73. Ibid., p. 57.
74. Ibid., p. 123.
75. Henri Bouillard, *Conversion et grâce chez S. Thomas d' Aquin,* (Aubier: Paris, 1944), p. 158.
76. John Freccero, *Dante: The Poetics of Conversion*, (Harvard University Press: Cambridge, Mass. 1986), p. 83.
77. Ibid., p. 297.
78. Ibid., p. 173.
79. Ibid., p. 174.
80. Ibid., p. 306, nn. 14 and 15.
81. M. Flick, *L'attimo*, p. 87: L'argomento è basato sul criterio che serve a distinguere tra loro, realmente, due mutazioni: Le mutazioni, si spiega, si distinguono secondo i loro termini. Si distinguono dunque realmente quelle mutazioni i cui termini sono realmente opposti, in forza di una realtà positiva come bianco e nero. Invece si distinguono solo con la ragione quelle mutazioni in cui l'uno dei termini è semplicemente la negazione dell'altro, come bianco e non bianco. "Ora, prosegue L'Angelico, il termine dell'infusione della grazia è la presenza della grazia nell'animo (gratiam inesse), il termine della remissione della colpa è l'assenza della colpa (culpam non esse) . . . È chiaro quindi che se la colpa in nessun modo è qualcosa di positivo, realmente l'infusione della grazia s'identifica con la remissione della colpa, da cui si distingue solo con una distinzione di ragione. Se invece la colpa pone qualche cosa di positivo non solo secondo la ragione ma realmente, la remissione della colpa si distingue dall'infusione della grazia, se si consideri come mutazione, per quanto come moto sia con essa una cosa sola, come è stato già detto. Ma la colpa pone qualche cosa di positivo e non solo l'assenza della grazia."
82. Ibid., pp. 88-89: Dobbiamo ora determinare quale sia quella realtà positiva a cui si termina la remissione del peccato, in forza della quale si può parlare di una corruzione dello stato di peccato, distinta dalla generazione della giustizia e la giustificazione del peccatore viene ad essere un vero moto comprendente due mutazioni. Non si può certo pensare all'atto stesso del peccato che è essenzialmente transitorio e che perciò non può appartenere ai costitutivi dello stato di peccato. Bisogna però notare che, passato l'atto del peccato, l'uomo resta reo del peccato stesso agli occhi di Dio finchè non l'abbia riparato. A questa "reità" che è una realtà di ordine morale, fa appello S. Tommaso nel *Commento* per spiegare l'opposizione che vige tra lo stato di giustizia e lo stato di peccato. Ad una difficoltà infatti che vuol provare l'inutilità di enumerare la remissione della colpa dopo l'infusione della grazia, in quanto la rimozione di una privazione non è altro che la posizione dell'abito opposto, egli così risponde: "Il peccato e la grazia non sono tra loro in relazione come un'affermazione e una negazione o come una privazione e un abito. Uno infatti può essere senza la grazia e tuttavia non avere il peccato, come si può vedere in Adamo secondo l'opinione di coloro i quali dicono che egli non sarebbe stato creato in grazia, perchè il peccato suppone che qualche cosa vi sia o vi sia stato nel peccante (peccatum aliquid ponit vel esse vel fuisse in peccante). Passato infatti l'atto del peccato rimane ancora in qualche modo il reato del peccato precedente nello stesso peccante, in quanto per esso egli è fatto reo presso Dio, come anche rimangono gli atti meritori, come è stato detto sopra nella distinzione XIV."
83. Ibid., pp. 92-93: "L'espulsione di una forma, egli spiega, dice il termine di quel moto che è ordinato alla corruzione, e l'introduzione di una forma dice similmente il termine di quel moto che precede la generazione, perchè tanto generazione quanto la corruzione sono termini di moto. Ora, tutto ciò che si muove, quando è nel termine del moto è disposto secondo ciò a cui il moto è ordinato. Perciò poichè il moto di corruzione tende al non essere e quello della generazione all'essere, nell'istante in cui la forma s'introduce è, nell'istante in cui si espelle non è. Poichè poi si dice che la forma s'introduce quando è per la prima volta e che si espelle quando per la prima volta non è, non può essere la materia senza questa o quella forma e perciò insieme e quivi l'espulsione di una forma e l'introduzione dell'altra. Poichè dunque sim-

ilmente l'anima non può essere senza colpa e senza grazia, insieme avviene l'espulsione della colpa e l'infusione della grazia."

84. J. Freccero, *Dante,* p. 185.
85. Ibid., p. 265.
86. Ibid., p. 305, n. 2.
87. Ibid., p. 109.
88. Ibid., p. 86.
89. Ibid., p. 68.
90. Ibid., p. 266.
91. Ibid., p. 266.
92. Ibid., p. XI.
93. Leo Spitzer, "Addresses to the reader in the *Commedia,*" *Italica,* vol. 23, 1955, p. 15.
94. J. Freccero, *Dante,* p. 266.
95. Ibid., p. 176.
96. Giuseppe Mazzotta, *Dante: Poet of the Desert,* (Princeton University Press: Princeton, 1979), p. 50.
97. Ibid., p. 36.
98. Etienne Gilson, *The Christian Philosophy of St. Thomas Aquinas,* (Random House: New York, 1956), p. 339.
99. Ibid., p. 347.
100. G. Mazzotta, *Dante,* p. 269.
101. Ibid., p. 16.
102. Garrigou-LaGrange, *Grace,* p. 35.
103. *S.T.* I-II, q. 9, a. 6, R.Obj. 3. Quoted by R. Garrigou-LaGrange, *Christian Perfection and Contemplation,* (B. Herder: St. Louis, 1951), p. 286.
104. Ibid., p. 290.
105. Ibid., p. 290.
106. Ibid., p. 290-91.
107. Ibid., p. 287.
108. Ibid., p. 286.
109. Ibid., p. 288.
110. Ibid., pp. 291-92.
111. *S.T.* I-II, q. 111, a. 2, (Also in Garrigou-LaGrange, *Christian Perfection,* p. 292, n. 56).
112. Ibid., p. 292.
113. Ibid., p. 292, n. 58. (*S.T.* I-II, q. 10, a. 4, R.Obj. 1).
114. Rocco Montano, *Storia della Poesia di Dante,* (Quaderni di Delta, Napoli, 1962), vol. 2, p. 174: "Stazio darà l'aiuto di una filosofia che, pur rimanendo sul piano della dimostrazione razionale, grazie alle indicazioni date dalla parola rivelata, può andare più avanti nella conquista della verità. Il momento è appunto quello della filosofia cristiana che S. Tommaso nel mondo medievale aveva formulata con più rigore di ogni altro ed era stata la base della grande confutazione filosofica degli errori dei Gentili che è la *Summa Contra Gentiles.*"
115. Garrigou-LaGrange, *Christian Perfection,* pp. 281-82.
116. Ibid., p. 331.
117. Ibid., p. 331.
118. Ibid., p. 331.
119. Garrigou-LaGrange, *Grace,* p. 373.
120. Dante, *Dante's Eleven Letters,* p. 195.
121. Garrigou-LaGrange, *Grace,* p. 379.
122. Ibid., p. 367.
123. Ibid., p. 367.
124. Singleton, *Journey,* p. 107.
125. Garrigou-LaGrange, *Grace,* p. 380.
126. Ibid., p. 380.
127. Ibid., p. 381.
128. Ibid., pp. 381-82, and n. 6.
129. Singleton, *Journey,* p. 257.
130. Garrigou-LaGrange, *Grace,* p. 378.
131. Ibid., p. 356.
132. Garrigou-LaGrange, *Christian Perfection,* p. 356.
133. Ibid., p. 321.

134. St. Thomas Aquinas, *Summa Theologica*, (Christian Classics: P.O. Box 30, Westminster, Maryland, 1981), vol. 2, pp. 696-97.

135. Etienne Gilson, *The Christian Philosophy of St. Thomas Aquinas*, p. 239.

136. Eric D'Arcy, *Summa Theologiae*, (Blackfriars and McGraw-Hill Book Company, New York, 1967), vol. 19, p. 107.

137. E. Gilson, *The Christian Philosophy*, p. 281.

138. Ibid., pp. 285-86.

139. Dante, *Monarchy*, III, 4, (Oxford University Press, 1916), p. 57.

140. Ibid., p. 3.

141. Garrigou-LaGrange, *Christian Perfection*, p. 400, n. 35.

142. Ibid., p. 289.

143. Ibid., p. 292.

144. Ibid., p. 293.

145. Singleton, *Journey*, p. 244.

A Pastel by Dinah Mastrobuono

This is the day
the Lord has made

In the third essay of my book *Essays on Dante's Philosophy of History*, I have endeavored to show that the first day in Dante's Purgatory is not Easter Sunday, as traditionally maintained, but simply a day that corresponds to the night of the Vigil between Holy Saturday and Easter Sunday in Jerusalem. In the present study, I will introduce new evidence to suggest further that Dante considers the second day as if it were Easter Sunday. Note that I say: "as if it were" and not "it is." There is a good reason for this. First of all it should be kept in mind that the Mountain of Purgatory is situated in the southern hemisphere, that is to say in the uninhabited part of the world. If no human beings dwell there, then no human measurement of time, such as a Sunday or a Monday can be ascribed to those days. Easter Sunday takes place in the northern hemisphere and is celebrated by living human beings. Human measurement of time applies only in this world and not in the regions of the world beyond. This much is confirmed for us on the Terrace of the Wrathful when Marco Lombardo asks Dante: "Who are you that speak of us as if you still measured time by calends (i. e. as if you were still alive)?"

> "Or tu chi se' che il nostro fummo fendi,
> e di noi parli pur come se tue
> partissi ancor lo tempo per calendi?"
>
> *(Purg.* XVI, 25-27)
>
> "Now who art thou that cleaver our smoke,
> and speakest of us even as if thou didst still
> measure time by calends?"

It is obvious from this quotation that hours and days can have meaning only to Dante, who is making the journey while still in this life. What can be said, therefore, is that Dante considers the second day as if it were Easter Sunday. If we keep in mind that, for Dante, the sun rotates around the earth, we may further say that the dawn of the second day coincides with the sunset of Easter Sunday in Jerusalem. To see how this may be so, before proceeding with my new study, I shall give a synopsis of the above-mentioned third essay of my book concentrating solely on some highlights since the chapter encompasses almost one hundred pages.

At sunset of the first day on the shore of Purgatory, Dante is in the Valley of the Negligent Princes, where a dramatic scene is about to take place. Two angels come down to guard the valley; they both come from Mary's bosom—we are told:

> "Ambo vegnon del grembo di Maria"
>
> > *(Purg.* VIII, 37)
>
> "Both come from Mary's bosom"

Dante is gazing at three stars (faith, hope, and charity) that have enflamed the whole pole:

> Li occhi miei ghiotti andavan pur al cielo,
> . . . .
> . . . "A quelle tre facelle
> di che 'l polo di qua tutto quanto arde."
>
> > *(Purg.* VIII, 85, 89-90)
>
> My yearning eyes again turned towards
> heaven
> . . . .
> . . . "At those three torches,
> wherewith the whole pole here is flaming."

Then comes the evil serpent (the same one, perhaps, that gave Eve the bitter food):

> Da quella parte onde non ha riparo
> la picciola vallea, era una biscia,
> forse qual diede ad Eva il cibo amaro.
>
> > *(Purg.* VIII, 97-99)
>
> On that side where the little vale hath no
> rampart, was a snake, perchance such as gave
> to Eve the bitter food.

At this point the angels, like celestial hawks, come down to put the serpent to flight. All during the assault, Currado Malaspina has not stopped gazing, even for a moment, at Dante's living body:

> L'ombra che s'era al giudice raccolta
> quando chiamò, per tutto quello assalto
> punto non fu da me guardare sciolta.
>
> > *(Purg.* VIII, 109-11)
>
> The shade that had drawn close to the judge
> when he called, through all that assault was
> not loosed a moment from gazing at me.

Currado Malaspina had been called by Nino Visconti to witness something truly extraordinary. In fact, Nino's own words unmistakably define it as
an act of God's grace:

> ..."Sù, Currado!
> vieni a veder che Dio per grazia volse."
>
> (*Purg.* VIII, 65-66)
>
> ... "Up, Conrad, come
> and see what God by his grace hath willed."

What is this act of grace that God has willed? In the literal sense of the
poem, this has to do with Dante the Pilgrim, who has been given an infusion
of grace, which allows him to make the journey through the world beyond in
his own body in order to gain his eternal salvation:

> "venni stamane, e sono in prima vita,
> ancor che l'altra, sì andando, acquisti."
>
> (*Purg.* VIII, 59-60)
>
> "from within the places of
> woe came I this morn, and am in my first life,
> albeit by this my journeying I gain the other."

At this revelation by Dante something quite unexpected takes place,
something that deserves to be called a "colpo di scena." In fact, upon hearing
Dante's words, Nino Visconti and Sordello stand back like people suddenly
bewildered:

> E come fu la mia risposta udita,
> Sordello ed elli in dietro si raccolse
> come gente di sùbito smarrita.
>
> (*Purg.* VIII, 61-63)
>
> And when my answer was heard, Sordello
> and he shrank back like folk suddenly be-
> wildered.

What should come as a surprise, even to the reader, is the fact that Sordello, who has been with Dante and Virgil for the entire afternoon, is unaware that the Pilgrim is making the journey in his own body—he is alive.
How could this be? But if we retrace our steps and go back to where Dante
first meets Sordello, we realize how masterfully Dante the poet has orches-
trated the fusion of the literal and symbolical meanings of this climactic
scene. The action, we should recall, is unfolding during the sunset of the first
day in Purgatory.

For now, we note that Dante, just before calling attention to the soul of
Sordello, informs the reader that the Pilgrim does not cast a shadow, and this

is the reason why Sordello has gone the entire afternoon without noticing that Dante is alive:

> "Prima che sie là sù, tornar vedrai
> colui che già si cuopre de la costa,
> sì che ' suoi raggi tu romper non fai.
> Ma vedi là un'anima che, posta
> sola soletta, inverso noi riguarda:
> quella ne 'nsegnerà la via più tosta."
>
> (Purg. VI, 55-60)
>
> "Ere thou art above, him shalt thou see return that
> now is being hidden by the slope, so that thou
> makest not his rays to break.
> But see there a soul which, placed alone, solitary,
> looketh towards us; it will point out to us the
> quickest way."

This leads to an important question: Why does Currado Malaspina fix his eyes on Dante's living body, as if spellbound? We would naturally expect him to be interested in the dramatic scene of the battle between the angels and the serpent, which is taking place at the very same time. What does he see in Dante's living body? To Currado Malaspina, I submit, Dante's body is the reflection (as in a mirror) of the symbolical meaning conveyed by the battle between the angels and the serpent. This battle may, therefore, be taken as a symbolical representation of the Resurrection. The angels come from Mary's bosom. The serpent is the same one, perhaps, that gave Eve the bitter fruit. The symbolical meaning is too obvious: it was Christ who came from Mary's bosom and it was He, through His Resurrection, who defeated both Satan and death and delivered mankind from Original Sin. And in this connection, we should now consider one of the most celebrated terzine of the entire *Comedy*. Early in the canto Dante addresses the reader directly and asks him to sharpen well his eyes to the truth because the veil is now indeed so thin that certainly to pass within is easy:

> Aguzza qui, lettor, ben li occhi al vero,
> ché 'l velo è ora ben tanto sottile,
> certo, che 'l trapassar dentro è leggero.
>
> (Purg. VIII, 19-20)
>
> Reader, here sharpen well thine eyes to the
> truth, for the veil now is indeed so thin,
> that of a surety to pass within is easy.

According to Sapegno:

Gli antichi commentatori, fino al Landino e al Daniello, intendono:

aguzza la tua mente a passare oltre il senso letterale, che qui è tanto sottile, trasparente, che non è difficile trapassarlo e cogliere il significato vero della finzione allegorica. Questa spiegazione è piaciuta alla maggior parte dei moderni; ma non si capisce perché il poeta sentisse il bisogno di richiamare il lettore a una speciale attenzione, ove veramente il senso dell'allegoria fosse in tutto così chiaro ed agevole a penetrarsi.

Ancient commentators, up until Landino and Daniello, understand it to mean: sharpen your mind to pass beyond the literal sense, which is here so thin, so transparent, that it is not difficult to pierce through it and capture the true meaning of the allegorical fiction. This explanation has received acceptance by the great majority of modern critics; but one fails to understand why the poet would feel the need to call the reader's special attention to it, when really the allegorical sense is, in every way, so clear and easy to penetrate.[1]

From the above quotation it is clear that I am not alone in saying that the symbolical truth is much too obvious, or "agevole a penetrarsi," as Sapegno says. I therefore believe that the essence of the story is given by the literal meaning, that is, by what actually takes place on the scene. In fact, the reader is informed that as the angels came down, Dante did not see, and therefore cannot tell, how the celestial falcons moved; he saw full well, however, that they had moved:

> Io non vidi, e però dicer non posso,
> come mosser li astor celestïali;
> ma vidi bene e l'uno e l'altro mosso.
>
> (*Purg.* VIII, 103-5)
> I saw not, and therefore cannot tell, how the
> celestial falcons moved; but full well I saw
> both in motion.

This, I suggest, is the literal truth to which Dante has invited the reader to sharpen his eyes. The central message here is that the Resurrection is a mystery. No human eyes witnessed the Resurrection, and this is the reason why Dante, who is here in the flesh, is not made to see how the angels defeated the serpent. The battle between the angels and the serpent should therefore be taken as a symbolical representation of the Resurrection, that Resurrection which is being commemorated at about the same time in Jerusalem. In fact, I have maintained that starting with the first canto of the *Purgatorio*, it is not Easter Sunday morning as traditionally interpreted

Since there is a thematic, symmetrical, correspondence between Limbo and Ante-Purgatory, it would now be helpful to compare the nature of these two places. Professor N. Iliescu, in a paper delivered at an annual conference of the Dante Society of America, has shown that there is no dogma of the Church that explains and defines the nature of Limbo. Christian tradition is divided as to where Limbo should be; some place it in Hell, others outside of it. Dante has chosen to place Limbo beyond the Gates of Hell, but has ascribed to it a suspended, spiritual reality, as we learn from Virgil, who says: "I was amongst them who are in suspense" (*Inf.* II, 52). From this we might infer that for Dante, as also for Christian tradition, Limbo is not necessarily eternal, and that the spirits who inhabit it may be said to be suspended until the end of time, when Christ will come again to judge the living and the dead.

What of the spirits of the Ante-Purgatory? They too are said to be spiritually suspended outside the Gates of Purgatory. Some of them must wait, we are told, thirty times the time that they delayed in repenting, before they are admitted into the world of purgation. In Limbo we encounter the spirits of unbaptized children and those of the great sages of antiquity who "non peccaro" (who did not sin). Dante says their only shortcoming was to have lived before Christ. In the Ante-Purgatory we meet the spirits of those who died outside the Church: the excommunicated, the late repentants, the violently slain, and the negligent rulers.

What is puzzling, however, is that Limbo has a long Christian tradition of interpretation, but the Ante-Purgatory has almost none. It has been suggested therefore that Dante simply invented the Ante-Purgatory. One such opinion was expressed by D'Ovidio:

Le curiose remore escogitate dal poeta per certe categorie di anime, quella specie di alunnato d'aspiranti alla purgazione, il teologo non può coglierle che con una stretta di spalle ed un sorriso.[2]

The curious impediments excogitated by the poet for certain categories of souls, that kind of apprenticeship for those aspiring to purgation, the theologian can only receive with a shrug of the shoulders and a smile.

This means that there is no theological justification for the existence of the Ante-Purgatory. But even if we grant this, we have no reason to deride Dante for his supposed naïveté. On the contrary, I believe there is a profound historical basis for Dante's Ante-Purgatory.

We must start with the chronology of Dante's journey through the world beyond. The journey begins on Good Friday of the year 1300, and by the time Dante reaches the shore of Purgatory it is supposedly Easter Sunday morning. As I said above, this is one of those commonplace pieces of information given without exception, I believe, by all editions of the *Comedy*; we simply take it for granted. How do we know that the journey takes place during Easter-time of the year 1300? One would expect to find this information in the very first canto of the *Comedy*. However this is not the case. The reader is not informed of this fact until Canto XXI:

Ier, più oltre cinqu'ore che quest' otta,
mille dugento con sessanta sei
anni compié che qui la via fu rotta.

(Inf. XXI, 112-14)

Yesterday, five hours later than this hour, completed a thousand two hundred and sixty-six
years since the way here was broken.

An exact date: one thousand two hundred and sixty-six years ago. A precise day: yesterday. A particular hour: five hours later than now—the bridge
was broken. It was broken by Christ when He descended into Hell after He
died at the age of thirty-three (thirty-four years after His conception), 1266
years ago, yesterday (Good Friday), five hours later than now, 7:00 A.M.,
Saturday April 9, 1300. Now, what have I done with this information? Quite
simply, I have allowed myself to be surprised by it, and since it is highly im-
probable that Dante might have ascribed to it only a casual meaning, I have
proposed an organic reinterpretation of both the Prologue Scene and the
Ante-Purgatory in terms of one unifying idea: the drama of redemption.
Therefore, I have suggested that there may be analogical contemporaneity
between Dante's personal redemption as it unfolds within the context of the
poem, and mankind's drama of redemption as it took place on the stage of
history. The philosophical justification for this approach is given by the principle of analogy which, according to Gilson, totally permeates the medieval
mind.[3] More specifically, Singleton says that the dimension of analogy may be
shown to be the "comprehensive principle by which the poem is related to
existence and exhibits truth."[4] Finally this is the very same principle given by
Dante himself in the Letter to Cangrande: "as a thing is in respect of being,
so is it in respect of truth."[5]

Thus we should recall that the journey starts on the eve of Good Friday,
after the commemoration of the Crucifixion:

Lo giorno se n'andava, e l'aere bruno

(Inf. II, 1)

The day was departing, and the brown air

and by nightfall of Saturday we find the two poets at the center of the earth:

"Ma la notte risurge, e oramai
è da partir, ché tutto avem veduto."

(Inf. XXXIV, 68-69.)

"But night is reascending; and now
must we depart: for we have seen the whole."

The descent into Hell has taken one complete day (24 hours), from Friday evening to Saturday evening according to the time of Jerusalem. At this

point, as they cross the center of the earth, the poets have to begin counting
time according to the island of Purgatory: but since Jerusalem and Purgatory
are on opposite sides of the earth (180 degrees from each other), the difference in time between the two places will be exactly twelve hours. Therefore,
while it is morning in Purgatory, it is still Saturday evening in Jerusalem, and
Dante seems surprised by the sudden change:

> "sì sottosopra? e come, in sì poc'ora,
> da sera a mane ha fatto il sol tragitto?"
>
> (Inf. XXXIV, 104-5)
>
> "thus upside down? and how, in so short a time,
> has the Sun from eve to morn made transit?"

But Virgil explains that they are now in the opposite hemisphere and
that, while it is morning here, over there it is still evening:

> "Qui è da man, quando di là è sera"
>
> (Inf. XXXIV, 118)
>
> "Here is morn, when it is evening there"

We should recall here the very important piece of information that
Dante himself is careful to point out concerning their ascent to the shore of
Purgatory. They went up the winding passage without caring for rest:

> e sanza cura aver d'alcun riposo
>
> (Inf. XXXIV, 135)
>
> and, without caring for any rest

We should consider, moreover, that in the first nine cantos of Purgatory
there are at least six major references to time, some of which unequivocally
suggest that we are to view the unfolding action according to Jerusalem time.
The sheer insistence is revealing. In the second canto, we are informed that,
as the day is rising in Purgatory, the night is setting in Jerusalem:

> Già era 'l sole a l'orizzonte giunto
> lo cui meridian cerchio coverchia
> Ierusalèm col suo più alto punto.
>
> (Purg. II, 1-3)
>
> Already had the sun reached the horizon, whose
> meridian circle covers Jerusalem with its
> highest point.

This, as we have seen, is still Saturday evening; in fact, from the above
quotations we might safely propose that the first day in Purgatory corre-

sponds to the night between Holy Saturday and Easter Sunday in Jerusalem.

We should now inquire whether the spiritual reality of the Ante-Purgatory has any historical justification. We know, for example, as Virgil will also inform us, that the Mountain of Purgatory became a place of purgation only after Christ's Resurrection. And I have said that, by analogy, as Dante's personal redemption is made possible on Good Friday evening—after the commemoration of the Crucifixion—so mankind's redemption on the stage of history was made possible on that Friday when Christ actually died on the Cross. But Dante crosses the Gates of Purgatory only in the ninth canto, an indication that throughout the first day in Purgatory the Resurrection of Christ has not yet been commemorated in Jerusalem.

For proof of this, it should now be said that by the "Te Deum"[6] the Church wishes to express the hour of Resurrection of Easter Sunday morning, as we read in the *Gemma Animae* of Honorius of Autun: "Per 'Te Deum Laudamus' exprimatur hora qua resurrexit Dominus."[7] Furthermore, according to Parsch[8] the "Te Deum" is not chanted for the entire Holy Week. My argument will then be as follows: if the mountain of Purgatory became a place of purgation only after Christ's resurrection, starting with the first canto of the *Purgatorio* it could not possibly be Easter Sunday morning since the "Te Deum" is heard nine cantos and twenty-four hours later. As Dante crosses the gates, his promise of salvation is being fulfilled—now—as mankind's was fulfilled—then—on that Sunday morning long ago, with Christ's Resurrection. Therefore, we may infer that the suspended spiritual reality of the Ante-Purgatory corresponds to the pathos of the Vigil Night in Jerusalem, and that its historical justification is, in fact, that reality on the stage of history between the Crucifixion and the Resurrection, when the world hung spiritually suspended.

There is more: we find it confirmed also in Durandus, a contemporary of Dante, that it was indeed by a long-established liturgical practice that the Church conveyed the hour of Christ's resurrection by chanting the "Te Deum" on Easter Sunday morning: "Te Deum Laudamus exprimit horam qua resurrexit."[9] It seems obvious therefore that Dante chose to employ a liturgical text of wide acceptance in order to convey to the reader that the second day should indeed be considered as Easter Sunday. As the sun is rising on the second day in Purgatory, it is setting in Jerusalem, which means that in the northern hemisphere it is still Vespers of Easter Sunday. Analogically, this was also the case for the morning of the first day in the Ante-Purgatory, which corresponded with Vespers of Holy Saturday, as the lines, "Vespero è già colà dov'è sepolto / lo corpo dentro al quale io facea ombra" (It is already evening there, where the body buried / lies within which I made shadow—*Purg*. III, 25-26), unmistakably confirm.

Easter-time is a time of returning, says Durandus, when, by the mercy of God, we return to the state of life that we lost through Adam;[10] and indeed this is the dominant theme in the *Purgatorio* as we learn in the very first canto when Dante says: we paced along the lonely plain, as one who returns to his lost road ("Noi andavam per lo solingo piano / com'om che torna a la perduta strada" (*Purg.* I, 118-19)). Once the "lost road" is found, man will begin his return to his primitive state; it is therefore a question of regeneration, which will bring him to the dignity of his first birth.[11] This is precisely Dante's condition: as he crosses the Gate of Purgatory he has actually found the road he had lost—"ché la diritta via era smarrita" (*Inf.* I, 3); therefore his ascent up the Mountain is at one and the same time a punishment and a regeneration. So much so, says Virgil, that his ascending will become to him an experience as pleasant and easy as going downstream in a boat: "com' a seconda giù andar per nave" (*Purg.* IV, 93).

The day of Easter itself can be discussed on four different levels. Considering the literal sense, Durandus points out that the Greek word "πασχα" means "phase" in Hebrew, while in Latin it signifies "transitus," "passage." This literal sense is historical, and it is true since it refers to the exterminating angel who passed over the doors the Israelites had marked with blood and also to the people who went out of Egypt and then passed through the Red Sea.[12]

As we turn to Purgatory and are attentive to what actually takes place on the scene—the historical events—during this morning of the second day, we realize that indeed a literal passage does take place: Dante crosses the Gates of Purgatory. All the other meanings depend on this one. The gate is called the "sacred portal" ("porta sacrata") and its nature is such that whoever is allowed to enter may not look back; if he does, he will have to go back outside:

> Poi pinse l'uscio a la porta sacrata,
> dicendo: "Intrate; ma facciovi accorti
> che di fuor torna chi 'n dietro si guata."
>
> (*Purg.* IX, 130-32)
>
> Then he pushed the door of the sacred portal,
> saying: "Enter, but I make you ware that
> he who looketh behind returns outside again."

On the allegorical level, the time of Easter is a passage from faithlessness to faith in virtue of the sacrament of baptism that the Church administers at this time.[13] This allegorical sense is also clearly present during the second morning in Purgatory. The sun is already more than two hours high, "e 'l sole er' alto già più che due ore" (*Purg.*, IX, 44), when Dante, awaking from sleep, is told that S. Lucia, when the day was bright, had transported him from the valley to the gate "ella ti tolse, e come 'l dì fu chiaro" (*Purg.* IX, 59). At this time Dante is like the man whose fear changes to comfort once the truth is revealed to him: "e che muta in conforto sua paura, / poi che la verità li è discoperta" (*Purg.* IX, 65-66). Note we are dealing here with "fear," "comfort," and "truth." Fear was caused by a strange dream Dante had had during the morning hours. He had dreamed of being snatched up by an eagle that had carried him to the sphere of fire. That imaginary fire ("lo 'ncendio imaginato" v. 32) was so intensely real that he awoke. As for the truth, we should recall that the eagle was used in Christian art "to represent the new life begun at the baptismal font,"[14] and since baptism is the door to faith, "ch'è porta de la fede che tu credi" (*Inf.* IV, 36), the truth here referred to could only be the truth of faith, the gift of baptism—the allegorical sense of Easter, according to Durandus.

The third sense of Easter, the tropological meaning, is that of a passage from vice to virtue; this is the time when the faithful make an act of contrition and confession.[15] Similarly, on this second day, acts of contrition and confession on the part of Dante are clearly discernible in the context. Before he is allowed to pass through the gate, Dante has, first of all, to ask humbly that the bolt be loosed: "Chiedi / umilemente che 'l serrame scioglia" (*Purg.* IX, 107-8). He then devoutly flings himself down at the holy angel's feet: "Divoto mi gittai a' santi piedi " (v. 109)—and asks, in the name of mercy, that the angel open to him: "misericordia chiesi ch 'el m'aprisse" (v. 110). Kneeling devoutly is the ordinary posture for confession; but, for a confession to take place, a true act of contrition is required. This in fact occurs when Dante smites his breast three times: "ma tre volte nel petto pria mi diedi" (v. 111). The angel carves with a sword seven "P"s ("peccata," sins) on Dante's forehead, and tells him to make sure that these wounds are washed once he is within: "Fa che lavi, / quando se' dentro, queste piaghe" (vv. 113-14). The sword is probably symbolic of divine justice and the angel most likely symbolizes the priest-confessor. The angel opens the gate of Purgatory with two keys that, we are told, he has received from St. Peter: "Da Pier le tengo" (v. 127). One of the keys is made of gold, the other of silver. According to St. Thomas, these two keys are symbolic of the power to absolve on the part of the priest and of the fitness of the one to be absolved,[16] as the angel confirms: "pur che la gente a' piedi mi s'atterri" (v. 129). This refers to the fitness of the penitent, whereas the key that unties the knot—"perch' ella è quella che 'l nodo disgroppa" (v. 126)—clearly refers to the power to absolve. This is the tropological meaning of the day of Easter. This tropological sense is unmistakably present on the second day in Purgatory. Dante's meaning could not be clearer—he considers this second day as Easter Sunday.

As further evidence of this, it should be pointed out that "contrition" and "confession" are two integral parts of the sacrament of penance, which the Church administers at Easter-time. The third integral part of the sacrament of Penance is constituted by "satisfaction," which is also clearly present on the scene. Dante is here symbolically receiving this sacrament. This is so because Dante is returning to God: "Noi andavam per lo solingo piano / com' om che torna a la perduta strada" (*Purg.* I, 118-19) and, according to St. Thomas, "the first thing to be faced by those returning to God is Penance"

(III, q. 84, a. 6, R.Obj. 2). We should distinguish, however, the sacrament of penance from the virtue of penance. This is of considerable importance since, as I have shown, Dante is justified and has received sanctifying grace in the second half of the Prologue scene (*Inf.* II). The virtue of penance is simply an act of repentance which, however, is absolutely necessary for justification, as St. Thomas says:

> But remission of sin can be caused by God without the sacrament of Penance, not however without the virtue of repentance, as has been said above. Hence before the time of the sacraments of the New Law God forgave sins to those who repented. Therefore pardon from sins is an effect of the virtue of penitence (III, q. 86, a. 6).

What distinguishes the sacrament of penance from the virtue of penance is the presence of the priest and his function of binding and loosing:

> And therefore it is impossible that a sin be forgiven anyone without the virtue of penitence. However, as has been said above, the sacrament of Penance is completed through the office of the priest binding and loosing. Now God can pardon sin without the priest, even as Christ forgave the sins of the adulteress, and the woman who was a sinner. Nevertheless, he did not forgive their sins without the virtue of penitence (III, q. 86, a. 2).

Dante's angel, at the gate of Purgatory, is clearly symbolic of the priest. The whole scene, in fact, unmistakably conveys a sacramental rite: "A sacrament consists in a certain ceremony in which the action is so performed that we take it to signify the sanctity it bestows" (III, q. 84, a.1). The effect of the sacrament of Penance is either an infusion of grace for the first time: "For the sacraments of the New Law not only signify, but also accomplish what they signify" (III, q. 84, a. 3, R.Obj. 5), or an increase of it: "As an interior willingness to atone, satisfaction does confer grace and increases it when carried over into action" (III, q. 90, a. 2, R.Obj. 2). This is so because: "Satisfaction is a part of the sacrament of Penance; a fruit of the virtue (III, q. 90, a. 2, R.Obj. 3). This is true not only of the sacrament of penance, but of all of them: "Sacraments, either cause grace where it was missing, or cause its increase."[17] The sacrament of penance may be received after justification: "Note that the penitent may be already justified as he approaches the sacrament" (cf IV *Sent.* loc cit, ii ad I).[18] Indeed, it may be received any number of times after justification: "But Penance has its power from Christ's Passion as a spiritual medicine, which can frequently be repeated" (III, q. 84, a. 10, R.Obj. 5). Dante's sins, as I have shown, were forgiven him even before he entered the world beyond. But a debt of punishment remains outstanding even after the sins are forgiven. This means that as Dante stands in front of the gate of Purgatory, the remaining balance of his debt of punishment is yet to be paid. This is the satisfaction to be rendered on the Mountain, and satisfaction is an integral part of the sacrament of Penance: "And therefore, the debt of all punishment is not taken away at once with the first act of repentance by which sin is pardoned, but only with the fulfillment of all the penitential acts" (III, q. 86, a. 4, R.Obj. 3). Throughout his descent into Hell and his ascent of Purgatory, Dante is in a continuous struggle against the disposition to sin left in his soul as an effect of sins he has committed even after these sins have been forgiven: "Therefore there is no reason why, once sin has been forgiven, certain dispositions caused from previous acts may not yet remain" (III, q. 86, a. 5). However, the struggle itself against the effects of sin is part of the expiation Dante has to endure in order to render satisfaction: "The struggle against the effects of sin itself becomes a way of conformity to Christ's suffering."[19] The form and matter of mortal sin are constituted by a turning away from God and a turning to a creaturely good. Dante's turning away from God was forgiven him by an infusion of sanctifying grace in the Prologue scene (*Inf.* II). However, Dante owes a debt of temporal punishment for having turned to a creaturely good:

> Mortal sin is both a turning away from God and a turning to a creaturely good. But, as we have seen in the *Secunda Pars*, the turning from God is the formal element there, and the turning to creaturely good the material. Remove the formal element of any thing, and the species goes, for instance humanity goes when you take away rationality. And therefore, mortal sin is said to be forgiven because through grace the soul's turning from God is taken away at the same time as the debt of eternal punishment. Nevertheless, there is still the question of the material, namely the inordinate turning to a creaturely good. The debt of temporal punishment is owed for this (III, q. 86, a. 4, R.Obj. 1).

Dante's inordinate attachment to a temporal thing is removed by temporal punishment, which takes away also the stain of venial sins—the "piaghe" Dante has been asked to cleanse by the angel: "Therefore, to take away the stain of mortal sin, an infusion of grace is needed. But to take away the stain of venial sin, some act under grace is called for; through this the inordinate attachment to a temporal thing is removed" (III, q. 87, a. 2, R.Obj. 3). Dante's stain of mortal sin and his debt of eternal punishment, as I have shown in the preceding chapter, were taken away by an infusion of sanctifying grace in the Prologue scene (*Inf.* II) and by his subsequent descent into Hell. The cleansing by Virgil of the infernal filth from Dante's face, as they emerge from Hell, is clear evidence that Dante is now free from the stain of his mortal sin.

The sacrament of Penance is actually made up of four integral parts. The matter, constituted by the acts of the penitent (confession, contrition, and satisfaction), and the form constituted by the absolution of the priest: "But the three parts mentioned stand as the matter of penance, since they are acts of the penitent, while the absolution of the priest serves as the form. Thus the absolution of the priest ought to be listed as a fourth part of penance" (III, q. 90, a. 2). In the context of the *Comedy*, as we have seen, absolution is symbolized by the angel's keys at the gate of Purgatory. But for Dante's act of repentance to be complete: "both contrition of heart, and confession in word and satisfaction in act, are required" (III, q. 90, a. 2, R.Obj. 4).

This brings us to the three steps of the gate of Purgatory, which convey unmistakably that Dante is here symbolically receiving the sacrament of Penance. The first step, we are told, is of white marble so clean and clear that Dante sees himself in it as in a mirror. This is the step of confession—Dante looking deeply into his soul:

> Là ne venimmo; e lo scaglion primaio
> bianco marmo era sì pulito e terso,
> ch'io mi specchiai in esso qual io paio.
>
> (*Purg.* IX, 94-96)
> There where we came, at the first step, was
> white marble so polished and smooth that I
> mirrored me therein as I appear.

The second step is of a dark purple color which, most importantly, is cracked in its length and in its breadth. This is the step of contrition, since: "Contrition is an act of the virtue of penance whereby the hardness of man's attachment to sin is crushed or broken. It is so called from the Latin *contritum* or *contritio*, which signify a crushing, breaking or undoing of something."[20]

> Era il secondo tinto più che perso,
> d'una petrina ruvida e arsiccia,
> crepata per lo lungo e per traverso.
>
> (*Purg.* IX, 97-99)
> The second darker was than perse, of a stone,
> rugged and calcined, cracked in its length and
> in its breadth.

The third step is of a red color, so flaming red as blood that spurts from a vein. Note that the step is not simply red, but of a flaming red similar to the red of blood spurting from a vein, which is clearly an allusion to Christ's blood. This is the step of satisfaction, since the sacrament of penance "associates the penitent in the satisfaction that Christ made for all, and gives renewed assurance that if we suffer with Christ we shall also be glorified with him."[21]

Lo terzo, che di sopra s'ammassiccia,
porfido mi parea, sì fiammeggiante
come sangue che fuor di vena spiccia.

(*Purg.* IX, 100-102)

The third, which is massy above, seemed to me
of porphyry so flaming red as blood that
spurts from a vein.

The association of the satisfaction of the penitent with the satisfaction paid by Christ is an idea also confirmed by St. Thomas who says that in the sacrament of penance: "The power of Christ's Passion works through the absolution of the priest, together with the action of the penitent who cooperates with grace for the destruction of sin" (III, q. 84, a. 5).

But it should be mentioned, at this time, that I am not the only one to maintain that Dante symbolically receives the sacrament of Penance at the gate of Purgatory. According to Sapegno, it was also held by most of the ancient commentators:

Lo scaglion primaio: the first step, of white marble, shiny like a mirror. It symbolically represents the first moment of the sacrament of penance, and that is to say the *contritio cordis*, "that each faithful must have before coming to confession, for, having examined himself and having mirrored himself in his own heart, he brings to mind all his sins and repents of them with good inner contrition; and at that point he remains white like marble, without any stain or darkness of sin" (Anonimo fiorentino). . . . "For this second step we must understand it to mean the confession [the *confessio oris*, second moment of penance]; since after a man is contrite and repentant of his sins, he must confess them to a priest. And the fact that the step is stained is there to signify the stain of shame that the sinner feels by confessing his sins. The stone being cracked in its length and in its breadth shows us that we must feel shame within as also without, and that very same man who hears himself in his heart confessing with words, will also hear the breaking of this stone of hardness and the obstinacy of his sins" (Anonimo fiorentino). Lana, Buti, Landino, and others reverse the order of the two symbols; they see oral confession as being symbolized by the first step, whereas contrition by the second. . . . "The third step is there to signify the satisfaction of his sins [*satisfatio operis*], because it is not enough to be repentant or, to have confessed his sins, a man must also do penance and satisfaction; he also says that the third step was flaming; and this color of fire is there to denote the ardor of charity and love that enflames men and drives them to do penance for the sins committed."[22]

The fourth meaning of the day of Easter is the anagogical sense. Inasmuch as Christ on that day passed from mortality to immortality, He will do the same for us,[23] which means that at the Last Judgment we too will triumph in His name over pain, suffering, and death. This meaning, as we might expect, is also clearly present in the *Comedy*, only now it is Dante the poet who explicitly calls our attention to it. This occurs when Dante sees a group of souls carrying boulders of such enormous size that the persons are barely recognizable as human figures, squashed as they are under the massive weight. These are the souls of the proud, who in life exemplified a behavior dominated by an inordinate desire for their own excellence. They might be envisioned to have walked the earth with head erect and furious hunger, "con rabbiosa fame" (*Inf.* I, 47), like the Lion in the Prologue scene. But somehow, while still alive, they must have humbled themselves before Christ with a true act of contrition, and therefore are saved. Nonetheless, by the Law of Contrapasso, they are now made to walk in humility in such a manner as to convey the disfiguring effect that pride had on their humanity. The scene is a visually powerful reminder of God's justice and, since these are the very first spirits we encounter in Purgatory proper, the effect on the reader may be somewhat disquieting. Thus Dante feels compelled to address the reader directly in order to assuage his fear at the spectacle of how God demands that the debt of punishment (satisfaction) be paid: "come Dio vuol che 'l debito si paghi" (*Purg.* X, 108). Heed not the form of the pain, Dante says, but think that at worst the suffering cannot go beyond the Last Judgment. Think of what follows, he insists, alluding directly to the everlasting beatitude in body and soul they will have gained in the name of Christ—here, again, is the anagogical sense of the day of Easter:

> "Non attender la forma del martìre:
> pensa la succession; pensa ch'al peggio,
> oltre la gran sentenza non può ire."
>
> (*Purg.* X, 109-11)
>
> "Heed not the form of the pain; think what
> followeth, think that at worst beyond the
> great judgment it cannot go."

Here we might ask why Dante's entrance into Purgatory, after he goes through the gate, should coincide with Vespers of Easter Sunday in Jerusalem. Is this correspondence intentional on the part of Dante the poet? And if so, was it dictated purely by his Gothic taste for symmetry, or is there a more profound reason involved? As we gradually attempt to answer these questions we will realize that the underlying structure of Dante's poem is laden with much meaning indeed. It is surprising for example, that of all canonical hours Dante should have chosen Vespers to be the mirror-image vehicle of the new spiritual order of Purgatory which, in turn, is symbolic of a new era. What possible relationship is there between Vespers and Christ? None, at least from the point of view of our twentieth-century mentality. In fact, we do not even suspect that these evening prayers might have been a treasure of symbolism for Dante, because we commonly associate not evening but dawn with Christ. Was He not, after all, called the Orient on High? And that deepest of all mysteries which we call the Resurrection, did it not take place at dawn? How are we to make this sudden shift in perspective from dawn to evening? That Dante should consider the second day in Purgatory as Easter Sunday, and that the morning of this day should correspond to Vespers of Easter Sunday in Jerusalem, are two elements sure to cause a certain amount of astonishment on the part of the reader.

The sense of astonishment, however, will soon fade away once we learn that the Church itself has explicitly established clear and unequivocal correspondences between Vespers and Christ. This, as we shall see, justifies Dante's entrance into Purgatory at a time that corresponds with the time of Vespers of Easter Sunday in Jerusalem. To clarify this correspondence I shall briefly treat Vespers in general, and Easter Vespers in particular. Durandus tells us that at the hour of Vespers the Church depicts the coming of the Lord, because this took place toward the evening of the world, that is, in the last age.[24] This is the reason why the Church in its songs renders thanks to God according to the words of the Apostle: "We are the ones upon whom the end of centuries has arrived";[25] it is in this sense that one speaks of the end. The Catholic Church gives thanks to Christ at this hour for other reasons as well. First, because it was at the hour of Vespers that Christ was taken down from the cross. Second, it was at this very same hour, during supper, that He instituted the sacrament of the Eucharist and washed the feet of the Apostles. Third, it was at this hour that He, in the form of a traveller, revealed Himself to the disciples going to Emmaus and again at the breaking of the bread.[26]

The office of Vespers receives its name from the star "Vesper" that appears at the beginning of the night[27] and comprises five psalms, which are sung according to the material furnished by the day itself (in our case, Easter Sunday).[28] But why precisely five psalms? Emile Mâle has remarked that the liturgy, like medieval art, is charged with endless symbolism. And this is the case even when nothing more than the number of these psalms is concerned, without for the moment considering their content. There are five psalms, we are told, because of the five wounds of Christ, who offered his sacrifice in the evening of the world. Second, there are five psalms for our correction, so that we may ask grace for the sins that enter into us each day through the five senses of the body. Third, by the five psalms the Church guards against the tribulations of the night (because this hour suggests the tears of those for whom the sun of justice has disappeared) and also because we beat our chest with the five fingers of the hand.[29]

A particular liturgical text will further help us in establishing a direct symmetrical correspondence between Dante's entrance into Purgatory and Vespers of Easter Sunday in Jerusalem. It is the canticle of Mary: the Magnificat. This canticle is a hymn of praise to God, and it starts with the words

"My soul magnifies the Lord." These words were spoken by Mary to Elizabeth, who had greeted her in a loud voice saying "Blessed art thou among women and blessed is the fruit of thy womb." Mary's soul magnifies the Lord because the Angel Gabriel had told her that she would bring forth a son (the Son of the Most High) and the Lord God would give him the throne of David and he would be king over the house of Jacob forever, and of his kingdom there would be no end. This canticle is taken from the Gospel of Luke, and its importance for us lies in the fact that it is a song of praise for the Annunciation. It is being chanted in Jerusalem at Easter Sunday Vespers just as Dante enters Purgatory. As Dante enters this new realm, the first thing he sees is a relief depicting the Annunciation to the Virgin Mary. The image of the Angel Gabriel is so real, "pareva sì verace" (X, 37), that it seems as if he were speaking: "non sembiava imagine che tace" (X, 39). This is the same angel who came to earth with the decree of that peace which had been wept for many a year: "col decreto / de la molt' anni lagrimata pace" (X, 34-35). It was precisely that peace which opened heaven from its long ban: "ch'aperse il ciel del suo lungo divieto" (X, 36) and has opened the gate of Purgatory for Dante on this second day in Purgatory, which coincides with Easter Sunday in Jerusalem, when that peace is being commemorated. The effect of the Resurrection and of Christ's death says Durandus, is the "opening of the gate of the realm of heaven."[30] One could have sworn that the angel in the relief was saying "Ave" to the one (Mary) who turned the key to open the supreme love: "ch'ad aprir l'alto amor volse la chiave" (X, 42). The Virgin Mary herself in her attitude showed the impression of these words, *Ecce ancilla Deï*," as expressly as a figure is stamped on wax: "come figura in cera si suggella" (X, 45).

The symmetrical correspondences could not be more self-evident. The thematic pattern of the second day in Purgatory may be said to be the mirror image of the thematic pattern of Easter Sunday in Jerusalem, especially if we consider the great theme of humility and the fact that, according to Durandus, the day of the Resurrection coincides with the day of the Annunciation. As he says: "Meanwhile, the Lord was truly risen on the sixth day of April, that is to say, on the same day on which he had been conceived, or that on which the Annunciation was made to the Virgin."[31] As for humility, understood as the great gesture and principle of the Kingdom of God, there are many clear instances that will unmistakably confirm a direct correspondence between the second day in Purgatory and the liturgy of Easter Sunday in Jerusalem. In the "Magnificat" Mary praises the mercy of God in the work of the Incarnation with the purest feelings of humility. "He has scattered the proud," she says, "in the conceit of their heart," and "has put down the mighty from their thrones, and has exalted the lowly" (Luke 1: 51-52). As far as she is personally concerned, her soul glorifies the Lord "Because he has regarded the lowliness of his handmaid" (Luke 1:48). Durandus points out that "she says 'Respexit humilitatem,' and not 'Respexit virginitatem' ("He has regarded my humility" and not, "He has regarded my virginity"). This is so because "Virginity of soul" is superior to "integrity of the body." She says "humilitatem because God opposes the proud and does not make them partake of the destiny of the just."[32] After Christ, the greatest human example of humility is therefore Mary. On the Terrace of Pride it is the intaglio of Mary, humbly accepting the Annunciation, that Dante sees. The images of Mary, David, and Trajan are in fact referred to by Dante as "l'imagini di tante umilitadi" (X, 98).

There is yet another meaning involved in these reliefs, but for now I should point out, as I have noted elsewhere,[33] that the theme of humility is also emphasized in one of the psalms of Easter Vespers:

> He raises up the lowly from the dust; from the
> dunghill he lifts up the poor
> To seat them with princes, with the
> princes of his own people.

(Ps. 113:7-8)

This is the principle of the Kingdom of God, proclaimed by the Church on Easter Sunday, and the very same principle is proclaimed by Dante on the second day in Purgatory when we hear the chanting of the first beatitude:

> "Beati pauperes spiritu!"

(Purg. XII, 110)

> "for theirs is the Kingdom of heaven"

(Matt. 5:3)

We are also told that these reliefs—this "visibile parlare" ("this visible speech," X, 95)—were made by God, "Colui che mai non vide cosa nuova" (X, 94). Dante says that this mode of speech is new to him because it does not exist here on earth, and that he rejoiced in looking at the images because they were precious to see, "a veder care" for the sake of the craftsman who had made them: "per lo fabbro loro" (Purg. X, 99). Sapegno cautions us not to assume, as some have, that these reliefs actually speak with a material sound. The miracle of this divine art, he says, consists in the fact that it does not represent a motionless situation, "una situazione immobile" (as a human sculptor's work might have), but a temporal series of affective situations, which appear simultaneous by the suggestive power of the words that correspond to the individual stages of that process.[34] Similarly, I would like to caution against a second possible assumption. It should not be assumed that these reliefs possess a three-dimensional, physical existence like the bas-reliefs of Ghiberti's panels at the Baptistry in Florence. God creates actual beings, i.e., men; man creates virtual beings, i.e., statues. This is what Dante means when he says that art, as it were, is the granddaughter of God:

"sì che vostr'arte a Dio quasi è nepote"

(Inf. XI, 105)

"so that your art is,
as it were, the grandchild of the Deity."

The world beyond, as conveyed by Dante's poem, is a non-dimensional, metaphysical reality; it is a state of being. It is presented to Dante as if it were physical because he is there, supposedly, with his live body, and this is the only way he could understand it. We are told this much in the *Paradiso*:

> Così parlar conviensi al vostro ingegno,
> però che solo da sensato apprende
> ciò che fa poscia d'intelletto degno.

(Par. IV, 40-42)

> Needs must such speech address your faculty,
> which only from the sense-reported thing
> doth apprehend what it then proceedeth to
> make fit matter for the intellect.

It should be immediately noted, however, that Dante has cast doubt on that very fact, i.e., whether he went to the world beyond in his body:

> S'i' era sol di me quel che creasti
> novellamente, amor che 'l ciel governi,
> tu 'l sai, che col tuo lume mi levasti.

(Par. I, 73-75)

> If I were only that of me which thou didst new-
> create, O Love who rulest heaven, thou
> knowest, who with thy light didst lift me up.

God alone knows whether he went there body and soul, or just in his mind. Dante himself does not know. He is certain however that the world beyond is metaphysically real, and for this reason he presents his journey as a vision.

So the reliefs could not possibly have a physical reality; they are, more properly, symbolic proclamations of the three essential offices of the Savior: Christ as King; Christ as High Priest; and Christ as Judge of the World throughout the history of mankind and at the Last Judgment. That this may be so will be confirmed by a comparison with the same offices proclaimed by the Church on Easter Sunday as belonging exclusively to the Messiah. All this is conveyed by the first psalm of Easter Vespers: Psalm 109. More importantly, it should be pointed out that Christ applied this messianic psalm to Himself in Matthew 22: 43.[35] This is a psalm of David[36]—"l'umile salmista" (*Purg.* X, 65)—whom we find depicted in the second relief.

In the first part of this psalm we read that Christ was called Lord, and that He sits on the right hand of the Lord. In Matthew 22: 41-45, Christ had asked the Pharisees:

> "What do you think of the Christ? Whose son is he?" They answered him: "David's." Whereupon He responded: "How then does David in the Spirit call him Lord, saying: The Lord said to my Lord: Sit thou at my right hand, till I make thy enemies thy footstool. If David, therefore, calls him 'Lord,' how is he his son?"

This is Christ Himself quoting from the psalm of David, where it is clear that "l'umile salmista" refers to Him as King:

> The scepter of your power the Lord
> will stretch forth from Zion:
> Rule in the midst of your enemies.
> Yours is a princely power in
> the day of your birth, in holy
> splendour;
> before the daystar, like the dew, I
> have begotten you.
>
> (Ps. 109: 2-3)

He was "begotten," not "created," therefore He could not be a temporal king, and His kingdom would not be of this world. But where in Dante's text do we find a correspondence with the idea that Christ is King? It should be emphasized that Dante's poem, like the Bible, exhibits truth through events, so that if we focus our attention on the action, we might perhaps be able to extract the proper symbolic meaning.

On the first terrace of Purgatory, Dante has had a profound experience. In sublime contemplation, he is made to experience a relief of the Annunciation made by divine art. Here is what I would like to suggest: the idea that Christ is King is conveyed by the miraculously "visibile parlare" of the relief of the Angel Gabriel and the Virgin Mary because that is exactly what happened at the Annunciation; the Angel announced that Mary would bring forth a child who would be King forever:

> And the angel said unto her, do not be afraid, Mary, for thou hast found grace with God. Behold, thou shalt conceive in thy womb and shall bring forth a son; and thou shalt call his name Jesus. He shall be great, and shall be called the Son of the Most High; and the Lord God will give him the throne of David his father, and he shall be King over the house of Jacob forever; and of his Kingdom there shall be no end.
>
> (Luke 1:30-33)

This, I believe, is the function of the relief of the Annunciation: it confirms, now in the world beyond, one of Christ's offices—that of Eternal King. The very same office is being proclaimed at about the same time in Jerusalem.

In the second relief we have the sacred Ark on a cart drawn by oxen: "lo carro e' buoi, traendo l'arca santa" (*Purg.* X, 56). In front of the cart there are people divided into seven choirs who look as if they are singing right now. Actually, Dante's senses (sight and hearing) are clashing; one says "no," the other says "yes, the people are singing." In like manner, the smoke of incense that is "imagined" there has a similar effect on Dante's eyes and nose. And before the blessed vessel there goes, dancing, the lowly psalmist—"l'umile salmista"—King David. At the window of a great palace there is figured Michal (David's wife) looking on, scornful and sad. This relief, I would like to propose, is here to convey the second office of the Messiah as proclaimed by the liturgy in Jerusalem, that is to say, Christ as High Priest, as we read in the psalm:

> The Lord has sworn, and he will not repent:
> You are a priest forever according to the order
> of Melchizedeck.
>
> (Ps. 109:4)

In Dante's poem, the whole scene is a religious, biblical spectacle; it commemorates the event of the Ark of the Covenant being brought to Jerusalem, as we read in 2 Samuel 6, where it is evident that David is offici-ating as high priest, not as king:

> Then David offered holocausts and peace offerings before the Lord. When he finished making these offerings, he blessed the people in the name of the Lord of Hosts. He then distributed among all the people, to each man and each woman in the entire multitude of Israel, a loaf of bread.
>
> (2 Sam. 6:17-19)

Similarly, in Dante's scene, David's dancing in front of the Ark should be understood as an act performed by a king who is officiating as a humble priest. In fact, Dante tells us that David was both more and less than a king in that case:

> e più e men che re era in quel caso
>
> (*Purg.* X, 66)
>
> and more and less than king was he in that case

Sapegno tells us that ancient commentators on the *Comedy*, followed by many moderns, understood the above line as follows: he was more than king, because he was wearing a priestly garment and was exercising the office of priesthood; he was less than king because his actions were not proper to his dignity and standing. Sapegno also says, and I agree, that the antithesis acquires a greater efficacy if we interpret the first term in a moral sense: David was more than king because he humbled himself to God precisely as king.[37]

But there is more. We have in Dante a line with an unmistakable reference to the office of priesthood. The very word "officio" is employed. In describing the sacred Ark being drawn by the oxen, he says:

> "per che si teme officio non commesso"
>
> *(Purg.* X, 57)

Singleton accurately translates the line as: "because of which men fear an office not given in charge"[38] There is general agreement among commentators that this line refers to the story of Uzzah, who presumptuously dared to assume the office of priesthood rightly belonging to David. The event took place when the Ark was being brought to Jerusalem:

> When they came to the threshing floor of Nodan, Uzzah reached out his hand to the Ark of God and steadied it, for the oxen were making it tip. But the Lord was angry with Uzzah; God struck him on the spot, and he died there before God.
>
> (2 Sam. 6:6-7)

As for the function of the relief representing King David officiating as High Priest in front of the Ark, I suggest that this be taken as a confirmation, in the world beyond, of a prophecy that "l'umile salmista" had made in life. King David is the author of Psalm 109, the very psalm that is being chanted in Jerusalem at about the same time that Dante contemplates the reliefs. In that psalm he had prophesied that the Messiah would be a priest forever, according to the order of Melchizedeck. As we have already noted, Christ had applied the substance of this psalm to Himself, and St. Paul tells us, in Hebrews 7, that the prophecy of David was fulfilled only by Christ. Melchizedek and Christ received the office of priesthood directly from God, not from Aaron, since neither one of them belonged to the tribe of Levi. Both kings as well as priests, and both offered bread and wine to God. The name "Melchizedek," says St. Paul, "means 'King of Justice'; he was also King of Salem, that is, 'King of Peace.' Without father, mother, or ancestry, without beginning of days or end of life, like the Son of God he remains a priest forever" (Heb. 7: 2-3). To be a "priest forever," as applied to Christ, has a very special meaning, and St. Paul explains this by focusing on the main difference between the old covenant and the new covenant brought about by the sacrifice of Jesus. In Psalm 109 (which St. Paul also quotes) we learned that Christ sits on the right hand of God, which means that he presides over a heavenly sanctuary established by God Himself: "The main point in what we are saying is this: we have such a high priest, who has taken his seat at the right hand of the throne of the Majesty in heaven, minister of the sanctuary and of that true tabernacle set up, not by man, but by the Lord. Now, every high priest is appointed to offer gifts and sacrifices; hence the necessity for this one to have something to offer" (Heb. 8: 1-3). Under the old covenant there were regulations for worship and an earthly sanctuary. A tabernacle was constructed, in the outer part of which there were: "the lampstand, the table, and the showbread" (Heb. 9: 1-3). This, we are told, was called the "holy place," but behind the second veil of the tabernacle there was the "holy of holies" in which there were "the golden altar of incense and the ark of the covenant entirely covered with gold. . . . In the Ark were the golden jar containing the manna, the rod of Aaron which had blossomed, and the tablets of the covenant. Above the Ark were the Cherubim of glory overshadowing the place of exploitation" (Heb. 9: 4-5). At this point St. Paul tells us: "we cannot speak now of each of these in detail" and goes on to say that priests performing their services used to go into the outer tabernacle continuously, while only the High Priest was allowed, once a year, to enter the inner one in order to offer the blood of a goat or a bull "for himself and for the sins of the people." But when Christ came as High Priest, St. Paul concludes—and this is the difference—he entered once and for all a tabernacle not made by human hands and, most importantly, "he entered, not with the blood of goats and calves, but with his own blood, and achieved eternal redemption" (Heb. 9: 11-12). This is the meaning of the prophecy given by David in Psalm 109—that the Messiah would be a "priest forever according to the order of Melchizedek"—and this is precisely what is proclaimed by the liturgy of Easter Vespers. Dante's relief of King David dancing in front of the Ark accomplishes what it signifies in the very act of signifying it: it confirms a prophecy that the historical King David had given in life. What Dante is conveying to us with these reliefs is a glimpse of biblical history as seen in retrospect, i.e., what had been only a hope for the Messiah is now an absolute certainty because the author of these reliefs is God Himself. We find further evidence for this in the *Paradiso* where, in the heaven of justice, we meet David himself—"il cantor de lo Spirito Santo" (as he is called)—who now knows (the verse is in the present tense) the merit of his song: "ora conosce il merto del suo canto" (*Par.* XX, 40).

As we now turn to the third part of the psalm we find expressions conveying the prophecy of Christ as Judge. He judges now as he judged then, and as he will judge on the Last Day. We are told that His day of Judgment is a day of wrath that neither kings nor nations will be able to escape:

> The Lord is at your right hand:
> he will crush Kings on the day of his wrath.
> He will do judgement on the nations.
>
> (Ps. 109: 5)

The same idea, of course, is also emphasized by Durandus, who says that the office of Sunday of the Resurrection belongs to the spirit of fear by which we dread the terrible sentence of Judgement.[39]

Thus far I have tried to show how the panel of the Annunciation in Dante's reliefs, and the one of King David, are confirmations of two prophesied functions of the Messiah, Christ as King and Christ as High Priest. The remaining panel is the one representing the Emperor Trajan doing justice to the humble widow. This relief, I suggest, conveys the third function, i.e., Christ as Judge. It should be said at once that the Emperor Trajan is also in the heaven of justice, immediately following the description of King David, whom we find in the eye of the eagle ("Colui che luce in mezzo per pupilla, / fu il cantor de lo Spirito Santo" (He who shineth midmost, as in the eye the / pupil, was the singer of the Holy Spirit—*Par*. XX, 37-38). Trajan is in the eyebrow of the eagle ("mi fan cerchio per ciglio"), which says of him (again the verb is in the present tense as in the case of David) that he now knows how dearly it costs not to follow Christ because he has had experience of this sweet life and of its opposite in Limbo:

> "ora conosce quanto caro costa
> non seguir Cristo, per l'esperïenza
> di questa dolce vita e de l'opposta."
>
> > (*Par*. XX, 46-48)
>
> "now knoweth he how dear it costs not to follow
> Christ, by his experience of this sweet life
> and of the opposite."

This is the soul of the historical Trajan, now in Paradise. What we have in the relief on the Terrace of the Proud in Purgatory is an "artistic analogue" of the historical person; and like all artistic analogues it may be called a "living form" in much the same way that we call Michelangelo's "Pietà" a living form. But there is a radical difference: The relief of Trajan, as also those of Mary and David, is denuded of materiality, as the "Pietà" is not. The world beyond is not physical but metaphysical. The three reliefs should be understood as three "events" that Dante is experiencing, because God speaks with events (the events of the journey are willed by God) as man speaks with words. Dante calls the reliefs a "visibile parlare" produced by God; they are not, therefore, works of art in the human sense or, better still, they are works of art such as only God could produce. This, in short, may be God's mysterious way of confirming to Dante at this stage of the journey that all functions prophesied of the Messiah have been fulfilled in Christ. For this reason the Church, in the liturgy of Easter Vespers, chants David's Psalm 109 to celebrate that truth. These reliefs therefore should be taken as a kind of "sacramental art" where a sign not only signifies, but it accomplishes what it signifies. They are both, a representation of the three prophesied offices of the Messiah and a confirmation that David's prophecy of those offices has been fulfilled in Christ, just as the water of baptism is not only the symbol of a cleansing, but it actually accomplishes the cleansing.

As to the specific justification for the statement that Trajan's relief conveys Christ's function as Judge, we should note that in the scene in question Trajan does in fact exercise the function of dispensing justice to the humble widow. That is precisely his duty, he seems to say: "ch'i' solva il mio dovere." He is moved at once by justice and also by pity: "giustizia vuole e pietà mi ritene" (*Purg.* X, 92-93). But all this is self-evident and may be there to indicate that Trajan was in life a just emperor. This alone, however, would not be enough to support the suggestion that the relief is there to convey the idea of Christ as Judge. The idea is not conveyed solely by Trajan the dispenser of human justice on earth, but also by Trajan the recipient of divine justice in the world beyond, and the dispenser of this divine justice is none other than Christ Himself. In a story which, to human reason, has all the ingredients of a classic paradox, Trajan has been judged by Christ not once but twice. He is the supreme, inscrutable Judge that no one can outguess, as the Eagle tells us in *Paradiso* XIX. Trajan is now a blessed soul in the heaven of justice, but the story of how he managed to get there is as unique as it is perplexing. So much so that even St. Thomas felt obliged to treat of it: "Concerning the incident of Trajan it may be supposed with probability that he was recalled to life at the prayers of blessed Gregory, and thus obtained the grace whereby he received the pardon of his sins and in consequence was freed from punishment." According to others, St. Thomas continues, it may be said "that Trajan's soul was not simply freed from the debt of eternal punishment, but that his punishment was suspended for a time, that is, until the Judgement Day" (III, Suppl., q. 71, R.Obj. 5).

In any event, in the *Comedy* we find the soul of Trajan already in Paradise, while in Purgatory we have a relief representing him in his function as emperor dispensing justice. Obviously he plays a major role in Dante's Christian conception of justice. The message is clear: human justice is nothing if it does not find itself in harmony with divine justice:

> "Lume non è, se non vien dal sereno
> che non si turba mai; anzi è tenèbra,
> od ombra de la carne, o suo veleno."
>
> (*Par.* XIX, 64-66)
>
> "There is no light unless from that serene which
> never is disturbed, else is it darkness or
> shadow of the flesh, or else its poison."

But when (as in the case of Trajan dispensing justice to the widow) the human effort to do justice finds itself mysteriously on the side of God, then the Supreme Judge alone is the absolute measure, even if it means that a pagan soul like Trajan should be brought back to life so that he may be converted and thus gain his eternal salvation. This is the reason why his relief is found here on the first terrace of Purgatory. Trajan's judgment of the widow and Christ's judgment of Trajan are intimately connected; they show Dante's profound understanding of the inner relationship between human and divine justice.

The theme of Christ as Judge throughout the history of mankind is further emphasized in the twelfth canto. The reliefs are clearly examples of exalted humility. Dante sees them sculpted on the rock. On the pavement of the same terrace, Dante later sees the lineaments (as a kind of relief) of the "defeated proud" of Jewish as well as pagan history (XII, 25-63). The examples are: Satan, Briareus, the Giants, Nimrod, Niobe, Saul, Arachne, Rehoboam, Eriphyle, Sennacherib, Cyrus, Holofernes, and Troy. Punished pride is underfoot, on the ground, in direct contrast to the upright panels of exalted humility.

One more detail from these panels should further confirm that there is indeed thematic correspondence between the second day in Purgatory and Easter Sunday in Jerusalem. This concerns the smoke of incense that Dante sees imaged on the rock. The impression is vividly real; so much so that Dante's eyes and nose are confounded by it:

> Similemente al fummo de li 'ncensi
> che v'era imaginato, li occhi e 'l naso
> e al sì e al no discordi fensi.
>
> *(Purg.* X, 61-63)
>
> In like wise, at the smoke of the incense which
> there was imaged, eyes and nose were made
> discordant with yes and no.

The smoke of incense rising toward heaven has had symbolic meaning ever since the origin of the Church. In fact, in his chapter on Vespers, we learn from Durandus that the priest incenses until all the people are perfumed by the odor, then the priest says:

"Let my prayer, Lord, ascend like incense at your presence."[40]

Immediately following the description of the incense, Dante presents to us King David, dancing in front of the sacred Ark, thus offering to God the good example of his prayers. Thus the smoke of incense can be taken as another, though minor, echo of Easter Vespers.

Now, in reference to the liturgical expression "This is the day the Lord has made," Durandus explains that Easter Sunday is a day of health, grace, eternity, and glory. "Let us rejoice and be transported with joy," he says, "because it is in being transported with joy and rejoicing that one goes to

Paradise, whereas it is in pain and anguish, and great affliction that one goes to Hell, because there is no peace for the impious, says the Lord, and for the good there is joy, peace and repose, above all because of the hope of the glorious resurrection."[41]

The very same concept may be found in Dante. On the second day in Purgatory he hears some voices chanting the first beatitude so sweetly as no words could tell:

> "*Beati pauperes spiritu!*" voci
> cantaron sì, che nol diria sermone.
>
> (*Purg.* XII, 110-11)
>
> "*Beati pauperes spiritu!*" voices
> so sweetly sang, that no speech would tell it.

Immediately following these lines, Dante breaks into a jubilant reflection concerning his journey, noting (like Durandus) that one enters Hell with fierce laments, whereas one enters here with sweet songs:

> Ahi quanto son diverse quelle foci
> da l'infernali! ché quivi per canti
> s'entra, e là giù per lamenti feroci.
>
> (*Purg.* XII, 112-14)
>
> Ah! how different are these openings from those
> in Hell! for here we enter through songs, and
> down there through fierce wailings.

Furthermore, Durandus says, today is the day when the Lord was raised; more specifically, this day, while it is in its dawn, or its beginning, is called day of health and grace; when it will be at its noon, it will be called day of eternity and glory. And this is so because this day has no decline.[42]

All this is symbolic of course, and I believe a similar symbolism may be found in the *Comedy* if we are willing to go beyond the literal meaning. Symbolism is conveyed by two terzine set in beautiful sequence both logically and poetically. Immediately following Dante's contemplation of the carvings on the pavement, Virgil exhorts him to lift his head since this is no time to go so "absorbed": "non è più tempo di gir sì sospeso" (*Purg.* XII, 78). Sapegno comments that "sospeso" here means "assorto a meditare, e quindi distratto dalle altre cose." (absorbed in meditating, and therefore distracted from other things).[43] In fact, Dante is distracted from the greater purpose of going up to Paradise, as Virgil reminds him by pointing to the guardian Angel who, they hope, will grant them passage:

> "Vedi colà un angel che s'appresta
> per venir verso noi; vedi che torna
> dal servigio del dì l'ancella sesta."
>
> (*Purg.* XII, 79-81)

"See there an angel who is making ready to come
towards us; look how the sixth handmaiden
is returning from the day's service."

In the above terzina, in one and the same breath, Virgil is telling Dante that the angel is approaching and that it is now about noontime; the sixth handmaiden (the sixth hour of daylight) is returning from the day's service. Noon of Easter Sunday, we have learned from Durandus, is symbolic of eternity and glory because this day has no end. And this is precisely what Virgil will allude to when he exhorts Dante to adorn with reverence his bearing and his face so that it may delight the angel to send them upward (to Paradise), and to reflect that this day never dawns again:

"Di riverenza il viso e li atti addorna,
sì che i diletti lo 'nvïarci in suso;
pensa che questo dì mai non raggiorna!"

(*Purg.* XII, 82-84)

"Adorn with reverence thy bearing and thy face,
so that it may delight him to send us upward;
reflect that this day never dawns again."

The expression: "Reflect that this day never dawns again" refers to the second day in Purgatory when Dante is in the act of purgating his sins and thus gaining his eternal redemption. The angel will soon erase from his forehead the "P" of pride, and Dante will feel as if a heavy weight has been lifted from him; so much so that he feels almost no toil in journeying upward:

Ond'io: "Maestro, dì, qual cosa greve
levata s'è da me, che nulla quasi
per me fatica, andando, si riceve?"

(*Purg.* XII, 118-20)

Wherefore I: "Master, say, what heavy thing
has been lifted from me, that scarce any toil
is perceived by me in journeying?"

Easter Sunday, says Durandus, is the day of grace that grants one the freedom of purgating one's sins thereby acquiring glory, i.e., of being eternally famous in the eyes of God. Being famous in the eyes of men, we are told on this second day in Purgatory, is nothing but a breath of wind: "Non è il mondan romore altro ch' un fiato / di vento" (*Purg.* XI, 100); and empty glory is the fruit of human powers: "Oh vana gloria de l'umane posse!" (v. 91). As I have previously stated, during the whole of the first day in the Ante-Purgatory, Dante is not purgating any sins; he, like all the spirits he encounters on the shore of Purgatory, is in a state of suspension. This is precisely as it should be since this state corresponds to the suspension of the Vigil Night in Jerusalem, and, most importantly, to that suspension between the Crucifixion and the Resurrection on the stage of history when humanity actually hung spiritually suspended.

One final point of considerable importance needs to be emphasized. Easter Sunday was the fulfillment of what Christ had promised to his disciples during the Last Supper. It was the fulfillment of the New Covenant of love: "Then he took a cup, gave thanks, and gave it to them. 'All of you must drink from it,' he said, 'for this is my blood, the blood of the Covenant, to be poured out in behalf of many for the forgiveness of sins," (Matt. 26:27-29). This was the covenant that established a new relationship between man and God—a relationship of love, since Christ's sacrifice was the supreme act of love. Through this act Christ also established a new relationship between man and man; this was his new gospel of fraternal love:

> My commandment to you is: love your enemies, pray for your persecutors. This will prove that you are sons of your heavenly Father, for his sun rises on the bad and the good, he rains on the just and on the unjust. If you love those who love you, what merit is there in that?
>
> (Matt. 5:45-6)

All this is now commemorated by the Church on Easter Sunday. Specifically, the Church proclaims the covenant by one of the psalms of Easter Vespers:

> He has given food to those who fear him;
> he will forever be mindful of his covenant.
> He has made known to his people the power of his
> works, giving them the inheritance of the nations.
> He has sent deliverance to his people;
> he has satisfied his covenant forever;
> holy and awesome is his name.
>
> (Ps. 111)

We find the proclamation that men should love each other as Christ had loved them in the thirteenth canto—the second day in Purgatory. As one might expect, this is done in a beautiful and moving fashion. We are on the second terrace, the Terrace of Envy, the vice opposed to love and generosity. We meet here the spirits of those who in life had envied the perfection and beauty of their fellow men, failing therefore to recognize them as brothers. They are now unable to see, for their eyes are sewn together with wire and they are forced to lean on each other for mutual support. A most pathetic scene indeed. But suddenly, sweet, beautiful voices are singing in the air: voices of spirits which, heard but not seen, are flying toward Dante, uttering courteous invitations to the table of love:

e verso noi volar furon sentiti,
non però visti, spiriti parlando
a la mensa d'amor cortesi inviti.

(Purg. XIII, 25-27)

and, flying towards us were heard, but not seen,
spirits, speaking courteous invitations to the
table of love.

One of the voices flying by calls out repeatedly the words of the Virgin Mary at the marriage in Cana:

La prima voce che passò volando,
"*vinum non habent*," altamente disse,
e retro a noi l'andò reïterando

(Purg. XIII, 28-30)

The first voice which passed by in its flight
loudly said, "*Vinum non habent*," and went
on repeating it behind us.

But then, most importantly for our purpose, another voice utters a direct quotation from Christ: "Love them from whom you have suffered evil":

"Oh!" diss'io, "padre, che voci son queste?"
e com'io domandai, ecco la terza
dicendo: "Amate da cui male aveste."

(Purg. XIII, 34-36)

"O Father," said I, "what voices are these?"
and as I was asking, lo the third saying:
"Love them from whom ye have suffered evil."

This, I believe, is an echo of Christ's new gospel of fraternal love being proclaimed by the liturgy of Easter Sunday in Jerusalem. We hear it on the second day in Purgatory; I submit, therefore, that Dante considers this day as Easter Sunday.

Again, this is the same conclusion that I reached in my earlier work, *Essays on Dante's Philosophy of History*, and I am grateful that my interpretation has won some acceptance among Dante scholars. In the previous study I attempted to show that there are strong thematic correspondences between the first day (in the Ante-Purgatory) and the liturgy of Holy Saturday in Jerusalem. In the present study I have tried to illustrate that there are even stronger correspondences between the second day of the cantica of Purgatory and the liturgy of Easter Sunday in Jerusalem. The first, most important element of this correspondence is constituted by the proclamation of Christ's new gospel of fraternal love, which occurs on the second day in Purgatory, and during the liturgy of Easter Sunday in Jerusalem. On this there can be no doubt; the correspondence is self-evident. The second important element is constituted by the fact that on Easter Sunday the Church proclaims, with the prophetic psalm of King David, the fulfillment of the three offices of the Messiah: Christ as King; Christ as High Priest; Christ as Judge. Most importantly, I have pointed out that Christ applied this psalm to himself. On the second day, as Dante goes through the gate of Purgatory proper, that is to say as he enters the Kingdom of God, he is confronted by three reliefs on the first terrace. The sculptor of these reliefs, we are told, is God Himself. The reliefs represent the Virgin Mary at the Annunciation, King David officiating as high priest, and the Emperor Trajan in his office as judge. My interpretation of these reliefs is that they proclaim the fulfillment of the three offices of the Messiah as they were prophesied by the psalm, which is being chanted in Jerusalem at Vespers of Easter Sunday. God is the author of these reliefs; He is, therefore, His own fulfillment because He is also the author of Mary, David, and Trajan, who were, in life, instruments, signs through which He chose to manifest Himself. We might ask ourselves the following questions: Why should God have chosen the Virgin Mary to bring forth His son who would be King forever? Why should God have chosen King David to prophesy that the Messiah would be a High Priest? Why should God have chosen Trajan (according to the legend) to exemplify that Christ is the Supreme Judge? We might say that to Dante, the answer in each case, quite simply, is that God, in His infinite wisdom has so chosen, just as He has also chosen that he (the poet) should thus represent them. We are here confronted with one of the most beautiful instances of Dante's profound understanding of biblical history. Dante, after all, tells us that he is God's scribe:

> Messo t'ho innanzi: omai per te ti ciba;
> ché a sé torce tutta la mia cura
> quella materia ond'io son fatto scriba.
>
> (Par. X, 25-27)
>
> I have set before thee; now feed thou thyself,
> for that matter whereof I have made me
> scribe, now wresteth to itself my total care.

NOTES

1. Natalino Sapegno, *La Divina Commedia*, (Milano: Ricciardi, 1957), p. 478.
2. Francesco D'Ovidio, *Nuovi Studi Danteschi*: "Il Purgatorio e il suo preludio," (Milano: V. Haepli, 1906), p. 422.
3. Etienne Gilson, *The Spirit of Medieval Philosophy*, (New York: Charles Scribener's Sons, 1940), pp. 84-108.
4. Charles S. Singleton, *Commedia: Elements of Structure*, (Cambridge: Harvard University Press, 1954), p. 61.
5. Paget Toynbee, *The Letters of Dante*, (Oxford: Oxford University Press, 1920), p. 198.
6. Professor Dino S. Cervigni (*Dante's Poetry of Dreams*: Florence-Olschki, 1986, p. 77, n. 2) has voiced the following objection to my essay: "The essay overlooks the fact that the *Te Deum* is also sung in extra-liturgical ceremonies: 'In addition to its liturgical use, the *Te Deum* is used in many extra-liturgical functions as a hymn of thanksgiving on occasions of great solemnity, such as the election of a pope, the consecration of a bishop [. . .] (M. Britt, *The Hymns of the Breviary and Missal*, New York, Benziger, 1936, p. 46).' " Now, since in Dante's text there is neither a pope being elected nor a bishop being consecrated, I honestly fail to see the validity or necessity of Cervigni's objection. What is of fundamental importance is the historical fact that both Durandus and Honorius of Autun concur in saying that the Church uses the *Te Deum* to signify the hour of Christ's resurrection on Easter Sunday morning. This was true at the time of Dante, as it is true today, as it was probably true for centuries before Dante. And since the unfolding action of the Ante-Purgatory clearly takes place within a context of Easter-time, it then becomes plausible to infer that Dante used the *Te Deum* to convey to the reader that he considers the second day as if it were Easter Sunday. The fact that the *Te Deum* is also used at the election of a pope or at the consecration of a bishop is simply extraneous to the problem. Also, Cervigni is not altogether accurate when he says: "According to A. C. Mastrobuono . . . one should situate the episode unfolding in the first eight cantos of the *Purgatorio* on Holy Saturday rather than on Easter Sunday." To be exact, my thesis is that the first day in Purgatory corresponds to the Vigil Night between Holy Saturday and Easter Sunday. To be more specifically exact, my study is one of thematic patterns between the *Exultet* of the Vigil Night and the unfolding action of the Ante-Purgatory, as is clear from what I said:

> The analysis of the cantos will therefore be made on three different levels:
> I. The Literal Level: What actually takes place in the context which has to be taken as true and historical.
> II. The Level of "Sacramental Representation": notably, the representation in the valley.
> III. The Level of Old Testament Literature: such as, "In Exitu Israel d'Egitto."
> These three levels are clearly discernible in the context. Now I have said that the first day in Purgatory may correspond to the night between Holy Saturday and Easter Sunday and, in this connection, we should call attention to the "Exultet" which is the single most important liturgical document for the Vigil Night because it is actually a proclamation of Easter; that is to say, it proclaims, in very moving language, the essence of Easter. It speaks of the mystery of Easter on three different levels which might find correspondence with Dante's three level narrative of the Ante-Purgatory: (1) Historical Fact; (2) Sacramental Representation; (3) Old Testament Type:
> No liturgical text speaks as eloquently and enthusiastically in praise of Easter as the "Praeconium Paschale" or "Exultet." Beneath the inspired words of this ancient Christian composition lies a spiritual world which makes us feel intuitively the nobility of Christianity. Words are bodies that have a soul; this soul must be known if the words are to be fully understood. What does the "Exultet" tell us about the Easter mystery? It approaches the subeject on three levels, that of Old Testament type, that of historical fact, and that of sacramental re-presentation here and now of the mystery of Redemption. The three levels coalesce in grand unity, minus the differentiation of time perspective[2] (*Essays*, pp. 84-85).

Finally, I take this opportunity to express my gratitude to Professor Cervigni for his kind consideration when he says: "Mastrobuono's thesis deserves the critics' close attention."

7. Honorius of Autun, (*Gemma Animae*), P.L., 172, col. 677.

8. Pius Parsch, *The Breviary Explained*, (St. Louis: B. Herder Co., 1952), p. 376.

9. Guglielmo Durando, *Rationale Divinorum Officiorum*, (Napoli: Apud Josephum Dura Bibliopolam, 1859), Book 6, chap. 87, section 5, p. 577.

10. *Rationale*, Book 6, chap. 86, section 1, p. 569: "Siquidem tempus paschale significat tempus illud quod erit post diem judicii, quando videlicet ad patriam vitae, quam per Adam amisimus, Deo propitiante, regrediemur: qua consideratione potest dici hoc tempus regressionis."

11. *Rationale*, Book 6, chap. 86, section 1, p. 569: "Sic restituetur homo in idipsum, et ad id quod fuerat conditus; imo supra primae originis reparabitur dignitatem."

12. *Rationale*, Book 6, chap. 86, section 2, pp. 569-70: "Sane πασχα graecum nomen est, quod hebraice dicitur *Phase*, quod latine *transitus* interpretatur . . . et hoc primo secundum historiam, ex eo quod exterminator Angelus videns sanguinem in foribus Israelitarum pertransiit, nec eos percussit; tunc etiam populus ex Ægypto transivit, idest exivit, tertiaque die mare rubrum pertransivit."

Also, in Honorius of Autun: "Phase Hebraice, pascha Graece, transitus dicitur Latine, eo quod illa nocte angelus percutiens Ægyptum transivit (Exod. XIV), et populos Dei illa die de Ægypto transiit, et die tertia mare Rubrum transiit, ac populus fidelis de infermi claustris illa nocte ad gaudia paradisi transivit, et exercitus baptizandorum de infidelitate ad lucem fidei transit" (*Gemma Animae*, Lib. III, Cap. CXXIV: De Pascha, P.L., 172, col. 676).

13. *Rationale*, Book 6, chap. 86, section 2, p. 570: "Secundo, secundum allegoriam, quia ecclesia in hoc tempore transivit per baptismum ab infidelitate ad fidem."

14. George Ferguson, *Signs and Symbols in Christan Art*, (Oxford: Oxford University Press, 1954), p. 17.

15. *Rationale*, Book 6, chap. 86, section 2, p. 570: "Tertio, secundum tropologiam, quoniam hoc tempore transimus per contritionem, et confessionem de vitiis ad virtutes."

16. P. H. Wicksteed, Temple Classics, *Paradiso*, (London: J. M. Dent and Sons Ltd.), pp. 56-57: "In popular estimate, 'the silver key of knowledge and the golden key of authority.' But Aquinas says more accurately: 'For either of these [i. e., to decide that the penitent is fit to be absolved, and actually to absolve him] a certain power or authority is needed; and so we distinguish between two keys, one pertaining to the judgment as to the fitness of him to be absolved, the other pertaining to the absolution itself.'"

17. Reginald Masterson O. P., T. C. O'Brien O. P., *Summa Theologiae*, (New York: McGraw-HIll Book Company, 1965), *Penance*, vol. 60, p. 108.

18. Ibid., p. 177.

19. Ibid., p. 188. And it is precisely on this aspect (that: "The struggle against the effects of sin itself becomes a way of conformity to Christ's suffering"), that Montano's application of the distinction between Dante the "poet" and Dante the "pilgrim" has proven to be the most valid, fundamental approach to Dante's poem, inasmuch as it captures the very essence of the pilgrim's journey to God: "Dante, the poet, has to narrate how he, after being on the verge of spiritual death and still being an infirm soul, passed through the world of perdition and how he was necessarily affected by the forms of evil with which he came into contact, and somehow he re-experienced and re-suffered certain states of blindness and perversion. For this reason it is clear that Dante, as a wayfarer in a journey from a state of perdition to light has to appear contaminated by the various forms of sin through which he passes" (Rocco Montano: *Dante's Thought and Poetry*, Chicago-Regnery Gateway, 1988, p. 151).

20. Thomas C. Donlan, O. P., *Christ, and His Sacraments*, (Dubuque: The Priory Press, 1958), p. 450.

21. Ibid., p. 459.

22. N. Sapegno, *La Divina Commedia*, pp. 496-97: *Lo scaglion primaio*: il primo gradino, di marmo bianco lucente come specchio. Rappresenta simbolicamente il primo momento del sacramento della penitenza, e cioè la *contritio cordis*, "che debbe avere ciascun fedele prima che venga alla confessione, che, esaminato in se medesimo et specchiatosi nel cuore suo, recasi a mente tutti i suoi peccati et di quelli pentesi interamente con buona contrizione; et in quel punto rimane bianco come il marmo, senza veruna macchia o oscurità di peccati" (Anonimo fiorentino). . . . "Per questo secondo grado si dee intendere la confessione [la *confessio oris*, secondo momento della penitenza]; ché, poi che l'uomo è contrito et pentuto de' suoi peccati, gli dee confessare al sacerdote. Et quello essere tinto ci ha a dimostrare la tinta della vergogna che riceve il peccatore confessando i suoi peccati. L'essere la pietra crepata per lungo et per traverso ci dimostra che dentro come di fuori si debbe vergognare, et quel medesimo che sente nel cuore dire colle parole, et rompere questa pietra della durezza et ostinazione de' suoi pec-

cati" (Anonimo fiorentino). Il Lana, il Buti, il Landino e altri invertono l'ordine dei due simboli, vedendo nel primo gradino la confessione orale e nel secondo la contrizione. . . . "Il terzo grado, hae a significare la satisfazione de' suoi peccati [*satisfatio operis*], però che non basta essere contrito, avere confessati i suoi peccati, se l'uomo non fa la penitenzia et la satisfazione; et però dice che 'l terzo grado era fiammeggiante: et questo colore di fuoco hae a denotare l'ardore della carità e dell'amore che accende gli uomini, et sospinge a fare la penitenzia de' peccati commessi" (Anonimo fiorentino).

23. *Rationale*, Book 6, chap. 86, section 2, p. 570: "Quarto, secundum anagogem, quia tunc Christus transiit a mortalitate ad immortalitatem, et faciet nos etiam transire."

24. *Rationale*, Book 5 chap. 9, section 1, p. 373: "In hora vespertina significat Ecclesia primum adventum Domini, qui fuit vergente mundi vespere, idest ultima aetate."

25. *Rationale*, Book 5, chap. 9, section 1, p. 373: "Nos sumus, *in quos fines seculum devenerunt.*"

26. *Rationale*, Book 5, chap. 9, section 1, p. 373: "Praeterea, Christus in vespere de cruce depositus fuit. Eadem quoque hora, in coena sacramentum corporis et sanguinis instituit, pedes discipulorum lavit, discipulis euntibus in Emmaus in habitu peregrini in fractione panis se manifestavit."

27. *Rationale*, Book 5, chap. 9, section 2, p. 373: "Unde vespertinum officium a Vespere stella nominatur, quae in principio noctis oritur."

28. *Rationale*, Book 5, chap. 9, section 3, p. 373: "Dicit autem Ecclesia in hac ora quinque psalmos."

Section 4, p. 374: "Quinque ergo psalmi in vespertinis hebdomadae officiis dicuntur, et cantantur psalmi secundum materiam diei."

29. *Rationale*, Book 5, chap. 9, section 3, p. 373: "Primo, propter quinque Christi vulnera, qui pro nobis obtulit sacrificium in vespera mundi. Secundo, ad correctionem, ut videlicet defleamus, et petamus veniam peccatorum, quae in die per quinque sensus corporis committuntur, et ad nos intrant . . . Tertio, per ipsos quinque psalmos munit se Ecclesia contra nocturnales tribulationes. Haec enim hora insinuat flectum eorum, quibus occidit sol justitiae . . . et propter easdem etiam causas pectus quinque digitis tundimus."

30. *Rationale*, Book 6, chap. 88, section 6, p. 580: "Post hoc dicitur Collecta, in qua ostenditur quis sit resurrectionis et mortis effectus, quoniam apertio januae regni coelestis est effectus."

31. *Rationale*, Book 6, chap. 86, section 11, pp. 571-72: "Dominus tamen vere surrexit in die sexto Calendas Aprilis, nam passus est octavo Calendas Aprilis, videlicet in die tali, in quali conceptus est, sive in quali annunciatio Virgini facta est."

32. *Rationale*, Book 5 chap. 9, section 7, p. 375: "Et nota quod dicit *respexit humilitatem*, et non dicit *respexit virginitatem*, innuens mentis virginitatem praevalere corporis integritati. Iterum, ideo dixit *humilitatem*, quia Deus superbis resistit, eosque a beatorum sorte secernens, per varia poenarum loca pro peccatorum impietate dispergit."

33. A. C. Mastrobuono, *Essays on Dante's Philosophy of History*, (Florence: Olschki, 1979), p. 184.

34. N. Sapegno, Op. Cit., p. 509.

35. Pius Parsch, *The Breviary Explained*, p. 382: "Psalm 109. This is a directly Messianic psalm which Christ applied to Himself. Its brilliant pictures describe the victory of the Savior. We may divide the psalm according to the following thoughts of the contents: 1. Christ as King; 2. Christ as High Priest; 3. Christ as Judge of the world, all during the history of mankind, as well as on the Last Day."

36. T. E. Bird, *A Commentary on the Psalms*, (London: Burns Oates & Washbourne Ltd., 1927), vol. 2, p. 238.

37. N. Sapegno, Op. Cit., p. 506.

38. Charles S. Singleton, *The Divine Comedy, Purgatorio*, (Princeton: Princeton University Press, 1973), p. 103.

39. *Rationale*, Book 6, chap. 96, section 2, p. 596: "Officium quidem dominicae resurrectionis pertinet ad timorem, quo timemus terribilem sententiam judicis."

40. *Rationale*, Book 5, chap. 9, section 5, p. 374: "*Dirigatur Domine oratio mea, sicut incensum in conspectu tuo.*"

41. *Rationale*, Book 6, chap. 88, section 10, p. 580: "Haec dies, quam fecit Dominus, exultemus et laetemur in ea, quia exultando et laetando itur in paradisum, sed cum labore et angustia, et cum maxima afflictione itur ad infernum, quia non est pax impiis, dicit Dominus, sed bonis est jucunditas, pax, et quies, maxime propter spem gloriosae resurrectionis."

42. *Rationale*, Book 6, chap. 88, section 10, p. 580: "Et hodie: Surrexit Dominus; sed haec dies, dum est in aurora vel in ascensu, vocatur dies salutis et gratiae, cum fuerit in meridie, vocabitur dies aeternitatis et gloriae. Haec declivium non sentit . . ."

43. N. Sapegno, Op. Cit., p. 533.

The Powerful Enigma:
A Mortification of the Intellect

It should be said at the outset that Ernest Robert Curtius is not alto-gether correct in saying that one can enjoy and understand Dante's poetry without ever knowing who the "Veltro" or the "Cinquecento diece e cinque" might be: "The deciphering of these hieroglyphics is irrelevant to an appreci-ation and comprehension of Dante's poetry."[1] For someone who is interested in Dante's philosophy of history, as I am, a plausible solution of these prob-lems assumes a role of considerable importance. The simple fact to keep in mind is that Dante himself has explicitly put these "prophecies" in the text, and until they are solved, his vision of history, as expressed in the *Comedy*, remains necessarily incomplete. Clearly, from this particular point of view, we are not confronted here with one of those problems we might otherwise easily dismiss as "irrelevant." If Dante may be said to be one of the greatest poets of the Christian era, it then becomes imperative that we establish to what extent his philosophy of history remains a Christian one.

One of the scholars who has recognized the interrelationship of these prophecies is R. E. Kaske, who maintains: "So far, I have tried to show that Beatrice's prophecy of the DXV foretells an advent of Christ; and that Vir-gil's prophecy of the Veltro foretells a decisive regeneration within Christen-dom, to be inspired by the preaching of Franciscan and Dominican orders."[2] I am in partial agreement with Kaske's thesis, since I also have come to the conclusion (though for different reasons as we shall see shortly) that Beat-rice's prophecy of the "Cinquecento diece e cinque" foretells Christ's Majes-tic Advent.

As for the Veltro, I have proposed elsewhere[3] that it be interpreted as Christ in His First Advent. There are many indications that would support this thesis. I shall limit myself, at present, to some highlights of this interpre-tation so as to provide a symmetrical balance to the study of the "Cinque-cento diece e cinque," which is the main theme of this essay.

First of all, I should like to mention that, unlike Charles Singleton, I have proposed a reading of the Prologue Scene of the *Comedy* in the allegory of Theologians, since every aspect of that scene may actually be grounded in sa-cred biblical history. This, I have said, constitutes the very premise and justi-fication for Dante's vision of the world beyond. The Allegory of Theologians demands that, within the fiction of the poem, the literal sense be taken as historically true. Thus, I have attempted to show that there may be analogical contemporaneity between Dante's personal redemption as it unfolds within the context of the poem during this Easter time of the year 1300, and mankind's drama of redemption as it took place on the stage of history.

Dante, we all agree, is symbolical of Humanity; yet, in the prologue scene, the three wild beasts have been identified with Incontinence, Violence, and Fraud, inasmuch as the sins of Hell fall under these general headings, or as Lust, Pride, and Avarice, respectively, which is to say that they are taken to represent moral evil. I have argued, however, that Mankind in the fallen state is confronted by moral evil (sin) as well as physical evil (death-pain), and that it is therefore inconceivable that Dante would represent himself confronted by moral evil alone since this would only be half the truth about Humanity.

The Leopard and the Lion, I have suggested, may be symbolical of Original Sin, whose cleansing is now being commemorated during this Easter time of the year 1300. The she-wolf deserves special attention and should be differentiated since she is the only beast explicitly tied in with the Veltro. What should be noted is that as Dante meets the Leopard, we are given a direct, most important reference to the time of Creation. It was the beginning of the morning and the sun was rising with those stars that were with Him when Divine Love first moved those fair things: "ch'eran con lui quando l'amor divino / mosse di prima quelle cose belle" (*Inf*. I, 39-40). This reference would naturally bring to our minds Adam and Eve in the Garden so that the symbolical meaning of the developing action might be seen in this manner: as Dante walks towards the Light on the Mountain, so Humanity walked toward the Messiah on Golgotha. On this journey Humanity then, like Dante now, was plagued by the Leopard and the Lion, that is, Original Sin.

To see how this may be so, we should point out that in the description of Original Sin (Gen. 3:2-6) there is an interplay between the order of Action and the order of Intention, which might correspond to Dante's order of encounter with the Leopard (Lust) and the Lion (Pride) and the she-wolf (the effects of Original Sin). The very same passage from Genesis is quoted by Dante in the *De vulgari eloquentia* (I, 4). In Genesis, Eve is first described as being sensually attracted by the forbidden fruit: "the woman saw that the tree was good for food, pleasing to the eyes" (Lust), but the motive was Pride since she also saw (with her mind this time) the fruit as "desirable for gaining wisdom," which amounts to a desire for a treacherous usurpation of God's Wisdom.

The Hill of the prologue scene should be identified, as I have also said, with a historical hill such as Golgotha, since it is demanded by the principle of analogy proposed by Dante himself: "As a thing is related to existence—so is it related to truth" (Letter to Can Grande). In fact, in the Judeo-Christian tradition, there are two mountains of major importance: Mount Sinai and Golgotha. They constitute the two major stages of mankind's relationship with God. On Mount Sinai, mankind received the Commandments: a covenant of Law. On Golgotha, mankind received the Sacrificial Lamb: a covenant of Love.

As for the Dark Wood, if we are willing to analyze the scene from a proper historical perspective, emphasizing the belief that Christianity is the fulfillment of the Jewish tradition, and that the time anterior to the Chosen People was a long, dark night without revelation, law, or faith,[4] we might then suggest that Dante's "selva oscura" may perhaps be symbolical of this time. Beatrice herself says that after the Fall the human race lay sick on earth for many centuries, in great error, until it pleased the Word of God to descend:

> onde l'umana specie inferma giacque
> giù per secoli molti in grande errore,
> fin ch'al Verbo di Dio discender piacque
>
> (*Par.* VII, 28-30)

There are many other indications that would support this thesis. Dante, like the Chosen People, may have succeeded in escaping the Dark Wood, but he is not yet completely out of danger. The rising sun may have given him hope of regaining the straight path (as the Jews were given a promise of Redemption), but the three wild beasts (Original Sin and its effects) still await him on the Mountain. What should be further considered is the important information we are given in Limbo. There Virgil tells Dante that many Jews were saved when "un possente" (Christ) descended into Hell (*Inf.* IV, 52-54). "And I wish thee to know"—Virgil is exacting—"that, before these, no human soul was saved"—"E vo' che sappi che, dinanzi ad essi, / spiriti umani non eran salvati" (62-63). This is to say that only the people who lived in hope of a Messiah were ultimately saved by Him. All the others, those who lived before the Chosen People, did not escape the Dark Wood of Perdition "che non lasciò già mai persona viva." In fact the Blessed Rose in Dante's Paradise is divided in those who believed in Christ to come and those who believed in Christ already come.

Of the three wild beasts, the most troublesome to Dante is the she-wolf. The Leopard and the Lion stay on the scene only briefly and disappear, as Original Sin in Dante's personal life disappears at baptism. Only the she-wolf (the effects of Original Sin) blocks Dante's path to the Mountain. We are told that she looks very hungry and lean: "Ed una lupa, che di tutte brame / sembiava carca ne la sua magrezza" (*Inf.* I, 49-50), that she has already made many people live in sorrow: "e molte genti fé già viver grame" (*Inf.* I, 51), and that her terrifying aspect has now caused Dante to lose hope of the ascent. Later, Dante is being told by Virgil that he had better take another road since she kills everyone that passes her way: "Non lascia altrui passar per la sua via, / ma tanto lo 'mpedisce che l'uccide" (*Inf.* I, 95-96). Her nature is one of such perversity and viciousness—"ha natura sì malvagia e ria" (*Inf.* I, 97)—that her craving is never quenched and after feeding she is hungrier than before: "Che mai non empie la bramosa voglia, / e dopo 'l pasto ha più fame che pria" (*Inf.* I, 98-99).

Now, a she-wolf that has made many people live in sorrow, and that kills everyone that passes her way, right here and now—on the stage of this life—within the fictional context of the prologue scene, may be symbolical not only of Avarice (death of the spirit, as traditionally interpreted), but also of the destruction of the body (physical death as we have proposed). These two meanings do not mutually exclude each other; on the contrary, they may be shown to be quite compatible. They are, in fact, inseparable if seen within the context of Original Sin. It was because of his sin that Adam lost the immortality of his body. As St. Paul says: "Therefore as through one man sin entered into the world and through sin death, and thus death has passed into all men because all have sinned" (Romans 5:12).

It should also be emphasized that Santa Lucia calls the she-wolf by name. When from Heaven she sees that Dante is down on earth struggling against the she-wolf, she goes to Beatrice to ask her why she does not help the one who loved her so greatly that for her he had left the vulgar crowd (*Inf.* II, 103-15). Then she adds:

> "Non odi tu la pieta del suo pianto,
> non vedi tu la *morte* che 'l combatte
> su la fiumana ove 'l mar non ha vanto?"
>
> (Inf. II, 106-8)
>
> "Hearest not thou the misery of his plaint? Seest
> thou not the *death* which combats him upon
> the river over which the sea has no boast?"[5]

This "morte che 'l combatte"—I have maintained—should be interpreted as both: spiritual death as well as physical death, that is, Evil or effects of Original Sin. And Dante, it will be remembered, does not cross the path of the she-wolf in order to enter the world beyond, but makes the journey with his live body like St. Paul.

There is more: Virgil goes on to say that a Greyhound will come to chase this she-wolf out of the earth and put her back into Hell from where envy first set her loose:

> Questi la caccerà per ogne villa,
> fin che l'avrà rimessa ne lo 'nferno,
> là onde 'nvidia prima dipartilla.
>
> (Inf. I, 109-11)
>
> He shall chase her through every city, till he
> have put her into Hell again; from which
> envy first set her loose.

How are we to understand that it was envy in Hell that set the she-wolf loose? If we compare the above passage to what is said in the Book of Wisdom, we cannot fail to note a striking similarity: "For God formed man to be imperishable; the image of his own nature he made him. But by the envy of the devil, death entered the world, and they who are in his possession experience it" (Wisd. of Sol. 2:23-24). This quotation is rather important since it comes from a very famous passage of the Book of Wisdom, considered to be a direct prophecy of Christ's Passion. What is especially revealing is the fact that it constitutes the main theme of the Fifth Lesson of Good Friday Matins; just as the supposed date of Dante's vision is Good Friday of the year 1300. The thematic correspondence is too striking; Virgil seems to be expressing the same concept in the very same words. The Book of Wisdom is referring to man's Original State. If man was ever imperishable, it must have been in the garden of Eden; and if death came to him there, it was because of Original Sin. The envy of the Devil may refer to the serpent's temptation, but Adam and Eve nonetheless remain responsible. Their death, spiritual as well as physical, was a consequence of Original Sin. What should also be pointed out is that we find King Solomon—the author of the Book of Wisdom—in Dante's *Paradiso* (XIV, 43-45). It would seem likely, therefore, that Dante, being familiar with the works of Solomon, could have had the Book of Wisdom in mind when he wrote about the she-wolf.

But if the she-wolf may be death, who then is the Veltro that will come to make her die in pain and send her back to Hell? He will not feed, Virgil says, on land or pelf, but rather on Wisdom, Virtues, and Love. All these qualities are clearly not material. They exclude, I would say, the possibility of interpreting the Veltro as a temporal ruler. I have proposed, therefore, that the Veltro may be symbolical of Christ in the First Advent since it was, in fact, said of Christ that He would come and destroy death forever: "On this mountain he will destroy the veil that veils all peoples, the web that is woven over all nations; he will destroy death forever" (Isaiah 25: 6-8). Furthermore, by the principle of analogy, Virgil's prophecy of the Veltro, here in the prologue scene, should be taken to echo something he might have said in life. He has first appeared to Dante early this Good Friday of the year 1300. These facts, I believe, point to something beyond themselves in the sense that Virgil is coming to Dante now, before the commemoration of the Crucifixion, as he came to Humanity—into the world—before Christ. He has come to Dante with the full force of his historical personality. And as such, he gives a prophecy of the Veltro just as he had actually given one in the fourth *Eclogue* in almost the same words. In the *Eclogue*, the serpent shall perish; in the *Comedy*, the she-wolf shall die; and in both cases, the one who will accomplish this shall have the gift of Divine Life (in the *Eclogue*) and feed on Wisdom, Love, and Virtues (in the *Comedy*).

Dante also believed that the founding of Rome was contemporary with the establishment of the house of Mary and, for this reason, was a sacred event in the course of history willed by God:

Per che assai è manifesto la divina elezione del romano imperio per lo nascimento de la santa cittade, che fu contemporaneo a la radice de la progenie di Maria.[6]

the divine predilection for the Roman empire is amply manifested by the birth of the holy city which was contemporaneous to the root of Mary's progeny.

The Roman Empire and the Jews' expectation of a Messiah are parallel events in the course of history, both sacred and providentially ordained to someday converge, as, in fact, they did: imperial Rome became the Holy Seat of Christianity. In fact, the concept of pagan Rome integrated into Christian Rome constitutes one of the most profound elements of Dante's vision of history, which sets him apart, as Rocco Montano says, from his contemporaries such as St. Thomas Aquinas, who was mostly concerned with the conduct of individuals in relation to Grace, and in many aspects ignored the problem of history. For Dante,

C'è un principio e una fine nella vicenda del mondo. Al centro è l'avvento di Cristo. L'impero romano, prima e dopo l'avvento, è come l'estrinsecazione del disegno divino.[7]

There is a beginning and an end to the vicissitude of the world. At the center there is Christ's Advent. The Roman Empire, before and after the Advent, is like the manifestation of the divine plan.

Rome is, therefore, both the unconscious preparation for Christ and the instrument for the propagation of the faith, which, according to Charles T. Davis,[8] Dante probably learned from Orosius.

All this is confirmed in the *Comedy*. In the second canto (which seems to be as devoid of action as the first is completely charged with it) we have Dante and Virgil talking to each other. The Virgin Mary, Santa Lucia, and Beatrice are referred to by Virgil, but they are not present on the scene. What actually takes place in the scene is that Dante is finally persuaded by Virgil to undertake the journey through the world beyond, a decision that should be taken as a conversion, since all the elements of the simile unmistakably suggest a joyful, inner movement of Dante's soul: "Quali fioretti dal notturno gelo . . . si drizzan tutti aperti in loro stelo, / tal mi fec'io di mia virtude stanca . . . ch'i' cominciai come persona franca" ("As flowerets, by the nightly chillness . . . erect themselves all open on their stems . . . thus I did, with my fainting courage . . . that I began as one set free,"(*Inf*. II, 127-32).

The parallel that I wish to point out is this: Virgil is sent by Beatrice to go and save Dante,

> I' son Beatrice che ti faccio andare;
> vegno del loco ove tornar disio;
> amor mi mosse, che mi fa parlare,
>
> (Inf. II, 70-72)
>
> I am Beatrice who send thee; I come from a
> place where I desire to return; love moved
> me, that makes me speak,

as God, we are told, established Rome for the Holy Seat through which humanity was to be saved:

> La quale e 'l quale, a voler dir lo vero,
> fu stabilita per lo loco santo
> u' siede il successor del maggior Piero.
>
> (Inf. II, 22-24)
>
> Both these, to say the truth, were established for
> the holy place, where the Successor of the
> greatest Peter sits.

It is quite revealing that Dante should inform the reader, in one and the same canto, of these two facts: that by a special, particular miracle performed for Dante, Virgil is made to go by Beatrice, and that, by special divine guidance, Rome was established for the Holy Seat. The parallel, I believe, could not be more explicit: Beatrice "loda di Dio vera" ("true praise of God") allows Dante (through Virgil) to exercise the freedom of his choice to redeem himself just as Christ, "true Son of God," allowed mankind (through Rome) to do the very same. The encounter between Virgil and Dante on this Good Friday of the year 1300, before the commemoration of the Crucifixion, may be symbolical of the encounter between Rome and Judaism on the stage of history. An imaginary curtain should fall between the first and the second cantos of the prologue scene so that we might better understand that Dante, in the first canto, may be symbolical of mankind, enslaved by Original Sin, leading up to the time of Christ; whereas, in the second canto, he may be symbolical of mankind set free by Christ (the expression: "I began as one set free"—"cominciai come persona franca"—is unmistakably clear), and converted through Rome. This interpretation—I am happy to point out—has been accepted by such a severe critic as Montano, who says:

> Ciò non esclude che Virgilio sia anche la Ragione, anche l'Impero. Ma è prima di tutto lui stesso, colui che aveva inteso e cantato la missione divina di Roma; e al di là di questo, è l'incarnazione del passaggio storico di Cristo dal mondo dei Gentili a quello di Cristo (un volume recente di un mio bravo allievo, Antonio Mastrobuono, *Essays on Dante's Philosophy of History*, edito da Olschki, offre giuste indicazioni in proposito).[9]

This does not exclude that Virgil may also be Reason, also the Empire. But he is first of all himself, the one who had understood and sung the divine mission of Rome; and beyond this, he is the incarnation of the historical crossing from the world of the Gentiles to that of Christ (a recent book by my able pupil, Antonio Mastrobuono, *Essays on Dante's Philosophy of History*, offers correct interpretations on this point).

Virgil's prophecy of the Veltro—I would like to reiterate—is the unconscious prophecy of Christ in His First Advent, just as he had actually given one in his famous fourth *Eclogue*, which, throughout the Middle Ages, was indeed taken as such. "Lactantius and St. Augustine believed this"—says T. S. Eliot—"so did the entire medieval Church and Dante."[10] It should be stressed, however, that for Dante, Virgil's prophecy remains an unconscious one, whereas the Jews' is the conscious prophecy of Christ. For this reason the latter are found in Dante's Paradise, while the former (Virgil) is in Limbo "among those who are suspended" until the end of time when, perhaps, his final destiny will be judged.

At the top of the Mountain of Purgatory, after Dante has witnessed a series of tableaux symbolically depicting the major calamities that have befallen the Church ever since her inception, Beatrice gives the following prophecy:

> Non sarà tutto tempo sanza reda
> l'aguglia che lasciò le penne al carro,
> per che divenne mostro e poscia preda;
>   ch'io veggio certamente, e però il narro,
> a darne tempo già stelle propinque,
> secure d'ogn' intoppo e d'ogne sbarro,
>   nel quale un cinquecento diece e cinque,
> messo di Dio, anciderà la fuia
> con quel gigante che con lei delinque.
>
> (Purg. XXXIII, 37-45)
>
> Not for all time shall be without heir the Eagle
> that left the plumage on the car, whereby it
> became a monster and then a prey;
>   for of a surety I see, and therefore do tell it, stars
> already nigh, secure from all impediment and
> from all hindrance, that shall bring us times
>   wherein a five hundred ten and five, sent by God,
> shall slay the thief, with that giant who sins
> with her.

Three things of great significance should be noted here: first, the expected "five hundred ten and five" is a messenger of God, "messo di Dio"; second, he is an heir to the Eagle, that is, to the Roman Empire, which presumably suggests a temporal ruler; third, he shall slay the Harlot and the Giant who sins with her. By the Harlot what is meant of course is Pope Clement V, and the French monarch Philip the Fair is understood to be symbolized by the Giant, who in the preceding canto has untied the Chariot of the Church from the Tree of Knowledge of Good and Evil and has dragged it away into the woods, which obviously represents the removal of the Papal Seat from Rome to Avignon in 1305. These are the major elements of the prophecy that must necessarily and successfully be explained by anyone who attempts a serious interpretation of the passage.

In reference to the prophecies of the *Comedy*, the eminent scholar, Curtius, as we have already noted, maintains that we do not need to know who the Veltro or the "Cinquecento diece e cinque" might be in order to appreciate and understand Dante's poetry. I would like to reiterate that I do not entirely agree with this since I think that Dante's poetry and his vision of history, of which the prophecies are an integral element, cannot be so easily separated without running the risk of impoverishing the integrity of the poem as a work of art and of ideas. If Dante may be said to be one of the greatest poets of the Christian era, then it becomes imperative that we should at least attempt to find a plausible solution to the age-old problem of his vision of history that remains incomplete to this day. And, in truth, I am perplexed but happy to note that Curtius himself does not altogether disregard these prophecies when he says:

> The liberation of mankind from the she-wolf requires a process of redemption in which the *tre donne benedette* act together as did the three persons of the Trinity in the "first" redemption. The explanation is unsatisfactory in this form. But it is in the right direction: Beatrice can be understood only as a function within the theological system. To this system belong the three beasts which block Dante's road and which have always been interpreted as three vices. These beasts draw the Veltro after them, and later the Cinquecento diece e cinque. With this the theological system becomes a prophetic system. No amount of ingenuity has yet succeeded in unraveling it. But it is there. No one should deny it. It was Dante's central message. It concerns a prophecy whose fulfillment he expected in the immediate future. . . . Dante believed that he had an apocalyptic mission. This must be taken into consideration in interpreting him. . . . Dante's system is built up in the first two cantos of the *Inferno*, it supports the entire *Commedia*.[11]

Dante believed indeed that he had a prophetic mission, and yet the majority of scholars today still maintain that the "Cinquecento diece e cinque" is to be interpreted as a temporal leader. As Singleton says:

> The one who is to come will be God-sent and, as has been suggested, will be a temporal monarch. But the problem of the DXV (to put the five

hundred, ten, and five into Roman numerals, as is commonly done) remains one of the most debated in Dante studies. The reader will find the latest summary of the many different attempts at a solution in the *Enciclopedia dantesca*. Perhaps the conclusion of this article (by P. Mazzamuto) may be quoted here in full as the most comprehensive statement of the most accepted general understanding of this riddle.[12]

Pietro Mazzamuto concludes as follows:

> Everything, however, leads us to believe that according to the authoritative opinion and the valid arguments of Parodi, the DXV is Henry VII, that is, the heir of the eagle, the same "sublime eagle" of the letter to the princes (V, II); and that in making the prophecy, Dante has followed the cryptographic method used by St. John in the Apocalypse (13:18), where in the number 666 Nero is indicated, and the method was reinstated by medieval symbolism; and that he thus celebrated the happy coincidence between the hoped-for triumph of Henry VII in the near future and the advent of the sixth epoch of Christ (1315) prophesied by the sacred texts of the Middle Ages.[13]

Note that both Singleton and Mazzamuto refer to the prophecy in Roman numerals—DXV. This, we are told, is what has been commonly done.

We should ask, however: Where is it written, where does Dante say, or remotely suggest in the poem or in any of his other works, that we should translate the prophecy into Roman numerals? Dante has at no time, in fact, and in no place suggested that this should be done. How then did this trend start? If we go back in time, we find that the first ever to give a commentary on the *Purgatorio* was Jacopo della Lana who, according to Mazzamuto, gives the first exhaustive explanation of the prophecy: "Ne dà la prima esauriente spiegazione." The first commentators of *Purgatorio*, he says, understood at once the symbolical value of the prophecy and considered DXV as an anagram of DUX, thinking generically without any historical identification, about an army leader, an emperor, a prince, who would be sent by God to the aid of corrupted humanity. We read in fact:

> I primi commentatori del *Purgatorio* ne compresero subito il valore di simbolo e considerarono il DXV come l'anagramma di DUX, pensando genericamente, senza alcuna indicazione di figure storiche, a un condottiero, imperatore o principe, che sarebbe stato inviato da Dio in soccorso della traviata umanità.

In Jacopo della Lana's own words the DXV is a:

> modo poetico de descrivere lo nome dell'ofizio dello executore della iustizia de Deo. E fecelo per numeri, "Cinque cento" se scrive per D,

cinque per V se scrive, dexe se scrive per X; ponendo queste tre lettere insieme relevano DUX; e perché nel verso siano altramente ordenade, çoè in prima D, seconda X, terzio V, no c'è força: ché li è conceduto de licenzia poetica a trasportare cussì le dizioni.[14]

The following is a paraphrase of the above quotation:

poetic way for describing the name of the office of the executor of God's justice. And he (Dante) did it by numbers, "Cinque cento" is written for D, "cinque" for V is written, "dexe" is written for X; by placing these three letters together they make up DUX; and since in the verse they are differently ordered, that is to say, first D, second X, third V, this is not forced: because it is conceded by poetic license to thus transpose them.

Note the subtle ways of Jacopo della Lana. He has first of all arbitrarily assumed that Dante's words should be translated into Roman numerals. He has subsequently made a second assumption to transpose DXV into DUX, which, to his mind, Dante should have done (but did not do) since, as a poet, he was free to use poetic license. I find this singularly contrived. Della Lana is more than ready to forgive Dante's supposed poetic license, which, in turn, becomes the justification for his own license by means of which he will cast the prophecy into a mold that will last for over six hundred and fifty years.

A rapid perusal of some proposals advanced throughout the centuries will confirm as much. *DXV equals: Christ; DXV equals: Gratian-Distinction XV; DXV equals: judge; DXV equals: Antichrist; DXV equals: a captain; DXV equals: Can Grande; DXV equals: Henry VII; DXV equals: Dante; DXV equals: a pope; DXV equals: an era; DXV equals: 1315,* and so on. What all these proposals have in common is that they repeat Della Lana's arbitrary translation of the prophecy into Roman numerals. But one should not hasten to make such an assumption, because it has only led to external solutions to the problem. I am deeply convinced that if a conclusive answer is ever to be found it has to be suggested first of all by the internal evidence of the poem itself. Let us therefore write the prophecy once again in the exact way that was given by Beatrice: "Cinquecento diece e cinque."

What should be noted is the fact that the prophecy begins and ends with the word "cinque." This, I believe, constitutes an important clue to the enigma. Also, as Edward Moore has pointed out, there is only one rhyme ending in "-inque" in the entire *Comedy*, which should be considered of primary importance since the poem is made up of well over fourteen thousand verses, and rhymes invariably repeat themselves. Moore continues:

Further, if "DUX" were intended either exclusively or even primarily, why should not Dante have said, "Un cinquecento cinque e diece," which would be closer also to the vernacular form, and "diece" would be a much easier rhyme? Thus, in the *Divina Commedia*,—ece occurs in ten terzine, and—inque in only one, viz. in the present passage.[15]

As for a probable symbolical meaning of "cinque," we should first of all admit that to a modern, twentieth-century mentality, this word has absolutely no significance. But for Dante and his contemporaries things were very much different. And if we are ever to understand Dante, somehow we have to become, as much as possible, his contemporaries. We must make, as Montano is fond of saying, "an intellectual pilgrimage to the world of the author." To this end we should mention that Kaske has pointed out that there are associations between the number five and Christ: "Associations of the number 5 with Christ can be found, of course, in popular devotional concepts like the five wounds, the five points of the Cross, and the five letters of the name Jesus."[16] Note that Kaske considers the five wounds one of many "popular devotional concepts." I will endeavor to show instead that the five wounds are of fundamental importance in the Liturgy, Theology, and Art of Dante's age, since they are directly connected with Christ's Majestic Advent at the end of time.

Of all liturgical events, the Easter Vigil is universally considered to be the most important. It is during this night that the blessing of the Paschal Candle takes place, which, according to Herbert Thurston, is the most perfect specimen of Christian symbolism.[17] We should, at this point, take note that the liturgy is made up of words as well as action and that, for our purpose, of the two elements it is the action which is charged with symbolism: "The value of the liturgical words depends on the accuracy with which they reflect what is taking place and to what extent they express the faith and piety of the Church; in the liturgical action it is the symbolism which counts."[18] This element is of considerable significance, and I shall refer to it again. For now, we should mention that in Italy the blessing of the Paschal Candle was so important that in many churches there were, in front of the pulpit, immovably fixed candlesticks of marble or bronze specifically for this purpose.

> In some parts of Europe in the eleventh and twelfth centuries more especially in Italy, there was a practice of using splendidly illuminated manuscripts or rolls which contained the Exsultet alone and were displayed only on this one day in all the year. The deacon sang from the pulpit or ambo, beside which in many Italian churches the paschal candlestick of marble or bronze is immovably fixed. As the deacon proceeded in his chanting, he allowed the loose end of the roll to fall over the pulpit, so as to hang before the eyes of the faithful gathered below. From this practice the curious arrangement has resulted that all the illuminations in these rolls are drawn up-side down with respect to the text which they illustrate.[19]

What should also be mentioned is the fact that this candle was of massive proportions—it easily surpassed the height of an average man (fig. 1). Dante surely must have witnessed the blessing of this candle time and again with keen interest as to the symbolism involved. Something beautiful and moving, in fact, takes place. From the *Pontificale* we read that the great candle which is to be blessed is put in a candelabra in front of the altar, and that after the people and clergy have congregated there, the deacon comes and with a stylus carves a cross into the wax. He then inscribes "Alpha" and "Omega," presumably at the top and bottom of the cross, and the year from the Incarnation of the Lord in the four corners of the cross as it is still done (fig. 2). The *Pontificale* does not say where "Alpha" and "Omega" and the current year are to be inscribed. I assume the practice to be the same as today's.

Haec est consuetudo ecclesiae romanae. Sed, iuxta institutionem beati Zosimi papae, cereus magnus qui benedicendus est ponitur in candelabro ante altare et, clero et populo ibi prope congregato, venit diaconus qui benedicere debet cereum et cum stylo facit crucem in ipso cereo et A et Ω et annum ab incarnatione domini describit. Postmodum vero humiliter inclinatus ad sacerdotem veniens recipit ab ipso benedictionem et tunc surgens et conversus ad chorum dicit ter, vocem exaltando: Lumen Christi.[20]

Now comes what is of special interest to us: we are also told that the deacon will insert in that same candle five grains of incense in the fashion of a cross:

1

4   **2**   **5**

3

"Infigat firmiter in ipso cereo quinque grana incensi in modum crucis."[21] If we should now ask: what is the symbolical significance of the five grains of incense, the answer is supplied to us by Durandus, a contemporary of Dante, who says that they signify the five wounds received on the Cross: "Quinque grana significant quinque plagas in Cruce receptas."[22] As for medieval art and the probable connection between the number five and the theme of the Last Judgement, Emile Mâle says that the Apocalypse was not the only source of inspiration for the medieval artist. There were at least two more of equal importance. One was Matthew's Gospel (XXIV and XXV),[23] and the other was a very famous book by Honorius of Autun:

The most valuable work of this kind was written by Honorius of Autun at the beginning of the twelfth century, with the title, *Elucidarium*. The third book, a form of catechism, deals almost entirely with the end of the world and the judgement of God. Composed at a time when the artistic formula for the Last Judgement had not yet been evolved, it may have supplied the painters and sculptors with several features. The fame of this manual, which was early adopted by the schoolman and was accessible to laymen in a French translation, supports such a theory. A century later Vincent of Beauvais summarized medieval belief with regard to the second coming of Christ in the epilogue to his *Speculum Historiale*, and as a contemporary of the sculptors of the tympanums of Amiens and Reims he supplies the best commentary on their work. In the *Summa* Aquinas deals with this subject after his accustomed manner, and the few concrete statements which stand out from the bristling phalanx of his syllogisms are in entire agreement with accepted doctrine. And lastly, in the first chapter of the *Golden Legend*, Jacobus da Voragine testifies that at the end of the thirteenth century the Church's teaching had not varied. There is then throughout the Middle Ages a real consensus of opinion on all those circumstances which it was held would accompany the second coming of Christ, and with guides such as ours there is no risk of misunderstanding the artist's intentions."[24]

Mâle goes on to say that the thirteenth century understood the Last Judgement as a great drama precisely divisible into five acts. The first concerns the setting of the stage, so to speak; that is to say, the calamities foretold in the Apocalypse are realized. Second, at the appointed hour, at the very time of the Resurrection, the Judge will appear in the clouds, as Matthew says: "Then shall appear the sign of the Son of Man in Heaven; and then shall all the tribes of the earth mourn: and they shall see the Son of Man coming in the clouds of Heaven with great power and majesty."[25] But to the all-important question, (and here is our point of interest), "How will He be recognized?" the answer is simple: "By the five wounds suffered on the Cross." And this is the reason that most of the Last Judgement scenes depict Christ showing His wounds, as figures 3 through 6 attest.

Mâle comments: "With a fine gesture He lifts his wounded hands, and through the open garment is seen the wound in His side. One feels that He has not yet spoken to the world, and the fateful silence is terrible."[26] But in medieval art, just as in the liturgy, an action, a gesture is always charged with symbolism. This question then naturally comes to mind: "What is the significance of this gesture?" "He shows His wounds to bear witness to the truth of the gospel and to prove that He was in truth crucified for us."[27] "His scars show His mercy, for they recall His willing sacrifice, and they justify His anger by reminding us that all men are not willing to profit by that sacrifice."[28] "His wounds prove His power, for they testify that He has triumphed over death."[29] And Mâle concludes, "Thus by this gesture Christ proclaims that He is Redeemer, Judge, and living God."[30]

So far we have been trying to establish that the word "cinque" may be an important, probable clue to Beatrice's prophecy. But a clue, by itself, is clearly not enough to solve this powerful enigma. Much more is needed. In fact, what is demanded is actually a key that would unlock the whole meaning of the prophecy. I now propose, therefore, that such a key does in fact exist, and that I believe it may be constituted by nothing less than the most basic of human acts—the act of knowledge. And to see how this may be so we should now return to Dante's poem and let the text itself guide us in the search for a new solution.

The canto in question opens as follows:

> "Deus, venerunt gentes," alternando
> or tre or quattro dolce salmodia,
> le donne incominciaro, e lagrimando.
>
> *(Purg.* XXXIII, 1-3)
>
> "Deus, vererunt gentes": now three, now four,
> alternately and weeping, a sweet psalmody the
> ladies began."

"Le donne" are, of course, the seven virtues: four cardinal (Prudence, Justice, Fortitude, Temperance) and three theological (Faith, Hope, Charity), and they are weeping and chanting alternately now three, now four, a sweet psalmody. The psalm they are chanting is of special significance and it begins as follows: "O God, the heathen are come into thine inheritance; thy holy temple have they defiled, they have laid Jerusalem on heaps" (Psalm 79). This psalm is particularly significant because it is recognized as one of the psalms written during the sack of Jerusalem by Nabuchodonosor.[31] The maidens are weeping and chanting because of what has just taken place: the Giant (the French monarch) has unbound the Chariot of the Church from the Tree of Knowledge, and along with the Harlot (Clement V, the Papal Curia) has dragged it into the woods. The analogy that Dante is establishing could not be more explicit: the Papal captivity of Avignon is analogous to the Babylonian captivity of the Jews. This, for Dante, is clearly an event of great calamity since he firmly believed that the Church was charged with the task of guiding mankind to its ultimate destiny. Dante must have felt himself to be standing at a crucial point in time and, without a doubt, to have been invested with a universal mission of helping mankind, as is unmistakably conveyed by Beatrice's words when she says:

> "Però, in pro del mondo che mal vive,
> al carro tieni or li occhi, e quel che vedi,
> ritornato di là, fa che tu scrive."
>
> *(Purg.* XXXII, 103-5)

> "Therefore to profit the world that liveth ill, fix
> now thine eyes upon the car, and look that thou
> write what thou seest, when returned yonder."

But there is more. While the seven virtues are chanting the above psalm, we are told that Beatrice is listening to them with a pious sigh resembling Mary at the Cross: "quelle ascoltava sì fatta, che poco / più a la croce si cambiò Maria" ("was hearkening to them so altered, that little / more did Mary change at the Cross" (*Purg.* XXXIII, 5-6). Then as the Maidens allow her to speak ("dier loco / a lei di dir"), Beatrice gets up on her feet and with her face "colorata come foco" ("in hue of fire") speaks to them with the very same words that Christ spoke to his disciples before His Crucifixion: "A little while and ye shall not see me; and again, a little while and ye shall see me, because I go to the Father" (John XVI, 16):

> "*Modicum, et non videbitis me*;
> *et iterum*, sorelle mie dilette,
> *modicum, et vos videbitis me*."
>
> (*Purg.* XXXIII, 10-12)

These are the mysterious words the disciples had so much trouble understanding. It was a promise of return, as Christ assured them: "But I shall see you again; then your hearts will rejoice with a joy no one can take from you. On that day you will have no questions to ask me. I give you my assurance . . ." (John XVI: 22-23).

But why, we might ask, is Beatrice addressing the Maidens with the words that Christ spoke when He wanted to instruct the disciples about His return? Is the day of Christ's return close at hand? Did Dante somehow believe in an imminent end of time? An affirmative answer to this last question cannot be given without this further, most important consideration: we are told by Beatrice that during the entire history of mankind, the Mystic Tree has been defiled only two times: once by Adam at the beginning of history and now by the Giant who has dragged the Chariot of the Church into the woods. Beatrice's words are exacting. Right after the prophecy she tells Dante to note her words and refer them to the living just as she has given them to him. Then, with rigor even more stringent, she admonishes Dante to bear in mind, when he so writes them, not to conceal the fact of how he has seen the Tree twice despoiled:

> "Tu nota; e sì come da me son porte,
> così queste parole segna a' vivi
> del viver ch'è un correre a la morte.
> E aggi a mente, quando tu le scrivi,

di non celar qual hai vista la pianta
ch'è or due volte dirubata quivi."

(Purg. XXXIII, 52-57)

"Note thou; and even as these words from me are
borne, so do thou signify them to those who
live that life which is a race unto death;
    and bear in mind when thou writest them, not to
conceal how thou hast seen the tree which
now twice hath been despoiled here."

Life is a running unto death ("del viver ch'è un correre a la morte"), as history is a running unto the Final Judgement. This further analogy is conveyed to us if we consider that Beatrice, immediately preceding the prophecy, refers to the corrupted Church with words echoing the Apocalypse: "The beast you saw was, and is not" (Revelation XVII: 8):

"Sappi che 'l vaso che 'l serpente ruppe,
fu e non è; ma chi n'ha colpa, creda
che vendetta di Dio non teme suppe."

(Purg. XXXIII, 34-36)

"Know that the vessel which the serpent broke,
was, and is not; but let him whose fault it is,
believe that God's vengeance fears no sops."

A judgement from God is clearly expected here. All these considerations are, of course, important, but only inasmuch as they serve to establish a thematic pattern to Beatrice's prophecy. By themselves they do not solve the enigma. And, in this connection, we shall now introduce some other fundamental elements that, hopefully, will in turn help us in formulating a new solution. Immediately following the prophecy, Beatrice, conscious that her words may be as obscure to Dante as the famous riddles of Themis and the Sphinx, assures him that soon the facts shall be the Naiads that will solve this powerful enigma without loss of flocks or of harvest:

"E forse che la mia narrazion buia,
qual Temi e Sfinge, men ti persuade,
perch' a lor modo lo 'ntelletto attuia;
    ma tosto fier li fatti le Naiade,
che solveranno questo enigma forte
sanza danno di pecore o di biade."

(Purg. XXXIII, 46-51)

"And perchance my prophecy, obscure as Themis
and Sphinx, doth less persuade thee, because
after their fashion it darkens thy mind;

> but soon the fact shall be that the Naiades will
> solve this hard riddle without loss of flocks
> or of corn."

According to most commentators, the word "Naiades" stands for "Laiades," that is to say, Oedipus, son of Laius, who solved the riddle of the Sphinx. Dante evidently read the passage in a faulty text. The meaning would therefore be the following: soon the facts will be the guessers that will solve this powerful enigma. C. H. Grandgent comments as follows:

> To emphasize the mysteriousness of his prediction, Dante compares it to the utterances of the goddess Themis, whose obscure oracle is recorded in *Met.*, I, 377-94, and to the riddle of the bloodthirsty Theban Sphinx, finally guessed by Oedipus (*Met.*, VII, 759-61; *Thebaid*, I 66-67). Dark though his words may be, he adds, the events shall ere long solve the problem—even as Oedipus, the son of Laius, unraveled the Sphinx's puzzle. Ovid, in *Met.*, VII, 759-60, relates that this son of Laius had cleared up the riddles which had never been understood before: "Carmina Laiades non intellecta priorum Solverat ingeniis" ("Oedipus, the son of Laius, had solved the riddle which had been inscrutable to the understanding of all before"). Dante, however, evidently read the passage in a faulty text, which substituted Naides for Laiades and solvunt for solverat, and was thus led to believe that Naiads, or water-nymphs, were the successful guessers. Therefore, instead of saying, "the events shall be the Oedipus (or Laiades) that shall explain the mystery," he puts it: "The facts shall soon be the Naiads that shall solve this hard enigma."[32]

This question should now be asked: What are the facts that will solve this powerful enigma? Are they to be understood as historical events, as Grandgent has suggested, or is there another more probable meaning we should be searching for? The answer to this question will be apparent later, only after we introduce one more most important element. For now, what we can say with complete confidence is that Dante is informing the reader that there are facts, whatever they may be, which will indeed solve the enigma without loss, we are told, of flocks or of harvest. This last particular is also important as we shall see later. From this point onward, however, it will be necessary to keep a line-by-line account of Beatrice's words so that we may follow the inner concatenation of her thoughts. For this reason we shall start again from her already quoted admonition to Dante:

> "Tu nota; e sì come da me son porte,
> così queste parole segna a' vivi
> del viver ch'è un correre a la morte."
>
> (*Purg.* XXXIII, 52-54)

What is of paramount importance here is that Beatrice is asking Dante to refer her words to the living just as she has given them to him, and to keep in mind, when he so writes them, not to hide what he has seen of the Tree that has been twice despoiled here:

> "E aggi a mente, quando tu le scrivi,
> di non celar qual hai vista la pianta
> ch'è or due volte dirubata quivi."
>
> (*Purg.* XXXIII, 55-57)

Whoever robs or rends the Tree with blasphemy of act offends God, who has created it holy for His own use:

> "Qualunque ruba quella o quella schianta,
> con bestemmia di fatto offende a Dio,
> che solo a l'uso suo la creò santa."
>
> (*Purg.* XXXIII, 58-60)

The first soul (Adam), for having eaten of that Tree, had to spend more than five thousand years in pain and in desire, longing for Christ:

> "Per morder quella, in pena e in disio
> cinquemilia anni e più l'anima prima
> bramò colui che 'l morso in sé punio."
>
> (*Purg.* XXXIII, 61-63)

Dante's wit is sleeping if he does not understand that the Tree has a special reason for being thus lofty and inverted at its top:

> "Dorme lo 'ngegno tuo, se non estima
> per singular cagione essere eccelsa
> lei tanto e sì travolta ne la cima."
>
> (*Purg.* XXXIII, 64-66)

And if Dante's thoughts had not been like Elsan waters about his mind (which waters have the virtue of quickly encrusting objects that fall into it), and their pleasantness as Pyramus to the mulberry, by so many circumstances alone Dante would recognize God's justice in the ban:

> "E se stati non fossero acqua d'Elsa
> li pensier vani intorno a la tua mente,
> e 'l piacer loro un Piramo a la gelsa,
> per tante circostanze solamente

> la giustizia di Dio, ne l'interdetto,
> conosceresti a l'arbor moralmente."
>
> (*Purg.* XXXIII, 67-72)

But since Beatrice sees Dante's intellect turned to stone and stonelike, such in hue that the light of her word dazes him:

> "Ma, perch' io veggio te ne lo 'ntelletto
> fatto di pietra e, impetrato, tinto,
> sì che t'abbaglia il lume del mio detto,"
>
> (*Purg.* XXXIII, 73-75)

she concludes:

> "voglio anco, e se non scritto, almen dipinto,
> che 'l te ne porti dentro a te per quello
> che si reca il bordon di palma cinto."
>
> (*Purg.* XXXIII, 76-78)
>
> "I also will that thou bear it away within thee,
> and if not written at least outlined, for the
> reason that the pilgrim's staff is brought back
> wreathed with palm."

"And I"—Dante finally responds—"Even as wax under the seal that does not change the imprinted figure, my brain is now stamped by you":

> E io: "Sì come cera da suggello,
> che la figura impressa non trasmuta,
> segnato è or da voi lo mio cervello."
>
> (*Purg.* XXXIII, 79-81)

This—I would like to propose—is the very key that will unlock the meaning of the "powerful enigma." The analogy could not be more revealing: Dante's brain is stamped by Beatrice's words as a piece of wax is stamped by a seal. In both cases an impression has been formed, and we shall be able to discover the true identity of Beatrice's prophecy only if we succeed in unveiling the imprint that she has left on Dante's brain. There is nothing mysterious about this. If we proceed methodically we shall see that there is a profound significance involved here. We must therefore ask: what is the origin of this image, and more important, what exactly does it mean? To answer the first part of the question, let it be said at once that the image may be traced back to Aristotle's *De anima* and, most important, the meaning of the image is intimately connected with the most basic of human acts—that is to say—the act of knowledge. In order to see how this may be so, let us first of all read the following passage from Aristotle's *De anima*:

> By a "sense" is meant what has the power of receiving into itself the sensible forms of things without the matter. This must be conceived of as taking place in the way in which a piece of wax takes on the impress of a signet ring without the iron or gold.[33]

It should be clear by now that the image in Dante and the one in Aristotle are one and the same. Before we attempt a full explanation, however, we might do well to point out that Dante was, of course, thoroughly familiar with Aristotle's *De anima*. More specifically, we find in the *Convivio* that Dante is quoting Book 2 of the *De anima* precisely where the image occurs:

> Dove è da sapere che, propriamente, è visibile lo colore e la luce, sì come Aristotele vuole nel secondo de *l'Anima* e nel libro del *Senso* e *Sensato*. . . . Ma colore e la luce sono propriamente, perché solo col viso comprendiamo ciò, e non con altro senso. Queste cose visibili, sì le proprie come le comuni, in quanto sono visibili, vengono dentro a l'occhio—non dico le cose, ma le forme loro—per lo mezzo (dia)fano, non realmente ma intenzionalmente, sì quasi come in vetro trasparente.[34]

From the above, we might say that Dante is discussing the very same problem, the problem of sense knowledge. Note especially the following: Dante says that visible things ("cose visibili") come into our eye ("vengono dentro a l'occhio"). Then, more exacting: "And I don't say the things themselves" ("non dico le cose"), "but their form" ("ma le forme loro"), "not actually" ("non realmente"), "but intentionally" ("ma intenzionalmente"). This is essentially the meaning of Aristotle's image of the wax and the seal.

But in order to fully appreciate the importance of Dante's position, it should be emphasized that philosophers all through the ages have given many and varied answers to the problem of how man acquires knowledge of the physical world. Dante, as we shall see shortly, has probed the problem even in the *Comedy*. For him, however, it was mainly a question of choosing between the theory of knowledge of Plato and that of Aristotle. And he, along with St. Thomas and many others, explicitly sided with Aristotle:

> Veramente Plato e altri filosofi dissero che'l nostro vedere non era perché lo visibile venisse a l'occhio, ma perché la virtù visiva andava fuori al visibile; e questa oppinione è riprovata per falsa dal Filosofo in quello del *Senso* e *Sensato*.[35]

Now what exactly is the difference between these two great philosophers? Plato maintained that man possesses innate knowledge. For him, therefore, knowing was a kind of remembering, as Etienne Gilson remarks:

The basic problem, the solution of which dominates all subsequent conclusions, is to know how the human intellect knows corporeal substances lower than itself. Plato teaches that the human soul has natural, innate knowledge of all things. No one, he says, can give the right answer about things he does not know. But a man in complete ignorance will always give the right answer to questions put to him, provided they are asked according to a proper method. This we find in the *Meno*. Therefore, everyone possesses knowledge of things even before acquiring science of them. This amounts to asserting that the soul knows all things, including bodies, by innate species that are in it by nature.[36]

To use Dante's own expression—"la virtù visiva andava fuori al visibile"—we might say that as far as Plato is concerned it may even be said that "we go to things," so to speak. A second approach is put forward by Democritus who maintains, on the contrary, that "things come to us" with their materiality. Again in the words of Gilson:

Opposed to Plato, who has the intellect directly participating in separate intelligible forms, we find Democritus who assigns no other cause to our knowledge than the presence within the soul of the image of the bodies about which we are thinking. According to Democritus, all action can be reduced to the influx of material atoms passing from one body to another. He imagines that little images are issuing from objects and penetrating into the matter of our soul.[37]

There is finally a middle approach offered by Aristotle, who resolves the problem by positing an agent intellect capable (by abstraction) of extracting the intelligible from the sensible:

But we know that the human soul has one operation in which the body does not share; namely, the intellectual operation. It is clearly impossible that corporeal matter should succeed in impressing its mark upon an incorporeal substance like an intellect and modifying it. Merely the impression of sensible bodies could never produce an operation like intellectual knowledge, and is not enough to explain it. We must appeal to some nobler principle of operation without however turning to the separated intelligibles of Plato. This is what we come to if we take the middle trail which Aristotle blazed between Democritus and Plato; that is, we posit an agent intellect capable of extracting the intelligible from the sensible by means of an abstraction whose nature we shall now analyze in some detail.[38]

We are now in a better position to appreciate Aristotle's image of the wax and the seal. Against Democritus, he maintains that things come to us denuded of their materiality. Against Plato's thesis of innate knowledge, he maintains that the mind is like an empty blackboard: "What it thinks must be in it just as characters may be said to be on a writing tablet on which as yet nothing actually stands written: this is exactly what happens with mind."[39] For Aristotle, there is sense knowledge and intellectual knowledge. The object of sense is particulars; the object of intellect is universals: "The ground of this difference is that what actual sensation apprehends is individuals, while that which knowledge apprehends is universals, and these are in a sense within the soul."[40] Aristotle insists that there is nothing in the mind that has not first passed through the senses, and that when the mind is aware of anything it is so by virtue of an image from which the universal is then abstracted:

Hence (1) no one can learn or understand anything in the absence of sense, and (2) when the mind is actively aware of anything it is necessarily aware of it along with an image; for images are like sensuous contents except that they contain no matter.[41]

It should be added that, above and beyond the five external senses, there are also internal powers such as "common sense," which distinguishes and unites the data of the special senses, and "imagination" or "fantasy," which is the power that preserves in us the images or phantasms of things existing outside of us. What we know is the thing. The image is that by which we know. What is important however (and this is a point directly connected with Dante's problem of the powerful enigma), is to keep in mind that at the level of imagination we are still dealing with knowledge of particulars rather than universals:

The same is true of the imagination, in which phantasms reside. But it is not the same when it comes to the possible intellect. As intellect, it receives universal species. The imagination, on the contrary, contains only particular species.[42]

As we now go back to Dante let us first turn our attention to some key passages of the *Comedy*, which further confirm to us that our poet was specifically acquainted with Aristotle's theory of knowledge. We shall then endeavor to illustrate how this theory may be integrally related to Beatrice's prophecy.

The first of these passages occurs in the *Purgatorio*, where Virgil is attempting to define the nature of love. Since to love a thing requires, first of all, that the thing be known, the problem of love viewed philosophically (as an attraction rather than a theological virtue) is found to be interrelated to the problem of knowledge. Your apprehensive faculty, says Virgil, draws an image from the real object, and unfolds it within you, so that it makes the mind turn to it:

"Vostra apprensiva da esser verace
tragge intenzione, e dentro a voi la spiega,
sì che l'animo ad essa volger face."

(Purg. XVIII, 22-24)

In the *Paradiso*, Beatrice explains to Dante that although the world beyond is a metaphysical place, it is presented to him in concrete terms as if it were a physical one because that is the only way he would understand it. This is so because he is there with his live body, and a human being can only learn through his body. Thus, she says, must we needs speak to your faculty, because it is only from the object of sense that it apprehends that which it then proceeds to make fit matter for the intellect:

"Così parlar coviensi al vostro ingegno,
però che solo da sensato apprende
ciò che fa poscia d'intelletto degno."

(Par. IV, 40-42)

After this brief perusal of the problem of knowledge, let us now return to Canto XXXIII. Here Beatrice, having already given the prophecy, and seeing that Dante's intellect (note the emphasis on the intellect) has turned to stone, so much so that the light of her words dazes him, finds necessary to make of Dante this most unusual request. She says: "And I would also want that you bear it away within you, if not written, at least depicted—for the reason that the pilgrim's staff is brought back wreathed with palm":

"Ma perch' io veggio te ne lo 'ntelletto
fatto di pietra e, impetrato, tinto,
sì che t'abbaglia il lume del mio detto,
     voglio anco, e se non scritto, almen dipinto,
che 'l te ne porti dentro a te per quello
che si reca il bordon di palma cinto."

(Purg. XXXIII, 73-78)

It should first of all be noted that the word "anco" (also) serves to add something to what has already been said. Accordingly, Natalino Sapegno has suggested that Beatrice is asking Dante to bear within himself, "almost in figures" ("quasi in figure"), all that he has heard from her:

> Voglio tuttavia che tu porti dentro di te il mio *detto*, se non proprio scolpito (*scritto*) nella mente in nitidi e comprensibili caratteri, almeno adombrato (*dipinto*)—quasi in figure e in geroglifici,—come un ricordo e un segno del viaggio che hai compiuto; per la stessa ragione (*per quello*), per cui il pellegrino reduce dalla Terrasanta porta a casa il bordone ornato di fronde di palma.[43]

A second interpretation is given by Singleton, who maintains instead that Beatrice is asking Dante to bear within himself all that he has seen. "This clearly refers to all that you have been shown here."[44]

I would like to suggest that neither of these interpretations is entirely acceptable. These two critics seem to be divided between the sense of hearing and the sense of sight. Sapegno's position may even be said to contradict the text. His contention is that the expression "if not written, at least depicted" refers to everything that Beatrice has said. This cannot be if we consider that twenty-four lines earlier Beatrice has specifically instructed Dante to note well her words so that he may refer them to the living exactly as she has given them to him.

> "Tu nota; e sì come da me son porte,
> così queste parole segna a' vivi
> del viver ch'è un correre a la morte."
>
> (*Purg.* XXXIII, 52-54)

We can safely say from the above that Beatrice does not wish that Dante should bear within himself figures of everything she says. As we have already noted, the exact words that the Pilgrim is asked to refer to the living have to do with how the Mystic Tree has been despoiled twice: once by Adam, and a second time by the Giant (the French monarch) who has dragged the Chariot of the Church into the woods, that is, the "Babylonian Captivity of the Papacy." Also, we should further note that if Beatrice were referring to all her words ("queste parole," as she says in verse 53), she would have said, "se non scritte, almen dipinte," feminine plural. Instead she says: "se non scritto, almen dipinto," masculine singular.

As for Singleton's argument, we should recall that Dante is a follower of Aristotle's, and as such he knows very well from the philosopher's theory of sense knowledge that we naturally carry within ourselves impressed images of what we see. This being the case, how could Beatrice request of the Pilgrim to perform an operation that occurs naturally in the first place? It simply cannot be.

It is a fact, however, that Beatrice is actually requesting that Dante should bear within himself a figure of "something." It is also clear that whatever may be involved will have to extend over and beyond what has already taken place, as "I also wish" ("voglio anco") unmistakably confirms. The question is, what is she referring to? I would suggest that a very specific "something" of which she has already spoken must be the crucial point here. This will be apparent if we consider that immediately preceding the terzina of "Tu nota . . . queste parole" (vv. 52-54), and immediately following the terzina of "un cinquecento diece e cinque" (vv. 43-45), in the intervening, symmetrically placed two terzine (vv. 46-51), Beatrice gives the following, most revealing information: "And perhaps my prophecy (narration), obscure as

Themis and Sphinx, persuades you less because, after their fashion, it darkens your mind; but soon the facts shall be the Naiads that will solve this hard enigma without loss of flocks or of harvest":[45]

> "E forse che la mia narrazion buia,
> qual Temi e Sfinge, men ti persuade,
> perch' a lor modo lo 'ntelletto attuia;
>   ma tosto fier li fatti le Naiade,
> che solveranno questo enigma forte,
> sanza danno di pecore o di biade."
>
> (*Purg.* XXXIII, 46-51)

The power of precision of these terzine and the unbroken line of Dante's concatenation of thought are of considerable help here. If we focus our attention on the expression "I also wish, and if not written, at least depicted" (v. 76), we realize that it cannot refer to anything following "Tu nota . . . queste parole" (v. 52), because Beatrice wants Dante to pass on these words to the living exactly as she has spoken them. By necessity the expression will have to refer to something before line 52. I would therefore suggest that it be taken as a direct reference to the "enigma forte" of line 49. In this connection it should be noted that the word "enigma" is of Greek derivation, and as such it constitutes an exception to the rule—it is a "masculine singular" rather than "feminine singular." The direct object pronoun of the line "che 'l te ne porti dentro"—"that you bear it within you,"(v. 77) is also a masculine singular, and the same is true of the past participles "scritto" ("written") and "dipinto" ("depicted"). Quite simply then we can say that Beatrice is asking Dante to bear within himself a visual image of the prophecy, "un cinquecento diece e cinque." The prophecy would have to be translated into a figure rather than Roman numerals as has traditionally been done. But how can this be done? Note well that Dante is being asked to translate what he has received through the sense of hearing into what can be retained only when received through the sense of sight. This is clearly impossible. A visual image of a sound is not within the natural order of things. Yet Beatrice insists that soon the facts shall be the Naiads (the guessers) that will solve this powerful enigma.

It would seem that the problem is not impossible to solve after all. There is, in fact, a special way that will enable the Pilgrim, Dante, to translate sounds into a figure; this is the way of analogy. What is required, however, is that Beatrice herself has to furnish the terms of the analogy, and the Pilgrim, by an act of the imagination will have to recall these terms as vividly present. These terms are none other than the facts that will solve the powerful enigma. Moreover, it should be remembered that in Aristotle's theory of knowledge, facts are particulars that become objects of sense knowledge. We are here at the level of "things seen." We therefore ask: what are these facts?

Let us quote Beatrice's request in its entirety. She says: "I also wish that you bear it within you, and if not written, at least depicted, for the reason that the pilgrim's staff is brought back wreathed with palm":

> "Voglio anco, e se non scritto, almen dipinto,
> che 'l te ne porti dentro a te per quello
> che si reca il bordon di palma cinto."
>
> (*Purg.* XXXIII, 76-78)

It should be clear by now that the facts may be constituted by the "pilgrim" and the "staff wreathed with palm." The unique importance of these facts, however, is not readily apparent. What is required is that we should focus our attention on the effects that they cause, and when this is done we realize at once that they have been charged with a very special significance. The direct effect of what takes place is that upon hearing these words, Dante's brain is immediately stamped by Beatrice's voice as a piece of wax is stamped by a seal. As he says: "And I: 'Even as wax under the seal, that does not change the imprinted figure, my brain is now stamped by you.' "

> E io: "Sì come cera da suggello,
> che la figura impressa non trasmuta,
> segnato è or da voi lo mio cervello."
>
> (*Purg.* XXXIII, 79-81)

And if we now recall that the image of the wax and the seal is of central importance in Aristotle's theory of knowledge, we should not fail to realize that an act of knowledge has taken place. Dante has learned something from Beatrice in much the same way that a student learns from his teacher—by instruction rather than by direct experience. The following passage from St. Thomas's theory of knowledge will further elucidate how Dante has been instructed by Beatrice:

> Now sense, imagination and the other powers belonging to the sensitive part make use of a corporeal organ. Therefore it is clear that for the intellect to understand actually, not only when it acquires new knowledge, but also when it uses knowledge already acquired, there is need for the act of the imagination and of the other powers. For when the act of the imagination is hindered by a lesion of the corporeal organ, for instance, in a case of frenzy, or when the act of the memory is hindered, as in the case of lethargy, we see that a man is hindered from understanding actually even those things of which he had a previous knowledge. Secondly, anyone can experience this of himself, that when he tries to understand something, he forms certain phantasms to serve him by way of examples, in which as it were he examines what he is desirous of understanding.

For this reason it is that when we wish to help someone to understand something, we lay examples before him, from which he can form phantasms for the purpose of understanding.[46]

It can be said at this time that Dante's brain has been imprinted with an image that might help him solve the prophecy. He has acquired this new knowledge by an act of his imagination. This means that, for a successful communication to have taken place between Beatrice and Dante, what is presupposed is for Dante to have had a vivid recollection of a past experience, of someone he has actually seen, that is to say, of having seen a pilgrim carrying a staff wreathed with palm.

We should therefore ask: what kind of a pilgrim is here indicated, and why is he charged with such unique significance? Luckily for us, Dante has spoken of these pilgrims in the *Vita nuova*, where he calls them "palmieri" (palmers) because they go beyond the sea to the Holy Land and often come back carrying a palm as a sign that they have been there:

> E però è da sapere che in tre modi si chiamano propriamente le genti che vanno al servigio de l'Altissimo: chiamansi palmieri in quanto vanno oltremare, la onde molte volte recano la palma (*Vita nuova*, chap. 60).

"Palmieri," Dante says, "are people who go to the service of the Most High." Dante is making a pilgrimage in the world beyond; he too is a pilgrim in the service of the Most High. This is explicitly revealed for the first time on the shore of Purgatory when Virgil, in answer to the spirits who inquire about the way to the Mountain, says, "Noi siam peregrin come voi siete" ("We are pilgrims even as you are," *Purg.* II, 63). The analogy is now complete. Beatrice also wishes that Dante should carry impressed on his brain an image pertaining to the prophecy as a confirmation to the living of his pilgrimage in the world beyond, just as a "palmiere" comes back from his pilgrimage to the Holy Land carrying a palm as a confirmation that he has been there. But the Pilgrim, as we shall see, does not know the meaning of the prophecy. It would seem therefore that the problem of solving the enigma is a task that falls on the reader.

But the question, however, still remains: what specifically constitutes this image? Before we attempt an answer to this question, let us first of all premise that Dante, the Pilgrim, is an analogue of all of us; he is symbolical of humanity. If, then, he has on his brain an image of something, we too can have one. What is required on our part is to have had a direct experience of actually seeing a pilgrim coming back from the Holy Land carrying a palm. For us to have within ourselves an image of anything, the thing itself must be, or must have been at least once, actually present to our senses. This is the requirement imposed by Aristotle's theory of knowledge and the famed image of the wax and the seal. But we have never seen such a pilgrim. The next best remedy would therefore be to have a painting or a description of such a pilgrim that would help us form an image of him. In other words, we need to know what the pilgrim looked like. And once again we are lucky in having the following description:

> Christian pilgrims had free access to the holy places; a pilgrimage to Palestine had long been a form of devotion or penance; everywhere in Europe one met "palmers" who, as a sign of pilgrimage accomplished, wore crossed palm leaves from Palestine; such men, said Piers Plowman, "had leave to lie all their lives thereafter."[47]

Now, if we turn to Dante's pilgrim carrying a staff wreathed with palm, and are mindful that, as a sign of pilgrimage accomplished, palmers everywhere in Europe wore crossed palm leaves, we should at once feel justified in proposing that, with a very high degree of probability, the palm on the staff was either shaped into a cross, or formed a cross with the staff. The central fact to be kept in mind is that Dante's brain is immediately stamped by Beatrice's voice as she mentions the pilgrim. In the line: "segnato è or da voi lo mio cervello" ("my brain is now stamped by you"), the emphasis is on "now." Dante has received the prophecy through the sense of hearing. Beatrice later asks that Dante should carry this powerful enigma within himself. Dante, the protagonist, has never seen the prophecy written out in letters the way we readers see it. He could, however, rely on his power of imagination in order to recall scattered instances of past experiences, that is to say, of actually having seen those numbers written out (not necessarily in that sequence, of course) at various times and places. This is indeed within the order of possibility. But this is clearly not what Beatrice wants of him. She is most exacting on this point. She does not wish that Dante should carry within himself a visual image of those numbers written out because, quite simply, she is aware that the numbers by themselves are utterly meaningless. In order to confer intelligibility to the prophecy, Beatrice has only one way open to her, the way of analogy. What is necessarily required is that she should lead Dante's mind into a train of thought whereby he can successfully translate the words "un cinquecento diece e cinque" into a self-evident, intelligible figure. And, in fact, she does this when she says that he should carry the enigma within himself, "if not written, at least depicted," just as—analogically—the pilgrim, on his return from the Holy Land, brings back his staff wreathed with palm. The staff and the palm, as we have suggested, were shaped into a cross, and the very same, I propose, can be done with the prophecy, since, in both cases, the figure is a sign of a pilgrimage accomplished.

But the Pilgrim, as already noted, does not know the meaning of the prophecy. This becomes clear when we consider that immediately following the words, "my brain is now stamped by you" (v. 81), Dante, in verse 82, asks the following, most revealing question: "But why doth your longed-for word soar so far beyond my sight, that the more it straineth the more it loses it?":

"Ma perché tanto sovra mia veduta
vostra parola disïata vola,
che più la perde quanto più s'aiuta."

(*Purg.* XXXIII, 82-84)

Beatrice's answer to this question stands in need of a full explanation. "That thou mayst know"—she says—"that school which thou hast followed, and see how its teaching can keep pace with my word":

"Perché cognoschi," disse, "quella scuola
c'hai seguitata, e veggi sua dottrina
come può seguitar la mia parola."

(*Purg.* XXXIII, 85-87)

"And"—she adds—"mayst see thy way so far distant from the divine way, as the heaven which highest speeds is removed from earth":

"E veggi vostra via da la divina
distar cotanto, quanto si discorda
da terra il ciel che più alto festina."

(*Purg.* XXXIII, 88-90)

The specific school that Dante may have followed, and for which he is now reproached, need not enter into our argument at present. What is important to consider is the fact that the school was a human school and, more important, that the human way of knowing is infinitely different from the divine way of knowing.

We would do well to inquire at this time as to the specific difference between these two ways of knowing. We should preface by pointing out that we are not real to God and neither is the universe. What is real to God is only Himself; more specifically, the three Persons of the Trinity are real to each other:

But when something proceeds from a principle of the same nature, then both the one proceeding and the source of procession communicate in the same order; and then they have real relations to each other. Therefore, as the divine processions are in the identity of the same nature, as was above explained, these relations, which are according to the divine processions, are necessarily real relations.[48]

We are ideas of God in much the same way that the "Six Characters in Search of an Author" are ideas of Pirandello. We say that the characters are children of Pirandello's mind and his relationship to them is necessarily one of idea—they are not real to him in the same way that his flesh and blood children are real to him. Similarly, we are like a play that God is writing:

Since, therefore, God is outside the whole order of creation, and all creatures are ordered to Him, and not conversely, it is manifest that creatures are really related to God Himself; whereas in God there is not real relation to creatures, but a relation only in idea, inasmuch as creatures are related to Him.[49]

We may conclude therefore that God knows us and the universe as His own ideas:

Ideas are exemplars existing in the divine mind, as is clear from Augustine. But God has the proper exemplars of all the things that He knows; and therefore He has ideas of all things known by Him.[50]

It can be further said that God's knowledge is the cause of anything that is:

Now it is manifest that God causes things by His intellect, since His being is His act of understanding; and hence His knowledge must be the cause of things, in so far as His will is joined to it. Hence the knowledge of God as the cause of things is usually called the *knowledge of approbation*.[51]

Conversely, in so far as man is concerned, the universe and God are very real to him. The human way of knowing must therefore be infinitely different from the divine way, as Beatrice has just proclaimed. In fact, man (Dante) acquires knowledge of the universe and God through a gradual process of abstraction of which there are three definite degrees.

In the first degree, the mind considers objects that cannot exist without matter, nor can they be conceived without it. An oak tree obviously cannot exist without matter; neither can it be conceived without the notion of wood, just as man cannot be thought of without flesh and blood. The first degree properly belongs to the natural sciences, inasmuch as scientific knowledge is knowledge of material objects:

The mind thus considers bodies in their mobile and sensitive reality, clothed with their experimentally verifiable properties. Such an object cannot exist without matter and the qualities which are bound up with it, nor can it be *conceived* without it. This is the great dominion of what the ancients called *Physica*: the knowledge of sensory nature. It is the first degree of abstraction.[52]

In the second degree of abstraction the mind considers objects that cannot exist without matter, but can nevertheless be thought of without matter. This degree belongs to mathematical sciences, inasmuch as the most typical examples of this kind of abstraction are numbers, figures, and lines. A triangle, for example, exists in a piece of pie, but it may also be thought of independently of matter—simply as an object of thought. Similarly, a cross exists in wood or bronze, but it may be conceived of apart from wood or bronze just as a sign:

> But the mind can also consider objects abstracted and purified from matter in so far as it is the general ground of the sensible properties, whether active or passive, of bodies. In this case it considers only one property which it detaches from bodies—what remains when all the sensible is removed—quantity, number and extension taken as such: an object of thought which cannot *exist* without sensible matter, but which can be *conceived* without it, e.g. nothing sensible or experimental enters into the definition of an ellipse or a square root. This is the great kingdom of *Mathematica*: the knowledge of quantity as such in its rightful relations of order and measurement. This is the second degree of abstraction.[53]

Last, in the third degree of abstraction, the mind considers objects of thought which can exist without matter and can be conceived of without it. For example, there is nothing in the nature of act as act that requires it to exist in matter:

> Finally, the mind can consider abstract objects from which matter has been entirely eliminated, where nothing remains of things but the being with which they are saturated, being as such and its laws: objects of thought which not only can be *conceived* without matter, but which can even *exist* without it, which may never have existed in material form at all, such as God and pure spirits, or which may equally exist in material and immaterial things, such as substance, quality, act and potency, beauty, goodness, etc. This is the great kingdom of *Metaphysica*: the knowledge of what is beyond sensible nature, or of Being as being. This is the third degree of abstraction.[54]

Of the above degrees of abstraction the one that concerns us is the second degree, since the typical examples of this kind of abstraction are constituted by numbers and figures. Beatrice—we should recall— has asked Dante to translate the prophecy into a figure, and has given him—by way of analogy—all that he needs for a successful translation. And yet the Pilgrim remains in the dark; he does not know the meaning of the prophecy. This is exactly as it should be, because a truth at the second level of abstraction does not happen by itself—the truth of a geometric figure must be actually worked out by making constructions, as Aristotle says:

> Obviously, therefore, the potentially existing constructions are discovered by being brought to actuality; the reason is that the geometer's thinking

is an actuality; so that the potency proceeds from an actuality; and therefore it is by making constructions that people come to know them (though the single actuality is later in generation than the corresponding potency).[55]

A mathematical truth, such as the axiom "two things that are equal to a third are also equal to each other," stands in need of direct measurements in order to be verified:

> Similarly with the knowledge of a general truth, such as that two things that are equal to a third are equal to each other. For this knowledge to be exercised it seems that its possessor must either enunciate it, or apply it say in the measurement of objects, or utilise it in some other way even if only in the artful manipulation of symbols.[56]

Jacques Maritain says that:

> The ancients held that in mathematics the judgement—by which knowledge is achieved—resulted not in the sensible, but in the imaginable. This should not be understood as meaning that each of the established conclusions needs to be directly verified by imaginative intuition: but that they need to be verified by it either directly or analogically.[57]

Guided by imaginative intuition, we should at this time attempt to verify Beatrice's Prophecy both directly and analogically. By way of analogy, we should consider that if the Pilgrim Dante and the palmer have in common a "pilgrimage accomplished" (as in fact they do), then the prophecy "un cinquecento diece e cinque" and the staff wreathed with palms must be equal to each other in symbolic value since they are respectively signs of a pilgrimage accomplished. A sign is that which signifies something other than itself. And if we consider that two things equal to a third are also equal to each other, it follows that as the staff with palm may be a sign of Christ inasmuch as they form a cross, the words "un cinquecento diece e cinque" may also be a sign of Christ, only if we succeed in forming a cross. But this is the very truth that needs to be directly verified.

Let us, therefore, consider the word "cinquecento." It contains eleven letters. We shall arrange the letters in the following fashion:

C I N Q U E C E N T O

The next word is "diece." It contains five letters. Where do we place these letters? Remember, we are not writing, we are drawing, which means that we can start anywhere on the page as long as we succeed in drawing an intelligible figure. We should start from the top of the page and arrange the letters vertically:

<pre>
               D
               I
               E
               C
        C I N Q U E C E N T O
</pre>

As you can see, I did not have to draw the fifth letter of "diece" because the letter "e" was already in place. The last word is "cinque." Continuing vertically, we will complete the figure in the following manner:

<pre>
               D
               I
               E
               C
        C I N Q U E C E N T O
               C
               I
               N
               Q
               U
               E
</pre>

For the Pilgrim to have known the meaning of the prophecy, he should have done what I have done. But he does not do it because he does not need to be assured about a journey that he knows he has undertaken. The image that the Pilgrim carries on his brain is a sign of a pilgrimage accomplished only to the reader just as the staff and the palm carried about by the palmer is a sign of a pilgrimage accomplished only to the people that he meets. The prophecy has acquired meaning inasmuch as it could be translated into a self-evident, immediately recognizable figure. This is in accordance not only with the requirements of the second degree of abstraction but also with the demands of Art and Liturgy. We have performed an action; we have drawn a figure. And this action has revealed a truth because in Medieval Art, as also in the Liturgy, the action is indeed that which is laden with symbolism.

Two more problems remain to be solved: first, Beatrice tells Dante that this Messenger of God will be the heir to the Eagle, that is to say, to the Roman Empire, and second, that he shall slay the thievish woman (the Papacy) and the Giant (the French monarchy) that sins with her. We have proposed that the Messenger of God should be taken to be Christ in His Second Coming. The question then naturally arises: how could it be said that He will come to slay the Papacy and the French monarchy? A satisfactory answer to this question will be reached only if we are willing to view the problems from a proper perspective. By this I mean that we should rise above factional considerations and interpret the facts from the point of view of universal history. To this end we should recall that for Dante, the Roman Empire and the Jews' expectation of a Messiah are parallel events in the course of history, both sacred and providentially ordained by God, as he says in the *Convivio*:

> Per che assai è manifesto la divina elezione del romano imperio per lo nascimento de la santa cittade, che fu contemporaneo a la radice de la progenie di Maria. (*Convivio* IV, 5).

All this is confirmed in the *Comedy* where we learn that Rome and her Empire—"a voler dir lo vero" ("to tell the truth")—were established for the holy place where the Successor of the Greatest Peter now sits:

> "La quale, e 'l quale, a voler dir lo vero,
> fu stabilita per lo loco santo
> u'siede il successor del maggior Piero."

(Inf. II, 22-24)

The concept of pagan Rome integrated into Christian Rome constitutes one of the most profound elements of Dante's vision of history. It may be said in fact that, for Dante, the Roman Empire fulfills three most important roles in universal history: the first deals with the function of Rome as a preparation for Christ's Advent (the so-called fulness of time); the second has to do with the Empire as a means for the propagation of the faith, which Dante probably learned from Orosius, as Davis has suggested; the third concerns the Empire as the dispenser of justice on earth.

This last function is of central importance to our purpose. And in this connection it should be recalled that in the Heaven of Jupiter, Dante meets the souls of the Just who come to him singing and arranging themselves in the shapes of letters that spell out the first verse of the Book of Wisdom: "Love righteousness, ye that be judges of the earth." "Diligite" and "iustitiam" are the first noun and verb of the text, and "qui iudicatis terram" are the last (*Par.* XVIII, 91-93). These souls who appear as writing in the sky later concentrate on the letter M and, after being joined by the other souls, all arrange themselves into the figure of an Eagle. This, to me, is quite revealing since it actually constitutes a factual justification for my proposed translation of "cinquecento diece e cinque" into the figure of a cross.

The Eagle, although made up of many souls, now speaks to Dante as if it were one person, and confirms to him that the function of the Roman Empire was indeed to be the dispenser of justice on earth: "In that I was just and piteous am I here exalted to this glory" ("Per esser giusto e pio / son io qui essaltato a quella gloria," *Par.* XIX, 13-14). The rightful heir to the Eagle—I would like to suggest—can be none other than Christ Himself—the dispenser of Divine Justice at the end of time. And it is, in fact, the Eagle who now speaks to Dante of Christ at the Last Judgement and of the inscrutability of Divine Justice: "As are my notes to thee who understand them not, such is the eternal judgement to you mortals . . . . To this realm never rose one who believed not in Christ, neither before nor after he was nailed unto the tree. But see, many cry 'Christ, Christ' who at the Judgement shall be far less near to him than he who knows not Christ":

> . . . "Quali
> son le mie note a te, che non le 'ntendi,
> tal è il giudicio etterno a voi mortali."
> . . . .
> . . . "A questo regno
> non salì mai chi non credette 'n Cristo,
> né pria né poi ch'el si chiavasse al legno.
> Ma vedi molti gridan "Cristo, Cristo!"
> che saranno in giudicio assai men *prope*
> a lui, che tal che non conosce Cristo."
>
> (*Par.* XIX, 96-98, 103-8)

Finally, how are we to understand that the Messenger of God shall come to slay the papacy and the French monarchy? Once again, if we view these facts from the perspective of universal history, we shall readily see that Christ, at the end of time, will in fact destroy both, inasmuch as He will abolish all human institutions. The French monarchy should be taken to signify the temporal institution of the State, whereas the papacy stands for the religious institution of the Church. We may speak, in fact, of three churches: the Church Militant on Earth; the Purgating Church in Purgatory; and the Celestial Church in Paradise. At the Last Judgement, the Militant and Purgating Churches will be abolished along with the State. In *Purgatory* XIX, 136-38, we find a direct allusion to the story of the Sadducees who told Jesus of a woman who had married seven brothers in succession. They then asked him:

Therefore in the Resurrection whose wife shall she be of the seven? for they all had her. Jesus answered and said unto them, Ye do err, not knowing the scriptures, nor the power of God. For in the Resurrection they neither marry, nor are given in marriage, but are as the angels of God in heaven (Matt. xxii: 23-30).

One final consideration: we recall that when the enigma of the Sphinx was finally solved by Oedipus, "Themis in anger sent a monster to ravage the flocks and fields of the Thebans."[58] Now, however, Beatrice tells us that when the facts will finally solve her powerful enigma, this will be done "without loss of flocks or of harvest":

"senza danno di pecore o di biade"

which is to say that when the missing link will be found, and Dante's vision of history will be at last complete, the end result will change absolutely nothing in the poem because the dogma of the Last Judgement constitutes the very premise that grounds and supports that vision.

NOTES

1. Ernest Robert Curtius, *European Literature and the Latin Middle Ages,* trans. Willard R. Trask (Princeton, N.J.; Princeton Univ. Press), p. 375.

2. Robert E. Kaske, "Dante's 'DXV' and 'Veltro,' " *Traditio* 17 (1961), p. 245.

3. A. C. Mastrobuono, "Analogical Contemporaneity in the Prologue Scene," in his *Essays on Dante's Philosophy of History* (Florence: Olschki, 1979).

4. Etienne Gilson, *The Spirit of Medieval Philosophy, trans.* A. H. C. Downes (New York: Charles Scribner's Sons, 1940), p. 384: "In the distant past, after the history of the Creation and the Fall, there was a multitude of men without faith or law; somewhat later the Chosen People, living under the Law, went through their long series of adventures; still more recently came the birth of Christianity, inaugurating a new era."

5. All quotations from the *Divine Comedy* are from Giorgio Petrocchi, ed. (Milan: Mondadori, 1966-67); translations are from The Temple Classics edition (London: J. M. Dent & Sons, 1964).

6. Dante, *Convivio,* ed. Maria Simonelli (Bologna: Riccardo Patron, 1966), IV, 5, p. 141.

7. Rocco Montano, *Storia della poesia di Dante* (Naples: Quaderni di Delta, 1962), II, p. 386.

8. Charles T. Davis, *Dante and the Idea of Rome* (Oxford Univ. Press, 1957), pp. 62-64.

9. Rocco Montano, "Virgilio e Dante," in *Miscellanea di studi in onore di Vittore Branca* (Florence: Leo Olschki, 1983), p. 246.

10. T. S. Eliot, *On Poetry and Poets* (New York: Noonday Press, 1964), p. 136.

11. Curtius, p. 377.

12. Charles Singleton, ed. and trans., *"Purgatorio," Divine Comedy* by Dante, Bolingen Series 80 (Princeton: Princeton Univ. Press, 1973), 2 *(Commentary)*, p. 813.

13. Singleton, *"Purgatorio,"* 2, p. 814.

14. Pietro Mazzamuto, "Cinquecento diece e cinque," in *Enciclopedia dantesca,* ed. Umberto Bosco (Rome, 1970), 2, p. 11.

15. Edward Moore, "The DXV Prophecy," in his *Studies in Dante*: Third Series (Oxford: Clarendon Press, 1968), p. 257.

16. Kaske, p. 197.

17. Herbert Thurston, S. J., *Lent and Holy Week* (London: Longmans, Green & Co., 1904), p. 412.

18. Ludwig Eisenhofer and Joseph Lechner, *The Liturgy of the Roman Rite* (New York: Herder & Herder, 1961), p. 17.

19. Thurston, p. 418.

20. Michel Andrieu, *Le pontificale romain au moyen age* (Vatican City: Biblioteca Apostolica Vaticana, 1938-40), 1, pp. 240-41.

21. Andrieu, p. 240.

22. Guglielmo Durando, *Rationale divinorum officiorum* (Apud Josephum Dura Bibliopolam, 1859), 5, p. 545.

23. Emile Mâle, *The Gothic Image: Religious Art in France of the Thirteenth Century,* trans. Dora Nussey (New York: Harper & Row, 1958), p. 365: "The evangelist's account is certainly less vivid, but it furnishes material more appropriate to plastic representation. God is no longer seen as a great precious stone whose brilliance no man can suffer, but as the Son of Man, who appears on His throne such as He was on earth, and whose face will be recognized by the people."

24. Mâle, pp. 366-67.

25. Matthew 24:30, as quoted by Mâle, pp. 368-69.

26. Mâle, p. 369.

27. Vincent of Beauvais, *Spec. Hist. Epil.* 112, as quoted by Mâle, p. 369.

28. Jacobus de Voragine, *The Golden Legend* 1:12, as quoted by Mâle, p. 369.

29. Thomas Aquinas, *Summa theologica,* supplement to part 3, Q. 90, a. 2, as quoted by Mâle, p. 369.

30. Mâle, p. 369.

31. T. E. Bird, *A Commentary on the Psalms* (London: Burn Oates & Washbourne, 1927), 2, p. 65: "The contents of the Ps. point to the sack of Jerusalem by Nabuchodonosor."

32. C. H. Grandgent, ed., *La divina commedia*, rev. ed. (Boston: D. C. Heath & Co., 1933), *"Purgatorio,"* p. 635.

33. Aristotle, *De anima*, ed. Richard Mckeon, in his *Basic Works of Aristotle* (New York: Random House, 1941), p. 580.

34. Dante, *Convivio*, 3.3-6, pp. 101-2.

35. Dante, *Convivio*, 3.9-10, p. 102.

36. Etienne Gilson, *The Christian Philosophy of St. Thomas Aquinas* (New York: Random House, 1956), p. 212.

37. Gilson, *Christian Philosophy*, pp. 216-17.

38. Ibid., p. 217.

39. Aristotle, *De anima*, III, chap. 4, p. 591.

40. Ibid., p. 566.

41. Ibid., p. 595.

42. Gilson, *Christian Philosophy*, p. 217.

43. Natalino Sapegno, ed., *La divina commedia* (Milan: Riccardo Ricciardi Editore, 1957), p. 773, n. 76-8.

44. Singleton, *"Purgatorio,"* 2, p. 819.

45. Singleton, *"Purgatorio,"* 1 (Text & Translation), p. 365.

46. Thomas Aquinas, *Summa theologica*, 1, Q. 84, a. 7, in *Basic Writings of St. Thomas Aquinas*, ed. Anton C. Pegis (New York: Random House, 1945), 1, pp. 808-9.

47. Will Durant, *The Age of Faith*, vol. 4 of *The Story of Civilization* (New York: Simon & Schuster, 1950), p. 585. Also, from *Piers The Ploughman*, by William Langland, trans. J. F. Goodridge (New York: Penguin Books, 1986), p. 77: "So they blundered on like beasts, over humps and hills, till at last, late in the day and far from home, they met a man dressed like a strange Saracen, as pilgrims are. He carried a staff, with a broad strip of cloth twisted round it like bindweed. By his side were slung a bag and begging-bowl, and souvenirs were pinned all round his hat—dozens of phials of holy oil, scallop-shells from Galicia, and emblems from Sinai. His cloak was sewn all over with devices—Holy Land crosses, cross-keys from Rome, and a St. Veronica handkerchief across the front—to let everyone know how many shrines he had seen."

48. Thomas, *S. Th.* 1, Q. 28, a. 1, p. 283.

49. Ibid., 1, Q. 13, a. 7, p. 124.

50. Ibid., 1, Q. 15, a. 3, p. 166.

51. Ibid., 1, Q. 14, a. 8, p. 147.

52. Jacques Maritain, *The Degrees of Knowledge*, trans. B. Wall and M. R. Adamson (New York: Charles Scribner's Sons, 1938), p. 45.

53. Maritain, pp. 45-46.

54. Ibid., p. 46.

55. Aristotle, *Metaphysics*, ed. Richard Mckeon, in his *Basic Works of Aristotle*, bk. 9, chap. 9, p. 833.

56. Anthony Kenny, "Intellect and Imagination in Aquinas," in *Aquinas: A Collection of Critical Essays*, ed. A. Kenny (Notre Dame: Univ. of Notre Dame Press, 1976), p. 291.

57. Maritain, pp. 68-69.

58. Singleton, *"Purgatorio,"* 2, p. 816.

THE DEACON SINGING THE 'EXSULTET' FROM THE AMBO.
(An illumination in an 'Exsultet' Roll of the eleventh century; copied from
Agincourt.)

FIG. 1 The Deacon singing the "Exsultet" from the ambo. An illumination in an "Exsultet"
Roll of the eleventh century; copied from Agincourt. From Herbert Thurston, S. J., *Lent and
Holy Week* (London: Longmans, Green & Co., 1904), p. 419.

FIG. 2 The paschal candle. From Pius Parsch, *The Church's Year of Grace* (Collegeville, Minn. : The Liturgical Press, 1953), p. 341.

FIG. 3 Chartres Cathedral, South façade, Central portal, The Last Judgment.

FIG. 4 Last Judgment, Tympanum. West façade, Notre Dame de Paris.

FIG. 5 Last Judgment by Giotto, Arena Chapel, Padua.

FIG. 6 Last Judgment, Baptistry, Florence.

APPENDIX

Review Article:
A Book Twenty-Five Years In The Making

John Freccero, *Dante: The Poetics of Conversion*. Edited, and with an introduction by Rachel Jacoff. (Cambridge: Harvard University Press, 1986. Pp. xvi, 328). A collection of essays published between 1959 and 1984.

In the first note of his first published essay "The Firm Foot on a Journey without a Guide" (1959), John Freccero acknowledges the fact that his interpretation of the structure of the *Comedy* as a whole is totally dependent on the studies of Charles Singleton: "The studies of Charles S. Singleton have examined this pattern in the poem and situated it in its historical context, and it is to those studies that this paper owes its view of the poem as a whole" (p. 278, n. 1). I shall, therefore, divide this review article in two parts; in the first part I will treat of Freccero's "view of the poem as a whole," and in the second, I will examine in some detail Freccero's interpretations of individual parts of the *Comedy*.*

I

I should like now to treat of Freccero's interpretations concerning individual parts of the *Comedy*. Accordingly, I shall focus my attention on the problem of the Prologue scene on which Freccero has written several essays.

In his first published article, "The Firm Foot on a Journey Without a Guide" (1959), Freccero's object of study is the following terzina from *Inferno* I, 28-30:

> Poi ch'èi posato un poco il corpo lasso,
> ripresi via per la piaggia diserta,
> sì che 'l piè fermo sempre era 'l più basso.

---

* I was commissioned to write a review article on Freccero's book by Professor Douglas Radcliff-Umstead (Editor-in-Chief of *Italian Culture*), but for obvious limitations of space the present second part of the review could not appear in that journal. I am publishing it here as an appendix just as it was written—without any changes.

> After I had rested my tired body a little, I again
> took up my way across the desert strand, so
> that the firm foot was always the lower (p. 33).

According to Rachel Jacoff, in this article Freccero

Took as its subject a phrase that made no sense if understood literally (nor was it even clear what its exact literal meaning was); no known gloss for it had yet convinced the majority of readers. Marshaling a wide variety of classical, patristic, and scholastic sources, Freccero arrived at an interpretation of the phrase as a figure for the pilgrim's wounded will, the crucial impediment to his desired journey toward truth. Understanding the precise meaning of this phrase required a reconstruction of its intellectual history, beginning with Aristotle and tracing its subsequent neoplatonic and Christian elaborations (p. XI).

Professor Jacoff is a student of Freccero's, and it is quite understandable that she should feel impressed by Freccero's marshaling of "a wide variety of classical, patristic, and scholastic sources." However, the truth of the matter is that Freccero's interpretation of the Prologue scene is entirely based on a confusion between the natural and the supernatural orders.

To begin with, Freccero correctly maintains that the summit of the mountain in the Prologue scene is symbolical of man's justification: "In the moral allegory, the summit of the mountain represents man's *justification*" (Freccero's italic—p. 279, n. 9). However, in order to solve the problem of the "firm foot," Freccero resolutely states that we must turn to philosophy rather than exegesis: "It is to the philosophy, rather than to the exegesis of the Middle Ages, that we must turn to arrive at the fullness of Dante's meaning" (p. 40). No doubt philosophy is involved in the Prologue scene, but in a way diametrically opposed (as we shall see shortly) to how Freccero understands the matter to be. However, if the summit of the mountain represents "man's justification" as Freccero correctly states, and justification is the proper domain of theology, then the ultimate resolution of the problem must be, by necessity, a theological one. This, as will be shown, is indeed the case.

Part of the confusion arises from the fact that Freccero postulates an analogy between Dante's spiritual state in Canto I of *Inferno* and St. Paul's spiritual state in the Letter to the Romans:

(Rom. 7: 18-19): "to will is present with me, but how to perform that which is good I find not. For the good that I would, I do not; but the evil which I would not, that I do." Canto I of Dante's poem dramatizes this situation, and the successful journey is the resolution of the problem (p. 30).

Freccero believes with Singleton that Dante receives sanctifying grace at the advent of Beatrice in the Earthly Paradise. I maintain, on the contrary, that Dante receives it in the second half of the Prologue scene (*Inf.* II). We are therefore in agreement that Dante in Canto I of *Inferno* has not yet received grace. However, the analogy between Dante's spiritual state in Canto I and St. Paul's spiritual state in the Letter to the Romans does not and could not hold for one very simple reason: Dante in Canto I is a man *"not yet healed by grace,"* whereas St. Paul in the Letter is a man *"already healed by grace,"* as St. Thomas points out:

But in the state of corrupted nature man needs grace to heal his nature in order that he may entirely abstain from sin. And in the present life this healing is wrought first in the mind, since the carnal appetite is not yet entirely healed. Hence the Apostle (Rom. vii. 25) says *in the person of one who is healed: I myself, with the mind, serve the law of God, but with the flesh, the law of sin*. And in this state man can abstain from all mortal sin, whose source is in the reason, as was stated above; but man cannot abstain from all venial sin because of the corruption of his lower appetite of sensuality. For man can, indeed, repress each of its movements (and hence they are sinful and voluntary), but not all, because, while he is resisting one, another may arise, and also because the reason is not always alert to avoid the movements, as it was said above (*S.T.* I-II, p.109, a. 8).

Note that Freccero is quoting Rom. 7:18-19. St. Thomas is quoting from the very same paragraph, Rom. 7:25. But St. Thomas correctly states that St. Paul is speaking as a man in the state of grace: "Hence the Apostle (Rom. vii.:25) says *in the person of one who is healed: 'I myself, with the mind, serve the law of God, but with the flesh, the law of sin.'*" This means that even after justification, which is to say, even after man (or Dante) has been healed by grace, his carnal appetite is not yet entirely healed because this will take place only with the resurrection of the glorified body. Dante's successful journey will not and could resolve the problem, as Freccero erroneously believes: "The successful journey is the resolution of the problem." Freccero's interpretation of Dante's journey is therefore an impossibility. St. Paul, in the very same paragraph, also says: "My inner self agrees with the law of God, but I see in my body's members another law at war with the law of my mind" (Rom. 7:22-23). In the preceding chapter, St. Paul explicitly states that he is living a new life in Christ: "Are you not aware that we who were baptized into Christ Jesus were baptized into his death? Through baptism into his death we were buried with him, so that, just as Christ was raised from the dead by the glory of the Father, we too might live a new life" (Rom. 6:3-4). Dante in Canto I of the poem is not in a state of grace. The *Comedy* opens with a confession. Dante confesses to having found himself in the dark wood of his personal sins because he had lost the straight path: "Nel mezzo del cammin di nostra vita / mi ritrovai per una selva oscura, / ché la diritta via era smarrita" (*Inf.* I, 1-3). But Freccero is adamant in his conviction that Dante, in the first canto, finds himself in a "Pauline situation":

> The pilgrim's metaphoric shore or slope is far from the Platonic plain of truth. It is the locus, in the moral landscape, of the Pauline situation, knowledge without virtue, where the spirit is willing but the flesh is fatally weak (p. 33).

The "Pauline situation" was one of "knowledge without virtue"? What a delusion! St. Paul's situation was not only one of knowledge and virtue but also of grace. Freccero, however, is convinced that Dante's firm foot "tells us something important about the condition of man left to himself" (p. 34). And since Dante, as he argues, is in a condition analogous to St. Paul's, Freccero evidently believes that serving the law of the flesh, as St. Paul says, is a "condition of man left to himself." That, on the contrary, is the human condition even for living saints who have already reached—through grace—a high degree of moral perfection. The analogy between Dante and St. Paul simply cannot hold because it is vitiated by a gross distortion of the historical facts. In fact, as we shall see later in detail, Freccero's analogies go so far as to violate the metaphysical principle of identity thereby destroying the very possibility of knowledge or meaning.

Elsewhere Freccero refers to the "Pauline situation" as the "Pauline malady" and erroneously identifies it as Dante's "wounded will":

> In another essay (chapt. 2 in this book), I attempted to explain the meaning of that verse in terms of the allegory of the "interior feet" of the soul. The "piè fermo" signifies the pilgrim's will, unable to respond to the promptings of the reason because of the Pauline malady, characteristic of fallen man whose mind far outstrips the ability of a wounded will to attain the truth. The fallen will limps in its effort to reach God (pp. 7-8).

On the contrary, as we have seen, St. Thomas has correctly stated that St. Paul's mind (intellect and will) has already been healed by grace: "in the present life this healing is wrought first in the mind." What is not yet entirely healed is St. Paul's sensuality. Also, the will attains a good, not the truth, as Freccero believes: "the ability of a wounded will to attain the truth." The intellect attains the truth.

In a more technical vein, Freccero establishes another analogy between the feet of Dante's body and the powers of the soul—intellect and will:

> But this is the journey of an "animo . . . ch'ancor fuggiva"(v. 25), and hence, when we read of the sudden intrusion of a body where there was

no body before—the "corpo lasso"(v. 28)—we are surely to understand this, to use the words of Charles Singleton, as the "vision made flesh." Here begins the journey of the "body" of the soul, accomplished, as St. Ambrose suggested, *pedibus interioribus*, and the feet are precisely the soul's two powers: *intellectus* and *affectus* (p. 43-44).

This must be so, according to Freccero, because:

> We have it on the authority of St. Thomas that the mind must move to God *et per intellectum et per affectum* (p.44).

Freccero gives no quotation here from St. Thomas. Instead, on page 284 he gives the following note (n. 61): "In IV *Sent.* d. xvii, q. I, a. 3, sol. 3; quoted by Singleton, *Journey*, pp. 13-14." So, Freccero has it on Singleton's authority that the mind must move to God by intellect and will. Freccero, of course, does not suspect that Singleton might have completely misunderstood St. Thomas. According to Singleton, sanctifying grace is a gift to intellect and will, whereas I have shown that, according to St. Thomas, sanctifying grace is a gift to the essence of the soul. Singleton's interpretation of the *Comedy* is vitiated by a reversal in the order of nature, which is like putting the cart in front of the horse. For a complete explanation of the problem, I refer the reader to chapter I of my book: *Dante's Journey of Sanctification*.

In any event, Freccero believes that Dante's feet are an analogue for his intellect and will. More specifically, the right foot is a symbol of the intellect, whereas the left is a symbol of the will. The left foot (the "piè fermo") is, for Freccero, symbolical of the pilgrim's wounded will:

> At any rate, it seems clear that Dante's *homo claudus* would have suggested, to a contemporary reader as learned as the poet, one of Adam's children, afflicted by the disease contracted by his father, unable to order his appetites to his mind (p. 45-46).

The word "mind" in the above quotation, is followed by footnote number "67." And as we turn to that note we read: ". . . Here are all the elements of *justificatio impii*, whose relevance to the *Purgatorio* has been traced by Singleton (*Journey*, pp. 57-71). . . . For *generatio* as *praeparatio ad gratiam*, see Singleton, ibid., pp. 43-54." Once again, I must refer the reader to my book where I have shown that Singleton performed an arbitrary surgical operation on St. Thomas's definition of justification. Here is St. Thomas's definition as quoted by Singleton:

> Justice is so called inasmuch as it implies a certain rectitude of order in the interior disposition of man, in so far as what is highest in man is subject to God || and the inferior powers of the soul are subject to the

superior, i.e., to the reason; and this disposition the philosopher calls justice metaphorically speaking (*Journey*, p. 268).

The two vertical bars after the word "God" were placed there by Singleton himself. They represent, for him, the line of demarcation between the "human justice" that Dante supposedly attains under Virgil's guidance ("In the journey with Virgil through Purgatory, right order is restored in the passions and lower powers") and the "transhuman justice attained with Beatrice," which for Singleton is "nothing less than the highest subjection of personal justice given through Christ's grace and through charity alone, and known only as the light of grace." Now, I have shown that for St. Thomas the justification of the ungodly takes place, literally, in one instant. Furthermore, the subjection of the inferior powers to the superior, in other words, to the reason, is caused by the subjection of the reason to God, since we hate sin because we love God. But at least, Singleton is aware that in justification right order is restored between the lower powers and reason. Freccero is not. He thinks that Dante, in the first canto of the poem, is "unable to order his appetites to his mind." However, he has identified "appetites" with Dante's will, and "mind" with Dante's intellect, or, with the left and right foot respectively:

> The summit of the mountain is the goal of both the itinerary led by Virgil and the attempted journey which the pilgrim undertakes on his own. It represents, in the moral allegory, an interior harmony in the soul, whereby the appetites, the movement of the left foot, are perfectly coordinated with reason, which, as the right, must always choose the objective and point the way (pp.46-47).

Freccero seems to be confused. When St. Thomas says that in justification "the inferior powers of the soul are subject to the superior," he does not mean that the appetites of the will ("the movement of the left foot") must be subjected to the intellect ("the right" foot). The "inferior powers" are the concupiscible and irascible appetites that must be subjected to the "superior," i.e., intellect and will. In justification it is not a question of ordering Dante's will to his intellect. It is a question of ordering Dante's passions (lower powers) to his reason, in other words, to his intellect and will. Freccero splits the will on the left foot and the intellect on the right foot. He does not seem to understand that the word "reason" for St. Thomas signifies the superior powers of both intellect and will. Dante's passions of his concupiscible appetite are: love-hate, desire-aversion, joy-sorrow; the passions of the irascible are: hope-despair, courage-fear, and anger. These are the passions that must be regulated by reason; and they will be so regulated only if Dante's reason (intellect and will) is subject to God. Freccero is convinced, however, that what is involved is an ordering of the will to the intellect, since man's ability to see the good outdistances his ability to do it on his own:

Ever since Adam's sin, man's ability to see the good has outdistanced his ability to do it on his own, for in the life without sanctifying grace, the middle ground of which St. Paul was so painfully aware, only one foot takes the forward step (p. 44).

Freccero's confusion is evidently due in part to his false assumption that St. Paul, in the Letter to the Romans, is a man "without sanctifying grace," and therefore his spiritual state is analogous, in Freccero's mind, to Dante's spiritual state in Canto I of *Inferno*. And we have seen, instead, that the analogy cannot hold because while Dante is, admittedly, a man "not yet healed by grace," the same cannot be said of St. Paul who is a man "already healed by grace." But there is yet another reason that will explain Freccero's confusion between the natural and supernatural orders. Freccero analyzes Dante's spiritual state in strict philosophical terms, completely ignoring that there is a theological dimension to the problem. On page 285, we read the following explanatory note (n. 68):

Dante, as a rationalist, had to believe in the priority of intellect in the act of choice. Thus the pilgrim begins the shorter journey with an apprehension of the truth, the glance up at the light. In the concatenation of apprehension and appetitive movements, represented by the footsteps, one or the other foot had to step out first, and this was *intellectus*. But even the *intellectus* had to have a prime mover, and this, like the prime mover in every causal chain, was God, who called the pilgrim to look up at the truth (cf. Thomas, *S.T.* I, 82, 4, ad 3; Singleton, *Journey*, pp. 48-56). Thus, grace is operative in some sense in every human act, and the complexities of this problem of actual grace were to vex Christian philosophers until well after the Renaissance.

Now, no one denies that the intellect has priority over the will inasmuch as "every movement of the will must be preceded by apprehension, whereas every apprehension is not preceded by an act of the will" (I, q. 82, a. 4, ad. 3). All this may be true in the natural order where the intellect, by an act of simple apprehension, abstracts a concept or an idea from a phantasm of a temporal good already present to the external senses. But in the first canto of the *Comedy*, we are dealing with the pilgrim Dante who looks up to the summit of the mountain and sees a light. This light, as Freccero correctly understands, pertains to the problem of man's justification. Therefore, it is either the light of faith or the light of grace which, in either case, cannot be the object of a natural apprehension on the part of the intellect for the very simple reason that they are absolute gifts from God. Faith is a supernatural theological virtue. The problem therefore is a theological problem. Freccero instead, does not speak of the truth of faith but simply of truth as if it could be reached by Dante by a natural apprehension of his intellect: "Thus the pilgrim begins the shorter journey with an apprehension of truth, the glance up at the light. In the concatenation of apprehensive and appetitive movements, represented by the footsteps, one or the other foot had to step out first, and this was *intellectus.*" If Dante has been called to see the light on the mountain, it must mean that he has received the gift of the theological virtue of faith. And this is possible even before Dante receives an actual infusion of sanctifying grace in the second canto of the poem, because faith and hope may be possessed without sanctifying grace: "If grace is a virtue, it would seem before all to be one of the three theological virtues. But grace is neither faith nor hope, for these can be without sanctifying grace. Nor is it charity, since grace fore-runs charity" (I-II, q. 110, a. 3). In the supernatural order, the intellect has priority over the will not because "every movement of the will must be preceded by apprehension, whereas every apprehension is not preceded by an act of the will." This is true in the natural order as far as natural knowledge and natural volition are concerned. But God, as the object of heavenly beatitude, cannot be reached by natural knowledge and natural volition. Therefore, in the supernatural order, the intellect has priority over the will because faith (a virtue of the intellect) "by its very nature, precedes all other virtues . . . Hence, as the last end is present in the will by hope and charity, and in the intellect, by faith, the first of all the virtues must of necessity, be faith, because natural knowledge cannot reach God as the object of heavenly bliss, which is the aspect under which hope and charity tend towards Him" (II-II, q. 4, a. 7). Dante, in the first canto of the poem, is in search of God as the object of heavenly beatitude. The problem therefore is entirely in the supernatural order involving not only faith, but also, as we shall see in detail later, hope; and hope is a supernatural virtue of the will. It should be stressed, however, that at this stage of Dante's journey, his faith as well as hope are still "unformed" in the sense that they are not yet perfected by charity, which will happen in the second canto: "Now it is evident from what has been said, that the act of faith is directed to the object of the will, i. e., the good, as to its end: and this good which is the end of faith, viz., the Divine Good, is the proper object of charity. Therefore charity is called the form of faith in so far as the act of faith is perfected and formed by charity" (II-II, q. 4, a. 3). Freccero, instead, analyzes Dante's search in strict philosophical terms whereby the footsteps are seen as a "concatenation of apprehensive and appetitve movements," as if Dante were in search of a crude temporal good.

That Freccero has confused the natural with the supernatural order may also be seen from the following passage:

> But even the intellectus had to have a prime mover, and this, like the prime mover in every causal chain, was God, who called the pilgrim to look up at the truth. Thus, grace is operative in some sense in every human act, and the complexities of this problem of actual grace were to vex Christian philosophers until well after the Renaissance.

It is simply false to say, as Freccero says, that "grace is operative in some sense in every human act." Freccero has confused God as Redeemer (supernatural order) with God as Prime Mover (natural order). Only God as the Redeemer could have called the pilgrim to look up at the truth. This is so because what distinguishes the natural from the supernatural order is the mode of God's love. God's love in the order of nature is an act of "common love," whereas his love in the order of grace is an act of "special love." By an act of common love, God confers upon man his natural being, whereas by an act of special love, He gives man, not the good of nature, but the Divine Good:

And according to this difference of good the love of God towards the creature is looked at differently. For one is common, whereby He loves all things that are (Wis. 11:25), and thereby gives things their natural being. But the second is a special love, whereby He draws the rational creature above the condition of its nature to a participation of the divine good . . . accordingly, when a man is said to have the grace of God, there is signified something supernatural bestowed on man by God (I-II, q. 110, a. 1).

This special act is the eternal act of love called the grace of predestination:

nevertheless, the grace of God sometimes signifies God's eternal love in which sense it is also called the grace of predestination, inasmuch as God gratuitously, and not from merits, predestines or elects some(I-II, q. 110, a.1).

God as Prime Mover is not the giver of grace. Therefore, grace is not "operative in some sense in every human act," as Freccero erroneously believes. The supernatural good of grace in one man, St. Thomas says, "is greater than the good of nature in the whole universe" (I-II, q. 113, a. 9, R. Obj. 2). The justification of the ungodly through grace is God's greatest work, even greater than creation, for creation terminates in a good of the natural order, whereas justification "terminates at the eternal good of a participation in God . . . Hence, Augustine, after saying that for a just man to be made from sinner is greater than to create heaven and earth, adds, *for heaven and earth shall pass away, but salvation and the justification of the predestined shall endure* (I-II, q. 13, a. 9).

But Freccero goes so far as to say that Dante's intellect is healed by beholding the rays of the sun:

Once the pilgrim beholds the rays of the sun, however, he has undergone an intellectual conversion, and is healed, so to speak, in one foot (p. 46).

This is yet another confusion. The rays of the sun, which most likely symbolize the light of faith, cannot heal Dante's soul. Dante's soul is healed only by sanctifying (healing) grace: "In this way, habitual grace, inasmuch as it heals and justifies the soul, or makes it pleasing to God, is called operating grace" (I-II, q. 111, a. 2). And since Freccero believes that Dante receives sanctifying grace with the advent of Beatrice in Purgatory, how can he say that Dante's intellect is healed in the first canto of the poem? The disclaimer "so to speak" is clear evidence that Freccero is proceeding by way of vague approximations. Four pages later, however, Freccero, with steadfast assurance, proclaims that Dante's glance at the light represents a conversion from ignorance and sin:

> According to our reading up to this point, the glance at the light and subsequent escape from the forest represent a conversion from ignorance and sin. One of the classic wounds of nature was thereby overcome, and there remained the other traditional affliction to which man in this life is subject: concupiscence, the wound of the affectus (p. 50).

A glance at the light represents "a conversion from ignorance and sin"? Freccero evidently ignores that not even sanctifying grace together with the theological virtues can entirely heal Dante's soul of the wound of ignorance. As I have shown in my book *Dante's Journey of Sanctification*, Dante's wound of ignorance may be entirely healed only by the gifts of the Holy Ghost:

> Whether we consider human reason as perfected in its natural perfection, or as perfected by the theological virtues, it does not know all things, nor are all things possible to it. Consequently, it is unable under all circumstances to avoid folly and other like things mentioned in the objection. God, however, to Whose knowledge and power all things are subject, by His motion safeguards us from all folly, ignorance, dullness of mind and hardness of heart, and the rest. Consequently, the gifts of the Holy Ghost, which make us amenable to His instigation, are said to be given as remedies to these defects (I-II, q. 68, a. 2, R. Obj. 3).

Freccero's interpretations of the Comedy are essentially characterized by a superficial understanding of fundamental philosophical and theological notions that constitute the very background to the poem. The mistakes seem to be, for the most part, honest mistakes. On some occasions, however, there seems to be a willful distortion of a given philosophical or theological notion in order to make it fit a preconceived assumption. The following is one example:

> The will, and the will alone, is the locus of sin, and hell therefore is patterned on its threefold division: the rational (*voluntas* properly speaking), the irascible, and the concupiscent appetite (p. 49).

Freccero does not give any quotations to substantiate the claim that the will has a "threefold division: the rational (*voluntas* properly speaking), the irascible, and the concupiscent appetite." The concupiscible and irascible appetites are not two divisions of the will—they are the two inferior powers of the soul, whereas intellect and will are the two superior powers of the soul. The concupiscible and irascible constitute the "sensitive appetite" whereas the will constitutes the "intellectual appetite." To the question "Whether the will is divided into irascible and concupiscible," St. Thomas answers in the negative, because the will is related to the good according to the common notion of good, whereas the concupiscible and irascible powers are differentiated by the different notions of particular good:

> The irascible and concupiscible are not parts of the intellectual appetite, which is called the will ... Now the sensitive appetite is not related to the common notion of good, because neither do the senses apprehend the universal. Therefore the parts of the sensitive appetite are differentiated by the different notions of particular good; for the concupiscible is related to its proper sort of good, which is something pleasant to the senses and suitable to nature; whereas the irascible is related to that sort of good which is something that wards off and repels what is hurtful. But the will is related to the good according to the common notion of good, and therefore in the will, which is the intellectual appetite, there is no differentiation of appetitive powers, so that there be in the intellectual appetite an irascible power distinct from a concupiscible power; just as neither on the part of the intellect are the apprehensive powers multiplied, although they are on the part of the senses (I, q. 82, a. 5).

But Freccero has arbitrarily decided to "lump together" the concupiscible, the irascible, and the will in one vague approximation, which he calls "the will in the broadest sense":

> Thus, man's appetite is composed of rational (i.e., volitive), irascible and concupiscent forces, the first of which is peculiarly human, while the other two are rational in man only because they are ruled by the first, and moved by it. The composite threefold appetite in man is what we call the will in the broadest sense (p. 48).

Freccero is apparently unaware that he has "lumped together" the inferior powers of the soul (concupiscible-irascible) with one of the superior powers of the soul, the will, which he arbitrarily ascribes to Dante's left foot. He ascribes to Dante's right foot only the intellect. The will, however, cannot be surgically split from the intellect, for the two of them together constitute the reason, and it is the reason that rules the concupiscible and irascible, as we shall see in detail shortly.

The same is true of his claim that "the will, and the will alone, is the locus of sin." But things are the very opposite of what Freccero claims them to be:

> Sin is contrary to virtue, and contraries are about one and the same thing. But the other powers of the soul, besides the will, are the subject of virtues, as was stated above. Therefore the will is not the only subject of sin.
>
> As was shown above, whatever is a principle of a voluntary act is a subject of sin. Now voluntary acts are not only those which are elicited by the will, but also those which are commanded by the will, as we have stated above in treating of voluntariness. Therefore not only the will can be a subject of sin, but also all those powers which can be moved to their acts, or restrained from their acts, by the will; and these same powers are the subjects of good and evil moral habits, because act and habit belong to the same subject (I-II, q. 74, a. 2).

Now, given these obvious distortions of fundamental philosophical notions, how can Freccero's interpretation of the three beasts in the first canto of *Inferno*, which depends on those notions, possess any degree of validity whatever?

Dante's "feet of the soul," according to Freccero, are the intellect (the right foot), which he believes to be healed of the wound of ignorance, and the will (the left foot), which he believes to be wounded. But it should now be pointed out that the intellect, as such, in its function as an apprehensive power, cannot really be a "foot of the soul," because an act of the apprehensive power "is not so properly called a movement as the act of the appetite":

> Now the sensual movement is an appetite following sensible apprehension. For the act of the apprehensive power is not so properly called a movement as the act of the appetite; since the operation of the apprehensive power is completed in the very fact that the thing apprehended is in the one that apprehends, while the operation of the appetitive power is completed in the fact that he who desires is borne towards the desirable thing. Hence it is that the operation of the apprehensive power is likened to rest; whereas the operation of the appetitive power is rather likened to movement (I, q. 81, a. 1).

So, if the function of the intellect, as an apprehensive power, is completed by the very fact that the object that is known is in the subject that knows, and the "operation of the apprehensive power is likened to rest," it follows that the intellect, as an apprehensive power, cannot be viewed as a "foot of the soul." And this is precisely what Freccero does, as we shall now see.

In the 17th canto of *Purgatory*, Virgil tells Dante that love is the universal law of the universe:

> "Nè creator nè creatura mai,"
> cominciò el, "figliuol, fu sanza amore,
> o naturale o d'animo; e tu 'l sai."
>
> (Purg. XVII, 91-93)
>
> He began: "Nor Creator, nor creature, my
> son, was ever without love, either natural or
> rational; and this thou knowest."

In the words of St. Thomas: "Every agent acts for an end, as stated above. Now the end is the good desired and loved by each one. Wherefore it is evident that every agent, whatever it be, does every action from love of some kind" (I-II, q. 28, a. 6). This love is a passion of our animal nature; specifically, a passion of the concupiscible appetite: "Since, therefore, love consists in a change wrought in the appetite by the appetible object, it is evident that love is a passion: properly so called, according as it is in the concupiscible faculty" (I-II, q. 26, a. 2). In the next canto, Dante is understandably perplexed. He argues that if love is offered to us from without (the natural attraction we experience for a desirable good), and the soul walks with no other foot, it is no merit of hers whether she goes straight or crooked:

> "ché, s'amore è di fuori a noi offerto
> e l'anima non va con altro piede,
> se dritta o torta va, non è suo merto."
>
> (Purg. XVIII, 43-45)

Note well that Dante is explicitly referring to the passion of love as a foot of the soul: "e l'anima non va con altro piede." Therefore, according to Dante himself, the concupiscible power of the soul is already a foot of the soul. This, I submit, is Dante's "firm foot" in the first canto of the poem:

sì che 'l piè fermo sempre era 'l più basso

The powers of the soul are divided into inferior sensitive powers (concupiscible-irascible) and superior rational powers (intellect-will). Dante's "piè fermo," which is always "il più basso," is an image for the "inferior powers" of Dante's soul. Those powers, we may recall, are the powers that, in justification, are subjected to the "superior powers" of the soul, i.e., intellect and will. The subjection of the superior powers of the soul to God causes, in turn, the subjection of the inferior to the superior, and not vice-versa, as Singleton believes and Freccero has uncritically accepted. Dante's inferior (sensitive) powers are referred to as "il piè fermo," which is always "il più basso," for the very simple reason that the concupiscible and irascible powers do not move by themselves. The inferior powers are moved by the superior powers of Dante's soul, in other words, intellect and will. To understand how this may be so, an important distinction must be made between the intellect as an "apprehensive power" and the intellect as a "reasoning power." The intellect has two functions, the first of which is apprehension, the second is reasoning:

> The human intellect must of necessity understand by composition and division. For since the intellect passes from potentiality to act, it has a likeness to generable things, which do not attain to perfection all at once but acquire it by degrees. In the same way, the human intellect does not acquire perfect knowledge of a thing by the first apprehension; but it first apprehends something of the thing, such as its quiddity, which is the first and proper object of the intellect; and then it understands the properties, accidents, and various dispositions affecting the essence. Thus it necessarily relates one thing with another by composition or division; and from one composition and division it necessarily proceeds to another, and this is reasoning (I, q. 85, a. 5).

Virgil refers to the "apprehensive power" of the intellect in his discourse on love, when he says:

> Vostra apprensiva da essere verace
> tragge intenzione, e dentro a voi la spiega,
> sì che l'animo ad essa volger face.
> (Purg. XVIII, 22-24)
> Your apprehensive faculty draws an impression
> from a real object, and unfolds it within you,
> so that it makes the mind turn thereto.

Later on, as we shall see shortly, Virgil will refer to the "reasoning power" of the intellect in conjunction also with the problem of love. For now, we should point out that Dante's intellect regulates his sensitive, inferior powers of concupiscible and irascible appetite, not as an "apprehensive power," but rather as a "reasoning power":

> In two ways do the irascible and concupiscible powers obey the higher part, in which are the intellect or reason, and the will: first, as to the reason, and secondly, as to the will. They obey the reason in their own acts, because in other animals the sensitive appetite is naturally moved by the estimative power; for instance, a sheep, esteeming the wolf as an enemy, is afraid. In man the estimative power, as we have said above, is replaced by the cogitative power, which is called by some *the particular reason*, be-

cause it compares individual intentions. Hence, in man the sensitive appetite is naturally moved by this particular reason. But this same particular reason is naturally guided and moved according to the universal reason; and that is why in syllogisms particular conclusions are drawn from universal propositions. Therefore it is clear that the universal reason directs the sensitive appetite, which is divided into concupiscible and irascible, and that this appetite obeys it. But because to draw particular conclusions from universal principles is not the work of the intellect, as such, but of the reason, hence it is that irascible and concupiscible are said to obey the reason rather than to obey the intellect. Anyone can experience this in himself; for by applying certain universal considerations, anger or fear or the like may be lessened or increased (I, q. 81, a. 3).

In the above quotation, what is of fundamental importance is the fact that the irascible and concupiscible "are said to obey the reason rather than to obey the intellect." This means that Dante's intellect regulates the inferior powers (the passions) not by virtue of its power of apprehension, but rather by virtue of its power of reasoning. This is of considerable importance since it is precisely here that Freccero has gone wrong. For now, let us point out that the irascible and concupiscible must also obey the will:

To the will also is the sensitive appetite subject in execution, which is accomplished by the motive power. For in other animals movement follows at once the concupiscible and irascible appetites. For instance, the sheep, fearing the wolf, flies at once, because it has no superior counteracting appetite. On the contrary, man is not moved at once according to the irascible and concupiscible appetites; but he awaits the command of the will, which is the superior appetite. For wherever there is order among a number of motive powers, the second moves only by virtue of the first; and so the lower appetite is not sufficient to cause movement, unless the higher appetite consents. And this is what the Philosopher says, namely, that *the higher appetite moves the lower appetite, as the higher sphere moves the lower*. In this way, therefore, the irascible and concupiscible are subject to reason (I, q. 81, a. 3).

Note: "The lower appetite is not sufficient to cause movement, unless the higher appetite consents." This is the function of the will. Therefore, in an act of choice, two things concur:

One on the part of the cognitive power, the other on the part of the appetitive power. On the part of the cognitive power, counsel is required, by which we judge one thing to be preferred to another; on the part of the appetitive power, it is required that the appetite should accept the judgement of counsel (I, q. 83. a. 3).

In an act of choice, the intellect gives "counsel," whereas the will gives "consent." The intellect has therefore priority over the will inasmuch as consent presupposes counsel in an act of choice. But if we consider the act of choice in reference to the two acts of the intellect, which is to say, the intellect as an "apprehensive power" and the intellect as a "reasoning power," the act of choice takes place at the second phase—at the phase of reasoning, since counsel is to "judge one thing to be preferred to another." Freccero, on the other hand, erroneously thinks that choice takes place at the level of apprehension:

> Dante, as a rationalist, had to believe in the priority of intellect in the act of choice. Thus the pilgrim begins the shorter journey with an apprehension of truth, the glance up at the light. In the concatenation of apprehensive and appetitive movements, represented by the footsteps, one or the other foot had to step out first, and this was *intellectus*.

Obviously, Freccero is under the mistaken impression that choice involves Dante's intellect only as an apprehensive power. Dante, however, is in perfect agreement with St. Thomas. We have shown that, according to Dante himself, the inferior powers of the soul (concupiscible-irascible) are already a foot of the soul. It remains now to be shown that, also according to Dante himself, the superior powers of the soul (intellect-will) constitute the other foot of the soul.

To Dante's question of merit or demerit concerning the passion of love of the concupiscible appetite as man's universal law—"e l'anima non va con altro piede"—Virgil answers that there is no question of morality at this primordial level, since it is after all a question of natural attraction: "e questa prima voglia / merto di lode o di biasmo non cape" ("and this prime love admits no desert of praise or of blame") (*Purg.* XVIII, 59-60). However, Virgil continues by suggesting that man's soul may yet have another foot inasmuch as man has an innate power that gives counsel, and ought to guard the threshold of assent:

> Or, perché a questa ogn' altra si raccoglia,
> innata v'è la virtù che consiglia,
> e de l'assenso de' tener la soglia.
>
> (*Purg.* XVIII, 61-63)

This "virtù che consiglia" ("the power that gives counsel") can be none other than the intellect in its function as a "reasoning power," whereas "assenso" can be none other than the "consent" of the will. In fact, Virgil says, those who by their reasoning were able to penetrate the very foundation of reality (the sages of antiquity), perceived this innate freedom in man, and therefore they left Ethics to the world:

Color che ragionando andaro al fondo,
s'accorser d'esta innata libertate;
però moralità lasciaro al mondo.

(*Purg.* XVIII, 67-68)

Therefore, according to Dante himself, the "piè fermo" is a figure of the inferior powers of the soul (concupiscible-irascible) and, by necessity, is always "il più basso," since "the lower appetite is not sufficient to cause movement, unless the higher appetite consents." The other foot of the soul is constituted by the superior powers of the soul (intellect and will) whose functions concur so intimately in the act of choice that Aristotle called election "either *an appetitive intellect or an intellectual appetite*" (I, q. 83, a. 3).

Is Freccero aware that Dante himself has spoken of the feet of the soul? Yes, as is evident in the following passage:

"S'io ti fiammeggio nel caldo d'amore / di là dal modo che 'n terra si vede, / sì che del viso tuo vinco il valore, / non ti maravigliar, ché ciò procede / da perfetto veder, che, come apprende, / così nel bene appreso move il piede" *(Par.* V, 1-6). Dante implies the analogy between the movement of the soul and the movement of the feet in *Purg.* XVIII, 43-45: "s'amore è di fuori a noi offerto, / e l'anima non va con altro piede, / se dritta o torta va, non è suo merto."

What should be noted about the above quotation is that it comes from page 284, footnote number 60. Freccero has looked everywhere for an explanation of the feet of the soul except in Dante's own poem. If Dante himself "implies the analogy between the movement of the soul and the movement of the feet," why, then, place that critically fundamental fact in a footnote? The normal scholarly approach would have been to make those passages of the *Purgatorio* the focal point of the inquiry. But had Freccero done so, he would have discovered that his naïvely simplistic theory of the feet of the soul as a "wounded will" and a "healed intellect" was utterly untenable. Or, it may be that Freccero is simply unaware that Virgil speaks of one foot of the soul as a figure of the passion of love of the concupiscible appetite. And, indeed, as we read elsewhere in the book, this seems to be precisely the case. Freccero refers to the definition of love in the *Purgatorio*, not as a passion of the concupiscible appetite, but as a spiritual motion of the mind:

According to Dante's own definition in the *Purgatorio*, love is a spiritual motion of the mind as it moves to God (p.107).

II

I should like to point out at this time that, so far, I have addressed the problem of the feet of the soul in strictly philosophical terms. But Dante, in the first canto of the poem, is not in search of a good of the temporal order. He is in search of God as the object of his heavenly beatitude. In other words, we are dealing here with Dante's spiritual-religious state. The solution of the problem, therefore, has to be elevated to the plane of theology. And, in point of fact, Dante is hoping to ascend the mountain. Hope can be both a passion of the irascible appetite and a theological virtue of the will. When Dante encounters the she-wolf, we are told that the terrifying aspect of this beast made him lose hope of ascending the mountain:

> Questa mi porse tanto di gravezza
> con la paura ch'uscia di sua vista,
> ch'io perdei la speranza de l'altezza.
>
> *(Inf.* I, 52-54)
>
> She brought such heaviness upon me with the
> terror of her aspect, that I lost the hope of
> ascending.

The passion opposed to hope is despair, and Dante falls briefly into despair until Virgil comes to rescue him seven verses later (v. 61). In any event, it stands to reason that if the she-wolf has made him lose hope, it means that he must have been hoping to ascend the mountain. We should distinguish, however, that hope as a passion of the irascible appetite is a desire of a future good, whereas hope as a theological virtue of the will is a certain expectation of a future glory:

The first of these pairs is hope and despair. Like all the passions of the irascible, hope presupposes desire. This is why we have already spoken of hope as the desire of a future good. However, hope is more than this, and rather different too. We do not hope for what we are sure to obtain. What characterizes hope is the feeling that difficulties stand between our desire and its fulfillment (E. Gilson, *The Christian Philosophy of St. Thomas Aquinas,* pp. 383-84).

Hope as a theological virtue of the will, in Dante's own terms, is a certain (firm) expectation of a future glory:

> "è uno attender certo / de la gloria futura"
> *(Par.* XXV, 67-68)

This is rather important since we are told by Beatrice that the Church Militant has no child with greater hope than Dante: "La Chiesa militante alcun figliuolo / non ha con più speranza" *(Par.* XXV, 52-53). This, according to Montano, constitutes the highest, most profound affirmation in praise of the Poet in the entire *Comedy*: "Ciò che egli voleva essere era soltanto questo: il santo, l'eroe della Speranza" (R. Montano, *Storia della poesia di Dante*, vol. II, pp. 573-74). As I have said, in the first canto of the poem, Dante is not in search of a temporal good. He is in search of God—a superintelligible, which is in fact the object of the virtue of hope: "The object of the irascible is an arduous sensible; whereas the object of the virtue of hope is an arduous intelligible, or rather superintelligible" (II-II, q. 18, a. 1, R.Obj. 1). Now, hope presupposes faith. Therefore, Dante can be said to be walking toward the light on the mountain in the hope of a future glory and in the hope for Divine assistance, which, in fact, comes with Virgil, since he is the first God-sent guide. The hope for future glory and for Divine assistance, St. Thomas says, are proposed to us by faith:

> Absolutely speaking, faith precedes hope. For the object of hope is a future good, arduous but possible to obtain. In order, therefore, that we may hope, it is necessary for the object of hope to be proposed to us as possible. Now the object of hope is, in one way, eternal happiness, and, in another way, the Divine assistance, as explained above: and both of these are proposed to us by faith, whereby we come to know that we are able to obtain eternal life, and that for this purpose the Divine assistance is ready for us, according to Heb. xi, 6: *He that cometh to God, must believe that He is, and is a rewarder to them that seek Him.* Therefore, it is evident that faith precedes hope (II-II, q. 17, a. 7).

In my book, *Essays on Dante's Philosophy of History*, I argued that there may be analogical contemporaneity between Dante's personal redemption as it unfolds within the context of the poem, and mankind's drama of redemption as it took place on the stage of history. This is what I said then:

> Our argument would, therefore, be as follows: If Dante is hoping (as in fact he is) to ascend the Mountain, and hope, to him, is expressly a certain expectation, then, in the first canto, he must consequently be expecting a personal deliverance by Beatrice (which in fact occurs) as fallen humanity was expecting a deliverance by the Messiah (*Essays*, p. 53).

More specifically:

> The encounter between Virgil and Dante on this Good Friday of the year 1300, before the commemoration of the Crucifixion, may be symbolical of the encounter between Rome and Judaism on the stage of history. Dante, in the first canto, may be symbolical of mankind enslaved by Original Sin, leading up to the time of Christ; whereas, in the second canto, he may be symbolical of mankind set free by Christ (the expression, "I began as one set free," is unmistakably clear) and converted through Rome (*Essays*, pp. 70-71).

What is clear, then, is that Dante, in the first canto, is walking toward the mountain in faith and hope for a personal deliverance. But Freccero in the essay "The Prologue Scene" (1966), is convinced that Dante's attempt at ascending the mountain involves a presumptuous philosophical attempt at conversion:

> There are some excellent reasons for believing Dante meant that first ascent to be read as a purely *intellectual* attempt at conversion, where the mind sees its objective but is unable to reach it (p. 5, Freccero's italics).

St. Bernard, Freccero says, being "an outspoken critic of philosophical presumption, speaks of the opposition between humility and pride in the itinerary to God" (p. 9). Freccero, then gives the following quotation from St. Bernard:

> Who dares climb the mountain of the Lord or who will stand in His holy place? . . . Only the humble man can safely climb the mountain, because only the humble man has nothing to trip him up. The proud man may climb it indeed, yet he cannot stand for long . . . The proud man has only one foot to stand on: love of his own excellence . . . Therefore to stand firmly, we must stand humbly. So that our feet may never stumble we must stand, not on the single foot of pride, but on the two feet of humility (p. 10).

Immediately following the above quotation from St. Bernard, Freccero concludes:

> There can be scarcely any doubt that Dante's pilgrim climbs the mountain in the same tradition (p. 10).

There is, of course, absolutely no evidence for all this. In reference to the Hill of the first canto, there is no act of pride anywhere expressed, as there are no expressions to indicate an inordinate desire for one's own excellence. The criticism that I levelled against Freccero in my first book, I believe is still valid. In that work I said: "Why then should a special miracle be given to Dante, who, through his own pride, thinks he can reach God's beatitude on the Mountain by a simple intellectual search? Should he not show some humility before he can be considered for—let alone merit—such a journey? In the context, Virgil, who is the first guide miraculously sent, comes to rescue him when Dante is in the act of ascending, that is to say, in the supposedly proud act of defying God" (*Essays*, p. 59). Freccero's thesis is simply inconsistent.

But why, we should ask, is Freccero so determined to prove that Dante, in the first canto, wants to reach God's beatitude on the mountain through a

supposedly proud, presumptuous, philosophical search? In Freccero's own
words, Dante's attempt at ascending the mountain is:

> A purely *intellectual* attempt at conversion, where the mind sees its ob-
> jective but is unable to reach it (p. 5).

Note that by the word "intellectual" Freccero means "philosophical."
But Dante's search goes beyond philosophy. It is a theological search inasmuch as faith is a theological virtue of the intellect, whereas hope is a theological virtue of the will. Freccero, however, could not even consider the possibility that Dante, in the first canto, may be walking toward the mountain in
faith and hope, for the very simple reason that Singleton's interpretation of
the structure of the *Comedy* excludes that possibility. Freccero accepts Singleton's thesis that Dante receives sanctifying grace with the advent of Beatrice in the Earthly Paradise. The whole area of Virgil's guidance is a preparation for sanctifying grace in the natural order, as Freccero says: "The implication seems to be that preparation for grace lies within the competence of
man, in the purely natural order" (p. 68). Now, Dante's journey to Beatrice
and Dante's journey to the summit of the mountain in the first canto are, for
Freccero, both in the natural order:

> The summit of the mountain is the goal of both the itinerary led by Virgil
> and the attempted journey which the pilgrim undertakes on his own (pp.
> 46-47).

The only difference is that the journey to Beatrice is a journey "with a guide,"
and the attempted journey to the mountain is a journey "without a guide."
Therefore, Freccero writes the essay "The Firm Foot on a Journey Without a
Guide." But there is much more. Singleton's interpretation of the structure of
the *Comedy* excludes that there may be faith and hope in the first canto of
the poem because Singleton erroneously believes that the theological virtues
of faith, hope, and charity may be had only with the advent of sanctifying
grace—with Beatrice:

> Neither charity nor any of the other infused virtues may be without sanc-
> tifying grace, which is as their root . . . The point is too clearly estab-
> lished everywhere in theology to require documentation (*Journey*, p.
> 220).

For a full explanation of Singleton's misunderstanding of the proper relationship between sanctifying grace and the infused virtues, I refer the
reader to my book: *Dante's Journey of Sanctification*. For now, it will suffice
to say that faith and hope may indeed be possessed without sanctifying grace:

> If grace is a virtue, it would seem before all to be one of the three theo-

logical virtues. But grace is neither faith nor hope, for these can be without sanctifying grace. Nor is it charity, since grace fore-runs charity (I-II, q. 110, a. 3).

And yet, Singleton says: "The point is too clearly established everywhere in theology to require documentation." Now, Freccero does not even suspect that Singleton was wrong on both counts: that Dante receives sanctifying grace with Beatrice, and that the infused virtues cannot be without grace (only charity cannot be without grace). Literally, every single essay by Freccero remains within the strict confines of Singleton's interpretations. Freccero's view of the *Comedy* as a whole—as he tells us—depends on Singleton's studies. So Freccero's predicament, for well over three decades, has been to build on Singleton's mistakes. Parenthetically, it should be added, however, that Freccero is not alone in having accepted Singleton's claim that Dante receives the theological virtues of faith, hope, and charity only with an infusion of sanctifying grace at the advent of Beatrice in the Earthly Paradise. This is a common belief shared by all scholars of Singleton's school of thought who have accepted his interpretation of the structure of the *Comedy*. G. Mazzotta (a student of Freccero) believes the same thing: "The second stage, *gratia sanctificans*, occurs when the soul in the Earthly Paradise is in possession of all the seven virtues" (*Dante, Poet of the Desert*, p. 36).

Everything then must be sacrificed to the altar of Singleton's truth, even if it means the distortion of supporting documentation. To prove that Dante's attempt in the first canto is "a purely intellectual attempt at conversion, where the mind sees its objective but is unable to reach it" (p. 5) because "the fallen will limps in its effort to reach God" (p. 8), Freccero gives the following quotation from Gregory the Great:

Indeed, one suffers initially after conversion, considering one's past sins, wishing to break immediately the bonds of secular concerns, to walk in tranquillity the ways of the Lord, to throw off the heavy burden of earthly desires and in free servitude to put on the light yoke of God. Yet while one thinks of these things, there arises a familiar delight in the flesh which quickly takes root. The longer it holds on, the tighter it becomes, the later does one manage to leave it behind. What suffering in such a situation, what anxiety of the heart! *When the spirit calls and the flesh calls us back.* On one hand the intimacy of a new love invites us, on the other the old habits of vice holds us back (p. 7).

Freccero believes that the above quotation "provides us with the kind of theological context in which I believe we are to read the 'animo' and 'corpo' of Dante's verses" (p. 7). But if there is a "theological context," how can Dante's attempt be "a purely intellectual attempt at conversion"? Freccero seems to be confused. The above quotation from Gregory the Great is followed by footnote number 12, in which we read:

> It is clear from the context that Gregory is talking about the first stage of conversion, presumably before the reception of sanctifying grace. In the figure of Exodus which he subsequently applies to his analysis (col. 301), this stage corresponds to the wandering in the desert, between the crossing of the Red Sea and the crossing of the Jordan. This is precisely the stage at which the pilgrim finds himself here. See Charles S. Singleton, "In Exitu Israel de Aegypto" . . . where Singleton quotes a passage further on in this chapter of the *Moralia* (p.276).

There you have it! Gregory the Great sacrificed on the altar of Singleton's truth. If in the essay, "The Firm Foot on a Journey Without a Guide," St. Paul was the object of Freccero's distortions, in the essay "The Prologue Scene," Gregory the Great has become the victim. For, where Gregory says: "Indeed, one suffers initially after conversion, considering one's past sins," Freccero, instead, says: "It is clear from the context that Gregory is talking about the first stage of conversion, presumably before the reception of sanctifying grace." But Gregory is specifically referring to his sins as "one's past sins." This means that they are no longer present in his soul for having been expelled by an infusion of sanctifying grace at the moment of conversion. Just like St. Paul, Gregory the Great speaks as a man "after conversion" already healed by grace. Gregory says: "When the spirit calls and the flesh calls us back." St. Paul had said: "I myself, with the mind, serve the law of God, but with the flesh, the law of sin." This means that both St. Paul and Gregory the Great have been healed in the mind (the mind includes both the intellect and the will) by sanctifying grace, but their flesh, their sensuality, their concupiscible appetite, are not entirely healed even after conversion, as St. Thomas has shown. When Gregory says: "the intimacy of a new love invites us," this "new love" could only refer to the love of charity, and there can be no charity without grace. Note also Freccero says: "It is clear from the context," and in the same breath he adds the disclaimer "presumably," which confirms, once again, that he is proceeding by way of nebulous approximations.

In the same essay ("The Prologue Scene"), Freccero maintains that the *Comedy* is essentially Augustinian in structure:

> If the point of departure, as well as the goal, of Dante's spiritual itinerary deliberately recalls the experience of Augustine in the *Confessions*, then it may be that we are to regard Dante's entire spiritual autobiography as essentially Augustinian in structure (p. 12).

This cannot possibly be for several reasons. First of all, St. Augustine is virtually absent from the *Comedy*; he is only barely mentioned in the *Paradiso*. However, according to Rachel Jacoff:

> While most scholars continued to gloss Dante's ideas primarily in relation to Aristotelian philosophy and Thomistic theology, Freccero's pro-

found grasp of neoplatonic thought and of Augustine's understanding of the relationship between language and desire allowed him to uncover the dynamism of such a paradigm; several essays explicitly return to these considerations, and each time the new context gives added density and intensity to our understanding of the centrality of the notion of conversion. The necessarily diachronic nature of such a narrative places temporality in the foreground (pp. xii-xiii).

The leading scholar who glossed: "Dante's ideas primarily in relation to Aristotelian philosophy and Thomistic theology" was, of course, Charles Singleton. Freccero obviously must have thought that Singleton had explored and exhausted all possible relations between Dante's poem and the Aristotelian-Thomistic background. In any event, Freccero did not discover the temporality of conversion in Augustine. The idea is already present in Singleton, who interprets Dante's conversion as a process in the order of time: "*Generatio* is essentially a movement toward form. Such, literally, is the most general definition of the term; 'generatio est motus ad formam'" (*Journey*, p. 46). And again: "One thus conceives a process which has extension in time and manifests two successive moments or phases. The first is the moment of *preparation*, the second the moment of *completion*, at the end, when form is attained" (Ibid., p. 58).

Now, following Singleton, Freccero also interprets Dante's conversion as a process in the order of time:

In their search to give the theology of grace a basis in natural philosophy, they turned to the teachings of Aristotle for a rationalization of the process of justification. Sanctifying grace was interpreted as an accidental form of the soul; justification was therefore a real change, a generation of a new form—"generatio ad formam." Charles Singleton has shown the relevance of the Aristotelian philosophy of becoming, "generatio et corruptio," to Dante's drama of justification, the *Purgatorio*. We need only review some of the principles established by Singleton's essay in order to show . . . (p. 173).

Singleton describes Dante's conversion in strict philosophical terms of a "corruptio" of the old form and a "generatio" of a new form. What Freccero discovered was that St. Augustine had spoken of that same temporality of conversion, not in metaphysical terms, but in psychological terms of a "death" and "resurrection" of the self:

Conversion, a death and resurrection of the self, is the experience that marks the difference between such confessions and facile counterfeits. In the poem, the difference between the attempt to scale the mountain, the journey that fails, and the successful journey that it prefigures is a descent in humility, a death of the self represented by the journey through hell. Augustine alludes briefly to a similar askesis in order to describe his suffering during his stay in Rome (p. 4).

In my book *Dante's Journey of Sanctification*, I have shown that Dante's conversion is not a process in the order of time, but a process in the order of nature for the very simple reason that the mind, which is being justified, is, in itself, above time:

> Now the human mind, which is justified, is, in itself, above time, but is subject to time accidentally, inasmuch as it understands with continuity and time, in keeping with the phantasm in which it considers the intelligible species, as was stated above. We must, therefore, decide from this about its change as regards the condition of temporal movements, i. e., we must say that there is no last instant that sin inhers, but a last time; whereas there is a first instant that grace inhers, but in all the time previous sin inhered (I-II, q. 113, a. 7, R.Obj. 5).

This, as I say in my book, is exactly Dante's condition in the Prologue scene (*Inf.* II). At the moment of justification, the same instant is the first non-existence of sin and the first existence of sanctifying grace. What all this means is that conversion for St. Thomas, as also for Dante, is a metaphysical problem before being a moral one, for the very simple reason that operation follows being:

> But if grace is taken, for the habitual gift, then again there is a double effect of grace, even as of every other form, the first of which is being, and the second, operation. Thus, the work of heat is to make its subject hot, and to give heat outwardly. In this way, habitual grace, inasmuch as it heals and justifies the soul, or makes it pleasing to God, is called operating grace; but inasmuch as it is the principle of meritorious works, which proceed from free choice, it is called cooperating grace (I-II, q. 111, a. 2).

Now, neither Singleton nor Freccero has ever distinguished between operating and cooperating grace, which means that they have never distinguished between the metaphysical and moral dimension of conversion. They speak of conversion only as a moral problem. And this is also the reason why Dante's "entire spiritual autobiography" cannot be regarded as "essentially Augustinian in structure" as Freccero claims. In the *Confessions*, St. Augustine speaks of conversion only as a moral problem. In fact, as Gilson points out, St. Augustine lacks a metaphysics:

> Perhaps as much ought to be said about the relation between St. Augustine's spirituality and his metaphysics. No one has felt more intensely

than he God's immanence in the soul which He transcends: "You were more interior than my own interior and higher that my highest self." Yet it is none the less true that Augustine was far better equipped to establish God's transcendence than to justify His immanence in the soul. The pathos of the *Confessions* depends in part upon its picture of a soul saturated with God's presence but failing to grasp it. Each time Augustine dares to say that God is within him, he hastens to add an *An potius . . .* "I should not be, O my God! I should absolutely not be, were Thou not within me. Or rather, I should not be, were I not in Thee, from Whom, by Whom and in Whom all things are." So it is that all his proofs for the existence of God, which are but so many impassioned searches for the divine presence, always bring Augustine to place God less within the soul than beyond it. Each proof tends to terminate in mystical experience, where the soul finds God only by escaping from its own becoming and rooting itself for the moment in the stability of the Immutable. These short experiences only serve to anticipate in time, by suspending its limitations, the final vicissitude of universal history in which the entire order of becoming will be transformed into the stable peace of eternity.

Augustine knows better than anyone that everything, even becoming, is the work of the Immutable. But it is precisely at this point that he finds the mystery most obscure. No doubt no one could have cleared it up. But, at least, it was possible to show what latent intelligibility lay locked in the mystery. This was only possible by reducing the antinomy of time and Eternity to the analogy of being to Being, that is, by moving from God as Eternity to God as Act-of-Being. "Eternity, it is the very substance of God"; these words of Augustine clearly mark the ultimate limits of his ontology. They explain how his thought had conceived as an antinomy of Eternity and Mutability the relation of man to God, which, his experience assured him, resembled the intimacy of a mutual presence. "God is his own act-of-being": these words of St. Thomas mark clearly the decisive progress attained by his ontology; they explain also the ease with which his thought could bind time to eternity, creature to Creator. For "He Who Is" signifies God's eternal present, and the immanence of the divine efficacy in His creatures is, at the same time, cause of their being and of their duration: "Being is innermost in each thing, and most fundamentally present within all things. . . . Hence it must be that God is in all things, and innermostly" *(S. T.* I, q. 8, 1). *(The Christian Philosophy of St. Thomas Aquinas,* pp. 135-36).

I hope the reader will forgive my quoting this lengthy passage from Gilson, but it was necessary in order to ask the following question: "Is Dante of the *Comedy,* Augustinian or Thomistic?" Dante is not only Thomistic, but eminently so. The *Divine Comedy* is not built upon the antinomy of "time and Eternity." The *Comedy* is built on the analogy of "being" to "Being." In the

Letter to Cangrande, Dante gives the following principle of analogy as the key for unlocking the entire meaning of the *Comedy*: "As a thing is related to being, so is it related to truth." The dimension of analogy (and in this Singleton was absolutely right) "can be seen to be the comprehensive principle by which the poem is related to existence and exhibits truth" (*Elements of Structure*, p. 61). Here is how Dante, in strict Thomistic terms, binds the universe to God with the same ease as St. Thomas:

> La gloria di colui che tutto move
> per l'universo penetra, e risplende
> in una parte più e meno altrove.
>
> *(Par.* I, 1-3)
>
> The All-mover's glory penetrates through the
> universe, and re-gloweth in one region more,
> and less in another.

It so happens that Dante himself, in the Letter to Cangrande, has given us, in strict metaphysical-Thomistic terms, an explanation of the above terzina:

> Therefore it is well said, when the author saith that the divine ray, or divine glory, *doth penetrate the universe and shine.* It *doth penetrate*, as touching the essence; it *shineth*, as touching the existence. Likewise what he doth append in regard to *more* and *less* is manifestly true, since we see one thing that existeth in a more exalted station and another in a more lowly; as is evident in regard to the heavens and the elements, the one of which is in truth incorruptible, but the others corruptible (*Letters*, Ed. & Tr. by C. S. Latham, p. 207).

Freccero, following St. Augustine, is under the impression that Dante's *Comedy* exhibits meaning by virtue of the antinomy of time and eternity:

> It was St. Augustine in his *Confessions* who first drew the analogy between the unfolding of syntax and the flow of human time. As words move toward their conclusion in a sentence in order to arrive at meaning and as the sentences flow toward the poem's ending in order to give it meaning, so the days of a man's life flow toward his death, the moment of closure that gives meaning to his life. Meaning in history is revealed in the same way, from the standpoint of the ending of history or Apocalypse, to use the biblical term. The same analogy is operative in Dante's poem, which is why the *Paradiso* is inseparable from the earlier *cantiche*. As we approach the poem's ending (and, incidentally, the literal ending of the poet's life), the closure that gives meaning to the verses and to the life that they represent, so all of history is reviewed under the aspect of eternity (p. 216).

This is the reason why Freccero's interpretation of the problem of conversion in the *Comedy* is expressed in terms such as: "the Dante who is" and "the Dante who was"; the "then" and the "now"; the "Old Testament and the New"; the "letter" and the "spirit"; "continuity" and "discontinuity"; a "beginning" and an "end"; "death" and "resurrection"; "conversion: the burial of the old man and the birth of the new" (pp. 132-33). These formulas, or a variation thereof, are repeated in virtually every article of the book. Freccero does not seem to realize that by adopting this mode of thinking, he has actually fallen into an intellectual trap. To see how this may be so we should consider the following. As the poem unfolds, the reader is made to witness a gradual self-evident, spiritual progress taking place in the soul of the pilgrim who goes from the Dark Wood to the Beatific Vision. Now, if Freccero has nothing but antinomies to work with, how does he account for Dante's spiritual progress? There is only one way open to him, which is to say, a mechanical repetition of the same formula. And in fact, this is precisely what he does: he postulates the absurd notion of Dante's journey as a "series of conversions":

> That Dante thinks of this movement as a series of conversions can scarcely be doubted. The ending of the *Inferno* is marked by a literal conversion, a turning upside-down of the pilgrim and his guide, providing a continuity and discontinuity in spatial terms as well as in spiritual terms. The second part of the journey also ends in a conversion, with the theological motifs of sanctifying grace whose presence has been convincingly demonstrated by Singleton (p. 265).

But Dante is a metaphysician, and as such, in perfect harmony with St. Thomas, he is aware of the metaphysical as well as the moral dimension of conversion. First of all, he is aware that conversion is a process in the order of nature that takes place, literally, in one instant as an effect of operating grace. There is one, and only one conversion in the *Divine Comedy*, not a series of them, as Freccero believes. This is the metaphysical level, as St. Thomas says: "There is a double effect of grace, even as of every other form, the first of which is being, and the second, operation." At the level of being God creates a new form (grace), which "inasmuch as it heals and justifies the soul, or makes it pleasing to God, is called operating grace." This is the time of justification in *Inferno* II. Once the soul is justified, the moral process (a process in the order of time) begins, whereby Dante in the exercise of the freedom of his choice, will cooperate with God by performing works of charity in order to earn the merit of his future glory: "But inasmuch as it is the principle of meritorious works, which proceed from free choice, it is called cooperating grace." Dante's journey takes place as an effect of cooperating grace, and this, precisely, accounts for his spiritual progress. Dante is aware that in order to earn the glory of heaven, grace alone is not enough. Merit (an effect of cooperating grace) is also required, as we see from the following terzina:

> "Spene," diss'io,"è uno attender certo
> de la gloria futura, il quale produce
> grazia divina e precedente merto."
>
> (Par. XXV, 67-69)
>
> "Hope," said I, "is a certain expectation of
> future glory, the product of divine grace and
> precedent merit."

Are we to regard "Dante's entire spiritual autobiography as essentially Augustinian in structure" as Freccero claims? Definitely not! Dante's entire spiritual journey is essentially Thomistic in structure. The above terzina is conclusive evidence that Dante is in perfect agreement with St. Thomas concerning the metaphysical and moral dimensions of sanctifying grace. For me there can be no doubt on this.

III

In the essay "The River of Death" (1966), Freccero's object of study is verse 108 of *Inferno* II:

> Non odi tu la pieta del suo pianto,
> non vedi tu la morte che 'l combatte
> su la fiumana ove 'l mar non ha vanto?

> Hearest not thou the misery of his plaint? Seest
> thou not the death which combats him upon
> the river over which the sea has no boast?

According to Freccero:

From the pilgrim's perspective, the final barrier on the difficult road to the summit seems to be the wolf; the view from heaven, however, refers to another, equally formidable, barrier. So we must assume from the words of Lucy when she calls upon Beatrice to help the pilgrim who finds himself blocked, *impedito*, on the desert slope (p. 56).

Freccero says: "So we must assume from the words of Lucy." This is not a simple assumption on the part of Freccero. We shall see shortly that he is actually doing violence to the text. Then he continues:

My purpose here is to show that when Lucy speaks of the wolf as though it were a *fiumana*, she is glossing the frustrated journey precisely as Beatrice will later gloss its successful counterpart in the *Paradiso* (p. 56).

What is involved here, according to Freccero, is a duality of imagery which indicates a dialectic between Dante the "pilgrim" and Dante the "poet":

The duality of the imagery in the prologue scene, with the pilgrim using the wolf and Lucy the river as descriptions of the same dramatic action, indicates a dialectic fundamental to this poem and to any novel of the self: the perspective of the self that was corrected and reinterpreted by the perspective of the author, the self that is (p. 57).

What should be noted is that Freccero claims that "Lucy speaks of the wolf as though it were a fiumana." He further claims that the pilgrim uses "the wolf and Lucy the river as descriptions of the same dramatic action," which is a double violation of the text, since it is Virgil, not the pilgrim, who refers to the wolf:

> e venni a te così com' ella volse:
> d'inanzi a quella fiera ti levai
> che del bel monte il corto andar ti tolse.
>
> (Inf. II, 118-20)
> and thus I came to thee, as she desired; took
> thee from before that savage beast, which bereft
> thee of the short way to the beautiful mountain.

Now, "quella fiera" ("that savage beast") is unmistakably "la lupa" ("the she-wolf") that blocked Dante's way. Therefore, the analogy established by St. Lucia is clearly between "la lupa" and "la morte," not between "la lupa" and "sulla fiumana." St. Lucia is not speaking of "the wolf as though it were a fiumana," as Freccero claims. St. Lucia is speaking of "la lupa" as though it were "la morte." The expression "sulla fiumana" is not one of the terms of the analogy. An analogy is always about a relation of functions between two subjects. "La morte" is performing the function of combatting Dante. St. Lucia is obviously speaking metaphorically. "Sulla fiumana" indicates a place, most likely the Dark Wood: "insomma un'altra immagine sostituita a quella della selva e della valle' (Torraca), immagine, del resto, di cui un primo accenno è già in *Inf.* I, 22-27" (Sapegno, *La Divina Commedia*, pp. 27-28). But Freccero has twisted the terms of the analogy established by St. Lucia in order to make it fit his own personal interpretation. In fact, he has arbitrarily identified the "fiumana" with the river Jordan: "Within a Christian context, to speak of a 'river over which the sea cannot boast' is necessarily to speak of the Jordan."

There are, on the other hand, very specific biblical and liturgical reasons that would explain why St. Lucia refers to "la lupa" as though it were "la morte." For an organic interpretation of the first two cantos of the *Comedy*, I refer the reader to my study "Analogical Contemporaneity in the Prologue Scene" in my book *Essays on Dante's Philosophy of History*. For now, it will suffice to point out a rather important piece of information concerning the she-wolf. Virgil tells us that a Greyhound will come to chase the she-wolf out of the earth and put her back into Hell from where envy first set her loose:

> Questi la caccerà per ogne villa,
> fin che l'avrà rimessa ne lo 'nferno,
> là onde 'nvidia prima dipartilla.
>
> <div align="right">(<i>Inf.</i> I, 109-111)</div>

This is, indeed, a rather perplexing statement on the part of Virgil, for how are we to understand that it was envy in Hell that set the she-wolf loose? In my study I proposed that the she-wolf be interpreted as the effect of original sin, that is to say, evil, of which we have two species: physical evil (death of the body) and moral evil (sin-death of the spirit). These are like the two faces of the same coin. It was, in fact, because of original sin that Adam and Eve lost the immortality of their body and integrity, the perfect subjection of the inferior powers of the soul to the superior and the subjection of the superior powers of the soul to God. The envy of Hell may therefore refer to the serpent's temptation in the Garden. If we take this line of interpretation, we might then realize that the most likely source for the above terzina is none other than King Solomon who says:

> For God formed man to be imperishable; the image of his own nature he made him. But by the *envy* of the devil, *death* entered the world, and they who are in his possession experience it (*Wisdom*, 2:23-24).

The above quotation is important for two reasons: First, it comes from a very famous passage of the Book of Wisdom considered to be a direct prophecy of Christ's Passion; second, it constitutes the main theme of the Fifth Lesson of Good Friday Matins, just as the supposed date of Dante's vision is Good Friday of the year 1300. The fifth lesson is taken from the treatise on the Psalms of St. Augustine, who, in fact, quotes from Solomon: "We recognize the words of these same men in the Book of Wisdom of Solomon."

But Freccero is not content to distort an already present analogy in the text, such as the one of St. Lucia. He is willing and able to construct his own original analogies, even if it means that in the process he will violate the metaphysical principle of identity, thereby destroying the very possibility of meaning.

In the essay "Manfred's Wounds and the Poetics of *Purgatorio*" (1983),

Freccero maintains that Manfredi is at last reconciled with the Church:

> The ideal of Empire lives on, but in matrilinear succession, outside the
> city of man, and reconciled at last to *Mater Ecclesia* (p.198).

Freccero overlooks the fact that Manfredi is in the Ante-Purgatory, outside the world of purgation, and therefore outside the world of *Mater Ecclesia*. Dante receives the Sacrament of Penance (administered by the Church
symbolized by the keys of the Angel) on the second day, just before he
crosses the gate of Purgatory. This means that only after Manfredi himself
has crossed the gate of Purgatory, can he be said to be "reconciled" with the
Church. The same is true for all the other souls in the Ante-Purgatory.

But Freccero is convinced that Manfredi's wounds "serve a deeper purpose than Dante's desire to hold up a mirror to reality" (p. 196). These
wounds, according to him, "are in fact a baptism, a rebirth into a new order,
with what St. Paul called "a circumcision of the heart" (p. 199). And finally, a
crowning analogy:

> At the same time, the wounds have served a providential purpose, in
> much the same way that sin can prepare the way for conversion (p. 205).

Note: "in much the same way that sin can prepare the way for conversion." How can this be possibly so? Philosophically, sin is something contrary
to reason, whereas, theologically it is essentially an offense against God:

> The theologian considers sin chiefly as an offense against God, and the
> moral philosopher, as something contrary to reason. Hence Augustine
> defines sin more fittingly with reference to its being *contrary to the eternal
> law* than with reference to its being contrary to reason; the more so as
> the eternal law directs us in many things that surpass human reason, e.
> g., in matters of faith (I-II, q. 71, a. 6, R.Obj. 5).

So, if sin is, by definition, a turning away from God, how can Freccero
say that "sin can prepare the way for conversion"? Sin cannot be at one and
the same time "a turning away from God" and "a turning toward God." This
is a violation of both the metaphysical principle of identity and the principle
of contradiction.

To an untrained ear, the metaphysical principle of identity may sound
like a useless tautology: "Si può formulare così: ogni ente è se stesso, è cioè
determinato a essere ciò che è" (*Enciclopedia Filosofica*, p. 724). In point of
fact, however, the metaphysical principle of identity is the supreme law of
thought because it guarantees the very possibility of knowledge—of all
knowledge: philosophical, scientific, poetic:

È il principio che esprime la legge suprema dell'essere, e quindi la legge suprema del pensiero, che è apprensione e riconoscimento dell'essere (Ibid., p. 724).

The metaphysical principle of identity presupposes the principle of contradiction because the necessity of not contradicting oneself in regard to the content is the very condition whereby a word may have a meaning:

Un ente infatti non può al tempo stesso essere e non essere quello che è, perchè essere e non essere allo stesso tempo non ha senso. La necessità di non contraddirsi nel proprio contenuto determinato è la condizione perchè la parola abbia un significato (Ibid., p. 725).

Sin, therefore, being an offense against God, is a preparation for damnation, not conversion as Freccero wants it to be. An analogy, Gilson says,

can be set up between beings which are out of all proportion, provided only that each of these is to itself what the others are to themselves (*The Spirit of Medieval Philosophy,* p. 448).

This means that an analogy can be set up between beings that are out of all proportion, provided that the metaphysical principle of identity is not violated. Freccero has set up an analogy in violation of this very principle. He has therefore postulated, literally, a non-sense.

Another, more serious, example of Freccero's violation of the metaphysical principle of identity involves the very nature of poetry and theology. In the essay "The significance of Terza Rima" (1983), Freccero starts off by paying a tribute to Charles Singleton:

In the field of Dante studies, it is the unique and permanent contribution of Charles Singleton to have brought poetics and thematics together in the interpretation of the poem. By refusing to accept the traditional dichotomy of poetry and belief, an older version of the opposition I have been describing, he demonstrated the relevance of theology not only to the literary archaeologist, but also to the literary critic. His formal criticism represents a dramatic departure from the tradition of the lectura Dantis, for it deals with the unity and coherence of the entire poem, rather than with single cantos or lyric passages. At the same time, that view of the whole necessarily involves accepting theology as part of that coherence. In this essay, I should like to extend his assertion of the relationship of theology to poetry in Dante's poem by offering one example where they are, quite literally, indistinguishable (p. 258-59).

The poignant irony of the above passage is that Freccero has not only violated, once again, the metaphysical principle of identity, but has also gone against the very best of Singleton's contribution to Dante studies.

Traditionally, Dante's *terza rima* has been understood as a symbol of the Trinity, as Gilson comments:

> The *Itinerary of the soul to God* is filled from cover to cover with this idea, and it has been maintained that even the *terza rima* of the *Divine Comedy*, that admirable mirror of the medieval world, was chosen by the poet so that the poem, like the world it describes, should be stamped in its very matter with the likeness of God (*Medieval Philosophy*, p. 99).

For Freccero, however, this means very little—to the point of being meaningless:

> The formal aspect of the poem that I have chosen to discuss is Dante's rhyme scheme, *terza rima*. Its significance has rarely been questioned because it has seemed too obviously to represent the Trinity. While this may be true, it tells us very little. For one thing, virtually everything represents God in this poem; the abstraction is so remote as to be meaningless (p. 260).

Freccero, however, will endeavor to give us a more profound truth; he will demonstrate that by virtue of the *terza rima*, Dante's poetry is "quite literally indistinguishable" from theology. He will prove this by affirming that the Word is the model of Dante's *terza rima*. Let us see how he does it.

According to Freccero, the central characteristic of *terza rima*, is the element of recapitulation. The *terza rima* is:

> A forward motion, closed with a recapitulation that gives to the motion its beginning and end. Any complete appearance of a rhyme . . . BA BCB . . . incorporates at the same time a recall to the past and a promise of the future that seem to meet in the now of the central rhyme (p. 262).

Similarly, history itself is characterized by an analogous recapitulation in the person of Christ:

> The term itself, *anakephalaiosis*, comes from Ephesians 1:10, where Christ is described as "the fullness of time." We are told that the eternal plan of the Father was realized by the Son: "and this His good pleasure He purposed in Him, to be dispensed in the fullness of time: to *re-establish* [recapitulate] all things in Christ, both those in the heavens and those on earth." Thus, Christ is the recapitulation, the fulfillment of the promise and the return to the beginning, as is said in the Gospel of John: "In the beginning was the Word" (pp. 266-67).

The source of inspiration for Freccero's analogy between the "realm of words" and the "theology of the Word" is, once again, St. Augustine:

> Of all the fathers of the Church, Augustine, orator and bishop, was most
> aware of the analogy between the realm of words and the theology of the
> Word. His discussion of the rule of recapitulation in the *De doctrina
> Christiana* moves from an understanding of the term as a literary device
> to its application to biblical exegesis. There is no conflict in his mind
> between literary interpretation and salvation history; on the contrary, po-
> etry was for him the emblem of intelligibility in the cosmos. Just as meter
> gave a pattern and regularity to the otherwise open-ended flow of our
> words, so God's providential intent gave meaning to the flow of time (pp.
> 269-70).

So far so good. Note well the four terms of the analogy: "Just as meter gave a
pattern and regularity to the otherwise open-ended flow of our words, so
God's providential intent gave meaning to the flow of time." The metaphysical principle of identity is here rigorously respected. The analogy holds perfectly well. As Gilson would say, "each of these is to itself what the others are
to themselves." The "pattern and regularity" are to the "meter," as the
"meaning of the flow of time" is to "God's providential intent." God's
"providential intent" is, of course, the Word. But Freccero, on the next page,
in the very last paragraph of the essay gives this closing argument:

> Whether the grounding of Dante's poem is in the formal, syllabic struc-
> ture of its cantos or in the *canticum* of the universe, its rhyme scheme
> remains the same. It begins and ends in duality, for there can be no
> memory in the first instant nor any further expectation at the last. Like
> the Hegelian dialectic, its modern analogue, *terza rima* represents a
> model for the synthesis of time and meaning into history (p. 271).

What has happened? Freccero has changed the meaning of one of the
terms of the analogy thereby violating the metaphysical principle of identity.
The *terza rima* is no longer viewed as conferring "pattern and regularity" of
sound to Dante's poem. Pattern and regularity of sound are elements pertaining to the physical dimension of poetry. The *terza rima* is now viewed as a
Hegelian dialectic conferring "meaning" to Dante's poem. And "meaning"
pertains to the metaphysical dimension of Dante's poem. The Hegelian dialectic does not confer "pattern and regularity" of sound to history. It confers, instead, patterns (thesis, antithesis, synthesis) of meaning to history. So
Freccero's analogy has now become: as the Hegelian dialectic confers meaning to history, so the *terza rima* confers meaning to Dante's poem. But the
original analogy was between the Word and the *terza rima*; therefore, we are
led to understand that as the Word confers meaning to history, so the *terza
rima* confers meaning to Dante's poem. Freccero has ascribed to the *terza*

rima a metaphysical function that does not properly belong to it. This metaphysical function belongs to Dante's faith. The *terza rima* is of the order of making. Faith is a theological virtue of the supernatural order. Once the *terza rima* is made to usurp the theological function of faith, then Freccero can strike a noble pose and thus declare that Dante's poetry is "quite literally indistinguishable" from theology. But, for Dante and his contemporaries, poetry is of the order of making, whereas theology is of the speculative order; to confuse one with the other is to show a radical misunderstanding of both.

That Dante's faith is the unifying element responsible for conferring meaning to the *Comedy* as an authentically "Christian poem," is something that Singleton has admirably demonstrated:

> And so, if we go beyond analogies, we shall have to answer that this is faith writing. This is a kind of knowing and seeing which begins as a moment of faith and culminates in vision. It is as though faith moved first and then the eye could see . . . It was a well-worn formula which one recognized immediately: *fides quaerens intellectum*, faith seeking understanding. Or there is another version: *praecedit fides, sequitur intellectus*, faith goes ahead, understanding follows (*Elements of Structure*, pp. 80-81).

Freccero is well aware of this. But in 1983 he must have been in a deconstructive mood, for he endeavors to bring about a reversal by suggesting that the coherence of Dante's belief is in part a projection of his poem:

> The coherence of Dante's poem is often taken to be a reflection of the coherence of his faith, which we take as the primary cultural reality, but the formula might well be reversed, by suggesting that the apparent coherence of Dante's belief is at least in part a projection of the coherence of his poem. The reversal is not meant to be cynically deconstructive (p. 260).

We should be willing to give Freccero the benefit of the doubt and exonerate him of the charge of cynicism. But of the charge of ignoring the proper theological facts he cannot be exonerated. The possibility of the reversal, according to Freccero, is ensured by the following analogy:

> What ensures the possibility of the reversal is the central tenet of Christianity, the doctrine of the Word, according to which language and reality are structured analogously (p. 260).

It should be pointed out, at this time, that the previous Augustinian analogy (as meter confers pattern and regularity of sound to poetry, so the Word confers meaning to history), was a valid analogy constructed in strict adherence to the metaphysical principle of identity. The above analogy, however, does not involve the Word as the "meaning" of history; it involves the Word as the Creator of "reality," which makes the analogy materially defective, since it is an analogy with a missing term—much like (if it can be imagined) a horse borne with only three feet. The Augustinian analogy involved the Word as truth, and properly remained at the level of truth since the Word is, in fact, the meaning of history. Freccero's new analogy is at the level of being (reality), which involves more than the Word; and at the level of being, as we have seen, St. Augustine cannot be of much help. Now, there is indeed a direct analogy between reality (God's creation) and poetry (man's creation) involving the Word, but in a way diametrically opposed to Freccero's understanding of the matter. For a full explanation of the problem we must turn, not to St. Augustine, but to St. Thomas. Here is how, in a beautifully symmetrical analogy of proportionality, St. Thomas speaks of the relationship between human and divine creativity:

> Nonetheless, the divine Persons, according to the nature of their procession, have a causality in relation to the creation of things. For as we said above, when treating of the knowledge and will of God, God is the cause of things by His intellect and will, just as the craftsman is the cause of the things made by his craft. The craftsman works through the word conceived in his intellect, and through the love of his will towards some object. So too God the Father made the creature through His word, which is His son; and through His Love, which is the Holy Ghost. And so the processions of the Persons are the model of the productions of creatures according as they include the essential attributes, namely, knowledge and will (I, q. 45, a. 6).

Dante's poetry (his *terza rima*) is of the order of making, it involves Dante's intellect and his will. Therefore, the model of Dante's poetry is both the Word and the Holy Ghost, not simply the Word, as Freccero mistakenly believes: "the doctrine of the Word, according to which language and reality are structured analogously." For a more extensive treatment of this problem, I refer the reader to my review article "Criticism on Ambiguity" on G. Mazzotta's book *Dante, Poet of the Desert* (*Italian Culture*, v. 5, 1984, pp. 15-37), where I show that Mazzotta's idea of Dante's poetry, as an analogue of the Word, is equally untenable. At this time, I would like to quote part of my closing argument from that review, which applies to Freccero as well. It should therefore be pointed out, that Dante is in perfect harmony with St. Thomas when he defines his poetry as the grandchild of God:

"Sì che vostr' arte a Dio quasi è nepote"

(*Inf.* XI, 105)

which is to say that as God created Dante, so Dante, analogically, creates poetry. But their mode of creating is infinitely different, for God creates from nothing while Dante creates from something. Dante is man in virtue of an idea that God has of him, and Dante exists because he is held in existence by an act of God's will. Similarly and analogically, the *Comedy* is a poem in virtue of an intuitive idea that Dante had of it, and the poem exists because Dante willed it to exist. God creates actual beings; Dante creates virtual beings and as Susan Langer notes, "such a virtual object is a work of art" (*Problems of Art*, N. Y., p. 148). What the poet creates out of words is an "appearance," a "poetic image," a "semblance" of a "perceptible human experience" (Ibid., p. 151), that is to say, the human experience of the pilgrim in his journey through the world beyond. Dante has created a "living form" which may live forever "insofar as it is form," as Pirandello says: "Hence, always, as we open the book, we shall find Francesca alive and confessing to Dante her sweet sin" (Preface to *Sei Personaggi In Cerca di Autore*). Therefore, like all true art, Dante's poetry is an analogue of life. It is "a new creature," says Jacques Maritain, "and the consequences is that art continues in its own way the labor of divine creation. It is therefore true to say with Dante that our human art is, as it were, the grandchild of God" (*Creative Intuition in Art and Poetry*, N. Y., 1957, p. 50).

But Freccero's attempt at postulating that Dante's *terza rima* is "quite literally indistinguishable" from theology is actually motivated by the philosophical ambition of wanting to create a new epistemological approach for interpreting the *Divine Comedy*:

> What ensures the possibility of the reversal is the central tenet of Christianity, the doctrine of the Word, according to which language and reality are structured analogously. We need not privilege either pole: thematics (that is, theology) and poetics might conceivably be joined in such a way as to offend neither historical understanding nor contemporary skepticism, for in either case we are discussing a coherence that is primarily linguistic. The traditional problem of poetry and belief would then be shifted onto a philosophical plane. Does the order of language reflect the order of reality or is "transcendent reality" simply a projection of language? What we had always taken to be a problem of Dante criticism turns out to be the central epistemological problem of all interpretation (p. 260).

Now, aside from the fact that the whole argument is based on a false analogy, since, as we have seen above, the analogy between poetry (man's creation) and reality (God's creation) involves both the Word and the Holy Ghost (not simply the Word, as Freccero claims), what should be observed is that Freccero has the uncanny ability of changing, almost imperceptibly, the terms of the argument under discussion. We have already noted how the *terza rima* suddenly became an analogue of Hegelian dialectic. Freccero now asks:

> Does the order of language reflect the order of reality or is "transcendent reality" simply a projection of language?

Note that Freccero has made a switch. The word "reality" (the second term of the first question) has suddenly become "transcendent reality" (the first term of the second question). But "reality" and "transcendent reality" are not the same thing. The reality of Dante's poem as a work of art, as an analogue of God's creation, involves Dante only as an artist, that is to say, it involves only his natural powers: As God creates reality through intellect (the Word) and will (the Holy Ghost), so Dante creates the poem through his natural powers of intellect and will. On the other hand, the transcendent reality of the world beyond portrayed by Dante in the *Comedy* is not, and could not be, "simply a projection of language," as Freccero claims, because it involves Dante as a Christian believer. No atheist poet, no matter how brilliant, could ever write the *Divine Comedy*; the transcendent reality of the *Comedy* is a projection of Dante's faith. Freccero has, once again, confused the natural with the supernatural order. Faith is not just an empty word. It is a supernatural virtue—a gift implanted in Dante's soul by God Himself. But Freccero says:

> If theology is words about God, wherein linguistic analogies are used to describe a transcendent divinity, then "logology" is the reduction of theological principles back into the realm of words (p. 260).

This is confusing theology as a speculative science with Revelation—the subject matter of theology. Revelation is an objectively (historically) existing body of truths whose validity does not depend on theological "linguistic analogies." "You have"—Dante says—"the New and Old Testament . . . this suffice you, unto your salvation" ("Avete il novo e 'l vecchio testamento, . . . questo vi basti a vostro salvamento"—*Par.* V, 76-78). Theology does not create the truth, it merely tries to understand and elucidate the truth of Revelation. Similarly, theology does not create the truth of Dante's poem. Theology may be used as a methodological tool in trying to understand the poem. The truth of the poem, however, is not only a direct effect of Dante's faith, but also, most importantly, of how Dante's vision of the world beyond (produced by that faith) remains authentically in adherence not with theology, but with Revelation. This is the proper meaning to be ascribed to Dante's principle of analogy: "As a thing is in respect of being, so is it in respect of truth." And faith to Dante is "the substance of things hoped for, and argument of things which are not seen; and this I take to be its quiddity":

fede è sustanza di cose sperate
ed argomento de le non parventi;
e questa pare a me sua quiditate.

(*Par.* XXIV, 64-66)

This means that faith has not only implanted in Dante's soul the first beginning (the substance) of his eternal beatitude (of things hoped for):

> In this way then faith is said to be the *substance of things to be hoped for*,
> for the reason that in us the first beginning of things to be hoped for is
> brought about by the assent of faith, which contains virtually all things to
> be hoped for. Because we hope to be made happy through seeing the un-
> veiled truth to which our faith cleaves (II-II, q. 4, a. 1).

but has also given him firm certitude concerning the hidden, mysterious ways
of God's workings (the evidence of things which are not seen):

> The relationship of the act of faith to the object of the intellect, consid-
> ered as the object of faith, is indicated by the words, *evidence of things
> that appear not*, where *evidence* is taken for the result of evidence. For
> evidence induces the intellect to adhere to a truth, wherefore the firm
> adhesion of the intellect to the non-apparent truth of faith is called evi-
> dence here . . . Accordingly if any one would reduce the foregoing words
> to a form of a definition, he may say that *faith is a habit of the mind,
> whereby eternal life is begun in us, making the intellect assent to what is
> non-apparent*. In this way faith is distinguished from all other things per-
> taining to the intellect. For when we describe it as *evidence*, we distin-
> guish it from opinion, suspicion and doubt, which do not make the intel-
> lect adhere to anything firmly; when we go on to say, *of things that appear
> not*, we distinguish it from science and understanding, the object of which
> is something apparent; and when we say that it is *the substance of things
> to be hoped for*, we distinguish the virtue of faith from faith commonly so
> called, which has no reference to the beatitude we hope for (II-II, q. 4, a.
> 1).

And so, I ask: How could all this be reduced, without destroying it, to the
level of philosophy, as Freccero proposes? "The traditional problem of poetry and belief would then be shifted onto a philosophical plane" (p. 260).
This would be like forcing the very essence of Dante's poetry to change
abode "dalle stelle alle stalle." But the truth of the matter is that the whole
argument is deficient simply on the level of formal logic. Freccero proposes
to shift the "traditional problem of poetry and belief . . . onto a philosophical
plane," because, according to him, the possibility of the reversal (that "the
apparent coherence of Dante's belief is at least in part the projection of the

coherence of his poem") is ensured by "the doctrine of the Word, according to which language and reality are structured analogously." But the doctrine of the Word is acceptable only by faith. So Freccero is proposing a "purely philosophical" reading of Dante's poem guaranteed by an act of faith in the "doctrine of the Word." It does not make any sense. No philosopher, or contemporary skeptic, in his right mind, would ever accept this for the very simple reason that philosophy, by definition, excludes faith. But Freccero is convinced that the "thematics (that is, theology) and poetics might conceivably be joined in such a way as to offend neither historical understanding nor contemporary skepticism." The philosopher, or the skeptic, might find all this simply quite amusing.

IV

In the essay "The Neutral Angels" (1960), Freccero's object of study is *Inferno* III, 37-39, pertaining to the angels of the vestibule:

> Mischiate sono a quel cattivo coro
> de li angeli che non furon ribelli
> nè fur fedeli a Dio, ma per sè fuoro

The preposition "per sè" in the above terzina is to be understood, according to Freccero, as meaning "by themselves":

> Some of the angels were for God, the others against Him and for themselves. Of the latter group, however, some stood apart and were by themselves. Part of the meaning of that preposition is the sense of separation. This is the *per sè* of the scholastic philosophers and the *da sè* of modern Italian (p. 112).

This is an important point to keep in mind since I will show later that the *per sè* of the scholastic philosophers refers to the concept of Being and its corollary, that is, the concept of perfection.

To begin with, it should be pointed out that Freccero has confused "natural love" with "supernatural love," as we see in the following passage:

> The movement is the movement of love, for fidelity and rebellion are the height and depth to which love can reach: "Però ti prego, dolce padre caro, / che mi dimostri amore, a cui reduci / ogne buono operare e 'l suo contraro" (*Purg.* XVIII, 13-15) (Wherefore, dear and gentle father, I pray that you expound love to me, to which you reduce every good action and its opposite). Fidelity is the perfection of that love, as rebellion is its perversion, and to be unmoved by love is to be a surd element in Dante's system. The "per sè" angels are creatures which have somehow managed

to break the bond of divine love without thereby embracing its contrary (p. 113).

Note that in the above quotation Freccero is referring to the concept of love as defined by Virgil in the *Purgatorio*. But that love, as we have already shown, is not the supernatural love of charity that both men and angels receive with an infusion of sanctifying grace. That love is the natural love with which both men and angels love God more than they love themselves for, if it were not so, it would not be perfected, but destroyed, by charity:

> Consequently, since God is the universal good, and under this good both man and angel and all creatures are comprised, for every creature in regard to its entire being naturally belongs to God, it follows that angel and man alike love God with a natural love before themselves and with a greater love. Otherwise, if either of them loved himself more than God, it would follow that natural love would be perverse, and that it would not be perfected, but destroyed, by charity (I, q. 60, a. 5).

God is therefore loved by two kinds of love, one natural, the other supernatural:

> God, in so far as He is the universal good, from Whom every natural good depends, is loved by everything with natural love. So far as He is the good which of its very nature beatifies all with supernatural beatitude, He is loved with the love of charity (I, q. 60, a. 5, R.Obj. 4).

But Freccero is under the mistaken impression that the angel merited his beatitude by his fidelity to his natural love of which Virgil spoke: "Fidelity is the perfection of that love, as rebellion is its perversion." The angel merited his beatitude by his fidelity to supernatural love, which is to say, charity:

> An angel did not merit beatitude by a natural conversion towards God; but by the conversion of charity, which comes through grace (I, q. 62, a. 4, R.Obj. 2).

Conversely, the bad angels sinned for their lack of fidelity to "infused love," i. e., charity:

> It is natural for the angel to turn to God by the movement of love, according as God is the source of his natural being. But for him to turn to God as the object of supernatural beatitude comes of infused love, from which he could be turned away by sinning (I, q. 63, a. 1, R.Obj. 3).

This is not all. Freccero also erroneously believes that the act of choice on the part of the angels involves two distinct, consecutive, acts of the will:

This initial division was only the first movement in the act of choice, the establishment of a predisposition for or against God, eternally separating the evil angels from the good. In this moment, the *fedeli* are logically opposed to both the *per sè* and the *ribelli*. In the second movement of choice, the *per sè* stand in logical opposition to both the *ribelli* and the *fedeli*. Those who had accepted the gift of grace moved toward God, while among those who rejected it, some rebelled and others remained within themselves, in a state of aversion (p. 116).

Freccero's scholarship seems to be characterized by a certain overconfidence in his ability to solve problems at the level of formal logic. This might explain why the word "logical" appears with ever increasing frequency throughout his essays. Now, the whole argument is not only based on a false assumption, as we shall see in a moment, but is also logically deficient. Note: "while among those who rejected it, some rebelled and others remained within themselves." The distinction does not hold since "those who rejected it" cannot be further subdivided into some who "rebelled" because the "rejection" was already the "rebellion." With the *Comedy*, however, one must always reason with the historical facts of Dante's time. And it is indeed an historical philosophical fact that for Dante and his contemporaries, choice does not involve two consecutive acts of the will. Theologically, sin is an offense against God. An act of sin is constituted by a movement of the will against God, and a movement of the will towards an inferior good. These two movements are simultaneous, not consecutive, in time and constitute therefore two aspects of one and the same act: "Mortal sin is both a turning away from God and a turning to a creaturely good (III, q. 86, a. 4, R.Obj. 1).

Specifically, choice involves the exercise of the act of the will tending toward an end, and the specification of an object as a means to that end:

> In like manner, on the part of the appetite, to will implies the simple appetite for something, and so the will is said to regard the end, which is desired for itself. But to elect is to desire something for the sake of obtaining something else, and so, properly speaking, it regards the means to the end (I, q. 87, a. 4).

The exercise of the act of the will (tending toward an end) and the specification of the object (as a means to that end) constitute one single act of the will:

> And thus the movement of the will to the end and its movement to the means are one and the same thing. For when I say: *I wish to take medicine for the sake of health*, I signify no more than one movement of my will, and this is because the end is the reason for willing the means to the end (I-II, q. 12, a. 4).

Moreover, these two aspects of the act of choice are not consecutive, but take place at the same time:

> There can be two operations of the same power at the one time, if one of them is referred to the other; as is evident when the will at the same time wills the end and the means to the end (I, q. 58, a. 7).

But it should be said, at this time, that Freccero has already been proven wrong on this subject by Professor Ernest Fortin who sagaciously says:

> La thèse de Freccero a l'avantage de rattacher le problème aux discussion qui avaient cours dans les milieux savants concernmant le pèchè des anges, mais elle n'est pas sans prèsenter de sèrieuses difficultès aussi bien du point de vue thèologique que du point de vue de la *Comédie*. Car on ne voit pas du tout à quoi correspondrait un acte de la volonté, que ce soit celle de l'ange ou de n'importe quel autre être, qui n'aurait aucun objet et qui se ramènerait à une "négation irréductible." Les scolastiques on bien distingué entre l'aspect négatif de l'acte mauvais, en vertu duquel la créature se détourne de son bien suprême, et son aspect positif, en vertu duquel elle se tourne vers un bien inférieur qui l'écarte de sa fin dernière. Mais il s'agit en l'espèce, non pas de deux actes consécutifs, mais de deux formalités distinctes d'un seul et même acte (*Dissidence et Philosophie au Moyen Age*, p.118).

Professor Fortin has not only proven that Freccero's argument is based on a false assumption, he has also proven that Freccero's conclusion regarding the problem of the "neutral angels" is actually a metaphysical impossibility. According to Freccero:

> For the angel, to avert from the vision of God is to ignore not only Him, but the self that depends upon Him. The rebellious angel will act on the basis of that aversion, but the "per sè" angel, having turned from the roots of its own being, refuses even this negative affirmation. It remains, locked tightly in the self, an irreducible negation, meriting not even classification among the damned, having done nothing to distinguish itself from the void out of which it was created. In the first moment of its existence, it saw God at the center of its being, and in the second moment, the moment of choice, it averted from that vision. It looked above itself to the angels who were elevated, below it to those who rebelled, and stood, undecided, as if it could really forge a destiny for itself, somehow different from the one God intended, and from the only other one the angel could elect in spite of its Maker. That hesitation was not so much an inability to choose as it was the result of a proto-choice, the choice for nothing, and because of it, the *per sè* angel was spewed forth from the supernatural cosmos (pp. 117-18).

Note Freccero's claim that the *"per sè"* angel's choice was a "proto-choice, the choice for nothing." This is a metaphysical impossibility for the simple reason that a choice is always a choice of this or that good for the sake of an end. It is simply inconceivable that "nothing" could be specified for the sake of the end, as Fortin points out:

La volonté a pour objet le bien et n'est jamais attirée que par lui. Même lorsqu'elle recherche le mal, ce ne peut être que parce qu'il lui apparaît comme un bien particulier vers lequel elle se précipite sans égard pour son bien total. Il est donc inconcevable que l'ange puisse poser un acte qu'aucun objet positif ne viendrait spécifier et qui se définirait par le pur néant (Ibid., p. 118).

I should like to propose, instead, that in order to come to a probable solution of the problem of the "per sè" angels, it would perhaps be advisable to also consider the problem of the slothful souls "che visser senza infamia e sanza lodo" (who lived without blame and without praise) that Dante encounters together with the angels in the vestibule of Hell. The ultimate problem to be resolved is to determine whether the spiritual status of both, the angels and the souls, is theologically tenable or untenable.

Accordingly, we should consider that man is endowed with a double freedom. He can will or not will, in the sense that the will is not compelled to act. And once a goal is established, he is free to specify this or that object that would lead to that goal:

Man does not choose of necessity. And this is because that which is possible not to be, is not of necessity. Now the reason why it is possible not to choose, or to choose, may be gathered from a twofold power in man. For man can will and not will, act and not act; and again, he can will this or that, and do this or that. The reason for this is to be found in the very power of the reason. For the will can tend to whatever the reason can apprehend as good. Now the reason can apprehend as good not only this, viz., *to will or to act*, but also this, viz., *not to will and not to act*. Again, in all particular goods, the reason can consider the nature of some good, and the lack of some good, which has the nature of an evil; and in this way, it can apprehend any single one of such goods as to be chosen or to be avoided. The perfect good alone, which is happiness, cannot be apprehended by the reason as an evil, or as lacking in any way. Consequently, man wills happiness of necessity, nor can he will not to be happy, or to be unhappy. Now since choice is not of the end, but of the means, as was stated above, it is not of the perfect good, which is happiness, but of other and particular goods. Therefore, man chooses, not of necessity, but freely (I-II, q. 13, a. 6).

Note: "man wills happiness of necessity, nor can he will not to be happy, or to be unhappy." This is quite true. But as Gilson elucidates on the problem, we are not free not to will our own happiness while our intellect is thinking about it; nevertheless, we are still free not to think about our beatitude:

> There is only one object which presents itself to us as good and suitable under all aspects—beatitude. Boethius defines it as *status omnium bonorum congregatione perfectus*. Obviously, this object does move our will necessarily. But let us note well that this necessity itself only concerns the determination of the act. It is limited strictly to this: that the will cannot will the contrary of beatitude. This reservation can be expressed differently. We can say that if the will performs an act while the intellect is thinking of beatitude, then this act is necessarily determined by such an object. The will will not will any other. But the actual exercise of the act remains free. If we cannot not will beatitude while we are thinking about it, we can, nevertheless, not will to think about beatitude. The will remains in control of its act and can use it as it pleases with reference to any object whatsoever: *libertas ad actum inest voluntati in quolibet statu naturae respectu cujuslibet objecti* (*The Christian Philosophy of St. Thomas Aquinas*, pp. 246-47).

This elucidation may prove to be of enormous importance for our purpose. Our beatitude may be natural as well as supernatural, so that, if it is possible to choose not to think about our natural happiness, it is equally possible to choose not to think about our supernatural happiness as well. This, in fact, may be the case of the souls in the vestibule of Dante's Hell. These are the slothful souls of the "ignavi," and spiritual sloth,

> according to Damascene is an *oppressive sorrow*, which, to wit, so weighs upon man's mind, that he wants to do nothing (II-II, q. 35, a. 1).

Sloth is therefore a kind of paralysis. However, it should be carefully noted that this is a kind of spiritual paralysis, which, moreover, does not pertain to any spiritual good whatsoever. It specifically pertains only to the Divine good:

> Sloth is not an aversion of the mind from any spiritual good, but from the Divine good, to which the mind is obliged to adhere (II-II, q. 35, a. 3, R.Obj. 2).

Note that the mind is "obliged to adhere" to the "Divine good," but we are free to choose not to think about our supernatural beatitude. In fact, conversely, we are free to choose to adhere to any number of particular, natural, spiritual goods—such as painting, music, poetry, philosophy and the like; and in these, indeed, our natural happiness may come to fruition. In so doing, however, we will have chosen our natural happiness to the exclusion of our supernatural one. An act of the will tending toward an end has been exercised. The end is our natural happiness. And an object, as a means to that end, has been specified. This object is ourselves—our own natural powers as a means for acquiring that end. This can hardly be called a "moral neutrality." We have deliberately chosen to remain content in the enjoyment of our natural happiness. Now, the question is: can this choice constitute a sinful act? The answer, strange as it may sound, is in the negative. It does not constitute a positive sinful act. To see how this may be so, we should consider that sloth, being a sorrow, is a passion of the concupiscible appetite. But passions are not sinful in themselves; they become sinful only when they are applied to something evil:

> Passions are not sinful in themselves; but they are blameworthy in so far as they are applied to something evil, just as they deserve praise in so far as they are applied to something good (II-II, q. 35, a. 1, R.Obj. 1).

So, inasmuch as the souls of the vestibule have not applied this passion of sorrow about Divine good to something evil, this passion has not become a positive sin. Therefore, St. Thomas says:

> Wherefore sorrow, in itself, calls neither for praise nor for blame (II-II, q. 35, a. 1, R.Obj. 1).

This is most likely the source for Dante's verse concerning these souls:

> che visser senza infamia e senza lodo

And since they could not be placed in any of the circles of Hell, Dante has relegated them to the vestibule. We might say, then, that these souls, theologically speaking, led a life of quiet despair. And as in life they had been overcome by sorrow, so are they in death. "Who are these people who seem to be so overcome by sorrow?" Dante asks:

> e che gente è, che par nel duol sì vinta?

to which Virgil answers: "These are the sorrowful souls (l'anime triste) of those who lived without blame and without praise." It would be a mistake, however, to think of these souls as being "morally neutral." Their condition is one of damnation; and this damnation is an indirect effect of a deliberate and complete act of choice. They, no less than the souls of Hell, have determined their own eternal destiny. The mind, says St. Thomas, has a twofold act:

> One is its proper act in relation to its proper object, and this is the act of knowing a truth; the other is the act of the reason as directing the other

powers. Now, in both of these ways there may be sin in the reason. First, in so far as it errs in the knowledge of truth, which error is imputed to the reason as a sin when it is in ignorance or error about what it is able and ought to know; secondly, when it either commands the inordinate movements of the lower powers, or deliberately fails to check them (I-II, q. 74, a. 5).

Therefore, inasmuch as these souls were in ignorance or error about what the mind is "able and ought to know" (that the mind is "obliged to adhere" to the "Divine good"), they have committed a sin of omission. A sin, St. Thomas says, is "fittingly defined as a word, deed or desire contrary to the eternal law." But since "affirmation and negation are reduced to one and the same genus," a "*word* and *deed* denote equally what is said and what is not said, what is done and what is not done" (I-II, q. 71, a. 6, R.Obj. 1).

This is so because the cause of a sin of omission is actually a voluntary act, inasmuch as a negation is always founded and caused by an affirmation:

But if we refer to the species in sins of omission and commission formally, they do not differ specifically, because they are directed to the same end, and proceed from the same motive. For the covetous man, in order to hoard money, both robs and omits to give what he ought; and, in like manner, the glutton, to satiate his appetite, both eats too much and omits the prescribed fasts. The same applies to other sins, for negation in things is always founded on affirmation, which in a way is its cause (I-II, q. 72, a. 6).

What all this means is that the affirmation (the choice) of the slothful souls to adhere exclusively to their natural happiness is also the indirect cause of their negation of the Divine good.

We should, however, distinguish between the spiritual status of the souls in the vestibule and the spiritual status of the souls in Limbo. Some of the inhabitants of Limbo are pagan souls who lived before Christ and who had never been given the opportunity of conversion. They did not sin: "ei non peccaro" (*Inf.* IV, 34), we are told, nonetheless they are lost since they did not receive the grace of baptism: "non ebber battesmo" (v. 35). The same cannot be said of the souls in the vestibule. Those souls may be said to be slothful who were in ignorance or error about what the mind is "able and ought to know," that is to say that the mind is "obliged to adhere" to the "Divine good." But the mind adheres to the Divine good through an act of charity. And since charity cannot exist without sanctifying grace, we must conclude that these are the slothful souls of Christians who have committed a sin of omission. This interpretation becomes all the more plausible if we consider that grace does not impose necessity, and that a man can sin simply by failing to make use of it:

Consequently the movement of grace does not impose necessity; but he who has grace can fail to make use of it, and can sin (I, q. 62, a. 3, R.Obj. 2).

The problem of the angels of the vestibule is more complex to explain. We should first of all point out, that Freccero thinks of the problem as one of political allegiance, as if it were a political contest. This is the major source of his misunderstanding. He thinks, in fact, that the "per sè" angels' choice was whether to side with the good or bad angels:

It looked above itself to the angels who were elevated, below it to those who rebelled, and stood, undecided, as if it could really forge a destiny for itself (p. 118).

The preposition "per sè" is understood by Freccero to mean "by themselves," in the sense that the angels of the vestibule sided neither with the good nor with the bad angels: "Part of the meaning of that preposition is the sense of separation. This is the per sè of the scholastic philosophers and the da sè of modern Italian" (p. 112). I shall propose, on the contrary, that the choice of the "per sè" angels was between themselves and God—the very same choice that the good and bad angels were confronted with.

We should begin by making a rather important distinction between a man's choice and an angel's choice. They do not take place in the same way. In fact, a man chooses with the "inquiring deliberation of counsel," whereas the angel chooses by the "immediate acceptance of truth":

Now just as a man's judgement in speculative matters differs from an angel's in that the one needs not to inquire, while the other does, so is it in practical matters. Hence there is choice in the angels, yet not with the inquiring deliberation of counsel, but by the immediate acceptance of truth (I, q. 59, a. 3, R. Obj.1).

This is so because man possesses discursive knowledge, whereas the angel possesses intuitive, innate knowledge:

So, likewise, the lower, namely, the human, intellects obtain their perfection in the knowledge of truth by a kind of movement and discursive intellectual operation. That is to say, they obtain their perfection by advancing from one thing known to another. But if from the knowledge of a known principle they were straightaway to perceive as known all its consequent conclusions, then there would be no place for discursiveness in human intellect. Such is the condition of the angels, because in the truth which they know naturally, they at once behold all things whatsoever that can be known in them (I, q. 58, a. 3).

This explains why the angel could decide his ultimate destiny of perfection in one single act, whereas man needs a lifetime to do the same:

> Man, according to his nature, was not intended to secure his ultimate perfection at once, like the angel. Hence a longer way was given to man than to the angel for securing beatitude (I, q. 62, a. 5, R. Obj. 1).

We might say then that man is in search of an absent God, whereas God was present to the angel at the moment of his choice. Therefore, an angel's choice takes place by "immediate acceptance" or "immediate rejection" of truth. The truth that the angel had to accept was that he could not reach his supernatural beatitude (his likeness to God) by the power of his own nature. This could be had only as a gift of sanctifying grace:

> Without doubt the angel sinned by seeking to be as God. But *to be as God* can be understood in two ways: first, by equality; secondly, by likeness. He could not seek to be as God in the first way, because by natural knowledge he knew that this was impossible; nor was there any habit preceding his first sinful act, or any passion fettering his mind, so as to lead him to choose what was impossible by causing him to fail in the order of the particular, as sometimes happens to ourselves . . . no creature of a lower order can ever covet the grade of a higher nature, just as an ass does not desire to be a horse; for were it to be so upraised, it would cease to be itself . . . consequently it is impossible for one angel of lower degree to desire equality with a higher, and still more to covet equality with God.
>
> On the other hand, to desire to be as God according to likeness can happen in two ways. In one way, as to that likeness whereby everything is made to be likened unto God. And so, if anyone desires in this way to be God-like, he commits no sin; provided that he desires such likeness in proper order, that is to say, that he may obtain it of God. But he would sin were he to desire to be like God even in the right way, but of his own power, and not of God's (I, q. 63, a. 3).

From the above we can say that the good angel exercised an act of the will tending toward an end. The end was his supernatural beatitude. At the same time, he specified an object as a means to that end. The object specified was sanctifying grace. These are the two aspects of one and the same act of choice. A deliberate and complete act of choice has been made. The good angel desires his supernatural beatitude and accepts the fact (the truth) that he can have it only through sanctifying grace. Therefore, by a single act of charity, he is elevated to his supernatural likeness to God.

The bad angel, on the other hand, also exercised an act of the will tending toward an end. The end, for him, like the good angel, was also his supernatural beatitude. At the same time he specified an object as a means to that end. The object specified, unlike the good angel, was not sanctifying grace, but the power of his own nature. These are, once again, the two aspects of one and the same act of choice. A deliberate and complete act of choice has been made. The bad angel desires his supernatural beatitude, but does not accept the fact (the truth) that he can have it only through sanctifying grace. Therefore, by a single act of pride, he descends to his eternal damnation of Hell.

Now, what of the angels of the vestibule? According to Freccero, these angels did not act:

> The angels of the vestibule underwent no such incarnation. They simply did not act, but remained frozen in a state of aversion from God . . . With the aversion from God, the bond of charity was smashed; with the abstention from action, they deprived themselves of the one positive element that could win them a place in the cosmos (p. 117).

Once again, Freccero splits the one single act of choice in two consecutive acts. As for the claim that these angels "did not act," this is another absurdity for the very simple reason that for Dante, as also for St. Thomas, the cosmic law of the universe is self-realization. This means that absolutely everything in the universe seeks its own perfection, and self-realization and perfection can be reached only in action inasmuch as perfection, or beatitude, "is not the nature of the creature, but is its ultimate end":

> Perfect beatitude is natural only to God, because to be and to be blessed are one and the same thing in Him. To be blessed, however, is not the nature of the creature, but is its ultimate end. Now everything attains its ultimate end by its operation (I, q. 62, a. 4).

This is so because to seek one's own perfection is actually to tend to a divine likeness:

> Because by tending to their own perfection, they tend to a good, since a thing is good in so far as it is perfect. And according as a thing tends to be good, it tends to a divine likeness, since a thing is like God in so far as it is good. Now this or that particular good is so far appetible as it bears a likeness to the first goodness. Therefore the reason why a thing tends to its own good is because it tends to a divine likeness, and not *vice-versa*. It is clear therefore that all things seek a divine likeness as their last end (*Contra Gentiles*, III, 24).

Also, the angels of the vestibule, like the good and bad angels, because of the perfection of their innate knowledge, had to attain, unlike men, their ultimate end of perfection by one single act of the will:

It is only for man that this very complex problem arises. In the case of the angels, their lot has been definitely decided from the first moment after their creation . . . The reason for this lies in the perfection of the angelic nature. The angel's nature is to live under the regime of direct intuition. It has no discursive knowledge. It can, accordingly, attain its end by one single act. Man, however, has to go searching. He needs time and a life of some duration to attain his end. The length of human life is based upon man's mode of knowing (E. Gilson, *The Christian Philosophy of St. Thomas*, pp. 251 & 478, n. 3).

But if the angels of the vestibule were not free to evade the choice before which they found themselves: "L'ange n'était pas libre de se dérober au choix devant lequel il s'est trouvé" (Fortin: p. 118), nonetheless, they remained free to choose, just like the slothful souls of the vestibule, between their natural and supernatural beatitude. My thesis, in fact, is that the alternative of the "per sè" angels was analogous to the alternative open to the slothful souls of the vestibule. That this alternative was open to the angel was recognized even by St. Thomas who says:

But he desired resemblance with God in this, that he desired as the last end of his beatitude something which he could attain by the virtue of his own nature, turning his appetite away from the supernatural beatitude which is attained by God's grace. Or, if he desired as his last end that likeness of God which is bestowed by grace, he sought to have it by the power of his own nature, and not from divine assistance according to God's ordering (I, q. 63, a. 3).

We might therefore say that as man is free not to think about his supernatural beatitude, so also the angel was free to turn "his appetite away from the supernatural beatitude which is attained by God's grace." The following, precise elucidation of the above passage by Kenelm Foster, is a clear confirmation of the possibility of such an alternative:

And we can conceive of this happening in one of two ways: either the angel, apprehending the supernatural life as a possibility for him, might have aspired to have it in the wrong way—that is, as the achievement of his own nature, not as a pure gift received from God—or else he might have refused to aspire to that which he could *only* have as a gift, preferring to rest in that joy to which his natural powers could bring him. St. Thomas states these alternatives at the end of his Reply in 63, 3 (*Summa Theologiae*, Blackfriars, v. 9, p. 318).

From the above passages, both from St. Thomas and Foster, we might say that the angel of the vestibule exercised an act of the will tending toward an end. The end, unlike that of the good and bad angels, was not his super-natural, but his natural beatitude. At the same time, he specified an object as a means to that end. The object specified, like the bad angel, was the power of his own nature. These are the two aspects of one and the same act of choice. Therefore, just like the souls of the vestibule, it would be a mistake to think of these angels as being "morally neutral." Their condition of eternal damnation is an indirect effect of a deliberate and complete act of choice. They, just like the angels of the rest of Hell, have determined their own eternal destiny. These angels have deliberately chosen to remain content in the enjoyment of their own natural happiness. Therefore, the same question should now be asked of these angels: Does this choice constitute a positive sinful act? And, once again, the answer is in the negative.

To see how this may be so, we should first of all mention that the angels were created in grace, and that grace may be "imperfect" or "consummate":

> The angel is above the time of corporeal things, and hence the various instants pertaining to the angels are not to be taken except as reckoning the succession of their acts. Now the act which merited beatitude could not be in them simultaneously with the act of beatitude which is fruition; since the one belongs to imperfect grace and the other to consummate grace. Consequently it is necessary to suppose a diversity of instants, in one of which the angel merited beatitude, and in another was beatified (I, q. 62, a. 5, R.Obj. 2).

This is rather important because we have to determine what exactly did the "per sè" angels do with the grace that they had received. It should be clearly understood however that in the first instant of their existence all angels were good. They were separated in the second instant: "Hence the first act was common to them all, but in their second they were separated. Consequently they were all of them good in the first instant, but in the second the good were set apart from the wicked (I, q. 63, a. 6, R.Obj. 4).

Secondly, we should consider that a sin of commission is constituted by the combination of two things: failure to consider things that ought to be considered, such as the rule of reason and the divine law, combined with the actual act of turning toward a mutable good:

> Accordingly, then, the will lacking the direction of the rule of reason and the divine law, and intent on some mutable good, causes the act of sin essentially (I-II, q. 75, a. 1).

But, as Professor Fortin has also noted, the failing of the will in not applying the rule of reason or the divine law is not, in itself, sinful before it is applied to the act:

> As was stated above, the will in failing to apply the rule of reason or of the divine law is the cause of sin. Now the fact of not applying the rule of

reason or of the divine law, has not in itself the nature of evil, whether of punishment or of guilt, before it is applied to the act (I-II, q. 75, a. 1, R.Obj. 3).

The problem of the angel was that he could reach his supernatural beatitude on condition (the rule of divine law) that it be accepted as a gift of sanctifying grace. The good angel, by accepting grace, applied the rule of divine law, turned to God, and was beatified by consummate grace. The bad angel, by rejecting grace, refused to apply the rule of divine law, turned to a mutable good (himself), and merited damnation. The bad angel therefore committed a complete sin of commission: "accordingly, then, the will lacking the direction of the rule of reason and the divine law, and intent on some mutable good, causes the act of sin essentially." The same cannot be said of the angel of the vestibule. He chose straightaway to remain in the enjoyment of his natural beatitude. So, if "not applying the rule of reason or of divine law, has not in itself the nature of evil, whether of punishment or of guilt, before it is applied to the act," this is all the more true in the case of the angel of the vestibule, who, in the exercise of the act of his will, is straightaway tending toward the end of his natural beatitude. This means that the question whether to apply or not to apply the rule of divine law does not even come into play because grace cannot be a means to his natural beatitude. The problem must therefore be posed in terms of indirect causality, such as: "For the covetous man, in order to hoard money, both robs and omits to give what he ought" (I-II, q. 72, a. 6). The affirmation (the choice) of the angel of the vestibule to adhere exclusively to his natural happiness is also the indirect cause of his negation of the Divine good, since as St. Thomas says: "Negation in things is always founded on affirmation, which in a way is its cause (I-II, q. 72, a. 6). We might say, then, that the good angel accepted grace. The bad angel rejected grace. The angel of the vestibule failed to make use of grace. Having grace, he was obliged to adhere to God with an act of charity; but since "grace does not impose necessity . . . he who has grace can fail to make use of it, and can sin" (I, q. 62, a. 3, R.Obj. 2). His sin, therefore, was a sin of omission inasmuch as, in the words of St. Thomas, "he desired as the last end of his beatitude something which he could attain by virtue of his own nature, turning his appetite away from the supernatural beatitude," or, in the words of Foster, inasmuch as "he might have refused to aspire to that which he could *only* have as a gift, preferring to rest in that joy to which his natural powers could bring him." In other words, the angel of the vestibule, like the slothful souls of that same vestibule, remained free to choose between his natural and supernatural beatitude. And since his sin, not being a sin of commission, did not correspond to any of the categories of the circles of Hell, Dante has relegated him to the vestibule.

But the bad angel had at least realized that he stood in potentiality to a supernatural perfection. The angel of the vestibule, on the other hand, must have thought that he was perfect just as he was. This brings us to the consideration of the proper meaning that should be ascribed to the preposition: *per sè*. Dante tells us that the angels of the vestibule were neither rebellious ("non furon ribelli"), nor faithful to God ("nè fur fedeli a Dio"), but were *per sè* ("ma per sè fuoro"). I would like to suggest, at this time, that this preposition should be understood in its strict philosophical connotation. In fact, when referred to God, *per se* refers specifically to the problem of aseity of being. Aseity means existence, originating from, and having no source other than, itself, which is to say that only God "exists in virtue of Himself (per se) in an absolute sense," as Gilson explains:

> Thus to say that God is being is equivalent to asserting His aseity. We must, once more, be quite clear as to the meaning of this last term. God exists in virtue of Himself (per se) in an absolute sense, that is to say as Being He enjoys complete independence not only as regards everything without but also as regards everything within Himself. Just as His existence is not derived from any other than Himself, so neither does He depend on any kind of internal essence, which would have in itself the power to bring itself to existence. If He is *essentia* this is because the word signifies the positive act itself by which Being is, as if *esse* could generate the present participle active *essens*, whence *essentia* would be derived . . . Now this complete aseity of God involves His absolute perfection as an immediate corollary . . . Thus the perfection of the Christian God is that perfection which being posits along with itself; we do not say that He is because He is perfect, but on the contrary, He is perfect because He is. And it is just that difference, so nearly imperceptible at its point of origin, and yet so fundamental, that carries with it such startling consequences, when at last it brings forth from the very perfection of God, His total freedom from all limits and His infinity (*Medieval Philosophy*, pp. 54-55).

Now, as St. Thomas has explained, the angels could not desire equality with God (aseity of Being) because by natural knowledge they knew this to be impossible, since they clearly saw that God was the sole source of their being. They could desire to be as God only by likeness—that is to say, by likeness of supernatural perfection. So, the good angel desired this likeness of supernatural perfection "in the proper order, that is to say, that he may obtain it of God," and was immediately elevated to a state of supernatural beatitude. The bad angel desired that very same likeness of supernatural perfection by "his own power, and not of God," and was immediately thrown into the deep Hell. The "per sè" angel, on the contrary, did not even begin to desire this likeness of supernatural perfection. He desired straightaway to remain in the enjoyment of his natural perfection as if, "in virtue of himself (per se) in an absolute sense," he possessed, like God, "aseity of perfection." His sin is one of omission, not of commission, he was therefore sent to the vestibule.

Thus Dante's meaning might be that these angels were neither rebellious, nor faithful to God, but unmindful of God. This might explain why, by contrapasso, both Heaven and the deep Hell are now unmindful of them: "Caccianli i ciel . . . né lo profondo inferno li riceve" (*Inf.* III, 40-41) ("Heaven chased them forth . . . and the deep Hell receives not"). And Virgil, in an obvious reference to both angels and souls, adds: "non ragioniam di lor, ma guarda e passa" ("Let us not speak of them, but look, and pass")—an exhortation advising Dante that he, himself, should be unmindful of them. So, these are not "The Neutral Angels," as Freccero claims to have proven. They are quite simply The Angels unmindful of God—an angelic analogue to the slothful souls of the human race.

Freccero seems to have fallen into an intellectual trap of his own making. The title itself of his essay "The Neutral Angels" already reveals an assumption. He has first assumed that these angels are neutral, and has then subsequently tried to prove how specifically they may be said to be so. To avoid the assumption altogether, he should have proposed writing an essay on "The Angels of the Vestibule" in order to inquire, in the first place, whether their spiritual status is theologically tenable or untenable. He does not realize that by calling these angels "neutral," he has already assumed that they are. Freccero's effort, therefore, was exclusively spent on proving how they are neutral. The possibility that they might not be neutral has not even entered his mind. But perhaps Freccero is not entirely to be blamed for this, since the tradition of Dante scholarship has always referred to these angels as the "neutral angels." Dante, however, does not call them so. In philosophy, as also in theology, the way a problem is posed already determines the outcome of the answer. Had Freccero posed the question the proper way, he might have discovered that, to the extent that it is theologically tenable, the spiritual status of these angels is not neutral. But perhaps Freccero is much too ingrained in his ways of thinking for we note that he wrote another essay on the subject (oddly enough not included in the present collection) revealingly entitled: "Dante's 'per sè' angel: The Middle Ground in Nature and in Grace" (*Studi Danteschi*, 1962, v. 39, pp. 5-38). And there is, of course, no such animal as a "middle ground" neither in nature nor in grace. It is simply a pure invention of Freccero's overworked imagination.

The idea of a moral "middle ground" was later taken up (with disastrous results) by Giuseppe Mazzotta (a student of Freccero) who maintains that Dante: "Takes the world of immanence seriously . . . and believes in the existence of a middle ground, a redeemed nature between fallen nature and the order of grace" (*Dante, Poet of the Desert*, p. 185). A "redeemed nature" redeemed by what? By free will ("*liberum arbitrium*" p. 185) Mazzotta says, which is another absurdity since "the entire justification of the ungodly consists as to its origin, in the infusion of grace. For it is by grace that *free choice is moved* and guilt is remitted" (I-II, q. 113, a. 7, italics mine). If what Mazzotta says were true (that: "the middle area is the region, on the contrary, of a *moral* middleness, the temporal and open-ended world where choices are made and the opportunity of transcending the order of nature is offered" p. 185), then Christ would have died in vain: "Hence with equal reason, if man has a nature whereby he can be justified, Christ died in vain, i. e., to no purpose" (I-II, q. 109, a. 7). And Dante is in perfect agreement with St. Thomas when he says: "e tutti li altri modi erano scarsi / a la giustizia, se 'l Figliuol di Dio / non fosse umilïato ad incarnasrsi" (Par. VII, 118-20). Mazzotta does not seem to understand that it takes a supernatural principle such as grace to transcend the order of nature. But he is quite sure of himself for he has his master's word on it: "The question has been treated, by focusing on angelology, by John Freccero, "Dante's 'per se' Angels: The Middle Ground in Nature and Grace" (p. 185, n. 62).

V

In the essay "Bestial Sign and Bread of Angels: Inferno XXXII and XXXIII" (1977), Freccero treats of the episode of Conte Ugolino, which, for him, "is rather a paradigm of death and salvation, stripped of comforting illusions and conventions, and so epitomizes the theme of the entire poem" (p. 152). This must be so because Freccero finds the clearest allusion to the passion of Christ in the lamentation of the children to the father:

> The clearest allusion to the passion of Christ is in verse 69: "Padre mio, che non m'aiuti?" echoing the words of Christ on the Cross: "My God, my God, why has thou forsaken me?" The children's words are the last words spoken by the Savior before his death (p. 156).

There is more. Freccero finds an equally strong Christological suggestion in the children's offer of themselves to the father:

> "Padre, assai ci fia men doglia
> se tu mangi di noi: tu ne vestisti
> queste misere carni, e tu le spoglia." (vv. 61-63)

> "Father, it will be far less painful to us if you
> eat of us; you did clothe us with this wretched
> flesh, and do you strip us of it!"

Freccero finds that these words:

> echo at once the eucharistic sacrifice and the words of Job: "The Lord giveth and the Lord taketh away. Blessed be the Name of the Lord" (p. 156).

These words are for Freccero the "key for the whole dramatic interpretation," since they carry "a redemptive possibility" (p.156-57) for Conte

Ugolino who, unfortunately, tragically fails to interpret the "spirit" of the offering:

> Ugolino's failure is an inability to interpret the Christian hope contained in the words of his children (p. 158).

Ugolino is therefore a literalist and is condemned by Dante, not only as a traitor but also for his "inability to grasp the spiritual meaning in the letter of his children's words" (p. 158).

To Ugolino and to the literalist critic (who, unlike Freccero, is like Ugolino in this case), the offering of the children can only suggest cannibalism:

> To Ugolino, as to the reader, a literal reading of their words suggests cannibalism (p. 163).

This is not all. Freccero goes so far as to say that the traditional interpretation of the episode in terms of cannibalism is simply an "unsophisticated reading" of it:

> He begins by not taking their offer seriously and ends, if we are to trust the traditional and unsophisticated reading of his last words, with a bestial literalism (p. 158).

But to Freccero, who claims to be both a non-literalist and a sophisticated reader of the episode, the children's offer to the father is the same as "Christ's offer to his disciples":

> The offer of the children to their father is the same as Christ's offer to his disciples (p. 163).

This must be so because, for Freccero, the offer of the children is a sacramental offer:

> The children's offer is sacramental, a sign that presents what it represents (p. 163).

This is nothing but an empty tautology and a gross misunderstanding of a sacramental sign. A sacrament, according to St. Thomas:

> consists in a certain ceremony in which the action is so performed that we take it to signify the sanctity it bestows (III, q. 84, a. 1).

As, for example, in baptism the water (the matter) and the words (the form) "I baptize you . . ." are not simply symbolical of "a cleansing," but they actually and literally cleanse the soul of original sin. A sacramental sign does not simply "present(s) what it represents" as Freccero claims, but it actually accomplishes what it signifies:

> For the sacraments of the New Law not only signify, but also accomplish what they signify (III, q. 84, a. 3, R.Obj. 5).

This is so because a sacrament is an instrumental cause of sanctifying grace: "Now it is as sacrament that it is a cause of grace" (III, q. 89, a. 1, R. Obj. 1). There is absolutely no evidence, not even remotely suggested, of the presence of grace in the episode of Ugolino. Only by a gross distortion of the text can Freccero say that the "children gloss Ugolino's grief, as he bites his own hand, as a figure for his spiritual hunger" (p. 164). In point of fact, the very opposite is true: the children gloss Ugolino's grief as a sign of biological hunger:

> ambo le man per lo dolor mi morsi;
> Ed ei, pensando ch'io 'l fessi per voglia
> di manicar, di sùbito levorsi
>   e disser: "Padre, assai ci fia men doglia
> se tu mangi di noi: tu ne vestisti
> queste misere carni, e tu le spoglia."
>
> (Inf. XXXIII, 58-63).
>
>   I bit on both my hands for grief. And they,
> thinking that I did it from desire of eating,
> of a sudden rose up,
>   and said: "Father, it will give us much less pain,
> if thou wilt eat of us: thou didst put upon us
> this miserable flesh, and do thou strip it off."

The children are just as blind as Ugolino. They are not offering their flesh as a "spiritual nourishment" for Ugolino's soul. Theirs is a bestial offer of their flesh for the nourishment of Ugolino's body. But Freccero says that this is only an apparent literalism on the part of the children: "The children, in their apparent naïve literalism, offer themselves as food" (p. 165). This is simply a case—it must be said—of interpretative perversion based on a gross distortion of both Dante's text and the proper meaning of a sacramental sign.

VI

In the essay "The Final Image: Paradiso XXXIII, 144" (1964), Freccero proposes to explain the precise meaning of the last four verses of the Comedy:

> A l'alta fantasia qui mancò possa;
> ma già volgeva il mio disio e 'l velle,

sì come rota ch'igualmente è mossa,
l'amor che move il sole e l'altre stelle.

(Par. XXXIII, 142-45)

Here power failed the lofty phantasy; but already my desire and my will were revolved,
like a wheel that is evenly moved, by the Love
which moves the sun and the other stars.

This meaning, Freccero tells us, depends on a precise definition of the words "disio" and "velle":

> For all its poetic immediacy, the final image makes considerable de-
> mands upon our learning. In the first place, although the vision itself
> transcended all human understanding, Dante does not hesitate to use a
> technical scholastic term, velle, as he describes its effect. There can be
> nothing vague about the word, for it is used in conjunction with disio, so
> close to it in meaning that unless we define both precisely, velle seems
> redundant and its use here pedantic (p. 246).

Then, in the same breath, Freccero declares that "disio" and "velle" constitute two powers of Dante's soul:

> The love that moves the sun and the other stars turned two powers, disio
> and velle, as a single wheel is moved. Either the final movement is not so
> simple as it appears to be, or disio and velle are not so distinct as poetic
> precision would seem to require (p. 246).

Now, velle (the will) is indeed a power of the soul. But disio (desire) is
not a power of the soul. Disio is an act belonging to the power of the will:
"desire is an act of the appetitive power" (I, q. 83, a. 3, and a. 2: "Whether
the will desires of necessity whatever it desires"). Elsewhere Freccero speaks
of "disio" as if it were the object of "velle":

> The pilgrim calls the souls in the name of the "amore" which impels
> them (v. 78) and they respond: "dal disio chiamate . . . dal voler portate"
> (called by desire . . . borne by their will). The flight of the doves, then, is
> literally "amore," the attempt to bridge the gap between the will (velle)
> and its object (disio) (p. 191).

If disio were really the object of velle, as Freccero seems to think, the
movement of our will would resemble the motion of a cat, running in circles,
forever trying to catch its own tail:

> Therefore the will's object is naturally prior to its act, and consequently
> its first object precedes its every act. Therefore an act of the will cannot

be the first thing willed. But this is the last end, which is beatitude. Therefore beatitude or happiness cannot be the very act of the will (Contra Gentiles, III, 26).

So much for Freccero's claim to philosophical precision! As for Freccero's claim to literary sophistication ("In a context such as this, combining a twofold human perfection with astronomical imagery, a sophisticated contemporary of Dante would associate the two expressions"—p. 252), we should point out that "disio" and "velle" constitute, for Freccero, two powers of Dante's soul (intellect and will) because he believes he has found confirmation for this erroneous assumption in the two movements of the wheel (circular-rectilinear) implied in the simile: "sì come rota ch'igualmente è mossa" (like a wheel that is evenly moved):

If it is true that reason and will are logically distinct, it is also true that they are ontologically one, just as their object is ontologically one. The rotating and revolving wheel therefore symbolizes them perfectly, and its uniformity of motion perfectly represents the exact proportion that exists between the two spiritual motions of the soul (p. 255).

The proper meaning of the simile, as we shall see later, is that Dante has by now become a "perfect image" of God. Freccero, however, believes that the proper meaning of the final scene in the Paradiso will be found in Plato's analogy between physical movement and spiritual development:

What concerns us now is the final scene of the drama of human perfection as Plato stages it, for it is against that Platonic background that Dante's final verses are to be understood. Because of the analogy established between physical movement and spiritual development, perfection in the spiritual order was symbolized in the Timaeus by perfect motion in the universe: the diurnal movement of the fixed stars. The soul began its pre-existence in the stars, and it is to the stars that the perfect soul will return, when the perfect "circlings" of its mind will exactly match the circlings of the universe (p. 250-51).

In fact, Freccero also believes that Dante's simile of the wheel is derived from Plato:

But assuming that the fixed stars not only revolve around the heavens but also rotate on their own axes, Plato provided himself with a perfect analogue of the twin aspect of intellectual perfection: perfect circling within, because of a fixity of knowledge and purpose, as well as perfect circling without, because of a perfect integration into a harmonious cosmic order. This representation of twofold perfection is the ancestor of Dante's celestial wheel (p. 251).

Accordingly, Freccero will say:

Dante's celestial wheel moves in two directions, and thus he calls it a wheel and not a circle. His personal fulfillment is represented by a perfect rotation around God, upon whom he is centered. At the same time, however, because he moves in harmony with the rest of creation, represented by the heavenly bodies, the forward motion is along the circular track that surrounds God. The pilgrim's motion is not only a rotation around the interior object of his desire, but also, because the contact with reality is never lost, a revolution around the spiritual center of the universe. The same revolution carries with it the angelic intelligences of the spheres; they in turn transmit the motive power of primal love to the sun and the other stars (pp. 249-50).

Evidently Freccero is giving a literal interpretation of a poetic simile. But the pilgrim is not an angel. The angels, for Dante (*Par.* XXVIII), whirl around God in a circular motion because they are actually and literally involved in God's chain of causality for the operation of the universe, as St. Thomas had maintained:

These angels are called Virtues, because they confer on the general causes the energy required that their numerous operations be carried out without fail. This order, then, presides over the operations of the universe as a whole; and to it is attributed not unreasonably the movement of heavenly bodies, universal causes from which proceed all the particular effects which take place in nature (Gilson: *The Christian Philosophy of St. Thomas Aquinas*, p. 171).

In the final scene of the *Paradiso*, we are dealing with the spiritual status of the pilgrim as given by a poetic simile, the interpretation, therefore, cannot be kept on a literal, naïvely mechanistic, level. The truth of the matter is that Plato's analogy has absolutely nothing to do with Dante's Beatific Vision, for the simple reason that Plato could not even begin to imagine the Christian concept of charity, which is at the core of the meaning of the last terzina of the *Comedy*. Freccero does not seem to know what is involved here; that is why he says that "*velle* seems redundant and its use here pedantic." The verse "ma già volgeva il mio disio e 'l velle" (but already my desire and my will were revolved) has absolutely nothing to do with Dante's intellect. It only concerns the power of the will (velle) and the act of the will (disio). Dante's intellect has already received all the truth it could possibly contain as given to him by a flash of insight—which is to say, by perfected consummate grace known as the light of glory:

ma non eran da ciò le proprie penne:
se non che la mia mente fu percossa

> da un folgore in che sua voglia venne.
>
> (*Par.* XXXIII, 139-41)
>
> but not for this were my proper wings, save
> that my mind was smitten by a flash wherein
> its will came to it.

It is simply not true to say, as Freccero says, that Dante's soul approaches God by "the intensity of his vision at the center of his being," or by a movement of "concentration":

> The movement by which the soul approaches God is thus a movement of "concentration" that is accomplished in the depths of the soul itself (p. 256).

Freccero, who has neglected to consider the above terzina, evidently thinks that Dante can reach God by a simple "concentration" of his soul. But concentration or intensity will not do:

> Now the natural power of the created intellect is not sufficient for the vision of the divine substance, as we have shown. Therefore its power needs to be increased in order that it attain to that vision. But increase through intensification of the natural power is insufficient, because that vision is not of the same kind as the natural vision of the created intellect; which is clear from the distance separating the things seen. Therefore there must be an increase of the intellectual power through its receiving a new disposition . . . Accordingly the disposition whereby the created intellect is raised to the intellectual vision of the divine substance is rightly called the *light of glory*; not indeed because it makes the object actually intelligible, as the light of the agent intellect does, but because it makes the intellect able to understand actually (*Contra Gentiles*, III, LIII).

In fact, Dante becomes most like God through that vision:

> It is through this vision that we become most like God, and participators of His blessedness, since God understands His substance through His essence, and this is His blessedness (*Contra Gentiles*, III, LI).

and in that vision Dante's intellect sees God "through the divine essence itself" so that "the divine essence is both the object and the medium of vision" (Ibid.,). But God is both Truth Itself and Goodness Itself, and since the object of the intellect is truth, whereas the object of the will is the good, Dante, having already received God as Truth, his will is now moved to desire Him as the Good, just as Dante himself says: "la mia mente fu percossa / da un fulgore, in che sua voglia venne" ("my mind was smitten by a flash wherein / its will came to it"). The verse "ma già volgeva il mio disio e 'l *velle*" means that now, for the first time ever, there is unity between Dante's will (velle) and its act (disio), because when the object of the will is the Supreme Good, there can only be one act of desire, since it becomes impossible to desire anything else. Dante is, of course, aware of this when, in the very same canto, he says:

> A quella luce cotal si diventa,
> che volgersi da lei per altro aspetto
> è impossibil che mai si consenta;
>   però che 'l ben, ch'è del volere obietto,
> tutto s'accoglie in lei, e fuor di quella
> è difettivo ciò ch'è lì perfetto.
>
> (*Par.* XXXIII, 100-105)
>   Such at that light doth man become that to turn
> thence to any other sight could not by possi-
> bility be ever yielded.
>   For the good, which is the object of the will, is
> therein wholly gathered, and outside it that
> same thing is defective which therein is perfect.

But Freccero, who, following Plato's analogy, is bent on having Dante take a spin around the universe, makes the following, ridiculous, statement:

> The final movement of the soul is not simply the private fruition of a per-
> sonal possession. In Dante's view, which is not the view of a solipsist, the
> complete fulfillment of the soul's desires is at the same time an integra-
> tion with the rest of creation. The circular turning of the soul does not
> shut out external reality but rather joins it in the majestic sweep of the
> final verse (p. 247).

A poetic simile cannot be taken literally. The verse "sì come rota ch'igualmente è mossa" ("like a wheel that is evenly moved") means that Dante has by now become a perfect image of God inasmuch as there is unity of "disio" and "velle" (power-act) with God, who is love itself, and whose love is the cause of that unity, as P. H. Wicksteed points out:

> Then the vision passes away and may not be recalled, but already all jar-
> ring protest and opposition to the divine order has given way in the seer's
> heart to oneness of wish and will with God, who himself is love (Temple
> Classics: *Paradiso*, p. 399).

In fact, the analogy is not between "disio" and "velle" on one side, and "circular" and "rectilinear" motions of the wheel, on the other, as Freccero

believes. Dante's simile is cast in the passive voice: "sì come rota ch'igualmente è mossa." The proper analogy established by Dante is, therefore, as
follows: Dante's "disio" and "velle" are moved by God's love, just as a wheel
is evenly moved by an agent's action. Or, we might say: God's love is to
Dante's "disio" and "velle," as an agent's action is to a wheel's uniform motion. And since a wheel may be moved by an agent either uniformly or non-
uniformly, what is involved are not the circular or rectilinear motions themselves, but only the "how" of motion—which is to say, the concept of uniformity. The uniformity between God's love and Dante's "disio" and "velle."
Freccero, however, is under the mistaken impression that the uniformity is
between Dante's intellect and will: "and its uniformity of motion perfectly
represents the exact proportion that exists between the two spiritual motions
of the soul" (p. 255), or "the soul is equally moved by its now *equal* intellect
and will" (p. 316, n. 25). The analogy of the last terzina, as we have shown,
does not involve Dante's intellect. In the Beatific Vision, Dante's will has become one with God's will inasmuch as there is uniformity (sameness) or
conformity between the human and divine will. And this, according to Gilson,
is also the essence of St. Bernard's mysticism:

> The essential character of Cistercian mysticism is now plain: it rests
> wholly upon a conscious effort to perfect the natural likeness of the soul
> to God, by means of a conformity, ever more fully realized, between the
> human will and the divine will. To love God is, in a way, to make God
> love Himself in us, as He loves Himself in Himself. That is the true
> meaning of the mystic marriage: "*Talis conformitas maritat animam
> Verbo, cum cui videlicet similis est per naturam, similem nihilominus se
> exhibet per voluntatem, diligens sicut dilecta est. Ergo si perfecte diligit,
> nupsit.*" The mutual embrace of God and the soul lies in the very union
> of their wills: "*Complexus, plane, ubi idem velle et nolle idem unum facit
> spiritum de duobus*" (*Medieval Philosophy*, p. 300).

The mutual embrace of God and Dante's soul lies—equally—in the very
union of their wills, and that union is given by the last terzina of the *Comedy*:

> ma già volgeva il mio disio e 'l *velle*,
> sì come rota ch'igualmente è mossa,
> l'amor che move il sole e l'altre stelle.

The pilgrim Dante has now become a true image of God because he
wills what God wills, just as Piccarda says:

> Anzi è formale ad esto beato *esse*
> tenersi dentro a la divina voglia,
> per ch'una fansi nostre voglie stesse;

sì che, come noi sem di soglia in soglia
per questo regno, a tutto il regno piace
com' a lo re che 'n suo voler ne 'nvoglia.

(Par. III, 79-84)

Nay, 'tis the essence of this blessed being to
hold ourselves within the divine will, whereby
our own wills are themselves made one.

So that our being thus, from threshold unto
threshold throughout the realm, is a joy to all
the realm as to the king, who draweth our
wills to what he willeth.

Dante's understanding of man's mystical union with God is in perfect harmony with St. Bernard's:

Now for man to become like God is to fulfill the desire of his true nature: "*Ipse enim imago Dei est. Et per hoc quod imago Dei est, intelligibile ei fit, et se posse et debere inhaerere ei cujus imago est.*" But to become like God is to will what God wills: "*Velle autem quod Deus vult, hoc est jam similem Deo esse. Non posse velle nisi quod Deus vult, hoc est jam esse quod Deus est, cui velle et esse idipsum est.*" One more step and we see that an image that attains to perfect resemblance attains, by definition, its own perfection. The author of the *Epistola* does not delay to take it: "*Et haec est hominis perfectio, similitudo Dei*: to be like God, that is man's perfection (Ibid., pp. 301-2).

And all this, of course, is also in perfect agreement with St. Thomas:

The well-known comparison between man's love for God and the love of the part for the whole has been pushed rather too far. Man is not a part of which God would be the whole, he is an analogue, a similitude, of his Principle: and that is why, according to the famous passage of the *Contra Gentiles*, III, 24: "*Propter hoc igitur tendit in proprium bonum, quia tendit in divinam similitudinem.*" If this is so, the conception of image, ruling even the philosophy of nature and orienting the desire of all created things, should secure in Thomism, as in Cistercian mysticism, that the perfection proper to man, and his complete submission to the divine will, shall converge to the same point (Ibid., 302-3).

But Freccero, who has undertaken the task of explaining to us Dante's mystical union with God, has not mentioned—not even once—the name of St. Bernard who, after all, is the guide that brings Dante to that final union. Instead, he says that Dante's mystical union should be understood in terms of human perfection as envisaged by Plato who knew, of course, absolutely nothing about charity: "What concerns us now is the final scene of the drama of human perfection as Plato stages it, for it is against that Platonic background that Dante's final verses are to be understood."

Of the Paradiso as a whole, in the only other essay ("The Dance of the Stars") dealing with the cantica, Freccero says:

> The representation points to no reality however fictive, beyond itself. The structure of the *cantica* depends, not upon a principle of *mimesis*, but rather upon metaphor: the creation of a totally new reality out of elements so disparate as to seem contradictory by any logic other than that of poetry (p. 222).

I will not enter into a detailed discussion of this most untenable position. It will suffice, however, at this time to give two brief remarks. To begin with, the above passage may be a strong indication of a radical misunderstanding of metaphor on the part of Freccero. The representation of the *Paradiso*, according to him, "points to no reality" since the structure of the *cantica* does not depend "upon a principle of *mimesis*, but rather upon metaphor." Freccero is apparently under the mistaken impression that metaphor has nothing to do with reality. The *Paradiso*, to him, is "the creation of a totally new reality out of elements so disparate as to seem contradictory by any logic other than that of poetry." Freccero is evidently unaware that the logic of poetry is ultimately the same as the logic of metaphysics. This is so because the cognitive value of metaphor is grounded in being—that is to say, in reality. A metaphor may be an immediate grasp of a truth seen by the mind in virtue of a non-discursive, intuitive, analogy. But the validity of an analogy is guaranteed by the metaphysical principle of identity. Therefore, poetry, no less than metaphysics, cannot violate that principle.

Also, it is simply not true to say, as Freccero says, that Dante's representation of the *Paradiso* "points to no reality however fictive, beyond itself." Dante's representation of the *Paradiso* points to, and is grounded in, the spiritual reality of this world; and the spiritual reality of this world is grounded in the mystery of God's Predilection, as it is confirmed by Piccarda, who informs us of the fact that God's grace is not poured into the souls of men "after one only fashion":

> Chiaro mi fu allor come ogne dove
> in cielo è Paradiso, etsi la grazia
> del sommo ben d'un modo non vi piove.
>
> (*Par*. III, 88-90)

Piccarda speaks of the supernatural order of grace involving God's "special love," whereby He makes the soul of man partake of His own supernatural beatitude. The same is true, analogically, in the natural order involving God's "common love," whereby He confers on the things of this world their natural being. And here, too, we are told, in the first terzina of the *Paradiso*, that the glory of the one that moves everything penetrates through the universe and re-glowes in one region more than in another:

> La gloria di colui che tutto move
> per l'universo penetra, e risplende
> in una parte più, e meno altrove.

One final consideration. We are told on the inside-jacket of the book that: "With these essays assembled for the first time, we can now see Freccero's stature: he is the best contemporary critic of Dante." Note that the claim is not that Freccero is "one of the best" contemporary critics of Dante. The claim is that Freccero is "the best." This is simply a shameless, if not shameful, example of advertising hype, altogether unbecoming in a scholarly book on Dante, whose *Comedy*, after all, is also a celebration of humility. It could be said, on the contrary, that these newly republished essays by Freccero are like "The Emperor's New Clothes," and the emperor, as we have seen, is naked.